Costa Rica
The Ecotravellers' Wildlife Guide

Costa Rica
The Ecotravellers' Wildlife Guide

Les Beletsky

Illustrated by:
Priscilla Barrett (Plates 71–80),
David Beadle (Plates 20–70),
David Dennis (Plates 1–20) and
John Myers (Figures 1–10).

ACADEMIC PRESS
SAN DIEGO   LONDON   BOSTON
NEW YORK   SYDNEY   TOKYO   TORONTO

AP Natural World is published by
Academic Press
525 B Street, Suite 1900, San Diego
California 92101–4495, USA

Academic Press
24–28 Oval Road, London NW1 7DX, UK

ISBN: 0–12–084810–4

Library of Congress Cataloging-in-Publication Data
Beletsky, Les, 1956–
The ecotravellers' wildlife guide to Costa Rica/by Les Beletsky,
p.   cm. — (Ecotravellers' guide)
Includes index.
ISBN 0–12–084810–4 (alk. paper)
1. Zoology—Costa Rica.   2. Ecotourism—Costa Rica.   I. Title.
II. Series.
QL687.C8845   1998
591.97288—dc21   97–45871
CIP

A catalogue record for this book is available from the British Library

Typeset by J&L Composition Ltd, Filey, North Yorkshire
Colour Separation by Tenon & Polert Colour Scanning Ltd.
Printed in Italy, Rotolito Lombarda, Milan
98 99 00 01 02 03 RL 9 8 7 6 5 4 3 2 1

Contents

Foreword

Throughout the world, wild places and wildlife are dwindling. Their conservation will require ever more intense protection, care, and management. We always value things more when we stand to lose them, and it is perhaps no coincidence that people are increasingly eager to experience unspoiled nature, and to see the great wildlife spectacles. Tourists are increasingly forsaking the package tour and the crowded beach, to wade through jungle streams, to dive on coral reefs, and to track elusive wildlife. But despite its increasing popularity, nature tourism is nothing new, and the attraction to the tourist is self evident – so why should a conservation organization like the Wildlife Conservation Society encourage it?

The answer is that nature tourism, if properly conducted, can contribute directly to the conservation of wild places and wildlife. If it does that, such tourism earns the sobriquet *ecotourism*. A defining quality of ecotourism is that people are actively encouraged to appreciate nature. If people experience wild areas, they can grow to appreciate their beauty, stability and integrity. And only if they do so, will people care about conserving these places. Before you can save nature, people need to know that it exists.

Another characteristic of ecotourism is that people tread lightly on the natural fabric of wild places. By their very definition, these are places with minimal human impact, so people must not destroy or degrade what they come to experience. Tourists need to take only photographs, leave only footprints – and ideally not even that. Wastes and pollution need to be minimized. Potential disturbance to animals and damage to vegetation must always be considered.

The third characteristic, and that which most clearly separates ecotourism from other forms of tourism, is that tourists actively participate in the conservation of the area. That participation can be direct. For instance, people or tour companies might pay fees or make contributions that support local conservation efforts, or tourists might volunteer to work on a project. More likely, the participation is indirect, with the revenues generated by the tourism entering the local economy. In this way, tourism provides an economic incentive to local communities to continue to conserve the area.

Ecotourists thus are likely to be relatively well informed about nature, and able to appreciate the exceptional nature of wild places. They are more likely to travel by canoe than cruise ship. They will be found staying at locally owned lodges rather than huge multi-national hotels. They will tend to travel to national parks and protected areas rather than to resorts. And they are more likely to contribute to conservation than detract from it.

The Wildlife Conservation Society was involved in promoting ecotourism since before the term was generally accepted. In the early 1960s, the Society (then known as the New York Zoological Society) studied how to use tourism to provide revenues for national park protection in Tanzania (then known as Tanganyika).

By the 1970s, the Society was actively involved in using tourism as a conservation strategy, focusing especially on Amboseli National Park in Kenya. The Mountain Gorilla Project in the Virunga mountains of Rwanda, a project started in the late 1970s, still remains one of the classic efforts to promote conservation through tourism. Today the Society continues to encourage tourism as a strategy from the lowland Amazonian forests to the savannas of East Africa.

We at the Wildlife Conservation Society believe that you will find these Ecotravellers' Wildlife Guides to be useful, educational introductions to the wildlife of many of the world's most spectacular ecotourism destinations.

John G. Robinson
Vice President and
Director of International Conservation
Wildlife Conservation Society

WCS
WILDLIFE CONSERVATION SOCIETY

● to sustain wildlife   ● to teach ecology   ● to inspire care for nature

The mission of the Wildlife Conservation Society, since its founding in 1895 as the New York Zoological Society, has been to save wildlife and inspire people to care about our nature heritage. Today, that mission is achieved through the world's leading international conservation program working in 53 nations to save endangered species and ecosystems, as well as through pioneering environmental education programs that reach more than two million schoolchildren in the New York metropolitan area and are used in 49 states and several nations, and through the nation's largest system of urban zoological facilities including the world famous Bronx Zoo. WCS is working to make future generations inheritors, not just survivors after Bronx Zoo.

With 60 staff scientists and more than 100 research fellows, WCS has the largest professional field staff of any US-based international conservation organization. WCS's field programs benefit from the technical support of specialists based at WCS's Bronx Zoo headquarters in New York. The Field Veterinarian Program sends experts around the globe to assess wildlife health, develop monitoring techniques, and train local veterinarians. WCS's curatorial staff provides expertise in breeding endangered species in captivity. The Science Resource Center helps researchers assess data through computer mapping, statistical treatments, and cutting-edge genetic analysis. The Education Department writes primary and secondary school curricula that address conservation issues and hosts teacher-training workshops around the world.

WCS's strategy is to conduct comprehensive field studies to gather information on wildlife needs, train local conservation professionals to protect and manage wildlife and wild areas for the future, and advise on protected area creation, expansion, and management. Because WCS scientists are familiar with local conditions, they can effectively translate field data into conservation action and policies, and develop locally sustainable solutions to conflicts between humans and wildlife. An acknowledged leader in the field, the Wildlife Conservation Society forges productive relationships with governments, international agencies and local organizations.

To learn more about WCS's regional programs and membership opportunities, please see our pages in the back of this book. And please visit our website at **www.wcs.org**.

Preface

This book and others in the series are aimed at environmentally conscious travellers for whom some of the best parts of any trip are glimpses of wildlife in natural settings; at people who, when speaking of a journey, often remember days and locations by encountered wildlife: "That was where we watched the monkeys," and "That was the day we saw the snake eat the frog." The purpose of the book is to enhance enjoyment of a trip and enrich wildlife sightings by providing identifying information on several hundred of the most frequently encountered animals of Costa Rica, along with up-to-date information on their ecology, behavior, and conservation. With color illustrations of about 80 species of amphibians and reptiles, 50 mammals, and more than 200 birds, this book truly includes almost all the vertebrate land animals that visitors are likely to encounter.

The idea to write these books grew out of my own travel experiences and frustrations. First and foremost, I found that I could not locate a single book to take along on a trip that would help me identify all the types of animals that interested me – birds and mammals, amphibians and reptiles. There are bird field guides, which I've used, but they are often large, heavy books, featuring information on every bird species in a given country or region. In Costa Rica, for instance, the bird guides detail more than 800 species, most of which are rarely seen. If I wanted to be able to identify mammals, I needed to carry another book. For "herps" – amphibians and reptiles – I was a bit astonished to learn, no good, small book existed that might permit me to identify these animals during my travels. Thus, the idea: create a single guide book that travellers could carry to help them identify and learn about the different kinds of animals they were most likely to see.

Also, in my experience with guided tours, I've found that guides vary tremendously in their knowledge of wildlife. Many, of course, are fantastic sources of information on the ecology and behavior of animals. Some, however, know only about certain kinds of animals, birds, for instance. And many others, I found, knew precious little about wildlife, and what information they did tell their groups was often incorrect. For example, many guides in Central America, when asked the identity of any large lizard, respond that it is an "iguana." Well, there certainly are iguanas in Central America, but there are also many other types of lizards, and people interested in wildlife need some way to identify more common ones. This book will help.

Last, like most ecotravellers, I am concerned about the threats to many species as their natural habitats are damaged or destroyed by people; when I travelled, I wanted current information on the conservation statuses of animals that I encountered. This book provides the traveller with conservation information on Costa Rica in general, and on many of the animal family groups pictured or discussed in the book.

A few administrative notes: because this book has an international audience, I present measurements in both metric and English system units. The scientific classification of common animals, you might think, by now would be pretty much established and unchanging; but you would be wrong. These days, what with new molecular methods to compare species, classifications of various animal groups that were first worked out during the 1800s and early 1900s are undergoing sometimes radical changes. Many bird groups, for instance, are being rearranged after comparative studies of their DNA. The research is so new that many biologists still argue about the results. I cannot guarantee that all the classifications that I use in the book are absolutely the last word on the subject, or that I have been wholly consistent in my classifications. However, for most users of this book, such minor transgressions are probably irrelevant.

Finally, let me say that I tried, in several sections of the book, to make the presented information at least mildly entertaining. So many books of this type are written in a dry, terse style. I thought a lighter touch was called for – after all, many of the book's readers will be on holiday, and should not have to plod through heavy material. When I anthropomorphize – provide plants and animals with human characteristics – I do so for fun; plants and insects, of course, do not actually think and reason. Readers who decide that they do not appreciate my sense of humor may simply ignore those sections; remaining still should be a solid natural history guide to Costa Rican animals.

I must acknowledge the help of a large number of people in producing this book. First, most of the information here comes from published sources, so I owe the authors of those books and scientific papers a great deal of credit. The source I most often consulted during writing this book, was *Costa Rican Natural History*, edited by Daniel Janzen (see reference page for complete citations); a great deal of the general information I present on tropical mammals, for instance, comes from this source. I freely acknowledge my debt to Janzen and the large numbers of contributors to that great compendium of information on the plants and animals of Costa Rica; without it, my job would have been much harder. Other good sources of information were *A Neotropical Companion*, by J. C. Kricher, *Neotropical Rainforest Mammals: A Field Guide*, by L. H. Emmons, *A Guide to the Birds of Costa Rica*, by F. G. Stiles and A. F. Skutch, and *Birds of the Mayas*, by A. L. Bowes, and I recommend all of these books for those wanting to delve deeper into their particular subjects.

I would like to take this opportunity to thank the many people who provided information for or helped in the preparation of this book, including Gordon Orians, Sharon Birks, Bruce Young, Luis Gomez, Gail Hewson, Eugenio Gonzalez, Fiona Reid, Dana Heller, Ananda Cooley, Rosa Sandoval and Orlando Vargas. Also thanks to my editor at Academic Press, Andrew Richford, and to the artists who drew the wonderful illustrations, Priscilla Barrett, David Beadle, David Dennis, and John Myers. Both the Burke Museum and the Department of Zoology at the University of Washington provided facilities during the book's preparation. Betty Orians provided the excellent habitat photos.

Please let me know of any errors, opinions on the book, and suggestions for future editions. I am interested in hearing of your travel wildlife experiences. Write care of the publisher or e-mail: Ecotravel/8@aol.com

Les Beletsky

Chapter 1

Ecotourism: Travel for the Environmentally Concerned

- What Ecotourism Is and Why It's Important
- The History of Ecotourism
- How Ecotourism Helps; Ecotravel Ethics

What Ecotourism Is and Why It's Important

People travel; always have, always will. Germans have wanderlust, college students at spring break have sunlust, retired people have recreational vehicles (RVs), Australians go walkabout, Japanese go everywhere. In the distant past, people travelled for the most fundamental reason – to find food. During 99% of human history, people were nomads or hunter-gatherers, moving almost constantly in search of sufficient nutrition. Then someone made the startling connection between some discarded seeds in the past and the sprouting seedlings of the present; she reported the discovery to her clan, and things have not been the same since. With the development of agriculture, travel, always an inherently risky undertaking, was less needed. Farming peoples could remain close to their familiar villages, tend crops, and supplement their diet with local hunting. In fact, we might imagine that long-distance travel and any venturing into completely unfamiliar territory would have ceased. But it didn't. People still travelled to avoid seasonally harsh conditions, to emigrate to new regions in search of more or better farming or hunting lands, to explore, and even, with the advent of leisure time, just for the heck of it (travel for leisure's sake is the definition of tourism). For most people, still, there's something irreplaceably satisfying about journeying to a new place: the sense of being in completely novel situations and surroundings, seeing things never before encountered, engaging in new and different activities.

During the final quarter of the 20th century arose a new reason to travel, perhaps the first wholly new reason in hundreds of years: with a certain urgency, to see natural habitats and their harbored wildlife before they forever vanish from the surface of the Earth. *Ecotourism* or *ecotravel* is travel to (usually exotic) destinations specifically to admire and enjoy wildlife and undeveloped, relatively undisturbed natural areas, as well as indigenous cultures. The development and increasing popularity of ecotourism is a clear outgrowth of escalating concern for conservation of the world's natural resources and biodiversity (the different types of animals, plants, and other life forms found within a region). Owing mainly to peoples' actions, animal species and wild habitats are disappearing or deteriorating at an alarming rate. Because of the increasing emphasis on the importance of the natural environment by schools at all levels and the media's continuing exposure of environmental issues, people have enhanced appreciation of the natural world and increased awareness of environmental problems globally. They also have the very human desire to want to see undisturbed habitats and wild animals before they are gone, and those with the time and resources increasingly are doing so.

But that is not the entire story. The purpose of ecotravel is actually twofold. Yes, people want to undertake exciting, challenging, educational trips to exotic locales – wet tropical forests, wind-blown deserts, high mountain passes, midocean coral reefs – to enjoy the scenery, the animals, the nearby local cultures. But the second major goal of ecotourism is often as important. The travellers want to help conserve the very places – their habitats and wildlife – that they visit. That is, through a portion of their tour cost and spending into the local economy of destination countries – paying for park admissions, engaging local guides, staying at local hotels, eating at local restaurants, using local transportation services, etc. – ecotourists help to preserve natural areas. Ecotourism helps because local people benefit economically as much or more by preserving habitats and wildlife for continuing use by ecotravellers than they could by "harvesting" the habitats for short-term gain. Put another way, local people can sustain themselves better economically by participating in ecotourism than by, for instance, cutting down rainforests for lumber or hunting animals for meat or the pet trade.

Preservation of some of the Earth's remaining wild areas is important for a number of reasons. Aside from moral arguments – the acknowledgment that we share the world with millions of other species and have some obligation not to be the continuing agent of their decline and extinction – increasingly we understand that conservation is in our own best interests. The example most often cited is that botanists and pharmaceutical researchers each year discover another wonder drug or two whose base chemicals come from plants that live, for instance, only in tropical rainforest. Fully one-fourth of all drugs sold in the USA come from natural sources – plants and animals. About 50 important drugs now manufactured come from flowering plants found in rainforests, and, based on the number of plants that have yet to be cataloged and screened for their drug potential, it is estimated that at least 300 more major drugs remain to be discovered. The implication is that if the globe's rainforests are soon destroyed, we will never discover these future wonder drugs, and so will never enjoy their benefits. Also, the developing concept of *biophilia*, if true, dictates that, for our own mental health, we need to preserve some of the wildness that remains in the world. Biophilia, the word coined by Harvard biologist E. O. Wilson, suggests that because people evolved amid rich and constant interactions with other species and in natural habitats, we have deeply ingrained, innate tendencies to affiliate with other species and actual physical need to experience, at some level, natural habitats. This instinctive, emotional attachment to wildness means that if we eliminate species and habitats, we will harm ourselves because we will lose things essential to our mental well-being.

If ecotourism contributes in a significant way to conservation, then it is an especially fitting reprieve for rainforests and other natural habitats, because it is the very characteristic of the habitats that conservationists want to save, wildness, that provides the incentive for travellers to visit and for local people to preserve.

The History of Ecotourism

Tourism is arguably now the world's largest industry, and ecotourism among its fastest growing segments. But mass ecotourism is a relatively new phenomenon, the name itself being coined only recently, during the 1980s. In fact, as recently as the 1970s, tourism and the preservation of natural habitats were viewed largely as incompatible pursuits. One of the first and best examples of ecotourism lies in Africa. Some adventurers, of course, have always travelled to wild areas of the Earth, but the contemporary history of popular ecotourism probably traces to the East African nation of Kenya. Ecotourism, by one name or another, has traditionally been a mainstay industry in Kenya, land of African savannah and of charismatic, *flagship*, mammals such as elephants, leopards, and lions – species upon which to base an entire ecotourism industry.

During most of the European colonial period in East Africa, wildlife was plentiful. However, by the end of colonial rule, in the middle part of the 20th century, continued hunting pressures had severely reduced animal populations. Wildlife was killed with abandon for sport, for trade (elephant ivory, rhinoceros horn, etc.), and simply to clear land to pave way for agriculture and development. By the 1970s it was widely believed in newly independent Kenya that if hunting and poaching were not halted, many species of large mammals would soon be eliminated. The country outlawed hunting and trade in wildlife products, and many people engaged in such pursuits turned, instead, to ecotourism. Today, more than a half million people per year travel to Kenya to view its tremendous wildlife and spectacular scenery. Local people and businesses profit more by charging ecotourists to see live elephants and rhinoceroses in natural settings than they could by killing the animals for the ivory and horns they provide. Estimates were made in the 1970s that, based on the number of tourist arrivals each year in Kenya and the average amount of money they spent, each lion in one of Kenya's national parks was worth $27,000 annually (much more than the amount it would be worth to a poacher who killed it for its skin or organs), and each elephant herd was worth a stunning $610,000 (in today's dollars, they would be worth much more). Also, whereas some of Kenya's other industries, such as coffee production, vary considerably from year to year in their profitability, ecotourism has been a steady and growing source of revenue (and should continue to be so, as long as political stability is maintained). Thus, the local people have strong economic incentive to preserve and protect their natural resources.

Current popular ecotourist destinations include Kenya, Tanzania, and South Africa in Africa; Nepal, Thailand, and China in Asia; Australia; and, in the Western Hemisphere, Mexico, Puerto Rico, Belize, Guatemala, Ecuador, and the Amazon Basin. Costa Rica, with more than half a million tourist arrivals annually and about 300,000 visits of foreigners to their national parks, is among the best and the most popular ecotourism destinations in the world; the reasons are explored in Chapter 2.

How Ecotourism Helps; Ecotravel Ethics

To the traveller, the benefits of ecotourism are substantial (exciting, adventurous trips to stunning wild areas; viewing never-before-seen wildlife); the disadvantages are minor (sometimes, less-than-deluxe transportation and accommodations that, to many ecotravellers, are actually an essential part of the experience). But what are the actual benefits of ecotourism to local economies and to helping preserve habitats and wildlife?

The pluses of ecotourism, in theory, are considerable (some negatives also have been noticed, and they are discussed in Chapter 4):

1   Ecotourism benefits visited sites in a number of ways. Most importantly from the visitor's point of view, through park admission fees, guide fees, etc., ecotourism generates money locally that can be used directly to manage and protect wild areas. Ecotourism allows local people to earn livings from areas they live in or near that have been set aside for ecological protection. Allowing local participation is important because people will not want to protect the sites, and may even be hostile toward them, if they formerly used the now-protected site (for farming or hunting, for instance) to support themselves but are no longer allowed such use. Finally, most ecotour destinations are in rural areas, regions that ordinarily would not warrant much attention, much less development money, from central governments for services such as road building and maintenance. But all governments realize that a popular tourist site is a valuable commodity, one that it is smart to cater to and protect.

2   Ecotourism benefits education and research. As people, both local and foreign, visit wild areas, they learn more about the sites – from books, from guides, from exhibits, and from their own observations. They come away with an enhanced appreciation of nature and ecology, an increased understanding of the need for preservation, and perhaps a greater likelihood to support conservation measures. Also, a percentage of ecotourist dollars are usually funnelled into research in ecology and conservation, work that will in the future lead to more and better conservation solutions.

3   Ecotourism can also be an attractive development option for developing countries. Investment costs to develop small, relatively rustic ecotourist facilities are minor compared with the costs involved in trying to develop traditional tourist facilities, such as beach resorts. Also, it has been estimated that, at least in Central America, ecotourists spend more per person in the destination countries than any other kind of tourists.

A conscientious ecotraveller can take several steps to maximize his or her positive impact on visited areas. First and foremost, if travelling with a tour group, is to select an ecologically committed tour company. Basic guidelines for ecotourism have been established by various international conservation organizations. These are a set of ethics that tour operators should follow if they are truly concerned with conservation. Travellers wishing to adhere to ecotour ethics, before committing to a tour, should ascertain whether tour operators conform to the guidelines (or at least to some of them), and choose a company accordingly. Some tour operators in their brochures and sales pitches conspicuously trumpet their ecotour credentials and commitments. A large, glossy brochure that fails to mention how a company fulfills some of the ecotour ethics may indicate an operator that is not especially environmentally concerned. Resorts, lodges, and travel agencies that specialize in ecotourism likewise can be evaluated for their dedication to eco-ethics.

Basic ecotour guidelines, as put forth by the United Nations Environmental

Programme (UNEP), the World Conservation Union (IUCN), and the World Resources Institute (WRI), are that tours and tour operators should:

1 Provide significant benefits for local residents; involve local communities in tour planning and implementation.
2 Contribute to the sustainable management of natural resources.
3 Incorporate environmental education for tourists and residents.
4 Manage tours to minimize negative impacts on the environment and local culture.

For example, tour companies could:

1 Make contributions to the parks or areas visited; support or sponsor small, local environmental projects.
2 Provide employment to local residents as tour assistants, local guides, or local naturalists.
3 Whenever possible, use local products, transportation, food, and locally owned lodging and other services.
4 Keep tour groups small to minimize negative impacts on visited sites; educate ecotourists about local cultures as well as habitats and wildlife.
5 When possible, cooperate with researchers; for instance, Costa Rican researchers are now making good use of the elevated forest canopy walkways in tropical forests that several ecotourism facility operators have erected on their properties for the enjoyment and education of their guests.

Committed ecotravellers can also adhere to the ecotourism ethic by disturbing habitats and wildlife as little as possible, by staying on trails, by being informed about the historical and present conservation concerns of destination countries, by respecting local cultures and rules, and even by actions as simple as picking up litter on trails.

Now, with some information on ecotourism in hand, we can move on to discuss Costa Rica.

Chapter 2

Costa Rica: Ecotourism, Geography, Habitats, Parks

A Brief Eco-history of Costa Rica

Costa Rica has a well-deserved reputation as a country sincerely interested in con-serving its natural resources and in fostering ecotourism. Many of its people have enlightened attitudes about using their lands to support themselves in ways other than traditional agriculture – the small farms and ranches for growing coffee, bananas, sugar, or raising cattle that have sustained the economy for generations – and one alternative money-earner with relatively benign effects on the envi-ronment is ecotourism. These attitudes are at least partly attributable to an edu-cated populace. Up to 25% of Costa Rica's national budget is directed toward education, and the country enjoys the highest literacy rate, 93%, in the Americas.

Without doubt, Costa Rica is a fantastic place to visit, particularly for the environmentally minded. People are friendly, the weather tropical, beaches wide and uncrowded, and, importantly, the nation's infrastructure (roads, towns, hotels, hospitals, etc.) is sufficiently developed to permit moderately fast, comfortable, and safe access to most parts of the country, yet undeveloped enough to have left untouched a large number of parks and other now protected areas that teem with wildlife and marvelous natural scenery. In fact, a total of about 75 protected areas (national parks, wildlife refuges, forest reserves) cover more than 1.1 million hectares (2.7 million acres), fully a quarter of the national territory – this in a country the size of the USA's West Virginia. The country is democratic and stable politically, and, in what must have been a burst of incredibly clear and forward thinking, Costa Ricans ("Ticos" as they refer to themselves) almost 50 years ago eliminated their army.

Costa Rica is one of the world's premier ecotourism destinations; a brief look at the country's extensive history with field biology and conservation tells why. Naturalists and field biologists, primarily interested in cataloging flora and fauna, have been attracted to Costa Rica for more than 100 years. The National Museum (Museo Nacional) opened in 1887 and ever since there has been an active exchange of field biologists between Costa Rica and the USA. Owing to its geographic location, rich biodiversity, educated people, stable politics, emerging commitment to preservation of wild areas, and openness toward science and ecology, Costa Rica long ago became a country of choice for many ecological, agricultural, and conservation research programs. The Organization of American States located its Inter-American Institute for Agricultural Science there in 1942 (in Turrialba, east of San José); renamed the Tropical Agricultural Research and Education Center, it has become a center for research into tropical agricultural practices, forestry, and wildlife management. The School of Biology and a zoology museum were initiated at the University of Costa Rica during the 1950s. The Caribbean Conservation Corporation was established in 1959 to protect sea turtle nesting on Costa Rica's beaches. The Ministry of Agriculture and Ranching operates a number of respected agricultural research stations. And, after demands by Costa Ricans for preservation of their disappearing natural habitats, the National Park Service (SPN, Servicio de Parques Nationales de Costa Rica) was formed in 1970. Soon after, more than 20 parks were established throughout the nation.

Meanwhile, North American scientists and educators were playing a role in putting Costa Rica on the path to becoming the training ground for a hefty percentage of the world's tropical biologists and the site of a significant amount of their research. During the early 1960s, a number of North American universities were seeking a tropical base from which to support faculty research and to train graduate students in tropical biology. Together with the University of Costa Rica, in 1963 the seven universities formed a non-profit educational and research consortium, The Organization for Tropical Studies (OTS, or, in Costa Rica, OET: Organización para Estudios Tropicales). Its aims are "to provide leadership in education, research, and the wise use of natural resources in the tropics ... by conducting graduate training, research, and environmental education programs in the tropics from a logistic support base in Costa Rica." Today it consists of more than 50 North American and six Central American colleges and universities. More than 2500 people have participated in OTS field classes and workshops in such areas as tropical ecology, agriculture, earth sciences, forestry, tropical diversity, and conservation biology; also, short courses in tropical biology are offered to governmental decision-makers from the USA and Latin America. It's now true that most of the leaders of tropical biology research, conservation, and governmental programs in the Western Hemisphere have been OTS-trained at some point in their careers. The organization has its administrative base at North Carolina's

Duke University (tel: 919–684–5774; www.ots.duke.edu) and a Central American office in San José (tel: 506–240–6696). The jewels of OTS, however, are the three field stations it operates in Costa Rica, stations that ecotravellers are encouraged to visit: La Selva, in Caribbean lowland rainforest to the north of San José; Las Cruces (which includes the Wilson Botanical Garden), in mid-elevation rainforest in the Southwest; and Palo Verde, in lowland deciduous dry forest on the Pacific side of the country, west of San José. More about these research stations in the Parks section.

Costa Rica may be the only country on Earth that has an organization dedicated to conducting an inventory of its entire biota – every plant and animal, probably a million species, give or take a few. A private, non-profit organization, The National Biodiversity Institute (Instituto Nacional de Biodiversidad, or, as usually referred to, INBio; www.inbio.ac.cr), was established in 1989 to survey and catalog on computer databases the country's flora and fauna. Its aim is to promote conservation and wise use of Costa Rica's natural resources by collecting and distributing information on its biodiversity and ecosystems. To obtain all the information necessary, INBio has taken a pioneering, innovative approach: it trains local people in all parts of the country as *parataxonomists*, research technicians that collect and begin to classify different species, sending their work eventually to a central facility located just outside the capital city. INBio has already established cooperative agreements with private companies, such as Merck Pharmaceuticals, one of the world's largest drug companies, to screen chemical substances found in Costa Rica's plant life for potential use in health-care products. Should profitable drugs eventually be found, INBio would stand to gain substantial amounts of money from royalties.

Costa Rica's national parks lure foreign visitors, but private conservation groups and ecologically oriented private resorts have also led the way to ecotourism growth in Costa Rica – facilities such as Rara Avis (in the mountains adjacent to Braulio Carrillo National Park; tel/fax: 506-253-0844; e-mail:raraavis@sol.racsa.co.cr), Hacienda la Pacifica (near Cañas, Guanacaste; tel: 506-669-0050), Marenco Biological Station/resort (near Corcovado National Park; tel: 506-221-1594), and La Selva and the other OTS research stations. The best example is Monteverde (green mountain), which is known worldwide as an exemplary case of ecotourism development. The main attraction near the small town of Monteverde (settled in 1949 by dairy-farming Quakers from Alabama, USA) is the Monteverde Cloud Forest Reserve (Reserva Bosque Nuboso Monteverde). In 1972, visiting scientists and local residents collaborated to establish the reserve as a 2500 hectare (6200 acre) wildlife sanctuary, protecting the land before it could be used for homesteading and agriculture. (Among the species the preserve was slated to save was the Golden Toad, a small amphibian that may now be extinct; see p. 66 and Plate 2.) Initially only tropical researchers used the site along with a few adventurous travellers. But a BBC documentary in 1978 publicized Monteverde, leading to significant growth in the number of tourist visits each year thereafter. Today, the reserve is owned and operated by the Tropical Science Center (tel: 506-253-3267), a Costa Rican conservation association and, although it is fairly remote, it has deservedly become what must be the nation's premier eco-attraction. The reserve and its surroundings include mid- and high-elevation rainforest areas with a rich, scenic beauty; at any time of the year the forests may be covered by low-lying clouds. There are now several reserves in the area (including the Children's International Eternal Rainforest, the Santa Elena Cloud Forest Reserve, and the

Monteverde Eco-Farm), bringing the total protected area above 10,000 hectares (25,000 acres). More than 500 tree species, 200 ferns, 300 orchids, 600 butterflies, 400 birds, 100 mammals, and 120 reptiles and amphibians have been noted there. Also, the beautiful setting has lured many creative people to be part-time or full-time residents, making Monteverde a kind of international artists' colony. The point is, Monteverde is a fantastic ecotourism success story. The entire economy of the area is based on ecotourism (well, OK, not the *entire* economy; there is still the Monteverde cheese factory, the end product of the original dairy industry in the area). Not only that, almost all the Monteverde business associated with tourists is in the hands of local people, many of them Costa Rican natives. They own stores, delivery services, taxis, hotels, guesthouses, restaurants, and guide services, and local people work for all these businesses. These people now have good economic incentive to preserve their precious rainforest – their livelihoods depend upon it. And talking to people there, one finds that that is exactly their attitude!

The figures in Table 1 show Monteverde's great success. Some say it has become too successful, and that the ecotravel experience is deteriorating: too many people in a small area leading to crowding, eroding trails, and diminished wildlife. Maybe. But on a recent trip I found that it is still a wonderful place. At the Cloud Forest Reserve, there is a limit on trails of 100 people per hour, which keeps people spaced, the experience pleasant. Most visitors are with larger groups, so those going off on their own will quickly find themselves alone. Also, partially to relieve crowding at the Cloud Forest Reserve, a number of other reserves have been established nearby. Information about Monteverde can be obtained from the Monteverde Cloud Forest Reserve office in San José (506-645-5122) or from the Monteverde Tourist Board (506-645-1001).

As for ecotourism in general, it had existed in Costa Rica at a low level for years, but, owing to a combination of factors, it reached a critical mass and took off in the mid-1980s. Some of the factors were increased use of the country by

Table I Growth of Ecotourism in Costa Rica. Numbers are Approximate.

	Number of international arrivals to Costa Rica	Number of visits to national parks by foreigners	Number of visitors to Monteverde Cloud Forest Reserve	Number of researcher/ visitor-days at La Selva Biological Station
1985	250,000	?	7,000	8,100
1986	250,000	?	9,000	9,600
1987	260,000	?	13,000	10,800
1988	320,000	125,000	15,000	12,400
1989	375,000	160,000	17,500	14,100
1990	425,000	220,000	26,000	15,200
1991	500,000	260,000	40,000	15,900
1992	580,000	325,000	49,000	?
1993	680,000	400,000	50,000	18,700
1994	750,000	375,000	49,800	?
1995	785,000	251,000	50,600	22,200
1996	779,000	269,000	47,500	21,700

tropical biology researchers (especially through OTS), some OTS-sponsored and led tours that exposed more people to the country's beauty and wildlife, more individuals making their way there as a result of word-of-mouth advertising, increased formal advertising internationally by the Costa Rican national airline and other groups, and directed marketing to North American conservation groups. As can be seen in Table 1, there was steady growth from the mid-1980s to the mid-1990s; growth has leveled off a bit, but international arrivals into Costa Rica are nearing a million a year; by 1995, ecotourism was pouring more than a half billion dollars per year into the Costa Rican economy.

Geography and Climate

Costa Rica is a long, narrow country (only 115 km, or 70 miles, wide in some spots) that spans the Central American isthmus (Map 1). Like even narrower Panama to its south and broader Nicaragua to its north, it borders both the Atlantic and Pacific. At 51,000 sq km (19,650 sq miles), it is slightly smaller than the USA's West Virginia, slightly larger than Switzerland. Costa Rica's population of about 3.5 million is concentrated in its capital's metropolitan area (San José, with nearly a million people) and a few other cities and larger towns – Alajuela to the capital's northwest, Cartago to its southeast, Limón on the Atlantic coast, Golfito on the Pacific.

The geography of Costa Rica can be summed up in a single sentence: A backbone-like central mountain range that runs the length of the country, northwest to southeast, separates eastern (Caribbean, or Atlantic) and western (Pacific) coastal lowlands. The land area is roughly evenly divided between lowland regions and middle and higher-elevation mountainous regions.

The Caribbean lowlands and foothills of the interior mountains (to 500 m, 1600 ft, in elevation) are wide in the north, near Nicaragua extending 120 km (75 miles) eastwards from the coast, and narrow in the south, in spots near Panama only a few km wide (Map 1). The vegetation over this entire region is (or was, before cutting) mainly tropical rainforest. Rainfall over the Caribbean lowlands is at least moderate all year (a total of 330 to 400 cm, 130 to 160 inches), with the heaviest rains occurring from November through January; the rainy season often lasts from May through early January. Temperatures are distinctly warm, daily *averages* ranging between 22 and 27°C (72 to 80°F); daily *maximum* temperatures, of course, are much higher – 30 to 35°C (86 to 95°F). Parks and reserves within this area that are detailed in this book are Caño Negro National Wildlife Refuge (CNWR), the lower-elevation portion of Braulio Carrillo National Park (BCNP), La Selva Biological Reserve (LSBR, which abuts BCNP), Tortuguero National Park (TONP), and Cahuita National Park (CHNP). Several of Costa Rica's major rivers flow from the mountains through the Caribbean lowlands to the ocean, including the San Carlos, Sarapiquí, and Reventazón.

The central mountainous region of the country consists of four separate ranges: from north to south, they are the Guanacaste Range (Cordillera de Guanacaste), the Tilarán Range, the Central Range, and the Talamanca Range (Map 1). San José, the capital, lies in the Central Valley, at a middle elevation (1170 m, 3840 ft), between the Cordillera Central and Cordillera de Talamanca. Elevations range from 500 m (1600 ft) to many peaks that rise above 3000 m (9800 ft); a Tala-

Map 1 Map of Costa Rica showing mountain ranges, selected cities and towns, and some major rivers.

mancan peak, Chirripó Grande, at 3820 m (12,530 ft), is the country's highest spot. Along the lower and mid-elevation slopes of the mountains the primary vegetation type is rainforest, some areas being wetter than others. In places, *cloud forest* predominates, where low-lying clouds bathe the forests most days, rendering them dark, cool, and moist. On the Caribbean side of the mountains, between 500 and 1600 m (1600 and 5200 ft), moderate temperatures prevail, with daily averages usually between 16 and 22°C (61 to 72°F); daily maximum temperatures are higher. Rainfall, often heaviest in September and October, varies from 150 to 250 cm (60 to 100 inches) per year. Temperatures are generally a bit warmer, and rainfall a bit less, at the same altitudes on the Pacific slopes. At high elevations, above 1600 m (5200 ft), average temperatures are cool (10 to 16°C, or 50 to 61°F). Parks of interest in this geographic region are Rincón de la Vieja National Park (RVNP), Arenal Volcano National Park (ARVL), Monteverde Cloud Forest Reserve (MVCR), Poás Volcano National Park (PONP), Braulio Carrillo National Park (BCNP), the Las Cruces OTS station and its Wilson Botanical Garden (WIBG), and La Amistad National Park (LANP).

The Pacific lowlands can be divided into two regions: the hot and dry northern half (including the Guanacaste Plains, Tempisque River Valley and the Nicoya Peninsula), and the wetter southern half, a narrow ribbon of coastal valleys and river basins that includes the Osa Peninsula (Map 1). In the North, a dry lowland climate that includes a severe 5- to 6-month-long dry season (November to April) supports tropical dry forests. Average rainfall per year over this area varies from 130 to 230 cm (50 to 90 inches; often heaviest in September and October), and daily average temperatures are in the 22 to 28°C (72 to 82°F) range. Daily maximum temperatures are in the low to mid 30s (°C; 90s, °F). Parks in this region are Santa Rosa National Park (SRNP) and Palo Verde National Park (PVNP).

The southern Pacific lowlands, from the Carara Biological Reserve (CABR) all the way to the Panamanian border, have a wet climate that supports tropical moist forests. Yearly rainfall is high, depending on location averaging between 250 and 400 cm (100 to 160 inches). In many parts, rains are most intense in October and November; between January and May there is a 2- to 4-month-long dry season. Average daily temperatures also vary, depending on region and elevation, but are in the range of 21 to 27°C (71 to 81°F); daily maximums average about 32°C (89°F). Parks in the southern Pacific lowlands include CABR, Manuel Antonio National Park (MANP) and Corcovado National Park (CONP).

Visitors should keep in mind that, even during rainy parts of the year, seldom does it rain all day. A typical pattern in the Caribbean lowlands, for instance, is sunny mornings but afternoon showers. Also remember that, in contrast to temperate regions, where season largely determines temperature, in tropical Costa Rica, elevation has the most important effect – the lower you are, the warmer you will be.

Habitats

Tropical Forest: General Characteristics

The most striking thing about tropical forests is their high degree of species diversity. Temperate forests in Europe or North America often consist of only several tree species. The norm in tropical forests is to find between 50 and 100 tree species (or more!) within the area of a few hectares or acres. In fact, sometimes after appreciating a specific tree and then looking around for another of the same species, it is not easy to locate one. Ecologists say tropical areas have a much higher *species richness* than temperate regions – for plantlife, as well as for some animals such as insects and birds. The reasons for geographic differences in species richness are not well understood, but are an area of current research interest (see Close-Up, p. 220).

During first visits to tropical forests, people from Europe, North America, and other temperate-zone areas are usually impressed with the richly varied plant forms, many of which are not found in temperate regions. Although not every kind of tropical forest includes all of them, a number of highly typical plant forms and shapes are usually seen:

Tree Shape and Forest Layering

Many tropical trees grow to great heights, straight trunks rising many meters before branching. Tropical forests often appear layered, or *stratified*, and several more or less distinct layers of vegetation can sometimes be seen. A typical tropical forest has a surface herb layer (ground cover), a low shrub layer, one or more lower levels of shorter trees, and a higher, or *canopy*, tree layer (Figure 1). In reality, there are no formal layers – just various species of trees that grow to different, characteristic, maximum heights. Trees are sometimes referred to as *emergent*, lone, very tall trees that soar high above their neighbors (emergents are characteristic only of tropical forests); *canopy*, those present in the upper layer; *subcanopy*, in the next highest layers; or *understory*, short and baby trees (Figure 1). Many of the *crowns*, or high leafy sections, of tropical trees in the canopy are characteristically-shaped, being short and very broad, looking like umbrellas (Figure 1).

Large-leaved Understory Plants

Tropical forests often have dense concentrations of large-leaved understory shrubs and herbs (Figures 1 and 2). Several plant families are usually represented (Figures 8 and 9): (1) Aroids, family Araceae, include plants such as *Dieffenbachia*, or Dumb Cane, and climbers such as *Monstera*, *Philodendron*, and *Syngonium*. (2) Marantas, family Marantaceae, including *Calathea insignis*, the Rattlesnake plant, which is a herb whose flattened yellow flowers resemble a snake's rattle. (3) Heliconia, family Helioconiaceae, which are large-leaved perennial herbs (see below).

Tree Roots

Any northerner visiting a tropical forest for the first time quickly stops in his or her tracks and stares at the bottoms of trees. The trunks of temperate zone trees may widen a bit at the base but they more or less descend straight into the ground. Not so in the tropics, where many trees are *buttressed* – roots emerge and descend from the lower section of the trunk and spread out around the tree before entering the ground (Figure 2). The buttresses appear as ridges attached to the sides of a trunk, ridges that in larger, older trees, are big and deep enough to hide a person (or a coiled snake!). The function of buttresses is believed to be tree support and, indeed, buttressed trees are highly wind resistant and difficult to take down. But whether increased support is the primary reason that buttressing evolved, well, that's an open question, one that plant biologists study and argue over. Another unusual root structure associated with the tropics is *stilt*, or *prop, roots*. These are roots that seem to raise the trunk of a tree off the ground. They come off the tree some distance from the bottom of the trunk and grow out and down, entering the ground at various distances from the trunk (Figure 2). Stilt roots are characteristic of trees, such as mangroves, that occur in habitats that are covered with water during parts of the year, and many palms. Aside from anchoring a tree, functions of stilt roots are controversial.

Climbers and Stranglers

Tropical trees are often conspicuously loaded with hanging vines (Figures 1 and 2). Vines, also called *climbers*, *lianas*, and *bush-ropes*, are species from a number of plant families that spend their lives associated with trees. Some ascend or descend along a tree's trunk, perhaps loosely attached; others spread out within a tree's leafy canopy before descending toward the ground, free, from a branch. Vines are surprisingly strong and difficult to break; many older ones grow less flexible and more woody, sometimes reaching the diamater of small trees. Common vines that climb trees from the ground up are Philodendrons and those of the genus *Monstera* (Mano de Tigre, in Spanish). Also likely to be seen and admired is a common vine with bright red flowers, *Passiflora spp.*, or Passion Flower (Figure 8). One group, known as strangler figs, (genus *Ficus*), begin their lives growing high on tree branches (that is, as epiphytes – see below), but their strong, woody roots grow down along a tree's trunk, attaching to and fusing with it, before entering the ground (Figure 9). The "host" tree, at the fig's center, eventually dies and rots away, leaving a tall fig tree with a hollow center. The manner in which the strangler kills the host tree is not well understood.

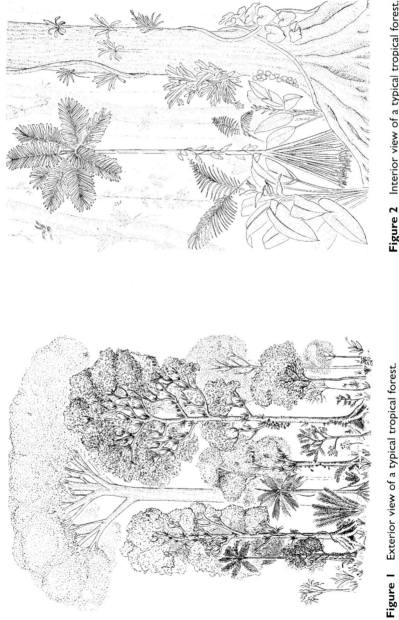

Figure 2 Interior view of a typical tropical forest.

Figure 1 Exterior view of a typical tropical forest.

Epiphytes

These are plants that grow on other plants (usually trees) but do not harm their "hosts" (Figure 2). They are not parasites – they do not burrow into the trees to suck out nutrients; they simply take up space on trunks and branches. (Ecologically, we would call the relationship between a tree and its epiphytes *commensal*: One party of the arrangement, the epiphyte, benefits – it gains growing space – and the other party, the tree, is unaffected.) How do epiphytes grow if they are not rooted in the host tree or the ground? Roots that grow along the tree's surface capture nutrients from the air – bits of dust, soil, and plant parts that breeze by. Eventually, by collecting debris, each epiphyte develops its own bit of soil, into which it is rooted. Epiphytes are especially numerous and diverse in middle and higher-elevation rainforests, where persistent cloud cover and mist provide them with ideal growing conditions. Orchids, with their striking flowers that attract bees and wasps for pollination, are among the most famous kinds of epiphytes. Bromeliads, restricted to the Americas, are common epiphytes with sharply pointed leaves that grow in a circular pattern, creating a central bucket, or *cistern*, in which collects rainwater, dust, soil, and plant materials. Recent studies of bromeliads show that these cisterns function as small aquatic ecosystems, with a number of different animals – insects, worms, snails, among others – making use of them. Several groups of amphibians are known to spend parts of their life cycles in these small pools (pp. 58 and 63), and a number of species of tiny birds nest in bromeliads. (Not all bromeliads are epiphytes; some grow on the ground as largish, spiny plants, such as *Bromelia pinguin* in dry forests, *Aechmea magdalenae* in wet forests, as well as pineapple.) Other plants that grow as epiphytes are mosses and ferns.

Palms

The trees most closely associated with the tropics worldwide are palms. Being greeted by palm trees upon exiting a jet is a sure sign that a warm climate has been reached. In fact, it is temperature that probably limits palms mainly to tropical and subtropical regions. They grow from a single point at the top of their stems, and so are very sensitive to frost; if that part of the plant freezes, the plant dies. Almost everyone recognizes palms because, for trees, they have unusual forms: they have no branches, but all leaves (which are quite large and called *fronds*) emerge from the top of the single trunk; and their trunks are usually of the same diameter from their bottoms to their tops. Many taller palms have stilt roots propping them up. Some palms have no trunks, but grow as small understory plants. Coconut Palms (Figure 10), *Cocos nucifera*, found throughout the world's tropical beaches, occur along both of Costa Rica's coasts, and a number of other palm species are quite common. The Pejibaye Palm (Figure 9), *Bactris gasipaes*, which occurs up to about 1000 m (3300 ft) in elevation, produces a small reddish fruit that is a popular food in Costa Rica, sold on city streets; they are common backyard and roadside trees. Travellers with a penchant for palms should not miss the collection at the Wilson Botanical Garden, which is probably the world's most extensive.

Major Habitats and Common Vegetation

Below are brief descriptions of Costa Rica's major habitats and listings of some of the more abundant and recognizable types of vegetation that visitors are almost sure to see. Note that many plant species occur in more than one habitat type, so although a tree like Balsa, for instance, occurs throughout Costa Rica's Atlantic lowland forests, it is also found in the southern Pacific lowlands and up to middle elevations on some mountain slopes. Some common plants do not have English names; in these cases, Spanish names are provided.

Lowland Wet Forest

Costa Rica's lowland wet forests are classic tropical rainforests with emergent trees and deciduous or evergreen canopy trees reaching 40 to 55 m (130 to 180 ft) in height. Canopy trees have broad crowns and sub-canopy trees broad or round crowns. Tree buttresses are very common and often extend high up on trunks. Palms are abundant, often with stilt roots. The ground in these forests is either mostly bare or sparsely covered with a herb layer. Vines and epiphytes are usually abundant. Biologically, these kinds of forests are probably the richest habitats on Earth, supporting the most species of both plants and animals per unit area (more plant species probably support greater animal richness). Lowland wet forest is found in both the northern and southern Caribbean lowlands (parks in this region include CNWR, LSBR, TONP, and CHNP) and in the southern Pacific lowlands (parks include CONP, MANP, and CABR).

Some common, recognizable trees and shrubs of Costa Rica's lowland wet forests are:

Welfia georgii: A very common palm, often with 70 or more trees per hectare (30 or more per acre). Figure 3.

Ochroma lagopus: Balsa is an abundant tree, up to 30 m (100 ft) tall, from which comes the light, soft wood familiar to model airplane builders and other hobbyists. Balsa grows rapidly in newly cleared forest patches – it is a forest *pioneer* species. Figure 3.

Pentaclethra macroloba: A legume (Gavilán, in Spanish) that is the most common tree in some forests, it often makes up a large percentage of the canopy at about 30 m (100 ft). Its fruits resemble green beans. Figure 3.

Piper: A very common and widespread genus of tropical forest understory shrubs, with more than 90 species represented in Costa Rica. Spanish name is Candela, after the candle-like, erect, flowering structures. Bats (p. 194), instead of insects or birds, act as pollinators on many of these shrubs. Usually 2 to 3 m (6 to 9 ft) high; occurs at elevations up to 2000 m (6500 ft). Figure 3.

Psychotria: Another genus of very common understory shrubs, in the coffee family, with a large number of species; for instance, LSBR has about 40 species. Most species have small white flowers. Figure 4.

Heliconia: A genus of striking flowering plants that is characteristic of tropical forests in the Americas; about 40 species occur in Costa Rica. They grow within forests along streams and in sunny gaps, around clearings, and in disturbed areas such as roadsides and overgrown agricultural fields. Heliconia (Plantanillo, in Spanish) have very large, banana-tree-like, leaves and their flowering structures are red, orange and yellow, large and flat, resembling nothing so much as lobster claws. Heliconia are pollinated by hummingbirds (p. 139). Occurs up to elevations of 2000 m (6500 ft). Figure 4.

Ceiba pentandra: Ceiba, or Kapok, are massive, often epiphyte-laden, trees, large enough to be emergents, with broad, flat crowns. Frequently they are the only trees left standing when pastures are cleared. Fibrous kapok from seeds is used to stuff cushions and furniture. Occurs in lowland areas along both coasts. Figure 4.

Cecropia: These are conspicuous trees as pioneer species – they grow very quickly in disturbed areas of a forest, particularly in large, sunny gaps or clearings. Generally they are thinnish trees with very large, umbrella-like leaves. Most Cecropias internally harbor teeming colonies of biting ants that apparently protect the tree in return for the right to feed on the nectar it produces. They grow at low and middle elevations over much of Costa Rica. Figure 4.

Mangroves: These are relatively short tree species of several unrelated plant families. They have in common the fact that they grow in areas exposed to salt water, usually around bays, lagoons, and other protected coastal infoldings. Mangrove trees occur along both coasts; most conspicuous, particularly along the Pacific, is the Red Mangrove, *Rhizophora mangle.* Figure 5.

Lowland Dry Forest

Lowland dry forests consist of relatively low, mostly deciduous, trees, usually in two layers, one 20 to 30 m (60 to 100 ft) high with large, broad crowns, and one 10 to 20 m (30 to 60 ft) high, more evergreen, with small crowns. Tree buttressing is relatively uncommon in dry forests. Vines are often present. Epiphytes are uncommon, but when present, bromeliads are the most conspicuous. The shrub layer is dense, ground cover sparse. These forests are not as species-rich as wet forests. Dry forest land also makes for excellent agriculture, and because of this, many of these forests throughout Central America have been cleared. Because dry forests have a more open, less dense, structure than wet forests, wildlife viewing in them is often much superior. Lowland dry forest occurs mainly in the northern Pacific lowland (Guanacaste) region; parks include PVNP and SRNP.

Some common, recognizable trees of lowland dry forests are:

Bursera simaruba: The Gumbo Limbo tree is very conspicuous owing to its smooth red/orange bark. Figure 5.

Acrocomia vinifera: A palm tree with spines on its lower trunk, sometimes called the Warree Palm. It occurs particularly in swampy areas and along roadsides, and in old fields and neglected pastures. Figure 5.

Enterolobium cyclocarpum: The Guanacaste, or Ear Fruit, is a legume tree with a very large, spreading crown. They are somewhat rare but still conspicuous because they are often left standing in pastures. Figure 5.

Scheelea rostrata: A palm (Palma Real, in Spanish) that prefers more upland areas, farther from water. Figure 6.

Swietenia macrophylla: Mahogany, source of fine furniture, is a large tree, up to 45 m (145 ft) high and 2 m (6 ft) wide, usually found few and far between in dry forests. Figure 6.

Crescentia alata: Gourd trees are conspicuous, largish, shrub-like trees. Their hard fruit, known as gourds, are eaten after they fall by rodents and horses, and are sometimes used by people for decorative purposes. Figure 6.

Tabebuia: These trees (Corteza, in Spanish), some of the most common in forests of the northern Pacific lowlands, are most conspicuous when they flower. They are *mass-flowerers* – all members of a species in an area burst into flower on the same day, and flowers last only about 4 days. Some species are yellow-flowered, and others, pink. Figure 6.

Gliricidia sepium: A small deciduous tree (Mandero Negro, in Spanish) that grows wild in forests of the northern Pacific lowlands; it can also be seen being used as a living fence there and in other parts of the country. Figure 7.

Highland and Cloud Forest

Under this heading I include a number of types of middle and high elevation rainforest that occur on the slopes and upper portions of Costa Rica's mountain ranges. These rainforests are mixed deciduous and evergreen in their lower reaches and uniformly evergreen in higher areas. Canopy height generally declines as elevation increases, being at between 30 and 40 m (100 to 130 ft) at lower levels and 20 to 30 m (60 to 100 ft) at higher elevations. These forests generally have two tree layers, canopy and subcanopy, and abundant vines. Tree buttressing is common in forest on mountains' lower slopes, but uncommon in higher-elevation areas. Epiphytes – orchids, bromeliads, mosses, and ferns – are profuse in most of these forests. *Cloud forest* occurs over the upper portions of mountains in areas where cloud and fog persistently enshroud the landscape. Cloud forests are evergreen forests, with vines and epiphytes (mosses, ferns, and orchids) being very common. At the highest mountain elevations in Costa Rica, *páramo* predominates, a treeless, subalpine habitat with grasses and shrubs.

Highland forests occur throughout the slopes of Costa Rica's mountain ranges; parks in these regions include ARVL, BCNP, Irazú Volcano National Park (IVNP), LANP, MVCR, PONP, RVNP, WIBG.

Some common and recognizable plants of highland forests are:

Treeferns: These plants are just what they sound like – very large ferns that attain the height of trees – some up to 20 m (65 ft) tall. They are common in many of Costa Rica's forested habitats, from coastal areas to high elevations, being especially prevalent in some of the highest elevation rainforests. Figure 7.

Erythrina spp: Coffee plants, *Coffee arabica*, do well in shade. Plantations, therefore, are often layered, with coffee plants as the understory and a canopy of *Erythrina*, trees that bloom with red or purple flowers. Figure 7.

Drimys winteri: The Winter's Bark tree, a very common plant at high altitudes, ranges from southern Mexico to Tierra del Fuego and is identified by large, leathery oval leaves that are yellow-green on top and waxy white underneath. The wax gives the tree a silvery appearance when the wind blows the leaves. It has clusters of little white flowers and the fruits are dark purple berries. Figure 7.

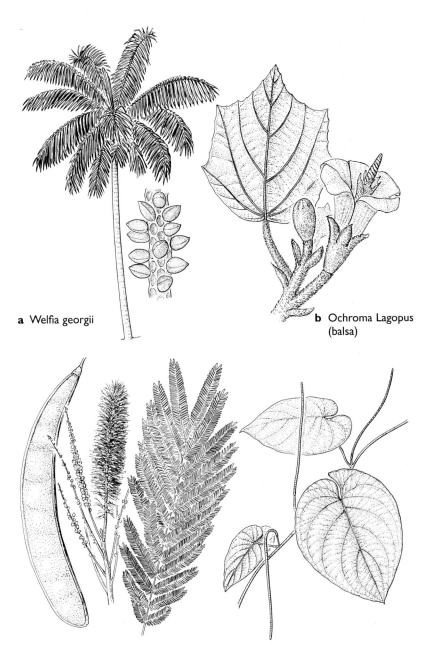

a Welfia georgii

b Ochroma Lagopus (balsa)

c Pentaclethra macroloba

d Piper auritum

Figure 3

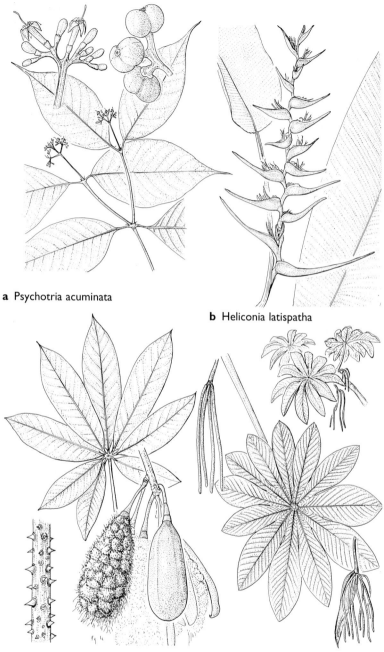

a Psychotria acuminata

b Heliconia latispatha

c Ceiba pentandra

d Cecropia obtusifolia

Figure 4

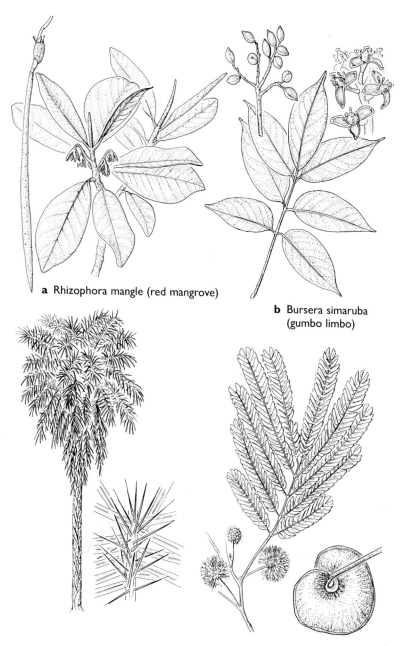

a Rhizophora mangle (red mangrove)

b Bursera simaruba
(gumbo limbo)

c Acrocomia vinifera
(warree palm)

d Enterolobium cyclocarpum
(guanacaste)

Figure 5

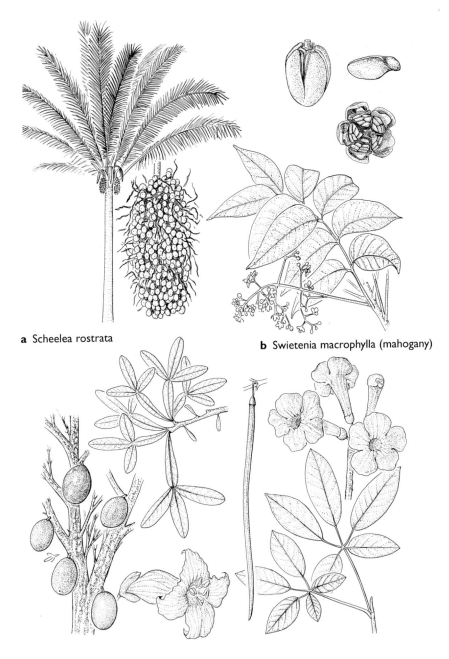

a Scheelea rostrata

b Swietenia macrophylla (mahogany)

c Crescentia alata (gourd)

d Tabebuia rosea

Figure 6

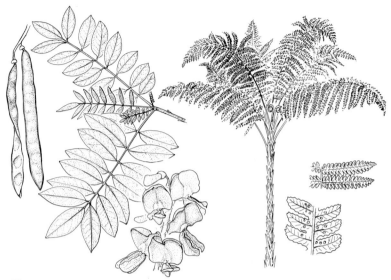

a Gliricidia sepium

b Cyathea multiflora (treefern)

c Erythrina poeppigiana

d Drymis winteri
(winter's bark)

Figure 7

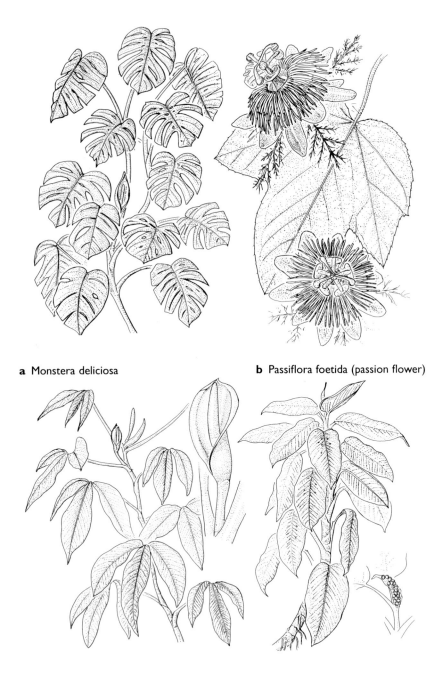

a Monstera deliciosa

b Passiflora foetida (passion flower)

c Philodendron tripartitum

d Dieffenbachia oerstedii
(dumb cane)

Figure 8

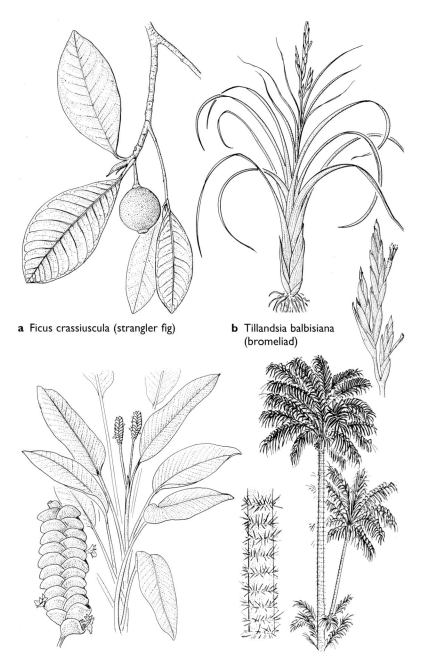

a Ficus crassiuscula (strangler fig)

b Tillandsia balbisiana (bromeliad)

c Calathea insignis (rattlesnake plant)

d Bactris gasipaes (pejibaye palm)

Figure 9

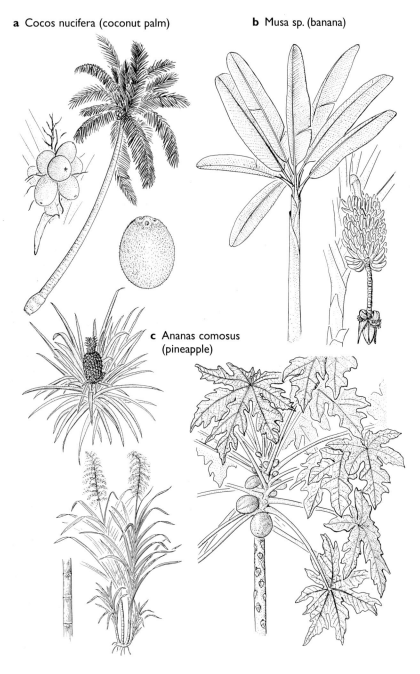

a Cocos nucifera (coconut palm)

b Musa sp. (banana)

c Ananas comosus (pineapple)

d Saccharum officinarum (sugarcane)

e Carica papaya (papaya)

Figure 10

Other major habitats in Costa Rica, and associated parks, include:

Freshwater
River and streamsides, lakes, wetlands. CNWR, CABR, PVNP, among many others.

Coastal Marine
Caribbean: TONP, CHNP; Pacific: CONP, MANP, SRNP.

Pastures, Farms, and Plantations (See Figure 10)
Agriculture in Costa Rica is split between traditional small family farms of, usually, 5 to 10 hectares (12 to 25 acres), which are still plentiful, and large corporate plantations. Family farms generally grow several crops, and plantations, single crops. The biggest export crops are coffee (cáfe), bananas (plátano or banano), pineapple (pina), and sugar. Frozen beef is also exported in large amounts. Coffee, native to Africa, was Costa Rica's first major export crop. Shrubby coffee plants, which can reach 5 m (15 ft) in height, grow over many parts of the country in various climates, but the best beans apparently come from elevations of 800 to 1500 m (2600 to 4900 ft); the crop is concentrated in the middle portion of the Meseta Central, around the capital, San José. Banana trees, with their large leaves and yellow fruit, have an Asian origin. They occur in gardens, but mostly on plantations along the Caribbean and Pacific Coasts. Sugar Cane (caña), grown in several regions of Costa Rica but particularly over the Pacific lowlands and middle elevations, is a perennial grass that may have originated in the New Guinea region. Pineapple plants are bromeliads, and are Neotropical in origin. They are grown mainly in the Meseta Central and mid-Pacific coastal area. Other common crops are corn (maíz), rice (arroz), black beans (frijoles negros), papaya, and chocolate (cacao). Of all of Costa Rica's agriculture, cattle ranching probably has had the greatest impact on the country's natural habitats. Before Columbus, most of Costa Rica was covered by forest; now much of it is covered in grasslands, the result of people cutting and burning forest to create rangeland for cattle. Ranching occurs in many regions of the country, but the cattle industry is centered in the dry Pacific northwest – Guanacaste Province. Cattle ranching is ecologically harmful in a number of ways (see Chapter 4).

Parks: Brief Descriptions and Getting Around

The parks and preserves described below and referred to in the wildlife profiles were selected primarily because they are the ones most often visited by ecotravellers in Costa Rica – by people who come on organized tours and also those who travel independently. Visitors who stay at private nature reserves or resorts in the same regions as the parks listed below can expect to encounter the same types of habitats and wildlife as described for the parks. Park locations are shown in Map 2. If no special information on reaching parks and on wildlife viewing is provided for a particular park, readers may assume that that site is fairly easy to reach and that wildlife can be seen simply by walking along trails, roads, beaches, etc. Tips on increasing the likelihood of seeing mammals, birds, reptiles, or amphibians are given in the introductions to each of those chapters.

In general, Costa Rica's main roads are kept in sufficient repair to permit safe and relatively fast passage. Drive within the speed limit (for safety and because

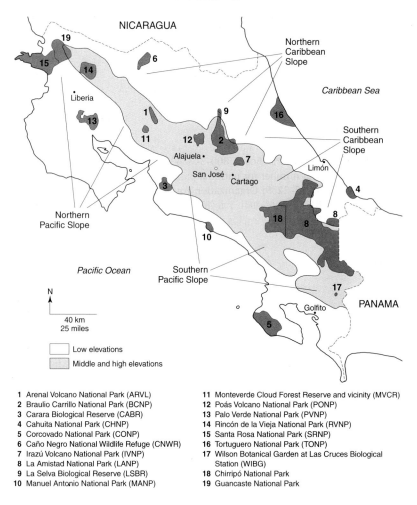

1 Arenal Volcano National Park (ARVL)
2 Braulio Carrillo National Park (BCNP)
3 Carara Biological Reserve (CABR)
4 Cahuita National Park (CHNP)
5 Corcovado National Park (CONP)
6 Caño Negro National Wildlife Refuge (CNWR)
7 Irazú Volcano National Park (IVNP)
8 La Amistad National Park (LANP)
9 La Selva Biological Reserve (LSBR)
10 Manuel Antonio National Park (MANP)

11 Monteverde Cloud Forest Reserve and vicinity (MVCR)
12 Poás Volcano National Park (PONP)
13 Palo Verde National Park (PVNP)
14 Rincón de la Vieja National Park (RVNP)
15 Santa Rosa National Park (SRNP)
16 Tortuguero National Park (TONP)
17 Wilson Botanical Garden at Las Cruces Biological
   Station (WIBG)
18 Chirripó National Park
19 Guanacaste National Park

Map 2 Map of Costa Rica showing locations of parks and reserves mentioned in the text and major cities and towns.

police constantly stake out roads). Let all the speeding local drivers and giant trucks pass, and watch for potholes. Secondary roads are often rife with potholes, greatly slowing driving times; often the phrase "more pothole than road" applies. As anywhere, condition of dirt and gravel roads varies tremendously, from OK to ones that require moving at a snail's pace. Standard sedans are fine for reaching many parks, particularly those approached via paved roads. Four-wheel drive vehicles, with their higher ground clearance, are recommended for remoter areas and for passage on dirt or gravel roads during rainy parts of the year.

A note on Costa Rica's road signs. When approaching a park's locale, slow down, because the sign for the park, if there is one, is probably small and inconspicuous. Usually there are no previous warning signs along the highway, just small signs at the intersections for important turns. Even exiting the main highway to approach the Monteverde Cloud Forest Reserve, one of Costa Rica's main eco-attractions, is adventurous – directions in books and from locals invariably take the form of "make the right turn just before crossing the so-and-so river. ..."

Describing San José, Costa Rica's capital, is outside the scope of this book. But because most foreign visitors to the country spend at least some time in the capital, I want to pass along a warning and a suggestion. The city is incredibly noisy and traffic is terrible. When driving yourself, the best way to avoid monumental traffic jams is to enter and leave the city in the very early morning or, failing that, Sunday almost anytime.

Important phone numbers and web-sites for visiting the parks and reserves: in the USA, Costa Rica Tourist Board, 800–343–6332 (www.tourism-costarica.com); in Costa Rica, central number for national parks and other protected areas, (506) 257–0922 or (506) 257–2239; Organization for Tropical Studies field stations, in the USA, (919) 684–5774 (e-mail: nao@acpub.duke.edu; www.ots.duke.edu); in Costa Rica, (506) 240–6696 (e-mail: reservas@ns.ots.ac.cr); Monteverde Cloud Forest Reserve, in Costa Rica, (506) 645–5122 or (506) 645–1001.

Northern Caribbean Lowlands

La Selva Biological Reserve (LSBR)

La Selva, which is both a world-class biological research station and a nature reserve, is owned and operated by the Organization for Tropical Studies. Less than two hours north of San José by good paved roads, this is a wonderful place to visit. Owing to their complete protection here, animals are a bit bolder than at other sites; visitors often see more wildlife just strolling around the station grounds for a few hours – agouti, coati, peccaries, and a host of birds including toucans, oropendolas, parrots, and bunches of tanagers – than during days of hiking along dank trails elsewhere. The reserve also has a beautiful arboretum and 57 km (35 miles) of trails, some of which require accompaniment by a La Selva guide. The rainforest here is one of the best-studied on Earth. It has more than 1900 species of plants, more than 400 bird species, 116 mammals (half are bats), 25 lizards, 56 snakes, at least 500 butterflies, and more than 400 ant species! A bonus is that La Selva always houses a number of working biology researchers who, during meals, can sometimes be prevailed upon to explain their research. Travellers can visit during the day or, with advance reservations, stay overnight (tel: 506–710–1515). (Area: 1510 hectares, 3700 acres. Elevation: 35 to 150 m, 100 to 500 ft. Habitats: lowland wet forest; forest edge; streams; some adjacent agricultural lands.)

Tortuguero National Park (TONP)

Tortuguero, northeast of Limón on Costa Rica's Caribbean coast, although reachable only by boat or airplane, nonetheless is a frequently visited park. It has rainforest and coastal habitats such as beaches and swamps. Most of the park is rather inaccessible, and there is little in the way of trails (there are one or two short ones). Most visitors tour parts of the park and look for wildlife from small boats which cruise along canals and lagoons. Many people go to Tortuguero (the word means *turtle catcher*) to view sea turtles coming ashore to lay eggs (p. 77); indeed, sea turtle conservation was the driving force behind the park's creation. (Area: 18,900 hectares, 46,000 acres, plus protected ocean reserve. Elevation: sea level. Habitats: lowland wet forest; mangroves; streams, canals, and lagoons; coastal marine/beaches.)

Caño Negro National Wildlife Refuge (CNWR)

This refuge, located several hours northwest of San José, near the Nicaraguan border, was established to protect wetlands particularly important to migratory birds. The prime attraction is Caño Negro Lake, a very shallow 800-hectare (2000-acre) freshwater lake that forms seasonally as overflow from the Frío River. There is little in the way of trails; wildlife viewing is by rented boats and canoes. Bird-watchers come to the refuge especially to see water-associated birds during migrations. The lake tends to dry during March and April, toward the end of the dry season. Roads near the refuge are rough. (Area: 9900 hectares, 25,000 acres. Elevation: 100 m, 300 ft, or less. Habitats: freshwater lake, river; wetlands; lowland wet forest; forest edge.)

Southern Caribbean Lowlands

Cahuita National Park (CHNP)

A fairly small park on the Caribbean, 42 km southeast of the coastal city of Limón, it was established to protect Costa Rica's largest coral reef (about 600 hectares, 1450 acres). Many more foreign visitors visit Tortuguero than visit Cahuita. Snorkeling the reef to view marine life is popular, and there are some trails. Cahuita (which means Mahogany Point) also protects sea turtle nesting beaches. (Area: 1100 hectares, 2600 acres, plus protected ocean reserve. Elevation: sea level. Habitats: lowland wet forest; swamp; coastal marine/beaches; coral reef.)

Southern Pacific Lowlands

Corcovado National Park (CONP)

This is one of the country's great natural attractions and, although a bit difficult to access, well worth a visit. The park is on the Pacific side of the Osa Peninsula, near Panama. Entry to Sirena, the main park station and the starting point of many trails, is by boat, airplane, or all-day walks either through magnificent rainforest or along the beach. The park was created to preserve one of Costa Rica's last (mostly untouched) wilderness areas. Many different habitats are contained within the large park, including lowland rainforest, swamp forest, mangroves, beach, and river. About half the park's interior encompasses higher-elevation rainforest. Trails are excellent and extensive, the beach, beautiful. This is one of the few places in the country where Jaguars are occasionally sighted; their tracks on the beach are common. It is also probably Costa Rica's best place to see Baird's Tapir and Scarlet Macaws, not to mention monkeys and fishing bats. A total of about 140 mammal species and 350+ birds occur there. *Caution*: Mosquitos are usually bad at night, and small ticks and chiggers abundant. Also, long beach walks in some areas need to be timed to tides, because when the tide is high, the beach is gone, and the only land left is impenetrable forest. (Area: 54,000 hectares, 130,000 acres, plus protected ocean reserve. Elevation: sea level to 750 m, 2500 ft. Habitats: lowland wet forest; highland/cloud forest; rivers and streams; mangrove swamp; coastal marine/beaches.)

Manuel Antonio National Park (MANP)

On the Pacific Coast, 3 to 4 hours south of San José, Manuel Antonio is the country's most visited national park. The attractions are the beach, the adjacent resort town of Quepos (with more than 100 hotels), and the wildlife, including one of Costa Rica's only populations of threatened Squirrel Monkeys (Plate 74). Other common animals seen along the sandy beach trails are seabirds and large lizards. To reduce environmental damage and over-crowding, the number of visitors per day to the park is now limited to 600. (Area: 680 hectares, 1650 acres, plus a large, protected ocean reserve. Elevation: sea level. Habitats: lowland wet forest, coastal marine/beaches.)

Carara Biological Reserve (CABR)

This is Costa Rica's most heavily visited wildlife reserve, probably because it is located only about 2 to 3 hours from San José along a main highway. Habitats include evergreen and deciduous forest, river (the Tárcoles) and marshland. Lizards and birds are abundant; Scarlet Macaws (Plate 36) are often sighted, as are White-faced Capuchins (Plate 74). Several trails. Early morning is best, for birds, but also to avoid the (small) crowds; even busloads of (gasp!) schoolchildren are known to visit. (Area: 4700 hectares, or 11,600 acres. Elevation: maximum 150 m, 500 ft. Habitats: lowland wet forest; river; marsh and lagoon.)

Northern Pacific Lowlands

Palo Verde National Park (PVNP)

A relatively lightly visited park about 3 hours northwest of San José, it is home to a number of habitats and diverse wildlife. Dry forests are evergreen and deciduous, and there is an extensive marsh area associated with the Tempisque River. There are also pastures and mangrove swamps. The Organization for Tropical Studies (OTS) leases land from the park for its Palo Verde Biological Research Station (at which travellers, with advance reservations, can visit and stay). Many trails start from the vicinity of the OTS station, and there is good access to the marsh from there. Weather is hot and often windy, especially during the dry season, but wildlife viewing makes a visit worthwhile. Frequently seen are monkeys, coati, peccaries, large lizards, snakes, and, in the marsh, good concentrations of marshbirds and waterbirds – including storks and spoonbills. The park takes its name from the light-green colored Palo Verde bush, or Horse Bean. *Caution*: The road through the park is rough. Also, Africanized honeybees ("killer bees") are common in the region. (Area: 16,800 hectares, 41,500 acres. Elevation: maximum 200 m, 650 feet. Habitats: lowland dry forest; freshwater marsh; river; mangroves; grassland/pastureland.)

Santa Rosa National Park (SRNP)

This park has a fairly high visitation rate because it is located along a main highway, about 4 hours northwest of San José, has beach access, and also national historical significance; the old hacienda located within the park is visited on weekdays by busloads of schoolchildren. Santa Rosa National Park is part of the Guanacaste Conservation district and adjoins Guanacaste National Park; the latter, however, is still little developed for visitors. The Guanacaste, or Ear Tree, is the national tree, and is common in the park. Most of Santa Rosa is dry deciduous forest, but some of the park is in grassland and open woodlands. There are about 20 km (12 miles) of trails, plus firebreak roads. Commonly seen wildlife includes large lizards, monkeys, peccaries, and coati; about 250 species of birds occur there. *Caution*: This area is hot and dry; take a lot of water along on hikes. (Area: 37,000 hectares, 91,000 acres, plus a large ocean preserve. Elevation: sea level to 300 m, 1000 ft. Habitats: lowland dry forest; grassland/pastureland; coastal marine/ beaches.)

Highlands

Monteverde Cloud Forest Reserve (MVCR)

This reserve in the Tilarán Mountains is one of Costa Rica's premier ecotravel destinations (see p. 8). Major habitats are middle- and high-elevation rainforest, and most of the reserve is cloud forest. As noted previously, the reserve supports more than 500 tree species, 200 ferns, 300 orchids, 400 birds, 100 mammals, and 120 reptiles and amphibians. Resplendent Quetzals (Plate 44) are still common. The forest is famous for its epiphytes, which sometimes grow so densely that it is difficult to see crowns of trees that support them. Monteverde's full-time human inhabitants are also of interest. A quirky lot, they are seemingly evenly divided between Quakers and artist-writer types. Long-haired European and North American youths walk the dirt roads lugging guitars. The appropriate question to ask locals that one meets is not "What do you do?" but "What sort of book are you writing?" or "What kind of artworks do you produce?" Advice to pass on about getting there is that, considering Monteverde's status as an important attraction for foreign visitors, the road to it is atrocious. Apparently local people want it that way to discourage mass tourism; and perhaps they are right. A standard sedan can make the 35 km (21 mile) trip from the main highway, but at so slow a speed that it takes about 3 hours; use a 4-wheel drive or take the bus. (Area: 10,500 hectares, 26,000 acres. Elevation: 1200 to 1800 m, 3900 to 5900 ft. Habitats: Highland/cloud forest; forest edge; streams.)

Braulio Carrillo National Park (BCNP)

A large, recently-created park in the rugged Central highlands just north of San José. The habitat is mostly mid- and high-elevation rainforest, dominated by evergreens. The park has many rivers and includes several peaks, the highest being Barva Volcano, at 2906 m (9500 ft). Of ecological interest is that the park extends down into the Caribbean lowlands, at 150 m (500 ft), and directly abuts the low-elevation La Selva Biological Reserve. The result is a protected corridor from low- to high-elevation rainforest, permitting safe migrations for animals that seasonally change altitude (for example, see p. 161). About 6000 plant species, 135 mammals, and more than 400 bird species are found in the park, including Resplendent Quetzals (Plate 44); frogs and toads are also abundant. Unfortunately, although a main highway runs through it, the park is not yet adequately developed for most ecotravellers. There are only a few short trails for day hikers, although some private companies operate ecotravel facilities such as elevated tree canopy walks. (Area: 47,500 hectares, 117,300 acres. Elevation: 150 to 2900 m, 500 to 9500 ft. Habitats: lowland wet forest; highland/cloud forest; rivers and streams.)

Wilson Botanical Garden (WIBG)

The Wilson Garden (part of the Las Cruces Biological Research Station) is owned and operated by the Organization for Tropical Studies (OTS), and although a bit out of the way, it is worth a trip. Located 6 or 7 hours southeast of San José, near the town of San Vito, the Wilson Garden is in the Coto Brus Valley of the Talamanca Mountains. Formerly a tea, then a coffee, plantation, the site, in mid-elevation rainforest, is stunning. The botanical garden proper, recognized as one of Central America's most important, occupies about 10 hectares (25 acres) and includes representatives of about 200 plant families, and 1000 genera (plural of *genus*). In the surrounding reserve, 2000 plant species, 320 birds, 100+ mammals, and about 3000 species of moths and butterflies have been identified. Travellers can visit during the day or, with advance reservations, stay overnight in beautiful rooms. OTS classes and researchers visit frequently. WIBG is considered part of the huge Amistad (*friendship*, in Spanish) Biosphere Reserve. (Area: 145 hectares, 350 acres; 1100 to 1800 m, 3600 to 5900 ft. Habitat: highland wet forest; planted gardens; adjacent agricultural areas.)

La Amistad National Park (LANP)

La Amistad is a huge, wild, remote, and largely unvisited park. It adjoins Chirripó National Park (home of Chirripó Peak, Costa Rica's highest at 3820 m, 12,530 ft), and between them, the two parks encompass much of the Talamanca Mountain Range. La Amistad is actually called an International Park, and it continues across the frontier into Panama. The habitat is middle- and high-elevation rainforest. Estimates are that fully 60% of the animal species in Costa Rica occur in the park, including 400 bird species and 260 species of reptiles and amphibians. The reason for La Amistad's light visitation is that it is difficult to reach and undeveloped for ecotravellers – there are few trails. LANP, together with Chirripó National Park, the Hitoy-Cerere Biological Reserve, and some other large parcels, are the main parts of the 600,000-hectare (1.5 million-acre) Amistad (*friendship*, in Spanish) Biosphere Reserve, a United Nations (UNESCO) declared World Heritage Site. (Area: 193,000 hectares, 476,000 acres. Elevation: 200 to 3800 m, 600 to 12,500 ft. Habitats: highland/cloud forest; marshes; streams.)

Rincón de la Vieja National Park (RVNP)

(Area: 14,100 hectares, 35,000 acres. Elevation: about 1000 to 1987 m, 3200 to 6520 ft.)

Poás Volcano National Park (PONP)

(Area: 5600 hectares, 13,800 acres. Elevation: about 2000 to 2700 m, 6500 to 8800 ft.)

Arenal Volcano National Park (ARVL)

(Area: 2900 hectares, 7200 acres. Elevation: about 1000 to 1633 m, 3200 to 5300 ft.)

Irazú Volcano National Park (IVNP)

(Area: 2300 hectares, 5700 acres. Elevation: about 2000 to 3400 m, 6500 to 11,200 ft.)

These parks are usually visited not for their wildlife but to view the active volcanos they contain: Rincón de la Vieja, Spanish for *Old Woman's Corner*, in the Guanacaste Range, with its peak at 1895 m (6217 ft); Arenal Volcano in the Tilarán Range, at 1633 m (5357 ft); Poás and Irazú Volcanos in the Central Range, at 2704 and 3432 m (8871 and 11,266 ft), respectively. Owing to their proximity to San José, Poás and Irazú are among the most heavily visited of Costa Rica's national parks. All these parks contain high-elevation wet forest and some trails. Of particular interest is stunted-growth forest, *elfin forest*, that grows at high elevations on the mountains' slopes; because of low rates of photosynthesis in the cool weather throughout the year, trees reach maximum heights of only 3 to 10 m (10 to 30 ft). If you visit these parks, remember that it is often quite cool at the higher altitudes.

Chapter 3

How to Use This book: Ecology and Natural History

- What is Natural History?
- What is Ecology and What Are Ecological Interactions?
- How to Use This Book
  Information in the Family Profiles
  Information in the Color Plate Sections

What is Natural History?

The purpose of this book is to provide ecotravellers with sufficient information to identify many common animal species and to learn about them and the families of animals to which they belong. Information on the lives of animals is known generally as *natural history*, which is usually defined as the study of animals' natural habits, including especially their ecology, distribution, classification, and behavior. This kind of information is important for a variety of reasons: Animal researchers need to know natural history as background on the species they study, and wildlife managers and conservationists need natural history information because their decisions about managing animal populations must be partially based on it. More relevant for the ecotraveller, natural history is simply interesting. People who appreciate animals typically like to watch them, touch them when appropriate, and know as much about them as they can.

What is Ecology and What Are Ecological Interactions?

Ecology is the branch of the biological sciences that deals with the interactions between living things and their physical environment and with each other. Animal ecology is the study of the interactions of animals with each other, with plants, and with the physical environment. Broadly interpreted, these interactions take into account most everything we find fascinating about animals – what they eat, how they forage, how and when they breed, how they survive the rigors of extreme climates, why they are large or small, or dully or brightly colored, and many other facets of their lives.

An animal's life, in some ways, is the sum of its interactions with other animals – members of its own species and others – and with its environment. Of particular interest are the numerous and diverse ecological interactions that occur between different species. Most can be placed into one of several general categories, based on how two species affect each other when they interact; they can have positive, negative, or neutral (that is, no) effects on each other. The relationship terms below are used in the book to describe the natural history of various animals.

Competition is an ecological relationship in which neither of the interacting species benefit. Competition occurs when individuals of two species use the same resource – a certain type of food, nesting holes in trees, etc. – and that resource is in insufficient supply to meet all their needs. As a result, both species are less successful than they could be in the absence of the interaction (that is, if the other species was not present).

Predation is an ecological interaction in which one species, the *predator*, benefits, and the other species, the *prey*, is harmed. Most people think that a good example of a predator eating prey would be a mountain lion eating a deer, and they are correct; but predation also includes interactions in which the predator eats only part of its prey and the prey individual often survives. Thus, deer eat tree leaves and branches, and so, in a way, they can be considered predators on plant prey.

Parasitism, like predation, is a relationship between two species in which one benefits and one is harmed. The difference is that in a predatory relationship, one animal kills and eats the other, but in a parasitic one, the parasite feeds slowly on the *host* species and usually does not kill it. There are internal parasites, like protozoans and many kinds of worms, and external parasites, such as leeches, ticks, and mites.

Some of the most compelling of ecological relationships are *Mutualisms* – interactions in which both participants benefit. Plants and their pollinators engage in mutualistic interactions. A bee species, for instance, obtains a food resource, nectar or pollen, from a plant's flower; the plant it visits benefits because it is able to complete its reproductive cycle when the bee transports pollen to another plant. In Central America, a famous case of mutualism involves several species of acacias and the ants that live in them: the ants obtain food (the acacias produce nectar for them) and shelter from the acacias and in return, the ants defend the plants from plant-eating insects. Sometimes the species have interacted so long that they now cannot live without each other; theirs is an *obligate* mutualism. For instance, termites cannot by themselves digest wood. Rather, it is the single-celled animals, protozoans, that live in their gut that produce the digestive enzymes that digest wood. At this point in their evolutionary histories, neither the termites nor their internal helpers can live alone.

Commensalism is a relationship in which one species benefits but the other is not affected in any way. For example, epiphytes (p. 15), such as orchids and bromeliads, that grow on tree trunks and branches obtain from trees some shelf space to grow on, but, as far as anyone knows, neither hurt nor help the trees. A classic example of a commensal animal is the Remora, a fish that attaches itself with a suction cup on its head to a shark, then feeds on scraps of food the shark leaves behind. Remora are commensals, not parasites – they neither harm nor help sharks, but they benefit greatly by associating with sharks. Cattle egrets (p. 108) are commensals – these birds follow cattle, eating insects and other small animals that flush from cover as the cattle move about their pastures; the cattle, as far as we know, couldn't care one way or the other (unless they are concerned about that certain loss of dignity that occurs when the egrets perch not only near them, but on them as well).

A term many people know that covers some of these ecological interactions is *symbiosis*, which means living together. Usually this term suggests that the two interacting species do not harm one another; therefore, mutualisms and commensalisms are the symbiotic relationships discussed here.

How to Use This Book

The information here on animals is divided into two sections: the *plates*, which include artists' color renderings of various species together with brief identifying and location information; and the *family profiles*, with natural history information on the families to which the pictured animals belong. The best way to identify and learn about Costa Rican animals may be to scan the illustrations before a trip to become familiar with the kinds of animals you are likely to encounter. Then when you spot an animal, you may recognize its general type or family, and can find the appropriate pictures and profiles quickly. In other words, it is more efficient, upon spotting a bird, to be thinking, "Gee, that looks like a flycatcher," and be able to flip to that part of the book, than to be thinking, "Gee, that bird is partly yellow" and then, to identify it, flipping through all the animal pictures, searching for yellow birds.

Information in the Family Profiles

Classification, Distribution, Morphology

The first paragraphs of each profile generally provide information on the family's classification (or *taxonomy*), geographic distribution, and *morphology* (shape, size, and coloring of the animals). Classification information is provided because it is how scientists separate animals into related groups and often it enhances our appreciation of animals to know these relationships. You may have been exposed to classification levels sometime during your education, but if you are a bit rusty, a quick review may help: *Kingdom* Animalia: all the species detailed in the book are members of the animal kingdom. *Phylum* Chordata, *Subphylum* Vertebrata: all the species in the book are vertebrates, animals with backbones. *Class*: the book covers several vertebrate classes: Amphibia (amphibians), Reptilia (reptiles), Aves (birds), and Mammalia (mammals). *Order*: each class is divided into several orders, the animals in each order sharing many characteristics. For example, one of the mammal orders is Carnivora, the carnivores, which includes mammals with teeth specialized for meat-eating – dogs, cats, bears, raccoons, weasels. *Family*: Families of animals are subdivisions of each order that contain closely related species that are very similar in form, ecology, and behavior. The family Canidae, for instance, contains all the dog-like mammals – coyote, wolf, fox, dog. Animal family names end in -dae; subfamilies, subdivisions of families, end in -nae. *Genus*: Further sub-divisions; within each genus are grouped species that are very closely related – they are all considered to have evolved from a common ancestor. *Species*: the lowest classification level; all members of a species are similar enough to be able to breed and produce living offspring.

Example: Classification of the Keel-billed Toucan (Plate 50):

Kingdom: Animalia, with more than a million species
Phylum: Chordata, Subphylum Vertebrata, with about 40,000 species
Class: Aves (birds), with about 9000 species
Order: Piciformes, with about 350 species; includes honeyguides, wood-peckers, barbets, and toucans
Family: Ramphastidae, with about 40 species; all the toucans (some newer classifications add the barbets into this group)
Genus: *Ramphastos*, with 11 species; one group of toucans
Species: *Ramphastos sulfuratus*; Keel-billed Toucan

Some of the family profiles in the book actually cover animal orders, while others describe families or subfamilies.

Species' distributions vary tremendously. Some species are found only in very limited areas, whereas others range over several continents. Distributions can be described in a number of ways. An animal can be said to be *Old World* or *New World*; the former refers to the regions of the globe that Europeans knew of before Columbus – Europe, Asia, Africa; and the latter refers to the Western Hemisphere – North, Central, and South America. Costa Rica falls within the part of the world called the *Neotropics* by biogeographers – scientists who study the geographic distributions of living things. A Neotropical species is one that occurs within southern Mexico, Central America, South America, and/or the Caribbean Islands. The terms *tropical*, *temperate*, and *arctic* refer to climate regions of the Earth; the boundaries of these zones are determined by lines of latitude (and ultimately, by the position of the sun with respect to the Earth's surface). The tropics, always warm, are the regions of the world that fall within the belt from 23.5 degrees North latitude (the Tropic of Cancer) to 23.5 degrees South latitude (the Tropic of Capricorn). The world's temperate zones, with more seasonal climates, extend from 23.5 degrees North and South latitude to the Arctic and Antarctic Circles, at 66.5 degrees North and South. Arctic regions, more or less always cold, extend from 66.5 degrees North and South to the poles. The position of Costa Rica with respect to these zones is shown in Map 3.

Several terms help define a species' distribution and describe how it attained its distribution: *Range*. The particular geographic area occupied by a species. *Native or Indigenous*. Occurring naturally in a particular place. *Introduced*. Occurring in a particular place owing to peoples' intentional or unintentional assistance with transportation, usually from one continent to another; the opposite of native. For instance, pheasants were initially brought to North America from Europe/Asia for hunting, Europeans brought rabbits and foxes to Australia for sport, and the British brought European Starlings and House Sparrows to North America. *Endemic*. A species, a genus, an entire family, etc., that is found in a particular place and nowhere else. Galápagos finches are endemic to the Galápagos Islands; nearly all the reptile and mammal species of Madagascar are endemics; all species are endemic to Earth (as far as we know). *Cosmopolitan*. A species that is widely distributed throughout the world.

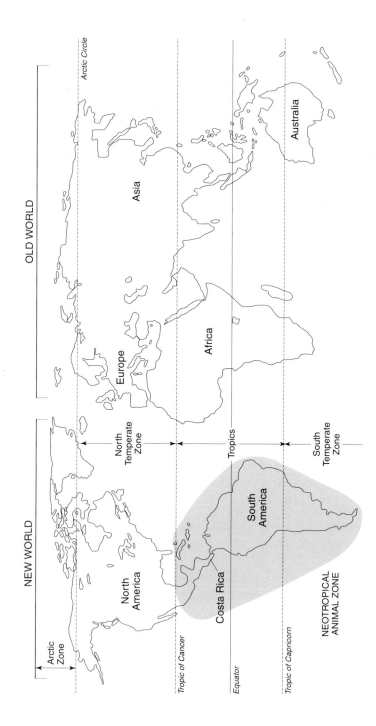

Map 3 Map of the Earth showing the positions of Costa Rica; Old World and New World zones; tropical, temperate, and arctic regions; and the Neotropical animal life zone.

Ecology and Behavior

In these sections, I describe some of what is known about the basic activities pursued by each group. Much of the information relates to when and where animals are usually active, what they eat, and how they forage.

Activity Location – *Terrestrial* animals pursue life and food on the ground. *Arboreal* animals pursue life and food in trees or shrubs. Many arboreal animals have *prehensile* tails, long and muscular, which they can wrap around tree branches to support themselves as they hang to feed or to move about more efficiently. *Cursorial* refers to animals that are adapted for running along the ground. *Fossorial* means living and moving underground.

Activity Time – *Nocturnal* means active at night. *Diurnal* means active during the day. *Crepuscular* refers to animals that are active at dusk and/or dawn.

Food Preferences – Although animal species can usually be assigned to one of the feeding categories below, most eat more than one type of food. Most frugivorous birds, for instance, also nibble on the occasional insect, and carnivorous mammals occasionally eat plant materials.

> *Herbivores* are predators that prey on plants.
> *Carnivores* are predators that prey on animals.
> *Insectivores* eat insects.
> *Granivores* eat seeds.
> *Frugivores* eat fruit.
> *Nectarivores* eat nectar.
> *Piscivores* eat fish.
> *Omnivores* eat a variety of things.
> *Detritivores*, such as vultures, eat dead stuff.

Breeding

In these sections, I present basics on each group's breeding particulars, including type of mating system, special breeding behaviors, durations of egg incubation or *gestation* (pregnancy), as well as information on nests, eggs, and young.

Mating Systems – A *monogamous* mating system is one in which one male and one female establish a pair-bond and contribute fairly evenly to each breeding effort. In polygamous systems, individuals of one of the sexes have more than one mate (that is, they have harems): in *polygynous* systems, one male mates with several females, and in *polyandrous* systems, one female mates with several males. (See Close-Up, p. 182)

Condition of young at birth – *Altricial* young are born in a relatively undeveloped state, usually naked of fur or feathers, eyes closed, and unable to feed themselves, walk, or run from predators. *Precocial* young are born in a more developed state, eyes open, and soon able to walk and perhaps feed themselves.

Ecological Interactions

These sections describe what I think are intriguing ecological relationships. Groups that are often the subject of ecological research are the ones for which such relationships are more likely to be known.

Lore and Notes

These sections provide brief accounts of folklore associated with the profiled groups, and any other interesting bits and pieces of information about the profiled animals that do not fit elsewhere in the account.

Status

These sections comment on the conservation status of each group, including information on relative rarity or abundance, factors contributing to population declines, and special conservation measures that have been implemented. Because this book concentrates on animals that ecotravellers are most likely to see – that is, on more common ones – few of the profiled species are immediately threatened with extinction. The definitions of the terms that I use to describe degrees of threat to various species are these: *Endangered* species are known to be in imminent danger of extinction throughout their range, and are highly unlikely to survive unless strong conservation measures are taken; populations of endangered species generally are very small, so they are rarely seen. *Threatened* species are known to be undergoing rapid declines in the sizes of their populations; unless conservation measures are enacted, and the causes of the population declines identified and halted, these species are likely to move to endangered status in the near future. *Vulnerable to threat* or *near-threatened*, are species that, owing to their habitat requirements or limited distributions, and based on known patterns of habitat destruction, are highly likely to be threatened in the near future. For instance, a fairly common bird species that breeds often in coastal mangrove swamps (such as Costa Rica's Mangrove Swallow, Plate 41) might be considered vulnerable to threat if it is known that people are cutting mangroves at a high rate. Several organizations publish lists of threatened and endangered species.

Where appropriate, I also include threat classifications from the Convention on International Trade in Endangered Species (CITES) and the United States Endangered Species Act (USA ESA) classifications. CITES is a global cooperative agreement to protect threatened species on a worldwide scale by regulating international trade in wild animals and plants among the 130 or so participating countries. Regulated species are listed in CITES Appendices, with trade in those species being strictly regulated by required licenses and documents. CITES Appendix I lists endangered species; all trade in them is prohibited. Appendix II lists threatened/vulnerable species, those that are not yet endangered but may soon be; trade in them is strictly regulated. Appendix III lists species that are protected by laws of individual countries that have signed the CITES agreements. The USA's Endangered Species Act works in a similar way – by listing endangered and threatened species, and, among other provisions, strictly regulating trade in those animals.

Information in the Color Plate Sections

Pictures

Among amphibians, reptiles, and mammals, males and females of a species usually look alike, although often there are size differences. For many species of birds, however, the sexes differ in color pattern and even anatomical features. If only one individual is pictured, you may assume that male and female of that species look exactly or almost alike; when there are major sex differences, both male and female are depicted. The animals shown on an individual plate, in most cases, have been drawn to the correct scale relative to each other.

Name

I provide the common English name for each profiled species, the scientific, or Latin, name, and local names and their English translations, if known. Often, in Costa Rica, the local name for a given species varies regionally. For some species, apparently there are no agreed upon Spanish names, or, as likely, I could not find them.

ID

Here I provide brief descriptive information that, together with the pictures, will enable you to identify most of the animals you see. The lengths of reptiles and amphibians given in this book are their *snout–vent lengths* (SVLs), the distance from the tip of the snout to the vent, unless I mention that the tail is included. The *vent* is the opening on their bellies that lies approximately where the rear limbs join the body, and through which sex occurs and wastes exit. Therefore, long tails of salamanders and lizards, for instance, are not included in the reported length measurements, and frogs' long legs are not included in theirs. I make an exception for snakes, for which I give total lengths. For mammals, measurements given are generally the lengths of the head and body, but do not include tails. Birds are measured from tip of bill to end of tail. For birds commonly seen flying, such as seabirds and hawks, I provide wingspan (wingtip to wingtip) measurements, if known. For most of the passerine birds (see p. 100), I use to describe their sizes the terms *large* (more than 30 cm, 12 in, long); *mid-sized* (between 15 or 18 cm, 6 or 7 in, and 30 cm, 12 in); *small* (10 to 15 cm, 4 to 6 in); and *very small* (less than 10 cm, 4 in).

Habitat/Parks

In these sections I list the regions and habitat types in which each species occurs, symbols for the habitat types each species prefers, and the initials of frequently visited parks and reserves where each species may be found. A species said to occur on the *Caribbean* (or *Atlantic*) *slope* occurs somewhere between the higher mountains in the central part of the country and the Caribbean; *Pacific slope* refers to the area between the higher mountains and the Pacific (see Map 2, p. 28). Note that the various species may also be found in other parks that are not listed, and outside of parks as well. For instance, many of the species that are found in Palo Verde and Santa Rosa National Parks in the northern Pacific lowlands also occur on the Nicoya Peninsula (Map 1). In general, *low elevation* refers to between 0 and 500 m (0 and 1600 ft) above sea level; *middle elevation* means between 500 and 1200 m (1640 and 4000 ft), and *higher elevation* means greater than 1200 m (4000 ft). The parks listed for a particular species are (1) those in which the species is known to occur and also (2) those in which it probably occurs, based on the known range of the animal, the elevation and type of habitat it prefers, and the elevations and types of habitats known to be present in the various parks.

Explanation of habitat symbols:

= Lowland wet forest.

= Lowland dry forest.

= Highland forest/cloud forest. Includes middle elevation and higher elevation wet forests and cloud forests.

= Forest edge/streamside. Some species typically are found along forest edges or near or along streams; these species prefer semi-open areas rather than dense, closed, interior parts of forests. Also included here: open woodlands, tree plantations, and shady gardens.

 = Pastureland/on-tree plantations/savannas (grassland with scattered trees, shrubs)/gardens without shade trees/roadside. Species found in these habitats prefer very open areas.

 = Freshwater. For species typically found in or near lakes, streams, rivers, marshes, swamps.

= Saltwater/marine. For species usually found in or near the ocean or ocean beaches.

Parks and reserves:

ARVL	Arenal Volcano National Park
BCNP	Braulio Carrillio National Park
CABR	Carara Biological Reserve
CHNP	Cahuita National Park
CONP	Corcovado National Park
CNWR	Caño Negro National Wildlife Refuge
IVNP	Irazú Volcano National Park
LANP	La Amistad National Park
LSBR	La Selva Biological Reserve
MANP	Manuel Antonio National Park
MVCR	Monteverde Cloud Forest Reserve and vicinity
PONP	Poás Volcano National Park
PVNP	Palo Verde National Park
RVNP	Rincón de la Vieja National Park
SRNP	Santa Rosa National Park
TONP	Tortuguero National Park
WIBG	Wilson Botanical Garden at Las Cruces Biological Station

Example

Plate 50a

Keel-billed Toucan
Ramphastos sulfuratus
Tucán Pico Iris = rainbow-billed toucan
Curré Negro

ID: A large, mostly black bird with yellow face and chest, yellowish green skin around eye and that amazing, rainbow-colored (green-orange-blue) toucan's bill; to 47 cm (18.5 in).

HABITAT: Low and some middle elevation forests, Caribbean and parts of northern Pacific slopes; found in tree canopy in more open habitats such as forest edges, tree plantations, and, in drier forests, along rivers and streams.

PARKS: BCNP, CHNP, CNWR, LSBR, MVCR, RVNP, SRNP, TONP

Chapter 4

Conservation in Costa Rica

- Environmental Threats
- Conservation Programs
- Ecotourism and Conservation
- Costa Rica's Special Role

Costa Rica holds a truly unique position among the world's tropical nations with regard to conservation. This small country simultaneously is among the nations facing severe environmental threats and the nation that is perhaps most active in conservation efforts. In this chapter I briefly describe some of the major threats to Costa Rica's ecosystems, as well as the country's conservation programs and initiatives.

Environmental Threats

Costa Rica is a wonderful country to visit but it is not an eco-paradise. Like any other country, there are problems, both socioeconomic and ecological. Costa Rica's population, about 3.5 million during the late 1990s, is growing quickly (2.6% per year), and will probably double before it stabilizes; most of the people are concentrated in a single region – in and around the capital, San José, and in the surrounding flat part of the Central Valley (the Meseta Central). Most environmental damage in the country is the result of generations of wasteful and polluting agriculture, practices that persist to this day.

The foremost cause for environmental concern is deforestation. Most forest cutting and burning is not to obtain timber but to clear land for cattle pastures, crop farming, and simply as a way to claim "unused" land. The entire country was once forested. Now most of it has been cleared, much of it recently. One-third of Costa Rica's forest cover was lost between 1950 and 1985, and the country still has one of the highest rates of deforestation in Central America and, in fact, in the world. According to the World Resources Institute, Costa Rica recently ranked 4th among the world's nations in rate of deforestation, with 3.9% of its forested area being cut each year (about 65,000 hectares, or 160,000 acres). As a result of past and present forest clearing, Costa Rica is among the Central American countries with the smallest percentage of its rainforests still intact. Perhaps only 5% of land outside of protected parks and reserves is still densely forested. Particularly hard-hit has been the tropical dry forest habitat that occupied Costa Rica's north-west Pacific lowlands. This habitat type, remnants of which are still found in Palo Verde, Santa Rosa, and Guanacaste National Parks, once stretched in a narrow belt along the Pacific from southern Mexico to Panama. Unfortunately, these dry forests lands were easily accessible and able to support several types of agriculture; by now, less than 1% remains of the original dry forests of Central America.

Cattle ranching, aside from large-scale deforestation required to create pastureland, is ecologically harmful in a number of other ways. Cattle grazing causes soil erosion, nutrient depletion of grazed lands, and ground compaction that prevents many plants from growing. Other agricultural practices have also led to environmental deterioration and dangers. The main plantation crops, coffee and bananas, are grown largely in *monoculture* – the entire plantation devoted to a single crop plant. This type of farming generally requires heavy use of pesticides and leads to depletion of soil nutrients. Also, large swaths of land populated by single plant species provide poor habitat for wildlife. The general rule is that the more complex the vegetation, the more animal species that can thrive in it. The species-rich wildlife of tropical forests cannot live in the pastures and monoculture plantations that replace cleared forest. The result of deforestation, therefore, is decreased plant diversity, which leads to decreased animal diversity.

Conservation Programs

Loss of the world's rainforests and the plant and animal species they contain – their biodiversity – is occurring at an alarming rate. People and governments are beginning to realize the scope of the problem and to take action. But the problems are long-established and severe, the possible solutions new, tentative, and difficult to introduce and enforce. To paraphrase one scientist who researches conservation strategies: It is difficult enough to change agricultural practices and implement conservation programs in the USA, a relatively rich, educated, technologically advanced, democratic country; imagine how much more difficult it must be for environmentalists in smaller, poorer countries to try to change long-standing agricultural and forestry policies, countries in which business concerns usually hold sway.

By most criteria, Costa Rica has a very good recent environmental record. By pursuing a number of conservation policies, by establishing and protecting parks, and by promoting ecotourism, the country is doing much to preserve its environmental heritage. Costa Rica has a long history of interest in biodiversity conservation, having enacted strict wildlife trade laws about 1970 and, in 1975, being the first Central American signer of the Convention on International Trade in Endangered Species (CITES) (see p. 40).

Costa Rica's system of national parks, initiated during the 1970s and added to regularly ever since, is the country's main effort at conservation. About 25% of the nation's land is included in parks and reserves that protect a healthy variety of ecosystems in diverse regions of the country. This park system is widely regarded as one of the world's finest. One national park, La Amistad (meaning *friendship*), adjoins a park in Panama, and another international park, adjoining a potential Nicaraguan park to Costa Rica's north, is being considered (the Peace Park).

A host of private conservation organizations based in Costa Rica or elsewhere have active biodiversity research or conservation programs in the country. I will mention just a few. The Neotropica Foundation (Fundación Neotropica) is Costa Rica's main nongovernmental, nonprofit conservation group. It buys ecologically important parcels of forested land to save them from imminent development and cooperates with international organizations. For instance, it collaborates with the World Wildlife Fund's Tropical Forestry Program on a forestry project on the Osa Peninsula. The project, named BOSCOSA, works to maintain the natural forests that surround Corcovado National Park by developing forest management and agricultural practices that are both ecologically and culturally suited to the region, and then teaching the practices to the local communities. The Neotropica Foundation is also collaborating on plans to establish a protected *greenway* wildlife corridor that will extend from Mexico to Colombia.

The Caribbean Conservation Corporation (CCC), established almost 40 years ago to protect sea turtles (see p. 77), is also involved in other conservation efforts, such as protecting the forests that surround Tortuguero National Park. INBio, the privately funded biodiversity organization (see p. 8) whose purpose is to collect, catalog, and disseminate information on Costa Rica's plant and animal species, has an important role to play in conservation because before conservation plans are made, it is always a good idea to know which species are in a country, and where they occur.

The Organization for Tropical Studies (OTS; see p. 7), in addition to foster-ing basic biological research at its three field stations, is also engaged in research into sustainable agricultural practices. (*Sustainable* means using plants and ani-mals in ways that are economically profitable for the local economy yet not eco-logically harmful; the use, in other words, will not lead to significant ecosystem damage or to decline in biodiversity.) At its La Selva research station, OTS carries out a project known as TRIALS that has attracted worldwide notice from govern-ments and conservation organizations. The project's purpose is to identify rapidly growing native tree species that might be used for sustainable forestry. Previously, no one really knew which native trees grew fastest and also provided high-qual-ity wood. Researchers at La Selva, by planting and monitoring large plots of land with almost 100 different tree species, eventually will be able to tell local tree pro-ducers which species are best to plant for tree farms (for eventual cutting and mar-keting) and also for reforesting old abandoned pastures. Already, near La Selva, applications of this research are being put into practice.

The TRIALS project brings up the subject of sustainable agriculture. For effec-tive, country-wide conservation, more than a large system of protected parks is necessary. What goes on outside of the parks, how nonprotected lands are treated, also matters a great deal. For example, consider two of Costa Rica's main export crops, coffee and bananas. These crops can be grown on plantations in environ-ment-damaging or environment-enhancing (*green*) ways. The traditional coffee crop on Costa Rica's family farms had low coffee plants growing beneath a canopy of trees (often *Erythrina*, p. 18), which provided shade as well as protec-tive ground mulch. When large corporations went into the coffee business, they increased yields by switching to *sun coffee*, growing coffee plants alone on large plantations, using fertilizers and pesticides extensively to do for their crop what shade trees used to. Many other growers also produce sun coffee. Unfortunately, monotonous rows of low coffee plants are a poor habitat for animal life, espe-cially birds. The drive to get large companies to produce only *shade-grown coffee* is concerned with having them add canopy trees to their plantations, thus improving the coffee's taste (as some insist), decreasing the amounts of chemicals needed, and, not incidentally, greatly enhancing the habitat for wildlife use. You might not think that simply planting shade trees above coffee plants would make much of a difference, but it does! It turns out that plantations with trees and understory crop plants provide habitats sufficiently complex to attract abundant wildlife, particularly migratory birds. The incentive for companies to produce shade-grown coffee is that they can advertise it as such and, hence, charge more for it. Many surveys have demonstrated that consumers, both in Costa Rica and in export countries, are willing to pay more for green products such as shade-grown coffee.

Costa Rica's banana industry, as well, is turning increasingly toward green production. Much of the new forest clearing in the country goes to establish new banana plantations, the result of a boom in international demand for Costa Rica's bananas. The ECO-O.K. Banana Project allows producers who comply with a wide range of green requirements to place ECO-O.K. stickers on their fruit and to use the term when advertising. To earn this green seal of approval, growers must not clear new forest for more plantations, must maintain greenbelts of natural vegetation along rivers and roads on their properties, and must store and manage pesticides and agricultural wastes in approved ways.

In addition to coffee and bananas, a broad range of Costa Rica's agricultural products can be grown in green ways, and marketed as green, or *organic* – fruits such as papaya, pineapple, oranges, and blackberries; spices and herbs such as cinnamon, vanilla, and pepper; and vegetables such as lettuce and radishes. Forest products likewise can be harvested in compliance with a green philosophy. One Costa Rican company that emphasizes strict sustainable forestry practices (harvesting specific trees without destroying the forests in which they grow) successfully markets wood products internationally under the trade name Royal Mahogany (actually a tree species in the mahogany family which is very abundant over Costa Rica's northern Caribbean lowlands). Buyers pay a premium price for the wood because they know it was harvested in an environmentally friendly way.

Ecotourism and Conservation

Ecotourism can contribute to sustainable development. In Chapter 1, I discussed ecotourism's economic and ecological advantages to Costa Rica and other destinations. But does ecotourism always help local economies and significantly preserve visited habitats and wildlife? This question is important because increasingly, the fostering of ecotourism is suggested by indigenous people in developing nations, by the nations themselves, and by international conservation organizations, as one of the best methods to preserve natural resources and biodiversity almost anywhere that they are threatened. Certainly it works to a degree – witness success stories in places such as Kenya and, especially, Costa Rica. However, as with any popular program that undergoes rapid growth, there are problems. Many people who monitor tourism – researchers and government officials – believe that in the rush to make money from ecotourism, benefits are often overstated and problems ignored.

Many private companies purporting to be "ecotour" operators are "eco-" in name only; they are interested solely in profits, and are not concerned about local economies or the wild areas into which they take tourists. There is increasing concern about monetary "leakage": despite attempts to keep most of the ecotourist revenues in local destination economies, many of those dollars, more than 50% by recent estimates, leak back to large urban areas of destination countries and even to developed nations; relatively little actually is spent on conservation. In some countries, ecotourism is an unstable source of local employment and economic well-being. Tour bookings are heavily dependent on seasonal trends, on the weather, on a country's political situation, and on worldwide currency fluctuations. Finally, popularity as an ecotourism site may inevitably lead to its failing. As ecotourism expands dramatically, sites that are over-used and under-managed will be damaged. Trails in forests gradually enlarge and deepen, erosion occurs, crowds of people are incompatible with natural animal behavior. Also, ecotourism's success harms itself in another way: when any area becomes too popular, many travellers wanting to experience truly wild areas and quiet solitude no longer want to go there; that is, with increasing popularity, there is an inexorable deterioration of the experience.

Thus, ecotourism is not a miracle cure-all for conservation; these days it is understood to be a double-edged sword. Clearly, large numbers of people visiting sites cannot help but have adverse impacts on those sites. But as long as operators of the facilities are aware of negative impacts, careful management practices can reduce damage. Leakage of ecotourist revenue away from the habitats the money was meant to conserve is difficult to control, but some proportion of the money does go for what it is intended and, with increased awareness of the problem, perhaps that proportion can be made to grow. Travellers themselves can take steps to ensure that their trips help rather than hurt visited sites (see p. 4).

Costa Rica's Special Role

In one respect, Costa Rica holds an enviable position for a small country with some serious environmental problems: many international organizations consider it to be the country of choice in which to begin conservation projects. Literally hundreds of environmental projects take place in the country, both those oriented toward research and actual conservation practice. In some years, more conservation programs are funded by foreign organizations in tiny Costa Rica than in relatively huge Brazil. Recently, the USA government alone sponsored 114 individual projects in Costa Rica; additionally, other countries sponsor programs in Costa Rica, as do many of the world's private international conservation organizations. The reasons for all the attention to Costa Rica are well-known: as the realization grows that the world's tropical forests are endangered, and money is increasingly available to try to preserve some of the forests, decisions need to be made about where to begin. Logically, the international community chooses to start in a place where they can operate in safety and security, preferably in a stable democratic country with good infrastructure and educated people, where there is a variety of species-rich ecosystems in need of conservation – a description that superbly fits Costa Rica.

A consequence of all the conservation attention is that Costa Rica has become a training and proving ground for tropical biologists and conservation research and programs. Conservation projects are often tried here first, under what most program managers would consider almost ideal conditions. If a project works in Costa Rica, it can then be tried elsewhere, in countries where conditions are more difficult and, perhaps, less friendly toward conservation.

Costa Rica's special role in the world conservation community sometimes brings criticism. Some conservationists and researchers have begun to question whether all the conservation work in Costa Rica has really made significant progress in conserving the country's natural resources. Certainly some progress has been made, and some programs will not show appreciable benefits for years. On balance, most agree that Costa Rica has a fine conservation record. But a crucial question being asked is: If Costa Rica, with its system of national parks and abundance of conservation programs, cannot stem the loss of its biodiversity, then what country can?

Chapter 5

Amphibians

General Characteristics and Natural History

Amphibians first arose during the mid part of the Paleozoic Era, 400 million years ago (although paleontologists are unsure if it was on a Thursday or Friday), developing from fish ancestors that had lungs and thus could breathe air. The word "amphibian" refers to an organism that can live in two worlds, and that is as good a definition of the amphibians as any: most stay in or near the water, but many spend at least portions of their lives on land. In addition to lungs, amphibians generally have wet, thin skins that aid in gas exchange (breathing). Amphibians were also the first animals to develop legs for walking on land, the basic design of which has remained remarkably constant for all other land vertebrates. Many have webbed feet that aid locomotion in the water.

Approximately 4500 species of living amphibians have been described. (Owing to their all-terrestrial existence, almost all reptiles, birds, and mammals living on Earth have been identified but, most experts agree, many more amphibians, with their aquatic ways, remain to be discovered.) They are separated into three groups. The *salamanders* (Order Caudata, or "tailed" amphibians) comprise 450 species (about 35 in Costa Rica), the mysterious *caecilians* (sih-SIL-ians; Order Gymnophiona) number about 160 species, and the *frogs* and *toads* (Order Anura, "without tails") make up the remainder, and the bulk, of the group (with about 120 species in Costa Rica).

Most amphibians live in the water during part of their lives. Typically a juvenile stage is spent in the water and an adult stage on land. Because amphibians need to keep their skin wet, even when on land, they are mostly found in moist habitats – in marshes and swamps, around the periphery of bodies of water, in wet forests. Adults of most species return to the water to lay eggs, which must stay wet to develop. Some amphibians – toads and some salamanders – are entirely terrestrial, laying eggs on land in moist places.

Relatively little is known of the caecilians. They are confined to tropical forests of Africa, Southeast Asia, and Central and South America, the latter two locations being their principal home (there are no Sicilian caecilians). They are legless with slender bodies up to 40 cm (15 in) long and up to 2.5 cm (1 in) in diameter, with ringed creases along their lengths – resembling nothing so much as a cross between a snake and an earthworm (Plate 1). Their skin is studded with small scales. Caecilian eyes are tiny and most are blind as adults. For sensing their environment they possess a pair of small tentacles at the head end that are continually extended out of and then withdrawn into the body. They feed on worms and other small invertebrate animals – termites, beetles, etc. – that they find underground. Because they spend much of their lives beneath the ground, caecilians are very rarely seen by people. However, they commonly leave their burrows at night during rains, moving along the ground, presumably foraging. Occasionally they are found in meadows and forests under logs and rocks, or buried deep in the leaf litter. I remember finding one, apparently bloodied and dropped by a predator, on a dirt road in South America. It was the first one another biologist and myself had seen outside of photographs, and it took quite a while for us to decide just what it was (a mutant worm from outer space, our first guess, turned out to be incorrect). Caecilians do not lay eggs, but give birth to live young.

Salamanders, intriguingly, are not much interested in the tropics. They are an almost exclusively temperate zone group. In the tropics they usually inhabit moist, cool areas, such as middle and higher elevation cloud forests. About 200 species are completely terrestrial. Females of these species lay eggs in moist places and then stay with the eggs, protecting them until hatching, sometimes coiling themselves around the eggs. *Newts* are a group of aquatic salamanders, often with rough-textured skin. Many lay their eggs singly on pond bottoms or on vegetation, but other aquatic salamanders lay their eggs in large, jelly-covered clusters, which they attach to sticks or plants in the water. The aquatic salamanders do not protect their eggs.

Most species of frogs and toads live in tropical or semi-tropical areas but some groups are abundant in temperate zone latitudes. Frogs can be either mostly aquatic or mostly terrestrial; some live primarily in vegetation on land. A few species of frogs live in deserts by staying underground, remaining moist enough to survive. At the arrival of periodic rains, they climb to the surface and breed in temporary ponds, before scampering back underground. Eggs hatch and the froglets burrow underground before the ponds dry. *Toads* constitute a group of frogs that have relatively heavy, dry skin that reduces water loss, permitting them to live on land. Most frogs and toads leave their eggs to develop on their own, but a few guard nests or egg masses, and some species actually carry their eggs on their backs or in skin pouches. One Australian species swallows its eggs and has them develop in the stomach, later having the live young emerge through the mouth.

Frogs and toads are known for the vocal behavior of males, which during breeding periods call loudly from the edges of lakes and ponds or on land, attempting to attract females. Each species has a different type of call. Some species breed *explosively* in synchronous groups – on a single night thousands gather at forest ponds, where males call and compete for females and females choose from among available suitors. Many frogs, such as *bullfrogs*, fight fiercely for the best calling spots and over mates. Because frogs really have no weapons to fight with, such as teeth or sharp claws, size usually determines fight outcomes. Some species of frogs and toads have developed *satellite* strategies to obtain matings. Instead of staking out a calling spot and vocalizing themselves (which is energy-draining and risky because calling attracts predators), satellite males remain silent but stay furtively near calling males, and attempt to intercept and mate with approaching females. Smaller males are more likely to employ such "sneaky-mater" tactics.

All amphibians as adults are predatory carnivores – as far as it is known, there is not a vegetarian among them. Many animals eat amphibians, although it is not as easy as you might think. At first glance amphibians appear to be among the most defenseless of animals. Most are small, many are relatively slow, and their teeth and claws are not the types appropriate for aggressive defense. But a closer look reveals an array of ingenious defenses. Most, perhaps all, amphibians produce toxins in the skin, many of which are harmless to humans and so not very noticeable, but a few of which are quite poisonous and even lethal. These toxins deter predators. Most amphibians are cryptically colored, often being amazingly difficult for people, and presumably predators, to detect in their natural settings. The jumping locomotion of frogs probably evolved as an anti-predator strategy – it is a much more efficient way of escaping quickly through leaves, dense grass, thickets, or shrubby areas than are walking or running. Some frogs hiss loudly and inflate their throat sacs when approached, which presumably makes predators think twice about attacking. Last, when grabbed by a predator, some frogs give loud screams, which are momentarily startling, creating opportunities for escape.

In general, amphibians are under less direct threat from people than are other vertebrate groups, there being little commercial exploitation of the group (aside from certain peoples' inexplicable taste for the limbs of frogs). However, amphibians are very sensitive to habitat destruction and, particularly, to pollution, because aquatic eggs and larvae are very susceptible to toxic substances. Many amphibian populations have been noticeably declining in recent years, although the reasons are not entirely clear. Much research attention is currently focused on determining whether these reported population changes are real and significant and, if so, their causes. Not all ecologists agree on what is going on (see Close-Up, p. 65).

Seeing Amphibians in Costa Rica

Costa Rica has been a center of interest for biologists who study amphibians because of its great diversity of habitats and rich number of species. For these same reasons, visitors to Costa Rica should be able to view a variety of amphibians, provided some effort is taken. First, an admonition: snakes have our respect, due to the evil reputations of the venomous ones, but many people, with little knowledge of tropical amphibians, improperly do not show them the same respect. Skin secretions of some terrestrial frogs, in particular the "poison dart" frogs, are highly toxic. The toxins can be dangerous if absorbed into the body through, for instance, a cut in your skin. The skin secretions of many frogs and salamanders, even if not harmful to humans, can sting badly. Take home message: when amphibians are located, enjoy them visually and leave their handling to experts.

With that warning in mind, here are the best ways to see amphibians. Look for them, of course, in moist habitats – wet forests, near bodies of water, in small pools and puddles, along streams. If you dare, and using your shoes, turn over rocks and logs in these habitats, or look through and under leaf litter. Most adult salamanders and most frogs are nocturnal, so a night walk with flashlight or head-lamp is often a good way to see amphibians. The best time is during a wet night (although not during torrential downpours), and especially during the rainy season, when most species breed. The calls of male frogs can be of assistance then in locating the little beasts.

Table 2 Amphibian Biodiversity Around Costa Rica: Where to See the Most Species (adapted from Janzen 1983).

| Site | Habitat type | Number of species of | | | Total |
		Caecilians	Salamanders	Frogs & toads	
La Selva Biological Reserve	lowland wet	1	3	44	48
Tortuguero National Park	lowland wet	1	2	30	33
Osa Peninsula; Corcovado National Park	low & middle elevation wet	1	4	43	48
San Vito area; Wilson Botanical Garden	middle elevation wet	2	14	62	78*
Monteverde Cloud Forest Reserve	middle & high elevation wet	2	5	51	58
Cañas area; Palo Verde National Park	lowland dry	1	0	22	23

* Some species have not been seen but are suspected to occur in this area.

Number of species known to occur in Costa Rica: Salamanders = about 35; Frogs and Toads = about 120; Caecilians = 3.

Family Profiles

1. Salamanders

Salamanders are long, generally slender amphibians with four limbs. They loosely resemble lizards in body plan, but their skin is smooth and wet – both from the aquatic or moist locales that they inhabit and the skin secretions that keep their skin wet for breathing. Worldwide they number perhaps 450 species, most of them being found within temperate zone regions. The group's largest family, however, containing about half the known species, is well-represented in the American tropics. This is the Family Plethodontidae, the lungless salamanders. All 30+ salamanders that occur in Costa Rica are members of this group. Being lungless, almost all gas exchange is through the moist skin (some occurs through the membranes of the mouth and throat). Most of the plethodontids are primarily terrestrial animals, inhabiting all but the very driest regions of Central America.

Plethodontid salamanders vary quite a bit in size and shape, from ones typically only 3 cm (1 in) long to those 25 cm (10 in) long. Some have webbed feet. Color patterns are often striking, and can vary within the same species between locations.

Salamanders are secretive and usually nocturnal in their activities; hence, unless looked for, they are only infrequently encountered.

Natural History
Ecology and Behavior
In contrast to frogs, with their vegetarian tadpole phase, all salamanders, both as juveniles and adults, are carnivores. They feed opportunistically, essentially snapping at and trying to ingest whatever squirms and will fit into their mouths – generally, on land, insects and spiders, but also small frogs and other salamanders. Because studying salamanders in the wild is difficult, relatively little is known about what eats them, but the list includes snakes, salamanders, frogs, fish, and a few birds and mammals. Although most of the plethodontids are considered terrestrial, some are *semi-arboreal*, regularly climbing into trees and shrubs, and others are *semi-fossorial*, usually burrowing into the leaf litter or underneath rocks or logs.

Breeding
Salamanders are known for their complex mating behavior. Unlike frogs, salamander males do not call to advertise territories or attract mates, but males do fight each other for females. Losers employ various strategies to try to interfere with the winners' mating – either physically inserting themselves between a female and a courting male, or approaching the mating pair, which distracts the male, causing him to pause or stop.

How sperm gain access to eggs in terrestrial salamanders is different from the way one might expect. Following a courtship ritual, the male deposits a tiny, cone-shaped packet containing sperm, called a *spermatophore*, on the ground. The female maneuvers until she can pick it up with her *vent* (the opening on her belly that provides entry and exit for both reproductive and excretory systems), which permits the sperm to gain access to her reproductive tract. She can then store the sperm for many months, having it always available to fertilize her eggs.

In the terrestrial salamanders, females typically lay a clutch of eggs – for instance, an average of 23 eggs in MOUNTAIN SALAMANDERS (Plate 1) – under logs, moss, or rocks. Then they coil themselves around the eggs and stay with them, protecting them and keeping them moist with their skin secretions. Males have also been found protecting eggs in this way, but it appears to be mainly a female role. Egg care is apparently necessary; eggs not protected by an adult are unlikely to hatch. Eggs hatch in 4 to 5 months. The young emerge looking like miniature adults – no larval stage after that in the egg exists – and must fend for themselves from the moment of birth. Growth proceeds very slowly, with many salamanders not sexually mature for at least 6 years. It is thought that all Costa Rican salamanders reproduce in this manner.

Ecological Interactions
Salamanders are usually inconspicuous and hidden to casual observers. Actually, however, they are integral parts of the forest animal community, often being very abundant in good habitat. Therefore, they are one of the predominant predators on forest insects, acting to keep many bug populations in check.

In addition to hiding, running and, in some species, biting, to prevent themselves from becoming another animal's dinner, salamanders employ chemical weapons. All of them apparently have skin secretions that are sufficiently toxic or distasteful to render them unpalatable to most potential predators, and some of the secretions contain potent poisons. Unfortunately for the salamanders, a few predators, such as some snakes, have evolved immunity from the secretions' noxious effects.

Lore and Notes
Many salamanders apparently lead long lives, as do several other groups of cold-blooded animals. They have low metabolisms and they grow slowly in cool habitats, at times eating infrequently and going through long periods of inactivity. In captivity, some salamanders – for instance, one species from Japan – live more than 50 years. Many New World species have lifespans that commonly range up to 20 to 25 years.

Status
None of the Costa Rican or other Central American plethodontid salamanders are thought to be rare or threatened. Several species of this group are threatened, however, in the USA, and three are endangered: DESERT SLENDER, SHENANDOAH, and TEXAS BLIND SALAMANDERS.

Profiles
Mountain Salamander, *Bolitoglossa subpalmata*, Plate 1b
Ring-tailed Salamander, *Bolitoglossa robusta*, Plate 1c

2. Toads

Scientists sometimes have trouble formally differentiating toads from frogs, but not so nonscientists, who usually know their toads: They are the frog-type animals with a rough, lumpy, wart-strewn appearance, not built for speed, that one finds on land. Actually, toads and frogs are both included in the amphibian group Anura; toads are a kind of frog. They have some special skeletal and reproductive traits that are used to set them apart (for instance, frogs lay eggs in jellied clusters, but toads lay them in jellied strings), but for our purposes, a modification of the common definition will do: Toads are squat, short, terrestrial frogs with thick, relatively dry skins that prevent rapid water loss, short limbs, and glands that resemble warts spread over their bodies. A few families of frogs are called toads, but the predominant group, hugely successful, is the *true* toads, Family Bufonidae (*bufo* is Latin for toad), which spread naturally to all continents except Australia (and has been introduced by people to that continent; all the toads occurring in the USA are in this family). *Bufonids* usually have two prominent "warts" on each side of the neck or shoulder area, called *parotoids*. Often shades of olive or brown, toads vary in size, with the largest in Central America, the MARINE TOAD (Plate 1), being anywhere from 9 to 20 cm (3.5 to 8 in) long, and weighing in at up to 1200 g (2.5 lb). Worldwide there are perhaps 300 bufonid toad species; 14 of them occur in Costa Rica.

Natural History
Ecology and Behavior
Although their relatively heavy, dry skin (as compared with that of other frogs) permits adult toads a permanently terrestrial existence, they experience some water loss through their skin, so unless they stay near water or in moist habitat, they dry out and die in just a few days. Although they are freed from an aquatic life, water still governs their existence. Many toads are primarily nocturnal, avoiding the sun and its drying heat by sheltering during the day under leaf litter, logs, or rocks, coming out to forage only after sundown. Toad tadpoles are vegetarians, feeding on green algae and bacteria in their aquatic habitats, but adult toads are all carnivorous, foraging for arthropods, mostly insects, amid the leaf litter. As one researcher defines the toad diet, "if it's bite-sized and animate it is food, no matter how noxious, toxic, or biting/stinging" (G. Zug 1983). Beetles and ants are frequent prey, as are small vertebrates such as small frogs, salamanders, and lizards.

Slow-moving toads (with their short legs they are capable of covering only very short distances per hop) have two methods to escape being eaten. They can be extremely hard to detect in their habitats, concealing themselves with their cryptic coloration and habit of slipping into crevices, under leaves, or actually burying themselves in the earth. Also, apparently quite effectively, they exude noxious fluids from their skin glands – the warts are actually a defense mechanism. If grabbed, a viscous, white fluid oozes from the warts. The fluid is very irritating to mucous membranes, such as those found in a predator's mouth and nose. Toads also have muscle control over the poison glands and some can squeeze them to spray the poison more than 30 cm (1 ft). Most predators that pick up a toad probably do not do it twice; people's four-legged pets that put toads into their mouths have been killed by the poisons. A few predators, however, such as raccoons and opossums, having learned their way around toad anatomy, avoid the warts on the back and legs by eating only the inside of the toad, entering through the mostly poison-gland-free belly.

Breeding
Many toads in Costa Rica breed at any time of year, but often there are breeding surges when seasons change. Fertilization is external, which means that it happens outside of the animal, in water. To breed, males migrate to ponds and streams, calling to attract females. After appropriate mating maneuvers of both sexes, sperm are released by a male in a cloud into the water, followed by a female releasing her eggs into the cloud. The eggs are laid within jellied strings, the jelly protecting the eggs physically and also, because it contains toxins, discouraging consumption by potential predators. Depending on species and size, a female

may lay from 100 to 25,000 eggs at a time. Eggs hatch in only a few days, releasing young in the larval feeding stage known commonly as *tadpoles*. They feed, grow, and develop, transforming themselves into *toadlets* after a few weeks, which then swarm up the banks and disappear into their terrestrial existences. Toads generally reach sexual maturity in a year or two, although the period before breeding is longer in some species.

Ecological Interactions

The MARINE TOAD, Central America's largest member of the Bufonid family, has somehow become semi-domesticated, and is now commonly found around human settlements at much higher densities than in wild areas. Adapting nicely to people's behavior, these toads will eat dog and cat food left outdoors for pets (which is quite a feat, given that most frogs will only eat live, moving prey). Because of their abundance around dwellings, they probably are the toad most likely to be seen by visitors to Costa Rica.

Lore and Notes

The claim that a person will contract warts by handling toads is not true. Human warts are caused by viruses, not amphibians. The glands on toads' skin that resemble warts release noxious fluids to discourage predators. In these fluids various poisons have been identified that, among other effects, cause increased blood pressure, blood vessel constriction, increased power of heartbeat, heart muscle tissue destruction, and hallucinations. Because these fluids minimally are irritants, a smart precaution is to avoid handling toads or, after such handling, make sure to wash your hands. Caustic irritation will result if the fluids are transferred from hands to eyes, nose or mouth. Some reports have it that voodoo practitioners in Haiti use the skin secretions of toads in their zombie-making concoctions.

Status

A number of New World bufonid species are known to be threatened or endangered. Costa Rica's GOLDEN TOAD (Plate 2), restricted to the Monteverde area, is considered highly endangered (CITES Appendix I and USA ESA listed) and may now be extinct. In fact, preservation of Golden Toads was one of the original reasons for the creation of the Monteverde Cloud Forest Reserve. The BLACK and HOUSTON TOADS of the USA and the SONORAN GREEN TOAD of Mexico and the USA are threatened, as are a few toads from Puerto Rico and Chile.

Profiles

Marine Toad, *Bufo marinus*, Plate 1d
Green Climbing Toad, *Bufo coniferus*, Plate 2a
Litter Toad, *Bufo haematiticus*, Plate 2b
Golden Toad, *Bufo periglenes*, Plate 2c
Harlequin Frog, *Atelopus varius*, Plate 2d
Mexican Burrowing Toad, *Rhinophrynus dorsalis*, Plate 3a

3. Rainfrogs

The *rainfrogs*, Family Leptodactylidae, also known as the *tropical frogs*, constitute a large New World group that is distributed from southern North America to throughout most of South America and the Caribbean. Primarily frogs of low and middle elevations, they occupy many different types of habitats, but especially forests. Often they are the most abundant kind of amphibian found in a given habitat. Species are variously land-dwelling, aquatic, or arboreal. About 40 of the more than 700 living species are represented in Costa Rica.

Rainfrogs vary extensively in size and color patterns, so much so that a general description of the group is difficult. One distinctive trait is the greatly enlarged finger disks – little suction cups – characteristic of many, the better to get around their arboreal habitats. Sizes in Costa Rica vary from the many small species that at their largest are only 2.5 to 3.0 cm (1 in) long, such as the common BRANSFORD'S LITTER and COMMON DINK FROGS (Plate 3), to the SMOKY JUNGLE FROG (Plate 4), which, at up to 16 cm (6 in) in length, is one of Costa Rica's largest amphibians (second in size only to the MARINE TOAD – Plate 1). Rainfrogs tend to be various shades of tan, beige, brown, gray, or pale yellow, often with dark markings such as bars or spots, particularly on the legs. Telling species apart by their markings is rendered more difficult because of the large amount of variation present within some species. For instance, Bransford's Litter Frog varies so extensively among individuals – even among those found in the same small area – in color, spotting pattern, and skin texture, that for many years even scientists were confused, repeatedly naming new species of litter frogs although they were actually all the same species (the way a newcomer to Earth might mistakenly assign species status to each breed of domestic canine, which, although they look very different, are all of the same species of marginal intelligence that we call dogs). The explanation for such extreme variability in color schemes within a single species is unknown, but is suspected to have to do with the advantages each kind has in blending in with various types of surroundings on the forest floor.

Natural History
Ecology and Behavior
Rainfrogs in Costa Rica are primarily terrestrial, arboreal, or both. Many small species typically coexist in the same area, making up a large portion of the *leaf litter amphibian community*. At one lowland forest, the La Selva Biological Reserve, the number of different amphibian (frog and salamander) species in the leaf litter at various sites ranges from 15 to 22, but rainfrogs always contribute the majority of species; that is, of all the amphibian families, a single family, the rainfrogs, always makes up more than 50% of the species inhabiting the region. Some are day-active on the ground, some are nocturnal on the ground, and some forage by day and breed at night (still other species, tree-dwellers, are not found in the litter). Besides contributing the majority of species to many Central American amphibian communities, one or another rainfrog species is usually the single most abundant amphibian in many habitats. For instance, in many Costa Rican forests, BRANSFORD'S LITTER FROG is the commonest amphibian in the forest litter.

Many rainfrogs are known as ant specialists, but typically a variety of insects, other arthropods, and even small vertebrates, are included in the diet – mites, beetles, spiders, small lizards, and others. Rainfrogs are *sit-and-wait* predators. Some, like the large SMOKY JUNGLE FROG, live in protective rock crevices or ground burrows, venturing out only to forage around the opening (or to breed), escaping back into the shelter at the first sign of trouble. These large frogs eat a variety of things, including other frogs and snakes up to half a meter (1.5 ft) long! Rainfrogs, especially the nocturnal ones, have reputations for being quite shy, which seems surprising for a night-active animal until one realizes that one of the chief predators on these frogs is also nocturnal – bats.

Breeding

These frogs breed in a variety of ways. One group (genus *Eleutherodactylus*, among which is BRANSFORD'S LITTER FROG) has become completely terrestrial in its breeding, females laying small clutches of eggs, often between 10 and 30, on land in moist sites. Embryos pass through a tadpole stage while still in the eggs, which hatch out fully-formed but tiny froglets. Another group (genus *Leptodactylus*, among which is the SMOKY JUNGLE FROG) deposits its eggs in foam nests which are placed in pockets in the ground near water. Males use their hindfeet to whip into foam a concoction of air, water, mucous from the female, and semen. Tadpoles that hatch out from eggs within the foam are washed into nearby temporary ponds by rainwater (perhaps providing the common name for these frogs), later to emerge as fully developed frogs. At least one species in Costa Rica builds its foam nests to float on water, another has no nest and gives birth to live young, and still others, such as the COMMON DINK FROG, lay their eggs in the little pools of water that collect in the central *cisterns* of bromeliad plants, which are often attached to tree limbs. The purpose of these exotic breeding tactics appears to be to keep eggs, or eggs and tadpoles, away from fish predators. Many rainfrogs breed at any time of year, but the ones that rely on rains to wash tadpoles into ponds often breed before heavy rains. Clutches vary in size from about 10 to several hundred eggs. Most rainfrogs reproduce at one year of age or younger.

Ecological Interactions

Interactions between predators and their prey sometimes have unintended consequences. SMOKY JUNGLE FROGS emit loud calls when captured whose function is probably to startle the predator, providing the caller with an opportunity to escape. Unfortunately for some of the predators, these calls also attract the attention of large, crocodile-like Caiman (Plate 9), which sometimes are successful at feeding on the frog predator. Thus, a hidden element of predation is exposed: except for the very largest and fiercest predators, many animals themselves become more exposed and so more vulnerable to predation when they search for, stalk, and handle prey.

Lore and Notes

Rainfrogs, like most amphibians, secrete poisons of varying degrees of toxicity from skin glands to discourage predation. The SMOKY JUNGLE FROG, in particular, has a potent poison, named leptodactylin, after the genus name, *Leptodactylus*. Its effects include blocking some neuromuscular activity and stimulating parts of the nervous system, particularly those that control blood vessels and hence, blood pressure. The secretions, very irritating to mucous membranes of the mouth, nose, and throat, presumably compel some predators to release the offending frog in their mouth.

Status

No Costa Rican rainfrogs are currently thought to be threatened, but as is the case with most amphibian groups, adequate monitoring on most species has yet to be done. Many rainfrogs of South America, particularly in Chile and Argentina, where a great number of species occur, are threatened or endangered, as are several from Jamaica and Puerto Rico.

Profiles

Common Dink Frog, *Eleutherodactylus diastema*, Plate 3b
Common Rain Frog, *Eleutherodactylus fitzingeri*, Plate 3c

Bransford's Litter Frog, *Eleutherodactylus bransfordii*, Plate 3d
Smoky Jungle Frog, *Leptodactylus pentadactylus*, Plate 4a
Mudpuddle Frog, *Physalaemus pustulosus*, Plate 4b

4. Treefrogs

The *treefrogs*, Family Hylidae, are an intriguing array of animals that, somewhat anomalously for amphibians, but owing to big eyes and bright colors, have joined toucans, parrots and other glamorous celebrities to become poster animals for tropical forests. Rarely these days is a book, poster, or calendar printed with pictures of tropical animals that does not include at least one of a treefrog. There are about 700 species of *hylids* worldwide, with some 39 species occurring within Costa Rica. They are distributed on all continents except Antarctica, but are most abundant and diverse in the American tropics. SPRING PEEPERS and CHORUS FROGS, their vocalizations familiar to so many North Americans, are hylids.

Most hylid treefrogs are small and elegantly slender-wasted. They have relatively large heads with long, rounded snouts, conspicuously large, bulging eyes, and long but skinny thighs and legs. Many have prominent, enlarged toe pads – sucking disks on the tips of their toes that permit them to cling to and climb tree leaves and branches. Most are between 3.5 and 8.5 cm long (1.5 to 3.5 in). Coloring is highly variable. Some are very cryptic, clad in greens and browns that produce virtual invisibility in their arboreal lodgings. Others, particularly ones that are poisonous, are brightly colored, presumably to warn away potential predators. For instance, the RED-EYED LEAF FROG (Plate 4), up to 7 cm (3 in) in length, is right out of a cartoon studio – bright leaf green above, with blue to purple sides, bright blue and green thighs, a white belly, orange hands and feet, and red eyes. Some species also have what biologists refer to as *flash* coloring – patches of bright blue, red, orange, or yellow on the hind legs or groin area that are concealed at rest but exposed as brilliant flashes of color when the frog moves. The purpose of flash coloring presumably is to startle predators as they attack, allowing a moment to escape.

Natural History
Ecology and Behavior

As their name suggests, most treefrogs are arboreal creatures, spending much of their time jumping and climbing among tree leaves and twigs. Although their skinny legs suggest weak muscles, they are good jumpers. Their adhesive toe pads allow them to climb even vertical surfaces. Some species are more ground-dwelling and some non-Costa Rican species are fully aquatic. The majority are nocturnally active, passing the daylight hours sheltered in tree crevices or among the plants that grow on trees (epiphytes), especially bromeliads. They emerge at night to forage for insects, their predominant food, and to pursue their romantic interests. Most species have the ability to change their skin color rapidly, like chameleons.

Breeding

Even the most jaded observer of animal behavior would be forced to admit that treefrog reproduction has some unusual features. As in most amphibians, one or both of the non-adult life stages, eggs and/or larvae (tadpoles), occur in water, but not just in any pond or stream. Females of one group of species lay eggs only in what ecologists term *arboreal water* – small, stagnant puddles present in tree cavities, on logs, or at the center of bromeliads and other epiphytic plants that have central *cisterns*, or bucket areas, that always hold rainwater. The eggs hatch in a few days, releasing tiny tadpoles that feed and develop within these isolated, protected ponds, eventually turning into *froglets*.

Another group of species – now, tell me this isn't fascinating – attach their eggs to tree leaves over water and, as the eggs hatch, the tadpoles drop into the water below. For example, in the RED-EYED LEAF FROG, a male in a reproductive mood moves to a tree branch overlooking a temporary pond or puddle and proceeds to call. A female approaches the vocalizing male and, after appropriate behaviors, the male clings to the female's back in the mating position. The female, with the male on her back, then climbs down to the pond to soak up some water into her bladder. She climbs back up into the tree and deposits a clutch of 30 to 50 eggs onto leaves and releases water over them; the male deposits sperm onto the wetted eggs as the female releases them, and fertilization occurs then. She climbs down again with the male to get some more water and repeats the process, sometimes 3 to 5 times in a night. In species that typically deposit eggs over streams, the eggs are particularly large, so that the tadpoles that hatch out and drop into the moving water are large and powerful enough to stand up to the currents. A number of other breeding methods exist within the hylid family as well – this is currently a hot area of animal research in Costa Rica. Some species lay 2000 or more eggs per clutch. Eggs generally hatch in 2 to 6 days. Sexual maturity is reached usually at about a year of age. Breeding can be at any time of year.

Ecological Interactions

Why do treefrogs live on land and often breed at least partially away from water? Evolutionary biologists believe that the most likely reason that some groups of frogs, such as the hylids, have developed terrestrial behavior is not that terrestrial existences are inherently better than aquatic ones, but that terrestrial life means a great reduction in the loss of eggs and tadpoles to predators. The chief culprit driving such predator-avoidance is thought to be fish, which eat copious amounts of frog eggs and tadpoles – when they can reach them. Eggs laid on leaves are obviously out of fish range, as are eggs and tadpoles that develop in fishless ponds and small, ephemeral ponds and puddles. The comparative distribution in Costa Rica of fish and frogs provides evidence for the claim. Above about 1500 m (5000 ft) in elevation there are no native fish but there is a large variety of stream-breeding treefrogs, which are distinctly rare below this elevation. This pattern suggests that where fish are present, treefrogs have evolved more terrestriality and its accompanying breeding away from streams; but where fish are absent, stream-breeding is less costly in terms of lost eggs and young, and so it continues. Avoiding fish predation by depositing eggs on land may be a good idea, but it is not without its own hazards: some snakes feed frequently on these egg clusters.

Lore and Notes

Treefrogs employ a number of methods to deter predation, including cryptic coloring that allows them to blend into their environments, rapid leaping (what must be, aside from flying or gliding, the most efficient way to move around quickly in trees), loud, startling screams or squalls emitted when grabbed by predators, and poisons. Some species are cryptic but not poisonous, some are brightly colored and poisonous, and some are both cryptically colored and poisonous. One Costa Rican species produces in its skin secretions toxins that cause sneezing in people, even if they are not handling a frog, and that cause pain and paralysis when ingested or when penetrating the body via an open wound.

Status

No hylid treefrogs outside of Australia are known positively to be immediately threatened or endangered. However, for many New World species, there is currently insufficient information to determine population sizes and trends. Some Brazilian species are thought to be rare and, hence, vulnerable, as is the USA's PINE BARRENS TREEFROG. As far as it can be known, Costa Rican treefrogs are not currently threatened.

Profiles

Red-eyed Leaf Frog, *Agalychnis callidryas,* Plate 4c
Misfit Leaf Frog *Agalychnis saltator,* Plate 4d
Meadow Treefrog, *Hyla pseudopuma,* Plate 5a
Variegated Treefrog, *Hyla ebraccata,* Plate 5b
Boulenger's Snouted Treefrog, *Scinax boulengeri,* Plate 5c
Gladiator Frog, *Hyla rosenbergi,* Plate 5d
Masked Treefrog, *Smilisca phaeota,* Plate 6a
Drab Treefrog, *Smilisca sordida,* Plate 6b
Mexican Treefrog, *Smilisca baudinii,* Plate 6c

5. Other Frogs

There are a number of groups of frogs that, although not represented by many species in Costa Rica, nonetheless are important members of the country's amphibian community and are often conspicuous to observant visitors. Frogs of the Family Ranidae are known as *true frogs* not because they are better frogs than any other but because they are the most common frogs of Europe, where the early classification of animals took place. Over 650 species strong, the true frogs now have a worldwide distribution, excepting Antarctica (the ones in Australia were introduced there by people); most are in Africa, 250 species occur in the New World, but in Costa Rica there are only about five. True frogs include many of what most people regard as typical frogs – green ones that spend most of their lives in water. Among frogs familiar to many North Americans, BULLFROGS and LEOPARD FROGS (Plate 7) are members of the Ranidae. Typically *ranids* are streamlined, slim-wasted frogs with long legs, webbed back feet, and thin, smooth skin. They are usually shades of green. Size varies extensively. VAILLANT'S FROG (Plate 6), a typical Costa Rican true frog, reaches lengths of 11 cm (4.5 in), excluding the long legs, of course.

Frogs of the Family Centrolenidae, known as *glass frogs* owing to their transparent abdominal skin, are limited in their distributions to humid regions of the Americas from southern Mexico to Bolivia and northern Argentina. There are about 100 species in the group, 13 of which occur in Costa Rica. These arboreal frogs are usually small, most in the range of 2.5 to 3 cm (an inch or so) long, and most come clad in a variety of greens, including lime, blue-green, and dark green. Various body organs and bones can be seen through the transparent skin of their bellies.

The *poison-dart frogs* of the Family Dendrobatidae, best-known for the deadly poisons some species produce in their skin glands, are a mid-sized group of about

115 species that are confined to tropical and subtropical Central America and northern South America. There are 7 species in Costa Rica. These amphibians are considered to be the most colorful of the treefrogs, not to mention the most dangerous. Usually quite small, most being less than 5 cm (2 in) long and many about half that, these frogs take on some brilliant hues. Some are a shiny black overall with bright red, orange, green, or blue markings. The very common STRAWBERRY POISON-DART FROG (Plate 8) has a red back, sometimes with black spots, and dark-colored limbs.

Natural History
Ecology and Behavior

True frogs. These are aquatic frogs that are good swimmers and jumpers. With their webbed toes and long, muscular hind legs, they are built for speed on land or in water. This is fortunate for the frogs because most lack the poison glands in their skins that many other types of frogs use to deter predation. They have thin skin through which water evaporates rapidly and thus they tend to remain in or near the water, often spending much of their time around the margins of ponds or floating in shallow water. Except during breeding seasons, they are active only during the day. True frogs feed mainly on bugs, but also on fish and smaller frogs. In turn, they are common food items for an array of beasts, such as wading birds, fish, turtles, and small mammals. Because they are such tasty morsels to so many predators, these frogs are very alert to their surroundings, attempting escape at the slightest movement or noise; the splashing heard as you walk along a pond or lakeshore is usually made by these frogs on the shore leaping into the water.

Glass frogs. Glass frogs are treefrogs of tropical moist forests. They are found along streams in lowland areas and all the way up to 3800 m (12,000 ft). Typically active during the day, glass frogs eat mainly insects, opportunistically taking whatever bugs they encounter. Males are highly territorial, defending sites to which, with their calls, they will attract females for mating. When another male intrudes into a resident's territory and will not leave, fighting ensues.

Poison-dart frogs. These treefrogs are usually ant and mite specialists, although other small arthropods are also eaten; they hunt actively during daylight hours. One theory of the development of their lethal poisons is that, because they eat such small items – ants – they need to forage for many hours each day to meet nutritional needs. Therefore they are exposed to predators for extended periods each day, and so, in response to heavy predation, have evolved protective toxic skin secretions. Poison-dart frogs are also highly territorial, and the resource that males are defending from other males with their aggressive behavior has been identified. Bromeliad plants figure prominently during breeding in some of these species (see below), and it is these plants that males are defending by excluding other males from their territories. Field experiments in which bromeliads were added to certain sites led to more male poison-dart frogs living together amicably at those sites, because each had a bromeliad for breeding.

Breeding

True frogs. These frogs reproduce under what most would consider the standard amphibian plan. Eggs are released by the female into the water in ponds or streams, and are fertilized then by sperm released by the male. Eggs and tadpoles develop in the water. In some species, the jellied egg masses float, but in others, they are attached to the undersides of rocks in streams. Clutch size varies tremendously, but large females can release thousands of eggs. Sexual maturity occurs in from 1 to 4 years.

Glass frogs. Glass frog males call, attracting females to their territories. Females deposit their eggs on leaves that hang over puddles and temporary pools. Some species of glass frogs stay near their eggs, guarding them. Males have been observed to sit on eggs during the night and near them during the day. Eggs hatch in 8 to 20 days, the released tadpoles dropping into the water below. Often hatching occurs during heavy rain, which is thought to help increase the chances that tadpoles make it to the pools. Tadpoles develop in the pools, finally emerging as frogs.

Poison-dart frogs. These frogs show some of the most complex parental care behavior of any non-bird or non-mammal. Males call to attract females to their territories. When a female arrives, the male searches for a good egg-laying site – usually a leaf in a moist area; the female follows him around the vegetation. After some courtship rubbing and touching, the female lays eggs and the male fertilizes them. The male or female then stays with the eggs to guard them. When hatching occurs, the female, but sometimes the male, carries the tadpoles on her back and places them into the pools of water that collect in the central parts, or *cisterns*, of bromeliad plants. Males will carry up to 6 tadpoles at a time, females usually just one or two. In the small, protected bromeliad pools the tadpoles develop into frogs. Recently it has been discovered that the female's role in caring for her young is not finished after transporting the tadpoles; she also periodically returns to the pool and drops unfertilized eggs into it, feeding her young this nutritious resource.

Ecological Interactions

The way that biologists view how animals distribute themselves within an area has been partially worked out by thinking about how true frogs might arrange themselves in a pond. Predation is a major worry for many animals, including aquatic frogs, and it doubtless influences many aspects of their lives. Often, there is safety in numbers, the rationale being that, although a group is larger than a single animal and therefore more easily located by a predator, the chances of any one animal in the group being taken is low, and so associating with the group, instead of striking out on one's own, is advantageous to an individual. But within the group, where should an individual frog, say one named Fred, position himself to minimize his chances of being eaten? Imagine a round pond around which frogs tread in the shallow water near shore or sun themselves on the bank. If the predator is a snake or a bird that for lunch will take one frog, the best place for Fred is between two other frogs, so that his left and right are "protected," the neighbor frogs there to be eaten first. To gain such advantageous positioning, clearly Fred's best move would be to find two frogs near each other and move into the gap between them. If such a strategy exists, then the neighboring frogs should move in turn, also trying to fit into small gaps. Eventually, all the frogs in the pond, if playing this game, should end up in a small heap, the best protected frogs at its center. And indeed, as any small child who hunts frogs will tell you, they are often found in tight groups at the edges of lakes and ponds. This *selfish herd* explanation for the formation of frog and other animal aggregations was first proposed about 30 years ago.

Lore and Notes

The true frogs have always provided a minor source of protein to people through-out the world – a bit revolting to this writer, but there's no accounting for national and ethnic taste. These frogs are often non-toxic, abundant, and large enough to make harvesting and preparation economically profitable. In much of Europe and pockets of the USA, the long muscles of the rear legs, often dusted with flour and fried in butter, are eaten by otherwise civilized people. Tastes like chicken breast, so I gather.

Far less palatable, and the most toxic of Costa Rican frogs, the poison-dart frogs can pack a wallop. The poison in their skin secretions affect nerves and muscles, causing paralysis and, eventually, cessation of breathing. (Recently, the mixture of chemicals secreted from the skin glands of one South American species has been found to be an excellent pain-blocking drug, 200 times more effective than morphine.) Several groups of native American peoples, notably in Colombia and Ecuador, apply the skin secretions from some of these frogs onto their blow-gun darts (hence, the name), using the poison's formidable toxicity to paralyze and kill the animals they hunt. Even large ants and large spiders avoid poison-dart frogs: in experiments in which ants or spiders that normally eat small frogs were presented in cages with either rainfrogs (p. 56) or poison-dart frogs, they attacked and consumed the rainfrogs, but attacked and rejected the poison-darts. Not all poison-dart frogs avoid predation. Some are taken by snakes immune to their poisons and some have been observed to be eaten by spiders, which avoid the skin by puncturing the body and sucking out the innards.

Status

As far as it is known, no species of true, glass, or poison-dart frogs are currently endangered in Costa Rica or other parts of the Americas. At least three species of true frogs are threatened in the USA. As is the case for many of the amphibia, rel-atively little is known about the sizes and health of the populations of many of these frogs; therefore, authoritative assurance that some are not threatened is impossible to provide. To regulate trade in the beautiful poison-dart frogs, all species are CITES Appendix II listed.

Profiles

True Frogs

Vaillant's Frog, *Rana vaillant*, Plate 6d
Brilliant Forest Frog, *Rana warszewitschii*, Plate 7a
Leopard Frog, *"Rana pipiens"*, Plate 7b

Glass Frogs

Fleischmann's Glass Frog, *Hyalinobatrachium fleischmanni*, Plate 7c
Emerald Glass Frog, *Centrolene prosoblepon*, Plate 7d

Poison-dart Frogs

Green Poison-arrow Frog, *Dendrobates auratus*, Plate 8a
Granular Poison-arrow Frog, *Dendrobates granulifer*, Plate 8b
Strawberry Poison-dart Frog, *Dendrobates pumilio*, Plate 8c
Lovely Poison-dart Frog, *Phyllobates lugubris*, Plate 8d
Orange and Black Poison-dart Frog, *Phyllobates vittatus*, Plate 8e

Environmental Close-Up I
Frog Population Declines: Amphibian Armageddon or Alarmist Absurdity?

The Problem

Recently, there has been a spate of articles and programs about amphibians in the popular and scientific media, bearing titles and subtitles such as "The Silence of the Frogs," "Where Have All the Frogs Gone?," "Why Are Frogs and Toads Croaking?," "Playing it Safe or Crying Frog?," and "Chicken Little or Nero's Fiddle?" What's stimulating all the silly titles? The issue traces back just a few years, to 1989 to be precise, to a conference in Britain attended by many of the world's leading scientists who study reptiles and amphibians in the wild. Gabbing in the hallways of the convention center, as scientists will do, relating stories about their research and the respective species that they study, they noticed a common thread emerging: many of the populations of frogs, toads, and salamanders that had been monitored for at least several years seemed to be declining in numbers, often drastically. Where some species had been common 20 years before, they were now rare or near extinction. Suspecting that something important was afoot, the scientists met formally the next year in California to discuss the subject, compare notes, and try to reach some preliminary conclusions or, minimally, at least to phrase some preliminary questions. Such as:

1   Are amphibian populations really declining over a broad geographic area? Or are the stories just that – anecdotal accounts concerning a few isolated populations that, even if they are in decline, do not portend a general trend?
2   If amphibian population declines are, in fact, a general phenomenon, are they over and above those of other kinds of animals (many of which, after all, given the alarming rate of natural habitat destruction occurring over the globe, are also thought to be declining – albeit usually at a gentler pace than that ascribed to the amphibian drops); that is, is the amphibian decline a special case, happening for a reason unrelated to general loss of biodiversity? and
3   If there really is a generalized worldwide amphibian problem, why is it happening?

Most of the conferring scientists agreed that a widespread pattern of amphibian declines was indicated by available data: there were reports from the USA, Central America, the Amazon Basin, the Andes, Europe, and Australia. They speculated about two possible main causes. First, that habitat loss – continued destruction of tropical forests, etc. – was almost certainly contributing to general declines in population sizes of amphibians and other types of animals. That is, that amphibian declines could be at least partly attributed to worldwide biodiversity loss. Second, that owing to their biology, amphibians were doubtless more sensitive than other groups to pollution, especially acid rain (rain that is acidified by various atmospheric pollutants, chiefly from engine emissions, leading to lake and river water being more acidic). Amphibians are more vulnerable to this kind of pollution than, say, reptiles, because of their thin, wet skins, through which they breathe and through which polluting chemicals may gain entry to their bodies, and also owing to their highly exposed and so vulnerable early life stages – eggs and tadpoles in lakes, ponds, and streams. Changes in the acidity of their aquatic environments, or even changes in water temperature, are known to have dire consequences for egg and larval (tadpole) development – and therefore such changes could be the main culprits behind amphibian declines. Plainly, if their reproduction were compromised, population numbers would plunge precipitously. Although it sounded a bit far-fetched, some scientists also suggested that the increased bombardment of the Earth by ultraviolet (UV) light, a direct result of the thinning, protective atmospheric ozone layer, might likewise be taking a disproportionate toll on biologically vulnerable amphibians. (Indeed, recent studies have proved to the satisfaction of some, but not all, scientists that increased UV light in natural situations destroys frog eggs and can interact chemically with diseases and acid rain to increase amphibian mortality rates.)

The Controversy

As might be expected, not all herpetologists agree that pollution, UV light, or some other environmental factor is currently exerting lethal effects worldwide on frogs and salamanders. Some biologists point out that the amphibians that they study in some of the world's most pristine environments, having little or no detectable pollution, also have experienced catastrophic population crashes. One of the prime examples is a Costa Rican resident, the Golden Toad. It had been monitored for many years in the same 5 breeding ponds at the Monteverde Cloud Forest Reserve, and until the late 1980s, more than 1500 adults had bred each year in the ponds; but from 1988 through 1990, fewer than 20 individuals could be found each year and the toad is now thought by many to be extinct. In total, populations of 20 of the approximately 50 frog species that inhabit the Cloud Forest Reserve crashed dramatically during the late 1980s and, as of 1996, still had not recovered. Pollution was probably not a factor, although UV light and weather could have had effects – average water temperature had risen a bit and there was a decrease in rainfall during the late 1980s.

Still other scientists, those who study natural size oscillations in animal populations, point out that science is aware of many animals whose populations cycle between scarcity and abundance. For instance, several small rodents of the arctic tundra, *voles* and *lemmings*, have the famous reputations for one year being at low population densities (a few per hectare) but three or four years hence, being at very high densities (thousands per hectare, so many that it's difficult to walk without stepping on them). These biologists point out that, unless the herpetologists sounding the alarm of amphibian declines can show that the declines are not part of natural cycles, it is too early to panic. Further, that the only way to know about possible natural population cycles is to monitor closely amphibian populations during long-term studies, which at present, are few and far between. (They also point out that the ones that have been performed provide only equivocal support for general population crashes; see Table 3).

The side of the debate that takes the amphibian declines as established fact and suspects an *anthropogenic* cause (scientific jargon for *people-caused*), while agreeing that long-term studies are necessary, believes that it would be a grave mistake to wait for the conclusions of those studies, 10 or 20 years down the road, before decisions are reached about whether amphibians are declining on a broad

Table 3 Trends in Amphibian Population Sizes Noted During Studies that Monitored Populations for at least Four Years (from Blaustein *et al.*, 1994).

Amphibian species	Location	Number of years studied	Population trend
Common Toad	Europe	24	Declining*
Yosemite Toad	California	12	Declining
Natterjack Toad	Great Britain	9	Declining
Golden Toad	Costa Rica	4	Declining
Leopard Frog	Colorado	10	6 populations extinct
Wood Frog	Maryland	7	Fluctuating
Ornate Chorus Frog	South Carolina	12	Fluctuating
Coqui Frog	Puerto Rico	4	Increasing
Red-cheeked Salamander	North Carolina	5	Stable
Slimy Salamander	North Carolina	5	Stable
Red-backed Salamander	Virginia	14	Stable
Shenandoah Salamander	Virginia	14	Declining
Marbled Salamander	South Carolina	12	Fluctuating
Mole Salamander	South Carolina	12	Fluctuating
Tiger Salamander	South Carolina	12	Fluctuating
Spotted Salamander	Michigan	5	Fluctuating

* But many Common Toads are killed by cars.

scale and what to do about it – because at that point, they believe, it will be too late to do anything but record mass extinctions.

The Future

What will happen now is that the controversy will continue as long-term population studies are conducted. In one novel approach, current populations of frogs and toads in California's Yosemite National Park were compared with notes on their population sizes from a survey conducted in 1915; all seven native species were found to have declined, but the causes are unclear. Also, a group of Australian researchers recently proposed that catastrophic frog declines in the eastern Australian rainforests were caused by a rapidly spreading, water-borne epidemic viral disease – and other scientists will follow-up this study to determine if viruses are responsible for other amphibian declines. A major problem is that, even if the scientific consensus now was that disease, pollution, and the increased incidence of UV light were harming amphibians around the world, the will and resources are currently lacking to do anything about it on the massive scale that conservation would require. Unless peoples' worldview changes, preservation of amphibians and reptiles, save special cases like *sea turtles* (p. 77), will always lag behind preservation efforts made on the behalf of the "cuddlies" – birds and mammals. The best hope is that the recent conservation emphasis on preserving entire ecosystems, rather than particular species, will eventually benefit the disappearing amphibians.

One positive element of the amphibian declines, if it can be called that, is that some scientists have suggested that if it is determined that amphibians are particularly sensitive to pollutants, then perhaps they can be used as indicators of environmental health: ecosystems with healthy amphibian populations could be deemed relatively healthy, those with declining amphibians could be targeted for hasty improvement. As one biologist phrased it, amphibians could be used as "yardsticks for ecosystem vitality," (R.B. Primack 1993) just as canaries in cages indicated to the coal miners who carried them something of vital importance about their environments.

Chapter 6

Reptiles

- General Characteristics and Natural History
- Seeing Reptiles in Costa Rica
- Family Profiles
    1. Crocodilians
    2. Turtles
    3. Colubrids: Your Regular, Everyday Snakes
    4. Dangerous Snakes
    5. Geckos
    6. Iguanids
    7. Skinks and Whiptails
- Environmental Close-Up 2: Temperature and Turtle Sex: If the Eggs are Warm, Prepare for Daughters

General Characteristics and Natural History

Most people journeying to Costa Rica to experience tropical habitats and view exotic wildlife are ambivalent toward reptiles. On one hand, almost all people react with surprise, fear, and rapid withdrawal when suddenly confronted with reptiles anywhere but the zoo (which is quite understandable, given the dangerous nature of some reptiles). But on the other hand, these creatures are fascinating to look at and contemplate – their threatening primitiveness, their very "dinosaur-ness" – and many have highly intriguing lifestyles. Most reptiles are harmless to people and, if discovered going about their daily business, are worth a look. Unfortunately, to avoid predation, most reptiles are inconspicuous both in their behavior and color patterns and often flee when alerted to people's presence; consequently most reptiles are never seen by people during a brief visit to a region. Exceptions are reptiles that achieve a great deal of safety by being very large – crocodiles and iguanas come immediately to mind. Also, some small lizards are very common along forest trails. But overall, you should expect to see relatively few reptile species during any brief trip to Costa Rica. Still, it is a good idea to keep a careful watch for them, remembering not to get too close to any that you find, and count yourself lucky for each one you see.

Reptiles have been around for a long while, arising, so the fossil evidence tells us, during the late portion of the Paleozoic Era, some 300 million years ago. Descendants of those first reptiles include 6000+ species that today inhabit most regions of the Earth, with a healthy contingent in the American tropics. Chief reptile traits, aside from being scary-looking, are:

1   Their skin is covered with tough scales, which cuts down significantly on water loss from their body surface. The development of this trait permitted animals for the first time to remain for extended periods on dry land, and most of today's reptiles are completely terrestrial (whereas amphibians, which lack a tough skin, need always remain in or near the water or moist places, lest they dry out).

2   Their heart is divided into more chambers that increase efficiency of circulation over that of the amphibians, allowing for a high blood pressure and thus the sustained muscular activity required for land-living.

3   Some employ *oviparous* reproduction, placing their fertilized eggs in layers of tough membrane or in hard shells and then expelling the eggs to the external environment, where development of the embryos occurs; whereas others are *ovoviviparous* – eggs are not shell-encased or laid, but remain within the mother until "hatching," the young being born live; still others are *viviparous*, in which embryos are connected to the mother via a type of placenta and are nourished by her until being born live. Most reptiles do not feed or protect their young, but desert their eggs after they are laid.

Reptile biologists recognize three major groups:

The *turtles* and *tortoises* (land turtles) constitute one group, with about 240 species worldwide. Some turtles live wholly on land, the sea turtles live out their lives in the oceans (coming ashore only to lay eggs), but most turtles live in lakes and ponds. Although most eat plants, some are carnivorous. Turtles are easily distinguished by their unique body armor – tough plates that cover their back and belly, creating wrap-around shells into which head and limbs are retracted when danger looms.

The *crocodiles* and their relatives, large, predatory carnivores that live along the shores of swamps, rivers, and estuaries, constitute a small second group of about 20 species.

Last, and currently positioned as the world's dominant reptiles, the 3000 *lizard* species and 3500 *snakes* comprise a third group (lizards and snakes have very similar skeletal traits, indicating a very close relationship).

Lizards walk on all four limbs, except for a few that are legless. Most are ground-dwelling animals, but many also climb when the need arises; a fair number spend much of their lives in trees. Almost all are capable of moving quite rapidly. Most lizards are insectivores, but some, especially larger ones, eat plants, and several prey on amphibians, other lizards, mammals, birds, and even fish. Lizards are hugely successful and are often the most abundant vertebrate animals within an area. Ecologists suspect that they owe this ecological success primarily to their ruthlessly efficient predation on insects and other small animals and low daily energy requirements.

Most Costa Rican lizards are insectivores, also opportunistically taking other small animals such as spiders and mites. Lizards employ two main foraging strategies. Some, such as the small whiptail lizards, are *active searchers*. They move continually while looking for prey, for instance nosing about in the leaf litter of the forest floor. *Sit-and-wait* predators, highly camouflaged, remain motionless on the ground or on tree trunks or branches, waiting for prey to happen by. When they see a likely meal – a caterpillar, a beetle – they reach out to snatch it if it is close enough or dart out to chase it down.

Many lizards are territorial, defending territories from other members of their species with displays, such as bobbing up and down on their front legs and raising their head crests. Lizards are especially common in deserts and semi-deserts, but they are numerous in other habitats as well. They are active primarily during the day, except for many of the gecko species, which are nocturnal.

Snakes probably evolved from burrowing lizards, and all are limbless. Snakes are all carnivores, but their methods of capturing prey differ. Several groups of species have evolved glands that manufacture poisons, or *venom*, that is injected into prey through the teeth. The venom immobilizes and kills the prey, which is then swallowed whole. Other snakes pounce on and wrap themselves around their prey, constricting the prey until it suffocates. The majority of snakes are nonvenomous, seizing prey with their mouths and relying on their size and strong jaws to subdue it. Snakes generally rely on vision and smell to locate prey, although members of two families have thermal sensor organs on their heads that detect the heat of prey animals.

More snake species exist now than species of all other reptiles combined. This success is thought to be attributable to their ability to devour prey that is larger than their heads (their jaw bones are highly mobile, separating partially and moving around prey as it is swallowed). This unique ability provides snakes with two great advantages over other animals: because they eat large items, they have been able to reduce the frequency with which they need to search for and capture prey; and owing to this, they can spend long periods hidden and secluded, safe from predators. Like lizards, snakes use either active searching or sit-and-wait foraging strategies.

Snakes are themselves prey for hawks and other predatory birds, as well as for some mammals. While many snakes are quite conspicuous against a solid color, being decorated with bold and colorful skin patterns, against their normal backdrops, such as a leaf-strewn forest floor, they are highly camouflaged. They rely on their cryptic colorations, and sometimes on speed, to evade predators.

Mating systems and behaviors of snakes in the wild are not well known. In some, males during the breeding period remain in mating areas, where interested females tend to gather. Males may fight each other to gain the right to mate with a particular female. Male size seems to matter most in determining the outcomes of these fights. Males and females are known to engage in multiple matings with different individuals.

Seeing Reptiles in Costa Rica

As with amphibians, many reptiles are difficult to observe. They spend most of their time concealed or still. Most do not vocalize like birds or frogs, so you cannot use sound to find them. The superb cryptic coloration of snakes, including venomous ones, makes a motionless snake a dangerous snake. Because of the difficulty people have of seeing snakes before getting very close to them, the rule for exploring any area known to harbor venomous snakes or any area for which you are unsure, is never, *Never* to place your hand or foot anywhere that you cannot see first. Do not climb rocks or trees, do not clamber over rocks where your hands or feet sink into holes or crevices; do not reach into bushes or trees. Walk carefully along trails and, although your attention understandably wanders as new sights and sounds are taken in, try to watch your feet and where you are going.

With safety in mind, if you want to see reptiles, there are a few ways to increase the chances. Knowing about activity periods helps. Lizards and many snakes are active during the day, but some snakes are active at night. Thus, a night walk with flashlights that is organized to find amphibians might also yield some reptile sightings. Weather is also important – snakes and lizards are often more active in sunny, warm weather. If all else fails, one may look for small snakes and

Table 4 Reptile Biodiversity Around Costa Rica: Where to See the Most Species (adapted from Janzen 1983).

| Site | Habitat type | Number of species of | | | | |
		Turtles	Crocodilians	Lizards	Snakes	Total
La Selva Biological Reserve	lowland wet	4	2	25	56	87
Tortuguero National Park	lowland wet	5	2	22	28	57
Osa Peninsula; Corcovado National Park	low & middle elevation wet	2	2	23	43	70
San Vito area; Wilson Botanical Garden	middle elevation wet	5	0	28	60+	93+**
Cerro de la Muerte*	highland wet	0	0	3	6	9
Monteverde Cloud Forest Reserve	middle & high elevation wet	0	0	9	28	37
Cañas area; Palo Verde National Park	lowland dry	3	2	16	35	56

Numbers of species known to occur in Costa Rica: Turtles = 14 (6 are sea turtles); Crocodilians = 2; Lizards = 68; Snakes = 127.

* High in the Talamanca Mountains, along the Pan-American Highway (Route 2), between Cartago and San Isidro.

** Some species have not been seen but are suspected to occur in this area.

lizards by carefully moving aside rocks and logs with a robust stick or with one's boots, although such adventures are not for the faint-hearted.

Some of Costa Rica's national parks and wildlife preserves are particularly good places to spot reptiles – Jesus Christ lizards (p. 89) are extremely common in Corcovado National Park and its environs as well as parts of Tortuguero National Park, and iguanas and ctenosaurs (p. 89) are abundant in many of the parks and preserves along the Pacific Coast. Happy hunting!

Family Profiles

I. Crocodilians

Remnants of the age when reptiles ruled the world, today's crocodilians (*alligators, caimans,* and *crocodiles*), when seen in the wild, generally inspire awe, respect, a bit of fear, and a great deal of curiosity. Recent classification schemes include a total of 23 species, distributed over most tropical and sub-tropical areas of the continents. Only two are found in Costa Rica, one of them being common enough for most visitors to see: The CAIMAN (or SPECTACLED CAIMAN) is probably the most abundant crocodilian in the New World and is common over both Pacific and Caribbean lowland areas of Costa Rica. Caiman are relatively small members of the group, reaching 2.5 m (8 ft) in length. They range from southern Mexico south to Ecuador and Central Brazil. The AMERICAN CROCODILE, although not as abundant in Costa Rica as the Caiman, is the most widely distributed of the four New World crocodile species. There is a small population in southern Florida (USA), but mainly it ranges from Mexico, Central America and the Caribbean islands south to Colombia, Venezuela, Peru, and Ecuador. American Crocodiles can reach lengths of 7 m (21.5 ft), as large as any crocodilian species, but in the wild individuals over 4 m (13 ft) are now rare. Male crocodilians are larger than females of the same age.

Generally, differences in coloring are not a good way to distinguish crocodilians – most are shades of brown or olive-brown (juvenile American Crocodiles have dark banding on their bodies and tail). Anatomy and location are more useful clues. Snouts of alligators and caiman tend to be broad and rounded, whereas those of crocodiles are longer and more pointed. Also, in crocodiles, the fourth tooth of the lower jaw projects upwards outside the mouth and can be seen above the upper jaw. Alligators and caiman are generally considered to be freshwater dwellers. Costa Rica's caiman mostly occupy inland creeks, ponds, and slow rivers, but are occasionally found in brackish mangrove swamps. In contrast, American Crocodiles occur mostly in coastal areas, in both brackish and freshwaters habitats, but sometimes spread up rivers farther inland.

Natural History
Ecology and Behavior

Although not amphibians, crocodilians are amphibious animals. They usually move slowly over land but in short bursts can cover ground rapidly. Most of their time, however, is spent in the water. They adore basking in the sunshine along the banks of rivers, streams, and ponds. Crocodilians in the water are largely hidden, resembling from above floating logs. This unassuming appearance allows them to move close to shore and seize animals that come to the water to drink.

Crocodilians are meat-eaters. The foods taken depend on their age and size. Juvenile caiman eat primarily aquatic insects, whereas adults prey on fish and amphibians. Carrion is also eaten. The young of American Crocodiles feed on small aquatic and terrestrial vertebrates; adults specialize on fish and turtles. They often forage at night.

American Crocodiles sometimes excavate burrows along waterways, into which they retreat to escape predators and, when water levels fall too low, to *estivate* (sleep until water conditions improve). Crocodilians may use vocal signals extensively in their behavior, in communicating with one another, but their sounds have been little-studied. It is known that juveniles give alarm calls when threatened, and that parents respond by quickly coming to their rescue.

One might guess that among such primitive reptiles, parental care would be absent – females would lay eggs, perhaps hide them, but at that point the eggs and hatchlings would be on their own. Surprisingly, however, crocodilians show varying degrees of *parental care*. Nests are guarded and one or both parents often help hatchlings free themselves from the nest. In some species, such as the AMERICAN ALLIGATOR, parents also carry hatchlings to the nearest water. Females may also remain with the young for up to two years, protecting them. This complex parental care in crocodilians is sometimes mentioned by scientists who study dinosaurs to support the idea that dinosaurs may have exhibited complex social and parental behaviors.

Crocodilians are long-lived animals, many surviving 60+ years in the wild.

Breeding

During courtship, male crocodilians such as Caiman often defend aquatic territories, giving displays with their tails – up-and-down and side-to-side movements – that probably serve both to defend the territory from other males and to court females. Typically the female makes the nest by scraping together grass, leaves, twigs, and sand or soil, into a pile near the water's edge. She then buries 20 to 30 eggs in the pile that she, and sometimes the male, guard for about 70 days until hatching. Nests of the AMERICAN CROCODILE are a bit different. The female digs a hole in sandy soil, deposits her eggs, then covers them with sand, which she packs down. She guards the nest and often helps the young emerge. As in the turtles and some lizards, the sex of developing crocodilians is determined largely by the temperature of the ground around the eggs (see Close-Up, p. 94). Crocodile young from a brood may remain together in the nest area for up to 18 months. Breeding seasons for crocodilians vary, especially for Caiman, with nesting observed during both wet and dry parts of the year.

Ecological Interactions

Somewhat surprisingly, crocodilians are prey for a number of animals. Young, very small caiman and crocodiles are eaten by a number of predators, including birds such as herons, storks, egrets and anhingas, and mammals such as raccoons and possibly foxes. Large adults apparently have only two enemies: people and large anaconda snakes. Slow-movers on land, caiman and crocodiles are sometimes killed by automobiles. Cases of cannibalism have been reported.

One of the more surprising mutualisms between species is the case of an African wading bird that actually picks and eats parasites and bits of food from among a basking crocodile's teeth. What is so interesting is that the cleaners are plainly potentially yummy prey for the crocs, yet the reptiles refrain from crunching them. Presumably when the mutualism began, the birds were not always so fortunate. It may be that long ago the birds began cleaning crocs on far less lethal sections of their anatomy.

Lore and Notes

Larger CAIMAN and AMERICAN CROCODILES are potentially dangerous to people, but they are not considered particularly aggressive species. Caiman are usually inoffensive, most being below a size where they try to eat land mammals; local people may even unconcernedly swim near them. There are few documented cases of American Crocodiles killing people. Some species, such as the Nile Crocodile, *are* known to be aggressive. In one famous, historical collecting trip, 444 large ones were shot randomly and opened; four had human remains in their stomachs. True, this number represents only 1% of the crocodile population, but still....

Owing to their predatory nature and large size, crocodilians play large roles in the history and folklore of many cultures, going back at least to ancient Egypt, where a crocodile-headed god was known as Sebek. The Egyptians apparently welcomed crocodiles into their canals, possibly as a defense from invaders. It may have been believed by Egyptians and other African peoples that crocodiles caused blindness, probably because the disease called river blindness results from infestation with a river-borne parasitic roundworm. To appease the crocodiles during canal construction, a virgin was sacrificed to the reptiles. Indeed, providing crocodiles with virgins seems to have been a farily common practice among several cultures, showing a preoccupation with these animals. Even today, carvings of crocodiles are found among many relatively primitive peoples, from South America to Africa to Papua New Guinea. The ancient Olmecs of eastern Mexico also had a crocodile deity.

One Guyana Indian legend explains how the crocodile obtained its scaled, ridged back. The Sun, an avid fisherman, got angry when fish disappeared from his ponds at night. He charged the fierce crocodile with guarding the ponds, unaware that the reptile was the thief. When the Sun finally caught the crocodile in the act, he slashed his body, forming scales.

Status

Most crocodilian species worldwide were severely reduced in numbers during this century. Several were hunted almost to extinction for their skins. In the USA, hunting almost caused AMERICAN ALLIGATORS to go extinct. In 1961 hunting alligators was made illegal, but poaching continued. Thanks to the 1973 Endangered Species Act, which gave protection to the alligators, they have returned to most of the areas from which they were eliminated. Crocodile and alligator farms (with captive-bred stock) and ranches (wild-caught stock) in many areas of the world now permit skins to be harvested while wild animals are relatively unmolested. Many of the Latin American crocodilians were hunted heavily during the first half of the 20th century. Today, only the COMMON CAIMAN (a species separate from the Costa Rican caiman) is hunted in large numbers, particularly in the Pantanal region of Brazil. In Costa Rica, CAIMAN are abundant and AMERICAN CROCODILES less so; the crocs were much more common in mangrove swamps and coastal rivers up until the 1950s. American Crocodiles, considered by some agencies as vulnerable to threat, are nonetheless CITES Appendix I and USA ESA listed as endangered. In fact, most of the 23 crocodilian species worldwide are considered threatened or endangered, and all are listed by CITES Appendix I or II.

Profiles

Spectacled Caiman, *Caiman crocodilus*, Plate 9a
American Crocodile, *Crocodylus acutus*, Plate 9b

2. Turtles

It is a shame that *turtles* in the wild are relatively rarely encountered reptiles (at least at close range) because they can be quite interesting to watch and they are generally innocuous and inoffensive. It is always a pleasant surprise stumbling across a turtle on land, perhaps laying eggs, or discovering a knot of them basking in the sunshine on rocks or logs in the middle of a pond. The 240 living turtle species are usually grouped into 12 families that can be divided into three types by their typical habitats. Two families comprise the *sea turtles*, ocean-going animals whose females come to shore only to lay eggs. The members of nine families, containing most of the species, live in freshwater habitats – lakes and ponds – except for the exclusively terrestrial *box turtles*. Finally, one family contains the *land tortoises*, which are completely terrestrial.

Turtles all basically look alike: bodies encased in tough shells (made up of two layers – an inner layer of bone and an outer layer of scale-like plates); four limbs, sometimes modified into flippers; highly mobile necks; toothless jaws; and small tails. This body plan must be among nature's best, because it has survived unchanged for a long time; according to fossils, turtles have looked more or less the same for at least 200 million years. Enclosing the body in heavy armor above and below apparently was an early solution to the problems vertebrates faced when they first moved onto land. It provides both rigid support when outside of buoyant water and a high level of protection from drying out and from predators.

Turtles come, for the most part, in a variety of browns, blacks and greens, with olive-greens predominating. They range in size from tiny terrapins a few centimeters long to 250-kg (550-lb) GALÁPAGOS TORTOISES and giant LEATHERBACK SEA TURTLES (Plate 11) that are nearly 2 m (7 ft) long, 3.6 m (12 ft) across (flipper to flipper), and that weigh 550+ kg (1200+ lb). The Leatherbacks are the heaviest living reptiles. In many turtle species, females are larger than males.

Costa Rica has both marine and freshwater turtles. Two sea turtle and three freshwater families are represented. There are no land tortoises.

Natural History

Ecology and Behavior

The diet of freshwater turtles changes as they develop. Early in life they are carnivorous, eating almost anything they can get their jaws on – snails, insects, fish, frogs, salamanders, reptiles. As they grow the diet of most changes to herbivory. Turtles are slow-moving on land, but they can retract their heads, tails, and limbs into their shells, rendering them almost impregnable to predators – unless they are swallowed whole, such as by crocodiles. Long-lived animals, individuals of many turtle species typically live 25 to 60 years in the wild. (GALÁPAGOS TORTOISES routinely live 100 years, the record being 152 years.) Many turtle species grow throughout their lives.

Snapping turtles (Family Chelydridae, Plate 10) are large freshwater turtles with long tails, hooked, mean-looking jaws, and usually bad dispositions – they will bite people. They are found mainly in marshes, ponds, lakes, rivers, and streams. They are omnivorous, and often quite inconspicuous: sometimes algae grows on their backs, camouflaging them as they lunge at and snatch small animals that venture near. They remain predatory throughout their lives, even taking birds and small mammals, but they also eat aquatic vegetation.

The *aquatic* (or *pond*) *turtles* and *box turtles* (Family Emydidae) of Costa Rica occupy a variety of habitats. Some spend most of their time in lakes and ponds, but others leave the water frequently to bask in the sun during the day and to forage on land at night. Because they feed on land, they can occupy rivers that lack vegetation. BROWN LAND, BLACK RIVER, and RED TURTLES (Plates 9, 10) from this family are illustrated. Only one type of box turtle occurs in the country, inhabiting the Atlantic lowlands. It eats plants.

Semi-aquatic *mud turtles* (Family Kinosternidae) are generally found in swamps, ponds, and slow streams, and only occasionally on land. Many appear to favor a diet of aquatic snails, but they have been also observed feeding on land. WHITE-LIPPED and CENTRAL AMERICAN MUD TURTLES (Plate 10) from this family are illustrated.

Sea turtles are large reptiles that live in the open oceans, with the result that, aside from their beach nesting habits, relatively little is known of their behavior. Their front legs have been modified into oar-like flippers, which propel them through the water. Although they need air to breathe, they can remain submerged for long periods. At first, all sea turtles were assumed to have similar diets, probably sea plants. But some observations of natural feeding, as well as examinations of stomach contents, reveal a variety of specializations. GREEN TURTLES eat bottom-dwelling sea grasses and algae, HAWKSBILL TURTLES eat bottom sponges, LEATHERBACK SEA TURTLES eat mostly jellyfish, and OLIVE RIDLEY SEA TURTLES feed on crabs, mollusks, and jellyfish, as well as vegetation.

Breeding

Courtship in turtles can be quite complex. In some, the male swims backwards in front of the female, stroking her face with his clawed feet. In the tortoises, courtship seems to take the form of some between-the-sexes butting and nipping. All turtles lay their leathery eggs on land. The female digs a hole in the earth or sand, deposits the eggs into the hole, then covers them over and departs. It is up to the hatchlings to dig their way out of the nest and navigate to the nearest water. Many tropical turtles breed at any time of year.

Although the numbers of eggs laid per nest varies extensively among the Costa Rican freshwater turtles (from one to about 100), in general, these turtles, specialized for life in the tropics, lay small clutches, often only 1 to 4 eggs. The reason seems to be that, because of the continuous warm weather, they need not breed in haste like their northern cousins, putting all their eggs in one nest. The danger with a single nest is that if a predator finds it, a year's breeding is lost. Tropical turtles, by placing only one or a few eggs in each of several nests spread through the year, are less likely to have predators destroy their total annual breeding production. Also, it may pay to lay a few big eggs rather than many small ones because bigger hatchlings can run faster to the water and its comparative safety from predators.

All sea turtle species breed in much the same way. Mature males and females appear offshore during breeding periods (for example, GREENS, July to October; LEATHERBACKS, February to July; OLIVE RIDLEYS, July to December). After mating, females alone come ashore on beaches, apparently the same ones on which they were born, to lay their eggs. Each female breeds probably every 2 to 4 years, laying from 2 to 8 clutches of eggs in a season (each clutch being laid on a different day). All within about an hour, and usually at night, a female drags herself up the beach to a suitable spot above the high-tide line, digs a hole with her rear flippers (a half meter or more, 2 ft, deep), deposits about 100 golfball-sized eggs, covers them with sand, tamps the sand down, and heads back to the ocean. Sometimes females emerge from the sea alone, but often there are mass emergences, with hundreds of females nesting on a beach in a single night. Eggs incubate for about 2 months, then hatch simultaneously. The hatchlings dig themselves out of the sand and make a dash for the water (if tiny turtles can be said to be able to "dash"). Many terrestrial and ocean predators devour the hatchlings and it is thought that only between 2% and 5% survive their first few days of life. The young float on rafts of sea vegetation during their first year, feeding and growing, until they reach a size when they can, with some safety, migrate long distances through the world's oceans. When sexually mature, in various species from 7 to 20+ years later, they undertake reverse migrations, returning to their birth sites to breed.

Ecological Interactions

If turtles can make it through the dangerous juvenile stage, when they are small and soft enough for a variety of predators to take them, they enjoy very high year-to-year survival – up to 80% or more of an adult population usually survives from one year to the next. However, there is very high mortality in the egg and juvenile stages. Nests are not guarded, and many kinds of predators, such as crocodiles, lizards, and, especially, armadillos, dig up turtle eggs or eat the hatchlings. Although adult turtles have few predators because they are difficult to kill and eat, some turtles have additional defenses. Within the mud turtle family is a group known as *musk turtles*. When grabbed or handled they give off a musky smell from scent glands located on the sides of their bodies; in North America they are known as *stinkpots*.

There is an intriguing relationship between turtle reproduction and temperature that nicely illustrates the intimate and sometimes puzzling connections between animals and the physical environment. For many vertebrate animals, the sex of an individual is determined by the kinds of sex chromosomes it has. In people, if each cell has an X and a Y chromosome, the person is male, and if two Xs, female. In birds, it is the opposite. But in most turtles, it is not the chromosomes that matter, but the temperature at which an egg develops. (See Close-Up, p. 94.)

Lore and Notes

One legend involving turtles concerns the death of Aeschylus, the Greek tragic poet. It is said that he died 2500 years ago, as he neared 100 years of age, when an eagle dropped a turtle on his head from a great height. This story is particularly interesting because birds in modern times have not been observed picking up and dropping turtles from the air to split their shells, as, for instance, seabirds and crows will do with crabs and shellfish. Perhaps turtles are too heavy, or lack a good bill-hold.

Often there is some trans-Atlantic confusion over turtle names: Americans use the word *turtle* for many land species, whereas the British refer to them as *tortoises*.

Status

The ecology and status of populations of most freshwater and land turtle species are still poorly known, making it difficult to determine whether population numbers are stable or declining. However, it is mainly sea turtles, rather than freshwater or terrestrial turtles, that are exploited by people, and therefore that are most threatened. Sea turtle eggs are harvested for food in many parts of the world, including Costa Rica, and adults are taken for meat (only some species) and for their skins. Many adults also die accidentally in fishing nets and collisions with boats. Although sea turtle eggs are protected, and nesting beaches within Costa Rica's national parks are secure, egg poaching occurs elsewhere in the country. Park personnel and volunteers from Costa Rica and from around the world gather seasonally to protect egg-laying females and their eggs, for example, at Tortuguero and Cahuita National Parks. One of the sea turtles, the HAWKSBILL, is the chief provider of tortoiseshell, which is carved for decorative purposes; although protected, these turtles are still hunted. All sea turtles are listed as endangered by CITES Appendix I. Other than sea turtles, probably only two Central American turtles are known to be rare or threatened: the CENTRAL AMERICAN MUD TURTLE (Plate 10) of Costa Rica, Nicaragua, and Panama, and the CENTRAL AMERICAN RIVER TURTLE of Belize and Guatemala; several other mud turtles in Mexico may also be vulnerable.

Profiles

Brown Land Turtle, *Rhinoclemmys annulata*, Plate 9c
Black River Turtle, *Rhinoclemmys funerea*, Plate 9d
Red Turtle, *Rhinoclemmys pulcherrima*, Plate 10a
Snapping Turtle, *Chelydra serpentina*, Plate 10b
White-lipped Mud Turtle, *Kinosternon leucostomum*, Plate 10c
Central American Mud Turtle, *Kinosternon angustipons*, Plate 10d
Green Sea Turtle, *Chelonia mydas*, Plate 11a
Hawksbill Sea Turtle, *Eretmochelys imbricata*, Plate 11b
Leatherback Sea Turtle, *Dermochelys coriacea*, Plate 11c
Olive Ridley Sea Turtle *Lepidochelys olivacea*, Plate 11d

3. Colubrids: Your Regular, Everyday Snakes

All snakes, particularly tropical varieties, are thought by many people to be poisonous, and hence, to be avoided at all cost. This "reptile anxiety" is serious when it prevents people who are paying initial visits to tropical forests from enjoying the many splendors around them. The phobia is understandable because of the lethal nature of a small number of snake species, snakes' abilities to blend in with surroundings and to move and strike so rapidly, and the long history we have, dating back to the origins of the Bible and beyond, of stories and legends of evil snakes. It is much more than Western societies' legends that cause our fear of snakes. All people it seems, irrespective of geography or culture, recoil from images of snakes and regard the real thing as dangerous, indicating a long conflict over evolutionary time between snakes and people. The fact is, however, that everywhere except unfortunate Australia, the majority of snakes are *not* poisonous. Also, poisonous snakes in the American tropics tend to be nocturnal and secretive. Therefore, with a modicum of caution, visitors should be able to enjoy their days in Costa Rica without worrying unduly about poisonous snakes, and, again with caution, be able to watch snakes that cross their paths. Many of them are beautiful organisms, fairly common, and worth a look.

The largest group of snakes are those of the Family Colubridae – the *colubrid* snakes. Most of these are nonpoisonous or, if venomous, dangerous only to small prey, such as lizards and rodents; in other words, they are only mildly venomous. This is a worldwide group comprising over 1500 species, including about three-quarters of the New World snakes. About 100 different species occur in Costa Rica. Most of the snakes with which people have some familiarity, such as *water, brown, garter, whip, green, rat,* and *king snakes,* among a host of others, are colubrids, which have a wide variety of habits and lifestyles. It is not even possible to provide a general physical description of colubrid snakes because of the great variety of shapes and colors that specialize each for their respective lifestyles. Most people will not get close enough to notice, but an expert could identify colubrids by their anatomy; they have rows of teeth on the upper and lower jaws but they do not have hollow, venom-injecting fangs in front on the upper jaw.

Natural History
Ecology and Behavior
Because colubrids vary so much in their natural history, I shall concentrate on the habits of the species illustrated (Plates 12, 13, 14), which are representative of several general types. You should keep in mind that many snakes have not been much studied in nature. Such research is difficult for several reasons. Most snake species are not plentiful in the wild – even members of healthy populations often are found only few and far between – making it difficult to locate and study simultaneously more than a few individuals. Snakes also spend long periods being inactive and they feed infrequently, which means that to collect enough observations, studies of behavior need to be of long duration.

Typical lifestyles of various colubrids are terrestrial, burrowing, arboreal, and aquatic. Arboreal snakes spend most of their time in trees and shrubs. BROWN VINE SNAKES (Plate 12), for instance, are slender, elegant, grayish or brown snakes that inhabit dry areas of Costa Rica, feeding on lizards taken in trees. These snakes have a mild venom that helps subdue their victims. Their thin, long bodies look much like vines and if not moving, these snakes are very difficult to see. They rely on their camouflage for both hunting and protection: they freeze in place when alerted to danger. BLUNT-HEADED TREE SNAKES (Plate 12) are also arboreal. They possess exceptional heads – broad and squarish, relative to a long, thin body – and large, bulging eyes. They forage at night for small frogs and lizards that they locate in their special hunting preserve, at the very outer layer of leaves and branches of trees and shrubs. These light snakes, which are slightly sideways flattened, can move from branch to branch over open gaps that are half the length of their bodies. They hide during the day in trees.

The INDIGO SNAKE (Plate 12) is common throughout much of the American lowland tropics, inhabiting riverbeds, swamps, and marshes. It moves over the ground and sometimes through bushes or shallow water, searching for its varied prey, which includes small turtles, frogs, mammals, birds, fish, eggs, and even other snakes. These beige, brown, or greenish-brown snakes range up to 4.5 m (15 ft) in length. Having no venom, they simply grab prey with their strong jaws, hold it, and swallow it. Another common terrestrial snake is the MUSSURANA (Plate 12). It has a broad range in the Neotropics in wet and semi-dry lowland areas. Hunting nocturnally, Mussuranas specialize on eating other snakes and, in fact, they even take the deadly FER-DE-LANCE (Plate 15) (and are appreciated for this habit by knowledgable local people). Mussurana are also interesting because they subdue their prey with a combination of slow-acting venom and physical constriction.

Breeding

Relatively little is known of the breeding particulars of Costa Rican colubrids. For the group as a whole, the best information is available for the North American garter snakes. In these snakes, group mating assemblages, or *mating balls*, occur on warm days in spring. Many males – dozens and sometimes hundreds – and a few females swarm together and mating occurs. Some males are successful in mating with one or more females, while others are not. Each female probably mates with several males, and DNA tests on snake babies indicate that a single brood may have more than one father. Some of the males within a mating ball actually mimic females by releasing female courtship pheromones, which distract other males from the real females; the mimics then obtain more matings themselves. In other colubrid species, monogamous mating seems to be the case. Males make prolonged searches for mates, perhaps using their chemical senses to detect female pheromones. Once a female is located, a male may spend several days courting her before mating occurs. Because larger female snakes lay more eggs per clutch, males, when given a choice, prefer to mate with larger females. The typical number of eggs per clutch varies from species to species, but some, such as the BLUNT-HEADED TREE SNAKE, lay small clutches of one to three eggs. Most snakes that lay eggs deposit them in a suitable location and depart; the parents provide no care of the eggs or young. A few snakes guard their eggs.

Ecological Interactions

Body shape: Body shape of snakes nicely demonstrates how a single body scheme, in this case cylindrical and legless, can be modified superbly through evolution to cope with a variety of habitats and lifestyles. The colubrid *worm snakes* live primarily underground. Their bodies are for the most part uniformly round, like earthworms. The majority of colubrids are long and very thin, at least partly as an adaptation for speedy movement – they escape from predators by moving rapidly. This very light, slender body plan also permits many arboreal colubrids to cross broad gaps between tree branches. In contrast to the mainly-slender colubrids, most of the *vipers* (see p. 83) are heavy-bodied and rely on their bites, rather than speed, for protection and hunting. Being mostly *sit-and-wait* predators, they move around a lot less than do the colubrids. Finally, *sea snakes*, which spend their time in the water, have flattened tails that help with aquatic propulsion (N.G. Hairston 1994).

Body temperature: Biologists who study snakes know that temperature regulates a snake's life, and is the key to understanding their ecology. Snakes are cold-blooded animals – they inhabit a world where the outside temperature governs their activity. Unlike birds and mammals, their body temperature is determined primarily by how much heat they obtain from the physical environment. Simply put, they can only be active when they gather sufficient warmth from the sun. They have some control over their body temperature, but it is behavioral rather than physiological – they can lie in the sun or retreat to shade to raise or lower their internal temperatures to within a good operating range, but only up to a point: snakes must "sit out" hours or days in which the air temperature is either too high or too low. This dependence on air temperature affects most aspects of snakes' lives, from date of birth, to food requirements, to the rapidity with which they can strike at prey. For instance, in cold weather, snakes are less successful at capturing prey (they move and strike more slowly) and have less time each day when the ambient temperature is within their operating range, and so within the range in which they can forage. On the other hand, their metabolisms are slower when they are cold, which means that they need less food to survive these periods. At lower temperatures, snakes also probably grow slower, reproduce less often, and live longer (C.R. Peterson *et al.* 1993).

Lore and Notes

Snakes' limbless condition, their manner of movement, and the venomous nature of some of them, have engendered for these intriguing reptiles almost universal hatred from people, stretching back thousands of years. Myths about the evil power and intentions of snakes are, as they say, legion. But one need go no further than the Old Testament, where the snake, of course, plays the pivotal role of Eve's corrupt enticer, responsible for people's expulsion from the Garden of Eden. The ensuing enhanced evil reputation of snakes came down through the ages essentially intact – so much so that even people who should have known better, such as Linnaeus, the 18th century botanist who began the scientific system we currently use to name and categorize plants and animals, considered them an abomination. Linnaeus, lumping snakes with other reptiles and the amphibians, referred to them in his writings as "these foul and loathsome animals" that are "abhorrent because of their cold body, pale color, cartilaginous filthy skin, fierce aspect, calculating eye, offensive smell, harsh voice, squalid habitation and terrible venom." He concluded that, owing to their malevolence, "their Creator has not exerted His powers to make many of them."

One common myth about snakes that has its roots in antiquity – back at least to the Egyptians 4500 years ago – and also modern-day adherents, is that a female snake can protect her young when they are threatened by swallowing them. However, there is no evidence for it. The behavior has never been observed in captive snakes or in the wild, undigested young have never been found in snake stomachs, and they are unlikely to be able to survive in a digestive tract. But because some fish and crocodiles brood their young in their mouths, and because one endangered frog species of Australia broods its young in its stomach, one never knows....

Status

No Costa Rican snake species are currently considered threatened. On the other hand, most experts will concede that at this time little is known about the biology and population numbers of most snakes. Long-term studies are necessary to determine if population sizes are stable or changing. Because individual species of snakes normally are not found in great numbers, the truth is that it will always be difficult to tell when they are threatened. Worldwide, about 20 colubrids are listed as vulnerable, threatened, or endangered. The leading threats are habitat destruction and the introduction by people of exotic animals that prey on snakes at some point in their life cycles, such as fire ants, cane toads, cattle egrets, and armadillos. Considered a top priority now for research and conservation are the snakes of the West Indies. The islands of the Caribbean have hundreds of unique snake species, many of which appear to be declining rapidly in numbers – the result of habitat destruction and predation by mongooses, which were imported to the islands to control venomous snakes.

Profiles

Mussurana, *Clelia clelia*, Plate 12a
Indigo Snake, *Drymarchon corais*, Plate 12b

Blunt-headed Tree Snake, *Imantodes cenchoa,* Plate 12c
Brown Vine Snake, *Oxybelis aeneus,* Plate 12d
Roadguard, *Conophis lineatus,* Plate 13a
Speckled Racer, *Drymobius margaritiferus,* Plate 13b
Mica, *Spilotes pullatus,* Plate 13c
Green Parrot Snake, *Leptophis ahaetulla,* Plate 13d
Bird-eating Snake, *Pseustes poecilonotus,* Plate 14a
Tropical Kingsnake, *Lampropeltis triangulum,* Plate 14b
Skink-eater, *Scaphiodontophis annulatus,* Plate 14c
Harlequin Snake, *Scolecophis atrocinctus,* Plate 14d

4. Dangerous Snakes

In this section I group together what are usually considered the more dangerous snakes, those that are highly poisonous and large ones that kill by squeezing their prey. Few short-term visitors to Costa Rica encounter a poisonous snake because most are well camouflaged, secretive in their habits, or nocturnal and, therefore, they are really outside the scope of this book. However, most people are extremely leery of snakes and want to be well-informed about them, just in case.

Vipers. Vipers, of the Family Viperidae, comprise most of the New World's poisonous snakes. Among all snakes they have the most highly developed venom-injection mechanisms: long, hollow fangs that inject poison into prey when they bite. The venom is often *neurotoxic*; that is it interferes with nerve function, causing paralysis of the limbs and then respiratory failure. Other venoms cause hemorrhaging both at the site of the bite and then internally, leading to cardiovascular shock and death. (The answer to the question of why venomous snakes are not harmed by their own venom is that they are immune.) Typically, vipers coil prior to striking. They vary considerably in size, shape, color pattern, and lifestyle. Many of the *viperids* are referred to as *pit-vipers* because they have heat-sensitive "pits," or depressions, between their nostrils and eyes that are sensory organs. Pit-vipers occur from southern Canada to Argentina, as well as in the Old World. The familiar venomous snakes of North America are pit vipers – *rattlesnakes, copperheads, water moccasins,* as are most of Costa Rica's poisonous snakes.

   The deadly FER-DE-LANCE (Plate 15) is abundant in Costa Rica in lowland wet areas and along watercourses in drier areas. Most are shorter than the maximum length of 2.5 m (8 ft). As their name suggests, they resemble a lance or spear, being slender snakes with triangular heads. *Palm vipers,* such as the EYELASH VIPER (Plate 15), are common arboreal snakes of lowland areas. There are several species, all small (as long as 1 m, or 3 ft, but most are only half that long) with prehensile tails and large wide heads. Their color schemes vary extensively. The TROPICAL RATTLER (Plate 15) occurs in Costa Rica mostly in the drier northwestern part of the country. Reaching a length of 1.5 m (5 ft), it is a heavy-bodied snake with a slender neck and broad, triangular head. The rattles consist of loosely-interlocking segments of a horn-like material at the base of the tail. A new segment is added each time the snake sheds its skin. BUSHMASTERS (Plate 16), the largest venomous snakes of the Neotropics, inhabit lowland wet areas, such as the Osa Peninsula and La Selva area. They are the giants of the pit-vipers, slender, large-headed snakes reaching lengths of 2.5 to 3.5 m (9 to 12 ft).

Coral Snakes. The Family Elapidae contains what are regarded as the world's deadliest snakes, the Old World *cobras* and *mambas*. In the Western Hemisphere, the group is represented by the coral snakes – small, often quite gaily attired in bands of red, yellow and black, and, unfortunately, possessed of a very powerful neurotoxic venom. Four coral snake species occur in Costa Rica, one of which is a fairly common terrestrial animal of moist lowland areas. Coral snakes rarely grow longer than a meter (3 ft).

Boas. The Family Boidae, members of which kill by constriction, encompasses about 80 species that are distributed throughout the world's tropical and subtropical regions. They include the Old World *pythons* and the New World's *boas* and *anacondas*, the pythons and anacondas being the world's largest snakes. Four boa species, but not the Anaconda, call Costa Rica home. The BOA CONSTRICTOR (Plate 16), one of the four, occurs over a wide range of habitat types, wet and dry, from sea level up to about 1000 m (3300 ft). This boa reaches lengths of about 6 m (19 ft), but typical specimens are only 1.5 to 2.5 m (5 to 8 ft) long. They have shiny, smooth scales and a back pattern of dark, squarish shapes that provides good camouflage against an array of backgrounds.

Within a species male and female snakes usually look alike, although in many there are minor differences between the sexes in traits such as color patterns or the sizes of their scales.

Natural History
Ecology and Behavior
Vipers. FER-DE-LANCE as adults are terrestrial, but partially arboreal as juveniles. They inhabit moist forests but also some drier areas. They eat mammals such as opossums, and birds. Palm vipers move through trees, along vines and twigs, searching for treefrogs, lizards, and mice to eat. These snakes are often seen sunning themselves on leaves and branches. TROPICAL RATTLERS are denizens of the forest floor and of more open areas. They eat primarily mammals and lizards. Like other pit-vipers (and some other snakes), they can sense the heat radiated by prey animals, which aids their foraging. Searching by heat detection probably works for both warm-blooded prey (birds, mammals) as well as cold-blooded (lizards, etc.), as long as the prey is at a higher temperature than its surroundings. BUSHMASTERS are terrestrial snakes that feed chiefly on mammals. They are mainly nocturnal and therefore, even where common, are infrequently seen. In a recent Costa Rican study during which these snakes could be followed closely because they were affixed with radio transmitters, biologists learned that the Bushmaster diet consisted almost entirely of *spiny rats*, rather large rodents. Typically, a Bushmaster would lie in wait for several days or even weeks beneath a palm tree; after capturing a rat, a snake moved to a new site.

Coral Snakes. Coral snakes are usually secretive and difficult to study; consequently relatively little is known about their ecology and behavior in the wild. They apparently forage by crawling along slowly, intermittently poking their heads into the leaf litter. They eat lizards, amphibians including caecilians (see p. 50), and small snakes, which they kill with their powerful venom. They are often found under rocks and logs.

Boas. Boas are mainly terrestrial but they are also good climbers, and young ones spend a good deal of time in trees. When foraging, boas apparently search for good places to wait for prey, such as in a mammal's burrow or in a tree, near fruit.

The diet includes lizards, birds, and mammals, including domesticated varieties. Prey, recognized by visual, smell (chemical), or heat senses, is seized with the teeth after a rapid, open-mouth lunge. As it strikes, the boa also coils around the prey, lifting it from the ground, and then constricts, squeezing the prey. The prey cannot breathe and suffocates. When the prey stops moving, the boa swallows it whole, starting always with the head.

Breeding

Details of the breeding in the wild of most tropical snakes are not well known. Many of the vipers may follow the general system of North American rattlesnakes, which have been much studied. Males search for females. When one is located, perhaps by a pheromonal trail she lays down, the male accompanies and courts her for several days before mating occurs. Fighting between males for the same female is probably uncommon, because it is rare for two males to locate the same female at the same time. North American rattlers have distinct breeding periods, but many tropical vipers may breed at almost any time of year. Most snakes that lay eggs deposit the eggs in a suitable location and depart; the parents provide no care of the eggs or young. A few snakes guard their eggs.

Vipers. Most of the vipers give birth to live young. The FER-DE-LANCE has a reputation as a prolific breeder, females giving birth to between 20 and 70 young at a time. Each is about a third of a meter (1 ft) long at birth, fully fanged with active poison glands, and dangerous. Palm vipers have clutches of up to 20 live young, and TROPICAL RATTLERS, 20 to 40. The BUSHMASTER is the only egg-laying viperid of the New World, usually producing small clutches of 10 or fewer eggs.

Coral Snakes. Coral snakes lay eggs, up to 10 per clutch.

Boas. Boa Constrictors give birth to live young. Litters vary between 12 and 60, each snakelet being about half a meter (1.5 ft) long.

Ecological Interactions

Coral snakes hold a special place in snake biology studies because a number of nonvenomous or mildly venomous colubrid snakes (see p. 79), as well as at least one caterpillar species, mimic the bright, striking coral snake color scheme – alternating bands of red, yellow (or white), and black. In Costa Rica alone, at least 10 types (genera) of colubrid snakes imitate – to varying degrees – the color patterns of coral snakes (see Plate 14 for examples). The function of the mimicry apparently is to take advantage of the quite proper respect many predatory animals show toward the lethal coral snakes. Ever since this idea was first proposed more than a hundred years ago, the main argument against it has been that it implied either that the predators had to be first bitten by a coral snake to learn of their toxicity and then survive to generalize the experience to all snakes that look like coral snakes, or that the predators were born with an innate fear of the coral snake color pattern. It has now been demonstrated experimentally that several bird predators on snakes (motmots, kiskadees, herons, and egrets) need *not* learn that a coral snake is dangerous by being bitten – they avoid these snakes instinctively from birth. Thus, many snakes have evolved as defensive mechanisms color schemes that mimic that of coral snakes. (However, some biologists argue that this explanation falls apart because, they say, the alternating color bands of the coral snake's body function as camouflage and *not* to warn predators away, and also because the snakes' mammalian predators lack color-vision and therefore could not make use of the patterns to avoid the mimics.)

Nonvenomous snakes also mimic some of the behavior of poisonous snakes, the most obvious example being that a good many snakes, when threatened, coil up and wiggle the tips of their tails, as do rattlesnakes and some other vipers.

Lore and Notes

These snakes are dangerous! Remember: Snakes, like traffic cops, lack a sense of humor. All of the venomous snakes discussed in this section, if encountered, should be given a wide berth. Watch them only from a distance. Very few visitors to Costa Rica are bitten by poisonous snakes, even those that spend their days tramping through forests. One well-known tropical biologist, in fact, calculated that about 450,000 person-hours of field research were conducted at Costa Rica's La Selva Biological Reserve without a single poisonous snake bite, and field biologists certainly have greater chances of coming into contact with snakes than average visitors. (Ironically, the biologist in question reported his calculation after being bitten by a FER-DE-LANCE.) The biology of snake bites is an active area of study. Venomous snakes can bite without injecting any venom, and they can also vary the amount of venom injected – even if bitten, one does not necessarily receive a fatal dose. Within the same species, the toxicity of a snake's venom varies geographically, seasonally, and from individual to individual.

Vipers. Because of its aggressive nature, the Fer-de-lance is often said to be the most feared and dangerous of Central American snakes – when approached, it is more likely to bite than retreat. Stories abound attesting to the potency of its venom. One, out of Honduras, tells the sorry tale of a railway worker and his wife. The man, bitten by a Fer-de-lance at work, was brought home and ministered to by his wife. The venom killed the man two hours later and the wife the next day – she had scraped her finger the previous day while cooking, and the poison had entered through the open cut as she dressed his wound. These snakes killed so many sugar cane workers in Jamaica earlier this century that mongooses from the Old World were shipped to the island to kill them. They were somewhat successful, but unfortunately, the mongooses also killed many of the isle's nonvenomous snakes, not to mention domestic fowl. Also, unhappily for the mongooses, it turns out that the New World pit vipers are a good deal faster striking than are cobras, their Old World nemeses. A documentary motion picture maker trying to film a mongoose killing a Fer-de-lance had several dead mongooses on his hands before obtaining the pictures he wanted. Somewhat amazingly, there is a colubrid snake, the MUSSURANA (Plate 12), that kills and eats the Fer-de-lance by first injecting it with its own considerably less potent venom and then by constricting it.

Palm vipers, although small, pack a potent venom and are a serious threat because of their arboreal habits and highly effective cryptic coloration. They move and coil themselves among a tree's leaves and branches. Some species have the habit of coiling their tails around a branch and hanging down, then turning their body in the air so that it is parallel to the ground, their head in a position to strike at a passing animal. Therefore, pushing through vegetation or clearing a path with a machete can be dangerous pursuits. Several people each year are killed in Costa Rica by palm vipers. One type, the JUMPING VIPER (Plate 15), although possessing a weaker venom than others of its ilk, is particularly scary and dreaded by local people; when threatened, these snakes sometimes jump nearly a meter (2 or 3 ft) into the air, and as they jump, they bite. TROPICAL RATTLERS are usually more aggressive than the North American rattlers, and their venom is stronger and faster-acting. For some reason, they do not always rattle when approached. If threatened, a Tropical Rattler will coil, raise its head high and, if necessary, attack. BUSHMASTERS are large, aggressive snakes, and they inject into their prey what is probably the most powerful venom among Neotropical snakes. When threatened, they coil quickly so that they can strike, and their tail vibrates like a rattlesnake's and makes a rattling sound. Because they are so long, they can strike over a great distance, *so be careful!* As for the stories of them chasing people, there are no documented cases (of course, if true, the victims would not be around to produce those documents); however, they *are* one of only a few snakes in the world with reputations for unprovoked attacks on people. The Bushmaster's scientific name, *Lachesis muta*, translates as "silent fate." Enough said.

Coral Snakes. These small, pretty snakes are rarely seen by people because of their secretive habits. Reports are that they are usually quite docile and seldom go out of their way to bite people. However, if threatened they give a scary defensive display, "erratically snapping their body back and forth ... the head swinging from side to side with the mouth open, and any object that is contacted is bitten" (H. Greene & R. Seib 1983). Their venom is very powerful and coral snakes have killed a good many incautious people.

Boas. Boa personalities appear to vary, but some are notoriously bad-tempered and aggressive. A BOA CONSTRICTOR may hiss loudly at people, draw its head back with its mouth open in a threat posture, and bite. They have large sharp teeth that can cause deep puncture wounds. Therefore, even though boas present no real threat to most people, keeping a respectful distance is advised.

Status
None of Costa Rica's vipers or coral snakes are considered threatened by people (for once, we can say that it's the other way around!). BOA CONSTRICTORS may be threatened in some areas of the country by habitat destruction and by capture for the pet trade; otherwise these boas seem to do well living near people and are still common in many parts of Costa Rica and the rest of the American tropics. Several other boa species, particularly some island endemics, are endangered; all boas are CITES Appendix II listed.

Profiles
Fer-de-lance, *Bothrops asper*, Plate 15a
Eyelash Viper, *Bothriechis schlegelii*, Plate 15b
Jumping Viper, *Atropoides nummifer*, Plate 15c
Tropical Rattlesnake, *Crotalus durissus*, Plate 15d
Bushmaster, *Lachesis muta*, Plate 16a
Rainforest Hognosed Pit-viper, *Porthidium nasutus*, Plate 16b
Boa Constrictor, *Boa constrictor*, Plate 16c
Central American Coral Snake, *Micrurus nigrocinctus*, Plate 16d
Pelagic Sea Snake, *Pelamis platurus*, Plate 17a

5. Geckos

Geckos are most interesting organisms because, of their own volition, they have become "house lizards" – probably the only self-domesticated reptile. The family, Gekkonidae, is spread throughout tropical and subtropical areas the world over,

750 species strong. In many regions, geckos have invaded houses and buildings, becoming ubiquitous adornments of walls and ceilings. Ignored by residents, they move around dwellings chiefly at night, munching insects. To first-time visitors from northern climes, however, the way these harmless lizards always seem to position themselves on ceilings directly above one's sleeping area can be a bit disconcerting. Nine species occur in Costa Rica.

Geckos are fairly small lizards, usually gray or brown, with large eyes. They have thin, soft skin, covered usually with small, granular scales that produce a slightly lumpy appearance, and big toes with well-developed claws that allow them to cling to vertical surfaces and even upside-down on ceilings. The way geckos manage these feats has engendered over the years a fair amount of scientific detective work. Various forces have been implicated in explaining the gecko's anti-gravity performance, from the ability of their claws to dig into tiny irregularities on man-made surfaces, to their large toes acting as suction cups, to an adhesive quality of friction. The real explanation appears to lie in the series of miniscule hair-like structures on the bottoms of the toes, which provide attachment to walls and ceilings by something akin to surface tension – the same property that allows some insects to walk on water.

Adult geckos mostly report in at only 5 to 10 cm (2 to 4 in) in length, tail excluded; tails can double the length. Because lizard tails frequently break off and regenerate (see p. 93), their length varies tremendously; gecko tails are particularly fragile. Lizards, therefore, are properly measured from the tip of their snouts to their *vent*, the urogenital opening on their bellies, usually located somewhere near to where their rear legs join their bodies. The geckos' 5 to 10 cm length, therefore, is their range of "SVLs," or *snout–vent lengths*.

Natural History
Ecology and Behavior

Although most lizards are active during the day and inactive at night, nearly all gecko species are nocturnal. In natural settings, they are primarily ground dwellers, but, as their behavior in buildings suggests, they are also excellent climbers. Geckos feed on arthropods, chiefly insects. In fact, it is their ravenous appetite for cockroaches and other insect undesirables that renders them welcome house guests in many parts of the world. Perhaps the only "negative" associated with house geckos is that, unlike the great majority of lizards, which keep quiet, geckos at night are quite the little chirpers and squeakers. They communicate with each other with loud calls – surprisingly loud for such small animals. Various species sound different; the word *gecko* approximates the sound of calls from some African and Asian species.

Geckos are *sit-and-wait* predators; instead of wasting energy actively searching for prey that is usually highly alert and able to flee, they sit still for long periods, waiting for unsuspecting insects to venture a bit too near, then lunge, grab, and swallow.

Geckos rely chiefly on their *cryptic coloration* and their ability to flee rapidly for escape from predators, which include snakes during the day and snakes, owls, and bats at night. When cornered, geckos give threat displays; when seized, they give loud calls to distract predators, and bite. Should the gecko be seized by its tail, it breaks off easily, allowing the gecko time to escape, albeit tail-less; tails regenerate rapidly. Some geckos when seized also secrete thick, noxious fluids from their tails, which presumably discourages some predators.

Breeding

Geckos are egg-layers. Mating occurs after a round of courtship, which involves a male displaying to a female by waving his tail around, followed by some mutual nosing and nibbling. Clutches usually contain only a few eggs, but a female may lay several clutches per year. There is no parental care – after eggs are deposited, they and the tiny geckos that hatch from them are on their own.

Lore and Notes

The world's smallest reptile, at 4 cm (1.5 in) long, is a gecko, the CARIBBEAN DWARF GECKO. As reptile biologists like to say, it is shorter than its name.

Status

More than 25 gecko species are listed by conservation organizations as rare, vulnerable to threat, or endangered, but they are almost all restricted to the Old World. The MONITO GECKO, found only on Monito Island, off Puerto Rico, is endangered (USA ESA listed), as is Venezuela's PARAGUANAN GROUND GECKO. None of Costa Rica's geckos are currently threatened.

Profiles

Leaf Litter Gecko, *Lepidoblepharis xanthostigma*, Plate 17b
Central American Smooth Gecko, *Thecadactylus rapicauda*, Plate 17c
Yellowbelly Gecko, *Phyllodactylus tuberculosus*, Plate 17d

6. Iguanids

The Iguanidae, a large family of lizards, has an almost exclusively New World distribution. There are more than 600 species, 38 of which occur in Costa Rica. Most of the lizards commonly encountered by ecotourists or that are on their viewing wish-lists, are members of this group. It includes the very abundant *anolis* lizards, the colorfully named Jesus Christ lizards, and the spectacular, dinosaur-like GREEN IGUANA (Plate 18).

The iguanids are a rich and varied group of diverse habits and habitats. Many in the family are brightly colored and have adornments such as crests, spines, or throat fans. They range in size from tiny anolis lizards, or *anoles*, only a few centimeters in total length and a few grams in weight, to GREEN IGUANAS, which are up to 2 m (6.5 ft) long. CTENOSAURS (TEN-o-saurs), or black iguanas, (Plate 18) range up to a meter (3 ft) or more in length and can weigh up to 1 kg (2 lbs). The *basilisks*, or Jesus Christ lizards, brown lizards with prominent head crests, range up to a meter in total length and more than half a kilogram (1 lb) in weight. Most of the length in iguanid lizards resides in the long, thin tail; hence the paradoxically low weight for such long animals. *Spiny lizards* are a large group (80 species) of small to moderate-sized iguanids that range from southern Canada to Panama. The ones in Costa Rica are usually 6 or 7 cm (3 in) long, excluding the tail. They are quite common in natural areas and also around human habitations. Scales on their backs are often overlapping and pointed, which yield a bristly appearance.

Natural History
Ecology and Behavior

Green Iguana. You won't mistake this animal; it's the large one resembling a dragon sitting in the tree near the river. Iguanas are common inhabitants of many Neotropical rainforests, in moist areas at low to middle elevations. Considered semi-arboreal, they spend most of their time in trees, usually along rivers and streams. They don't move much, and when they do it's often in slow-motion. They are herbivores as adults, eating mainly leaves and twigs and, more occasionally, fruit; insects are favorites of youngsters. They are fun to discover, but boring to watch. When threatened, an iguana above a river will drop from its perch into the water, making its escape underwater; they are good swimmers. During their breeding season, males establish and defend mating territories on which live one to 4 females.

Ctenosaur. Ctenosaurs are sometimes confused with Green Iguanas, but they are darker-colored, lack the iguana's conspicuous head spines and crest, and are often found in drier habitats, such as fields, farms, scrubland, dry woodlands, savannas, and roadsides. Like iguanas, they are semi-arboreal, spending considerable time in trees, feeding and basking; when chased on the ground, they often run to a tree and climb to escape. They also burrow into the ground and under rocks. Ctenosaurs are territorial, each one defending its shelter and perch sites from all others. (Many of the drier campground areas in the national parks along Costa Rica's Pacific coast seasonally are chock full of displaying and chasing Ctenosaurs.) They are predominantly vegetarians, eating flowers, fruits, agricultural crops, but also the odd lizard or small mammal. Juvenile Ctenosaurs eat insects and, in turn, are preyed upon by a variety of animals, including snakes, hawks, jays, skunks, and raccoons.

Basilisk. Basilisks are medium to large, active lizards commonly found along watercourses in lowland areas. Often they are very abundant – one Costa Rican study estimated their numbers to be more than 200 per acre! They are classified as terrestrial but are also semi-arboreal – possessed of a tendency to climb. They are omnivorous, eating a variety of invertebrate and vertebrate animals (especially hatchling lizards), some flowers, and a good deal of fruit. The name "Jesus Christ lizard" refers to their ability to run over the surface of ponds or streams, really skipping along, for distances up to 20 m (60 ft) or more. They do it in an upright posture, on their rear legs, further inviting the divine comparison. The trick is one of fluid dynamics: some of the force to support the lizard comes from resistance of the water when the large rear feet are slapped onto the surface; the rest of the upward force stems from the compression of the water that occurs as the lizard's feet move slightly downwards into the water (their feet move so rapidly up and down that they are actually pulled from below the surface before the water can close over them). Juveniles are better at water-running than are adults, which, when too heavy to be supported on the surface, escape predation by diving in and swimming underwater.

Anole. Anoles are small, often arboreal lizards, and a good number of species are represented in Costa Rica. Many are frequently encountered, but others, such as ones that live in the high canopy, are rarely seen. Some are ground dwellers, and others spend most of their time on tree trunks perched head toward the ground, visually searching for insect prey. Anoles are known especially for their territorial behavior. Males defend territories on which one to three females may live. In some species males with territories spend up to half of each day defending their territories from males looking to establish new territories. The defender will roam his territory, perhaps 30 sq m (325 sq ft), occasionally giving territorial advertisements – repeatedly displaying his extended throat sac, or *dewlap,* and performing *push-ups*, bobbing his head and body up and down. Trespassers that do not exit the territory are chased and even bitten. Anoles are chiefly sit-and-wait predators on insects and other small invertebrates. Anoles themselves, small and presumably tasty, are frequent prey for many birds (motmots, trogons, and others) and snakes.

Spiny Lizard. Most spiny lizard species in the wild are ground-dwelling or semi-arboreal, but around buildings they are climbers of walls, fences, and rooftops. Sit-and-wait predators, they eat mainly insects, and many also consume some plant materials.

Breeding

Green Iguana. Breeding occurs during the early part of the dry season, in December and January. These large lizards lay clutches that average about 40 eggs. They are laid in burrows that are 1 to 2 m (3 to 7 ft) long, dug by the females. After laying her clutch, the female fills the burrow with dirt, giving the site a final packing down with her nose. It has been said that a female digging her nest burrow probably engages in the most vigorous activity performed by these sluggish reptiles.

Ctenosaur. Female Ctenosaurs annually lay a single clutch of between 12 and 88 eggs, older females producing more. Eggs are laid in burrows in open, sunny areas, from December to February; they hatch from April through July.

Basilisk. Female Basilisks produce clutches of 2 to 18 eggs several times each year. Smaller, younger females, have fewer eggs per clutch. Eggs hatch in about 3 months. Hatchling lizards, weighing only 2 g, are wholly on their own; in one study, only about 15% of them survived the first few months of life.

Anole. Female Anoles lay small clutches of eggs throughout the year; an individual female may produce eggs every few weeks.

Spiny Lizard. In contrast to most iguanids, some spiny lizard species in Costa Rica are *viviparous*, giving birth to live young once per year. Average brood size in one study was 6.

Ecological Interactions

Via interactions between the external environment and their nervous and hormonal systems, many iguanids have the novel ability to change their body color. Such color changes presumably are adaptations that allow them to be more *cryptic*, to blend into their surroundings, and hence, to be less detectable to and safer from predators. Also, alterations in color through the day may aid in temperature regulation; lizards must obtain their body heat from the sun, and darker colors absorb more heat. Color changing is accomplished by moving pigment granules within individual skin cells either to a central clump (causing that color to diminish) or spreading them evenly about the cell (enhancing the color). It is now thought that the stimulus to change colors arises with the physiology of the animal rather than with the color of its surroundings. Spiny lizards change color with temperature or light intensity, some being very dark, even black, in the cool early morning and green at midday. Even the large CTENOSAUR has skin that lightens or darkens with changing temperature or activity levels. Anolis lizards also change color. North American species, particularly CAROLINA ANOLES, owing to their color-changing ways, are hawked in pet stores as "chameleons" even though the real chameleons are Old World lizards.

Lore and Notes

The large iguanid lizards (GREEN IGUANA, CTENOSAUR) are not dangerous. They are not poisonous and they will not bite unless given no other choice. The iguana and ctenosaur are both hunted by local people for invitation to the dinner table. Give them a try if the meat is offered; but it's an acquired taste. Ctenosaur parts supposedly have great medicinal power, especially as an anti-impotence agent.

Status

None of the Costa Rican iguanids are currently considered threatened. Because CTENOSAURS and GREEN IGUANAS are hunted for meat, they are scarce in some localities. Several iguanids of the Caribbean are endangered, such as the JAMAICAN GROUND IGUANA and VIRGIN ISLANDS (ANEGADA) ROCK IGUANA (both are USA ESA listed). At least three iguana species in the Galápagos Islands are threatened, and two iguanids in the USA are known to be endangered.

Profiles

Green Iguana, *Iguana iguana*, Plate 18a
Basilisk, *Basiliscus basiliscus*, Plate 18b
Ctenosaur, *Ctenosaura similis*, Plate 18c
Big-headed Anole, *Anolis capito*, Plate 19a
Ground Anole, *Anolis humilis*, Plate 19b
Slender Anole, *Anolis limifrons*, Plate 19c
Green Spiny Lizard, *Sceloporus malachiticus*, Plate 19d

7. Skinks and Whiptails

The *skinks* are a large family (Scincidae, with about 700 species) of small and medium-sized lizards with a worldwide distribution. Over the warmer parts of the globe, they occur just about everywhere. Skinks are easily recognized because they look different from other lizards, being slim-bodied with relatively short limbs, and smooth, shiny, roundish scales that combine to produce a satiny look. Many skinks are in the 5 to 9 cm (2 to 4 in) long range, not including the tail, which can easily double an adult's total length. The LITTER SKINK, profiled here (Plate 20), is one of only three Costa Rican species. It is common to rainforests at low to moderate elevations, and is especially prevalent in forest edge areas.

Whiptails, Family Tiidae, are a New World group of about 200 species, distributed throughout the Americas. Most are tropical residents, inhabiting most areas below 1500 m (5000 ft) in elevation. Although only 11 species occur in Costa Rica, they are often quite abundant along trails, roads, beaches, and clearings and, hence, frequently conspicuous. Whiptails are small to medium-sized, slender lizards, known for their highly alert, active behavior. They have long, slender, whip-like tails, often twice the length of their bodies, which range from 7 to 12 cm (3 to 5 in) in length. Some whiptails are striped, others are striped and spotted.

Natural History

Ecology and Behavior

Skinks. Many skinks are terrestrial lizards, particularly appreciative of moist ground habitats such as sites near streams and springs, or of spending time under wet leaf litter. A few species are arboreal, and some are burrowers. Skink locomotion is surprising; they use their limbs to walk but when the need arises for speed, they locomote mainly by making rapid wriggling movements with their bodies, snake-fashion, with little leg assistance. Through evolutionary change, in fact, some species have lost limbs entirely, all movement being snake-fashion.

Skinks are day-active lizards, most activity in the tropics being confined to the morning hours; they spend the heat of midday in sheltered, insulated hiding places, such as deep beneath the leaf litter. Some skinks are sit-and-wait foragers, whereas others seek their food actively. They consume many kinds of insects, which they grab, crush with their jaws or beat against the ground, then swallow whole. Predators on Costa Rican skinks are snakes, larger lizards, birds, and mammals such as coati, armadillo, and opossum.

Skinks generally are not seen unless searched for. Most species are quite secretive, spending most of their time hidden under rocks, vegetation, or leaf litter.

Whiptails. Whiptails actively search for their food, usually insects, but also small amphibians. Typically they forage by moving slowly along the ground, poking their nose into the leaf litter and under sticks and rocks. Although most are terrestrial, many also climb into lower vegetation to hunt. Whiptails have a characteristic gait, moving jerkily forward while rapidly turning their head from side to side.

Breeding
Skinks. Skinks are either egg-layers or live-bearers. LITTER SKINKS lay eggs, usually small clutches of 1 to 3. They breed year round, with individual females laying several clutches annually.

Whiptails. Costa Rican Whiptails may breed throughout the year. They are egg-layers, females producing small clutches that average 3 to 5 eggs; individuals produce two or more clutches per year.

Ecological Interactions
Whiptails nicely demonstrate the ecological relationship known as *resource partitioning.* A close examination of the Osa Peninsula, for instance, will reveal that three closely related whiptail lizards live there in happy coexistence, all very common and about the same size. At first glance, their mutual survival appears to violate one of the basic tenets of ecological theory, which posits that when two or more species are very similar in their habits, that is, if they occupy the same *niche*, then the best competitor will win and the others will be driven to rarity and eventual extinction. The whiptails get around this rule by resource partitioning: although they coexist closely, each employs just a slightly different feeding behavior – differing in what, when, or where they eat; and that small amount of difference is sufficient to reduce competition to levels at which all three populations can thrive in the same locality.

Many lizards, including the skinks, whiptails, and geckos, have what many might regard as a self-defeating predator escape mechanism: they detach a large chunk of their bodies, leaving it behind for the predator to attack and eat while they make their escape. (True, the piece they desert, the tail, is not vital to their health, but still, it's an adaptation that I have always been glad that the higher primates have not emulated.) The process is known as *tail autotomy* – "self removal." Owing to some special anatomical features of the tail vertebrae, the tail is only tenuously attached to the rest of the body; when the animal is grasped forcefully by its tail, the tail breaks off easily. The shed tail then wriggles vigorously for a while, diverting a predator's attention for the instant it takes the skink or whiptail to find shelter. A new tail grows quickly to replace the lost one.

Is autotomy successful as a lifesaving tactic? Most evolutionary biologists would argue that, of course it works, otherwise it could not have evolved to be part of lizards' present day defensive strategy. But we have hard evidence, too. For instance, some snakes that have been caught and dissected have been found to have in their stomachs nothing but skinks – not whole bodies, just tails! Also, a very common finding when a field biologist surveys any population of small lizards (catching as many as possible in a given area to count and examine them) is that a hefty percentage, often 50% or more, have regenerating tails; this indicates that tail autotomy is common and successful in preventing predation.

Lore and Notes

Among the whiptails, a number of species exhibit what for vertebrate animals is an odd method of reproduction, one that is difficult for us to imagine. All individuals in these species are female; not a male amongst them. Yet they breed merrily away, by *parthenogenesis*. Females lay unfertilized eggs, which all develop as females that, barring mutations, are all genetically identical to mom. (Some fish and amphibians also reproduce this way.) This hardly seems a happy state of affairs; many people would argue that something important is missing from such societies. It is likely that parthenogenetic species arise when individuals of two different but closely related, sexually reproducing, "parent" species mate and, instead of having hybrid young that are sterile (a usual result, as when horses and donkeys mate to produce sterile mules), have young whose eggs can produce viable females.

Status

Costa Rican skinks and whiptails, as far as is known, are secure; none are presently considered threatened. As is the case for many reptiles and amphibians, however, many species have not been sufficiently monitored to ascertain the true health of populations. Many skinks of Australia and New Zealand regularly make lists of vulnerable and threatened animals and several Caribbean skinks and whiptails are endangered. In the USA, Florida's SAND SKINK (USA ESA listed) and the ORANGE-THROATED WHIPTAIL are considered vulnerable or threatened species.

Profiles

Litter Skink, *Sphenomorphus cherriei*, Plate 20a
Central American Whiptail, *Ameiva festiva*, Plate 20b
Barred Whiptail, *Ameiva undulata*, Plate 20c
Deppe's Whiptail, *Cnemidophorus deppei*, Plate 20d

Environmental Close-Up 2
Temperature and Turtle Sex: If the Eggs are Warm, Prepare for Daughters

Most biologists would concur that one of the most fascinating – and still mysterious – discoveries about reptiles during the past 30 years was the surprising finding that, in several groups, the temperature at which eggs develop in the ground largely determines the sex of the individuals that emerge from the eggs. All *crocodilians*, most *turtles*, and many *lizards* lack sex-determining chromosomes (like people's famous X and Y) and so instead of genetics being responsible, their sexes are determined by egg temperature. This method of sex determination is myste-rious for the basic reason that no one quite knows why it should exist; that is, is there some advantage of this system to the animals that we as yet fail to appreci-ate? Or is it simply a consequence of reptile structure and function, some funda-mental constraint of their biology?

The facts are these. In most turtles, for instance, eggs incubated at constant temperatures above 30°C (86°F) all develop as females, whereas those incubated at 24 to 28°C (75 to 82°F) become males. At 28 to 30°C, both males and females are produced. In some species, a second temperature threshold exists – eggs that develop below 24°C (75°F) again become females. In the crocodiles and lizards, the situation reverses, with males developing at relatively high temperatures and females at low temperatures. These findings have been confirmed both by lab experiments and in natural nests.

The exact way that temperature influences sex determination is not clear, but it is suspected that temperature directly influences a turtle's developing brain. Whatever the cause, the system has myriad implications for reptile reproduction and population sizes, as well as important consequences for conservation biology. First, and most interesting, is that a female's choice of nest site determines the sex of her offspring (in humans the analogous situation would be if the choice of delivery hospital determined a baby's sex). For example, female American Alliga-tors that make their nests on levees, which are usually much warmer than nests built in other areas such as marshes, have more sons than daughters. In other rep-tiles, it has been observed that nests in sunny, open areas tend to produce females, and those in the shade produce males.

Second, an egg's position within a nest can determine its sex. In shallow nests of Snapping Turtles (Plate 10), eggs near the top of the nest are warmer and pro-duce females, while eggs in a nest's cooler bottom region produce males. Third, as turtle females age and their egg-producing and laying habits change, so change the proportions of male and female offspring produced. When females first start breeding, they tend to lay relatively small eggs in shallow nests, which develop at warmer temperatures and tend to produce females. Later in life, the same females produce larger eggs in deeper nests, where cool conditions favor the development of males. Interestingly, small eggs have a lower probability of hatching than do larger eggs and, because smaller eggs produce smaller hatchlings, the young from smaller eggs have lower survival rates than those from larger eggs. In other words, a typical female turtle may spend her early reproductive years producing rela-tively unsuccessful broods of females, and her later years producing relatively more successful broods of males.

Fourth, reptiles with long nesting seasons may produce primarily one sex early in the season, when weather is warmer or cooler than later, and the other sex later in the season. This scenario opens the door to a potential problem with this system of sex determination. Suppose the nesting habitats of a species are reg-ularly exposed to seasonal floods, run-offs, or high tides that destroy reptile nests at about the same time each year? If that happened, nests developing into one sex would suffer higher mortality than nests of the other sex, with the result that in many years there would be more of one sex born than the other; when these young matured and reached reproductive age, there would also be more of one sex than the other. If the disparity in numbers between the sexes were sufficiently large, there could ensue difficulties for individuals finding mates and therefore, eventually, in maintaining healthy populations.

The discovery of this crucial relationship between temperature of egg development and sex determination has important consequences for reptile conservation efforts. For years conservationists concerned with saving *sea turtles* (p. 77) from the brink of extinction, for instance, would remove eggs from beach nests to protect them from predators, people, and bad weather. The eggs were placed in styrofoam boxes and incubated in shelters near the beach. Unwittingly, however, by having all the eggs develop under the same temperature conditions, the effect of these conservation efforts must have been to produce hatchlings that were almost all males. Artificially creating large numbers of male and few female sea turtles, of course, is a poor way to encourage reproduction and population growth. Thus, more recent efforts, fortified with knowledge of turtle physiological ecology, vary the conditions under which removed eggs are incubated, assuring mixed-sex groups of hatchlings.

Knowledge of turtle sex determination also provides important information for calculating the amount of beach habitat that needs to be preserved for sea turtles to maintain healthy populations. It turns out that temperature conditions vary from beach to beach, even when they are located near to each other. It is strongly suspected, for that reason, that some beaches traditionally produce female sea turtles and others, males. The point is, there is the danger that if only a single beach area is protected from development or poaching, even if it is an extensive area, the protective efforts will be for naught if hatchlings of only one sex are produced there. A better plan, in that case, would be to make sure to protect several different beaches, with different thermal properties, thus ensuring the production of both boy and girl turtles.

Not surprisingly, sex determination in reptiles is currently a hot area of biological research (no pun intended).

Chapter 7

Birds

- Introduction
  General Characteristics of Birds
  Classification of Birds
- Features of Tropical Birds
- Seeing Birds in Costa Rica
- Family Profiles

Introduction

Most of the vertebrate animals one sees on a visit to just about anywhere at or above the water's surface are birds, and Costa Rica is no exception. Regardless of how the rest of a trip's wildlife-viewing progresses – how fortunate one is to observe mammals or reptiles or amphibians – birds will be seen frequently and in large numbers. The reasons for this pattern are that birds are, as opposed to those other terrestrial vertebrates, most often active during the day, visually conspicuous and, to put it nicely, usually far from quiet as they pursue their daily activities. But why are birds so much more conspicuous than other vertebrates? The reason goes to the essential nature of birds: they fly. The ability to fly is, so far, nature's premier anti-predator escape mechanism. Animals that can fly well are relatively less predation prone than those which cannot, and so they can be both reasonably conspicuous in their behavior and also reasonably certain of daily survival. Birds can fly quickly from dangerous situations, and, if you will, remain above the fray. Most flightless land vertebrates, tied to moving in or over the ground or on plants, are easy prey unless they are quiet, concealed, and careful or, alternatively, very large or fierce; many smaller ones, in fact, have evolved special defense mechanisms, such as poisons or nocturnal behavior.

A fringe benefit of birds being the most frequently encountered kind of vertebrate wildlife is that, for an ecotraveller's intents and purposes, birds are innocuous. Typically, the worst that can happen from any encounter is a soiled shirt. Contrast that with too-close, potentially dangerous meetings with certain reptiles (venomous snakes!), amphibians (frogs and salamanders with toxic skin secretions), and mammals (bears or big cats). Moreover, birds do not always depart with all due haste after being spotted, as is the wont of most other types of vertebrates. Again, their ability to fly and thus easily evade our grasp, permits many birds, when confronted with people, to behave leisurely and go about their business (albeit keeping one eye at all times on the strange-looking bipeds), allowing us extensive time to watch them. Not only are birds among the safest animals to observe and the most easily discovered and watched, but they are among the most beautiful. Experiences with Costa Rica's birds will almost certainly provide some of any trip's finest, most memorable naturalistic moments. A visitor who stumbles across a tree filled with a squawking flock of feeding parrots, for instance, is in for a stunning tropical treat.

General Characteristics of Birds

Birds are vertebrates that can fly. They began evolving from reptiles during the Jurassic Period of the Mesozoic Era, perhaps 150 million years ago, and saw explosive development of new species occur during the last 50 million years or so. The development of flight is the key factor behind birds' evolution, their historical spread throughout the globe, and their current ecological success and arguable dominant position among the world's land animals. Flight, as mentioned above, is a fantastic predator evasion technique, it permits birds to move over long distances in search of particular foods or habitats, and its development opened up for vertebrate exploration and exploitation an entirely new and vast theater of operations – the atmosphere.

At first glance, birds appear to be highly variable beasts, ranging in size and form from 135 kg (300 lb) ostriches to 4 kg (10 lb) eagles to 3 g (a tenth of an ounce) hummingbirds. Actually, however, when compared with other types of vertebrates, birds are remarkably standardized physically. The reason is that, whereas mammals or reptiles can be quite diverse in form and still function as mammals or reptiles (think how different in form are lizards, snakes, and turtles), if birds are going to fly, they more or less must look like birds, and have the forms and physiologies that birds have. The most important traits for flying are:

1 feathers, which are unique to birds;
2 powerful wings, which are modified upper limbs;
3 hollow bones;
4 warm-bloodedness; and
5 efficient respiratory and circulatory systems.

These characteristics combine to produce animals with two overarching traits – high power and low weight, which are the twin dictates that make for successful feathered flying machines. (The flying mammals, bats, also follow these dictates.)

Classification of Birds

Bird classification is one of those areas of science that continually undergoes revision. Currently about 9000 separate species are recognized. They are divided into 28 to 30 orders, depending on whose classification scheme one follows, perhaps 170 families, and about 2040 genera. For purposes here, we can divide birds into *passerines* and *nonpasserines*. Passerine birds (Order Passeriformes) are the perching birds, with feet specialized to grasp and to perch on tree branches. They are mostly the small land birds (or *songbirds*) with which we are most familiar – blackbirds, robins, wrens, finches, sparrows, etc – and the group includes more than 50% of all bird species. The remainder of the birds – seabirds and shorebirds, ducks and geese, hawks and owls, parrots and woodpeckers, and a host of others – are divided among the other 20+ orders.

Features of Tropical Birds

The first thing to know about tropical birds is that they are exceedingly varied and diverse. There are many more species of birds in the tropics than in temperate or arctic regions. For instance, somewhat less than 700 bird species occur in North America north of Mexico, but about 3300 species occur in the Neotropics (Central and South America), most of those in the tropical regions, and about 830 species (roughly 600 year-round *resident*, 200 *migrant*) call comparatively tiny Costa Rica home. Many families of birds, such as the toucans, motmots, manakins, and cotingas, are *endemic* to the Neotropics – they occur nowhere else on Earth.

Many tropical birds rely for food on insects or seeds, but it is fruit-eating, or *frugivory*, that really distinguishes birds in the tropics. Frugivory has reached its zenith among tropical species, and the relationships between the birds that eat fruit and the plants that produce it have powerful implications for the biology of both (see Close-Up, p. 179).

The mating systems of tropical birds range from typical, familiar *monogamy*, a male and a female pairing and cooperating to raise a brood of young, to the so-called *promiscuity* of manakins, some hummingbirds and others, in which males of the species gather in groups called *leks* to display and advertise for mates. Females attracted to the leks choose males to mate with and then depart to nest and raise their young themselves (see Close-Up, p. 182). The social systems of birds in the tropics are also quite variable. Many are *territorial*, aggressively defending parcels of real estate from other members of their species (*conspecifics*), typically during the breeding season, although some seem to exhibit year-round territoriality. Often it is a mated pair that keeps a territory, but in some species (some of the cotingas, jays, wrens, tanagers, and woodpeckers), small family groups stay together throughout the year, even engaging in *cooperative breeding* in which all members of the group assist with a single nest. A number of species, such as the oropendolas, stay in small colonial associations, and build their nests together in the same tree. Tropical birds often participate in *mixed-species foraging flocks*, spending nonbreeding periods travelling around a large territory or semi-nomadically in the company of many other species – searching, for example, for trees bearing ripe fruit. Some of these flocks contain primarily *insectivorous* birds, others primarily *granivores* (seedeaters), and still others typically follow swarms of army ants, feasting on the insects and other small animals that bolt from cover at the approach of the predatory ants.

Breeding seasons in the tropics tend to be longer than in other regions. The weather is more conducive to breeding for longer periods. Also, unlike many temperate zone birds, those in the tropics need not hurry through breeding efforts because, being resident all year, they do not face migration deadlines. Breeding in the tropics is closely tied to wet and dry seasons. Most Costa Rican birds breed from March through August or September, timed to coincide with the greatest abundance of food for their offspring. March is usually when the months-long dry season ends, and spring showers bring heavy concentrations of insect life and ripening of fruit.

One notable aspect of bird breeding in the tropics that has long puzzled biologists is that clutches are usually small, most species typically laying two eggs per nest. Birds that breed in temperate zone areas usually have clutches of three to five eggs. Possible explanations are that:

1   small broods attract fewer predators;
2   because such a high percentage of nests in the tropics are destroyed by predators it is not worth putting too much energy and effort into any one nest; and
3   with the increased numbers of hours of daylight in northern areas, temperate zone birds have more time each day to gather food for larger numbers of growing nestlings.

Last, tropical birds include the most gorgeously attired birds, those with bright, flashy colors and vivid plumage patterns, with some of Costa Rica's parrots, toucans, trogons, and tanagers, among others, claiming top honors. Why so many tropical birds possess highly colored bodies remains an area of ornithological debate.

Seeing Birds in Costa Rica

Selected for illustration in the color plates are 214 species that are among Costa Rica's most frequently seen birds. The best way to spot these birds is to follow three easy steps:

1   Look for them at the correct time. Birds can be seen at any time of day, but they are often most active, and vocalize most frequently, during early morning and late afternoon, and so can be best detected and seen during these times.
2   Be quiet as you walk along trails or roads, and stop periodically to look around carefully. Not all birds are noisy, and some, even brightly colored ones, can be quite inconspicuous when they are directly above you, in a forest canopy. Trogons, for instance, beautiful medium-sized birds with green backs and bright red or yellow bellies, are notoriously difficult to see among branches and leaves.
3   *Bring binoculars* on your trip. You would be surprised at the number of people that visit tropical areas with the purpose of viewing wildlife and don't bother to bring binoculars. They need not be an expensive pair, but binoculars are essential to bird viewing.

A surprise to many people during their first trip to a tropical rainforest is that hordes of birds are not immediately seen or heard upon entering a trail. During large portions of the day, in fact, the forest is mainly quiet, with few birds noticeably active. Birds are often present, but many are inconspicuous – small brownish birds near to the ground, and greenish, brownish, or grayish birds in the canopy. A frequent, at first discombobulating experience is that you will be walking along a trail, seeing few birds, and then, suddenly, a mixed foraging flock with up to 20 or more species swooshes into view, filling the trees around you at all levels – some hopping along the ground, some moving through the brush, some clinging to tree trunks, others in the canopy – more birds than you can easily

Table 5 Bird Biodiversity Around Costa Rica: Where to See the Most Species (adapted from Janzen 1983).

| Site | Habitat type | Number of species of | | Total |
		Passerine birds*	Nonpasserine birds	
La Selva Biological Reserve & vicinity**	lowland wet	224	187	411
Osa Peninsula; Corcovado National Park	low & middle elevation wet	170	198	368
San Vito area; Wilson Botanical Garden	middle elevation wet	200+	130+	330+
Cerro de la Muerte***	highland wet	53	35	88
Monteverde Cloud Forest Reserve	middle & high elevation wet	145	90	235
Guanacaste area; Santa Rosa National Park	lowland dry	115	151	266
Palo Verde National Park	lowland dry	116	160	276
San José area	middle elevation wet	110	61	171

Total number of bird species known to occur in Costa Rica: About 600 resident breeders and 200 migrants.

* Passerines are the perching birds, most of which are songbirds (see p. 100).

** Includes most of Tortuguero National Park.

*** High in the Talamanca Mountains, along the Pan-American Highway (Route 2), between Cartago and San Isidro.

count or identify – and then, just as suddenly, the flock is gone, moved on in its meandering path through the forest (see p. 157).

It would be a shame to leave Costa Rica without seeing at least some of its spectacular birds, such as macaws, toucans, trogons, and tanagers. If you have trouble locating such birds, ask people – tour guides, resort employees, park personnel – about good places to see them.

Family Profiles

1. Seabirds

Along Costa Rica's rich coasts, as along coasts almost everywhere, seabirds, many of them conspicuously large and abundant, reign as the dominant vertebrate animals of the land, air, and water's surface. Many Costa Rican seabirds commonly seen by visitors from northern temperate areas are very similar to species found back home, but some are members of groups restricted to the tropics and subtropics and, hence, should be of ecotraveller interest. A few of these birds will be seen by almost everyone. As a group seabirds are incredibly successful animals, present often at breeding and roosting colonies in enormous numbers. Their success surely is owing to their incredibly rich food resources – the fish and invertebrate animals (crabs, mollusks, insects, jellyfish) produced in the sea and on beaches and mudflats. Further, people's exploitation of marine and coastal areas has, in many cases, enhanced rather than hurt seabird populations. Many gull species, for instance, which make good use of human-altered landscapes and human activities, such as garbage dumps, agricultural fields, and fishing boats, are almost certainly more numerous today than at any time in the past.

Three birds treated here (Plate 21) are members of the Order Pelicaniformes: the BROWN BOOBY of the Family Sulidae (9 species worldwide, with 4 occurring in Costa Rica), MAGNIFICENT FRIGATEBIRD of the Family Fregatidae (5 species with mainly tropical distributions; 2 occur off Costa Rican shores), and BROWN PELICAN, Family Pelicanidae (8 species worldwide, with only one in Costa Rica). A fourth species, the LAUGHING GULL (Plate 21), is in Family Laridae (more than 80 species worldwide, with relatively few occurring in tropical climes), which is allied with the shorebirds (p. 114), and is part of another order. *Boobies*, of which the Brown Booby is one of the most common, are large seabirds known for their sprawling, densely packed breeding colonies, spots of bright body coloring, and for plunging into the ocean from heights to pursue fish. They have tapered bodies, long, pointed wings, long tails, long, pointed bills, and often, brightly colored feet. The Magnificent Frigatebird is a very large soaring bird, mostly black, with huge, pointed wings that span up to 2 m (6 ft) or more, and a long, forked, tail. Males have red throat pouches that they inflate, balloonlike, during courtship displays. Brown Pelicans are large heavy-bodied seabirds, and, owing to their big, saggy throat pouches, are perhaps among the most recognizable of birds. They have long wings, long necks, large heads, and long bills from which hang the flexible, fish-catching, pouches. Laughing Gulls are mid-sized seabirds with long, narrow wings and heavy bills; they are largely white and grayish, but adults' heads are black, or *hooded*, during the breeding season.

Natural History
Ecology and Behavior

Most seabirds feed mainly on fish, and have developed a variety of ways to catch them. Boobies, which also eat squid, plunge-dive from the air or surface dive to catch fish underwater. Sometimes they dive quite deeply, and they often take fish unawares from below, as they rise toward the surface. Frigatebirds feed on the wing, sometimes soaring effortlessly for hours at a time. They swoop low to catch flying fish that leap from the water (the fish leap when they are pursued by larger, predatory fish or dolphins), and also to pluck squid and jellyfish from the wave-tops. Although their lives are tied to the sea, frigatebirds cannot swim and rarely, if ever, enter the water voluntarily; with their very long, narrow wings, they have difficulty lifting off from the water. To rest, they land on remote islands, itself a problematic act in high winds. Pelicans eat fish almost exclusively. BROWN PELI-CANS, in addition to feeding as they swim along the water's surface, are the only pelicans that also plunge from the air, sometimes from considerable altitude, to dive for meals. While underwater, the throat sac is used as a net to scoop up fish (to 30 cm, 1 ft, long). Captured fish are quickly swallowed because the water in the sac with the fish usually weighs enough to prohibit the bird's lifting off again from the water. Pelicans, ungainly looking, nonetheless are excellent flyers, and can use air updrafts to soar high above in circles for hours. These are large, hand-some birds; a flight of them, passing low and slow overhead on a beach, in per-fect V-formation or in a single line, is a tremendous sight. Of special note is that adult pelicans, so far as it is known, are largely silent. Gulls are highly gregarious seabirds – they feed, roost, and breed in groups. They feed on fish and other sea-life that they snatch from shallow water, and on crabs and other invertebrates they find on mudflats and beaches. Also, they are not above visiting garbage dumps or following fishing boats to grab whatever goodies that fall or are thrown overboard.

Breeding

Seabirds usually breed in large colonies on small islands (where there are no mam-mal predators) or in isolated mainland areas that are relatively free of predators. Some breed on slopes, cliffs, or ledges (boobies), some in trees or on tops of shrubs (pelicans, frigatebirds), and some on the bare ground (gulls, and also, if trees are unavailable, pelicans and frigatebirds). Most species are monogamous, mated males and females sharing in nest-building, incubation, and feeding young. In some groups, such as the pelicans, the male gathers sticks and stones for a nest, but the female carries out the actual construction (perhaps the male supervises). High year-to-year fidelity to mates, to breeding islands, and to particular nest sites is common. BROWN BOOBY females lay 1 or 2 eggs, which are incubated for about 45 days. Usually only a single chick survives to fledging age (one chick often pecks the other to death). MAGNIFICENT FRIGATEBIRDS lay a single egg that is incubated for about 55 days; male and female spell each other during incu-bation, taking shifts of up to 12 days. Young remain in and around the nest, dependent on the parents, for up to 6 months. BROWN PELICANS lay 2 or 3 eggs, which are incubated for 30 to 37 days; usually only one young is raised success-fully. LAUGHING GULLS lay 1 to 4 eggs, and incubation lasts 21 to 28 days; young fledge after 28 to 35 days at the nest. In most seabirds, young are fed when they push their bills into their parents' throats, in effect forcing the parents to regurgitate food stored in their *crops* – enlargements of the top portion of the esophagous. Seabirds reach sexual maturity slowly (in 2 to 5 years; 7+ years in frigatebirds) and live long lives (pelicans in the wild probably average 15 to 25 years, and some live 50+ years in zoos; frigatebirds and boobies live 20+ years in the wild).

Ecological Interactions

Frigatebirds are large, beautiful birds and are a treat to watch as they glide silently along coastal areas, but they have some highly questionable habits – in fact, patterns of behavior that among humans would be indictable offenses. Frigatebirds practice *kleptoparasitism*: they "parasitize" other seabirds, such as boobies, frequently chasing them in the air until they drop recently caught fish. The frigatebird then steals the fish, catching it in mid-air as it falls. Frigatebirds are also common predators on baby sea turtles (p. 77), scooping them from beaches as the reptiles make their post-hatching dashes to the ocean.

Lore and Notes

Boobies are sometimes called *gannets*, particularly by Europeans. The term *booby* apparently arose because the nesting and roosting birds seemed so bold and fearless toward people, which was considered stupid. Actually, the fact that these birds bred on isolated islands and cliffs meant that they had few natural predators, so had never developed, or had lost, fear responses to large mammals, such as people. Frigatebirds are also known as *man-of-war* birds, both names referring to warships, and to the birds' kleptoparasitism; they also steal nesting materials from other birds, furthering the image of avian pirates.

At least since medieval times in Europe, pelicans have been associated with the Christian concepts of piety and self-sacrifice; the legend is that when food is unavailable, pelican parents slit their breasts to feed their young with their own blood.

Status

The BROWN PELICAN is listed by USA ESA as endangered over parts of its range, but the species is still common in many areas. None of the other seabirds that occur along Costa Rica's shores are considered threatened or endangered. BROWN BOOBIES, MAGNIFICENT FRIGATEBIRDS, and LAUGHING GULLS are all abundant along one or both coasts. Some seabirds in other parts of the world are highly endangered. For example, for both the DALMATIAN PELICAN of Eurasia (CITES Appendix I listed) and the SPOT-BILLED PELICAN of India and Sri Lanka, only a few thousand breeding pairs remain. Also, ABBOT'S BOOBY (CITES Appendix I and USA ESA listed) is now limited to a single, small breeding population on the Indian Ocean's Christmas Island.

Profiles

Brown Booby, *Sula leucogaster*, Plate 21a
Magnificent Frigatebird, *Fregata magnificens*, Plate 21b
Laughing Gull, *Larus atricilla*, Plate 21c
Brown Pelican, *Pelecanus occidentalis*, Plate 21d

2. Waterbirds

Included under the vague heading of *waterbirds* is a group of medium to large birds, all with distinctive, identifying bills, that make their livings in freshwater and coastal saltwater habitats. Visitors to Costa Rican marsh or river areas are highly likely to encounter some of these species, particularly in the Guanacaste region. Some, such as *cormorants* and *anhingas*, swim to catch fish, whereas others, *storks* and *ibises*, wade about in marshes, shallow water areas, and fields in search of a variety of foods. Cormorants (Family Phalacrocoracidae) inhabit coasts and inland waterways over much of the world; there are 28 species, but only one occurs in Costa Rica. Anhingas (Family Anhingidae), closely related to cormorants, are fresh- and brackish-water birds mostly of tropical and subtropical regions; there are 4 species, one of which occurs in Costa Rica. Storks (Family Ciconiidae) are wading birds that occur worldwide in tropical and temperate regions; there are 17 species, but only 3 occur in the New World, 2 of them in Costa Rica. The 33 species of ibises and *spoonbills* (Family Threskiornthidae), also wading birds, are globally distributed; 3 ibises and a single spoonbill species occur in Costa Rica.

Cormorants are medium-sized birds, usually black, with short legs, long tails, and longish bills with hooked tips. ANHINGAS (Plate 22) are similar to cormorants, blackish with long tails, but they have very long, thin necks and their bills are longer and end with sharp points. Storks are huge, ungainly-looking – and so unmistakeable – wading birds. Those in Costa Rica are white with black or black and red heads; the head and neck area are featherless. Storks have very large, heavy bills. The JABIRU (Plate 22) is one of the largest of the world's storks, standing up to 1.5 m (5 ft) tall. Ibises and spoonbills resemble storks, but are smaller and have shorter necks. Most ibises are white, brown, or blackish, and in many, the head is bare of feathers. Ibis bills are long, thin, and curved downwards. Spoonbills are named for their straight, flat, spoon-shaped bills. The ROSEATE SPOONBILL (Plate 22), large, pink, and spoon-billed, must be one of the easiest birds on earth to identify. In most of these waterbirds, the sexes are similar in plumage, but males are often a bit larger.

Natural History
Ecology and Behavior
Diving from the surface of lakes, rivers, lagoons, and coastal saltwater areas, OLIVACEOUS CORMORANTS (Plate 21) and ANHINGAS pursue fish underwater. Cormorants, which take crustaceans also, catch food in their bills; Anhingas, which also take young turtles, caiman (p. 73), and snakes, use their sharply pointed bills to spear fish. Cormorants are social birds, foraging, roosting, and nesting in groups, but Anhingas are somewhat territorial, defending resting and feeding areas from other birds. Both Anhingas and cormorants are known for standing on logs, trees, or other surfaces after diving and spreading their wings, presumably to dry them (they may also be warming their bodies in the sun following dives into cold water.) Storks feed by walking slowly through fields and marshy areas, looking for suitable prey, essentially anything that moves: small rodents, young birds, frogs, reptiles, fish, earthworms, mollusks, crustaceans, and insects. Food is grabbed with the tip of the bill and swallowed quickly. Storks can be found either alone or, if food is plentiful in an area, in groups. These birds are excellent flyers, often soaring high overhead for hours during hot afternoons. They are known to fly 80 km (50 miles) or more daily between roosting or nesting sites and feeding areas. Ibises are gregarious birds that insert their long bills into soft mud of marshes and shore areas and poke about for food – insects, snails, crabs, frogs, tadpoles. Apparently they feed by touch, not vision; whatever the bill contacts that feels like food is grabbed and swallowed. Spoonbills, likewise, are gregarious birds

that feed in marsh or shallow-water habitats. They lower their bills into the water and sweep them around, stirring up the mud, then grab fish, frogs, snails, or crustaceans that touch their bills. Spoonbills are soaring birds, but ibises, although good flyers, do not soar.

Breeding
Most of these waterbirds breed in colonies of various sizes, although ANHINGAS sometimes breed alone, and JABIRU STORKS usually do so. Mating is monogamous, with both male and female contributing to nest-building, incubation, and feeding offspring. Cormorants, which begin breeding when they are 3 or 4 years old, construct stick nests in trees or on ledges. Two to 4 eggs are incubated for about 4 weeks, and young fledge 5 to 8 weeks after hatching. Anhingas breed at 2 or 3 years of age. They have stick and leaf nests in trees or bushes. Three to 5 eggs are incubated for 4 to 5 weeks, and chicks fledge 5 weeks after hatching. Storks first breed when they are 3 to 5 years old. They build platforms of sticks in trees or on ledges. Sometimes they add new material each year, which results eventually in enormous nests. Two to 4 eggs are incubated for 4 to 5 weeks and chicks remain in the nest for 50 to 90 days after hatching. Ibises and spoonbills also make stick nests, mixed with green vegetation, in trees. Two to 4 eggs are incubated for about 3 weeks, and young fledge 6 to 7 weeks after hatching.

Lore and Notes
ANHINGAS are also known as *darters*, the name owing to the way the birds swiftly thrust their necks forward to spear fish. Because of their long necks, they are also called *snakebirds*. Cormorants were so common and conspicuous to early European mariners that they were given the name *Corvus marinus*, or "sea raven." (The word cormorant derives from the term corvus marinus.) Cormorants have been used for centuries in Japan, China, and Central Europe as fishing birds. A ring is placed around a cormorant's neck so that it cannot swallow its catch, and then, leashed or free, it is released into the water. When the bird returns or is reeled in, a fish is usually clenched in its bill.

Europe's WHITE STORK, which nests on the roofs of buildings in villages, is highly respected by people and, because of its annual returns, is considered a symbol of continuity and reliability.

Status
All of the waterbirds considered here are widely or locally common in Costa Rica, although JABIRU STORK populations are declining. The Jabiru is considered threatened in Central America generally (CITES I listed even though it is not highly endangered), and its likeness serves in several countries (most notably in Costa Rica and Belize) as a conservation symbol. WOOD STORKS, although still somewhat common in Costa Rica, are threatened in other parts of their range, and are listed as endangered by USA ESA (there are small populations of Wood Storks in southeastern USA). Storks are declining because they are hunted for food over parts of their ranges (for instance, Jabiru are considered game birds in the Amazon Basin) and because nesting sites are disturbed by people. ROSEATE SPOONBILLS were almost elminated in the southeastern USA in the late 19th and early 20th centuries when they were hunted to turn their pink wings into feather fans.

Profiles
Olivaceous Cormorant, *Phalacrocorax brasilianus*, Plate 21e
Anhinga, *Anhinga anhinga*, Plate 22a

Jabiru Stork, *Jabiru mycteria*, Plate 22b
Wood Stork, *Mycteria americana*, Plate 22c
Roseate Spoonbill, *Ajaia ajaja*, Plate 22d
White Ibis, *Eudocimus albus*, Plate 22e

3. Herons and Egrets

Herons and *egrets* are beautiful medium to large-sized wading birds that enjoy broad distributions throughout temperate and tropical regions of both hemispheres. Herons and egrets, together with the similar but quite elusive wading birds called *bitterns*, constitute the heron family, Ardeidae, which includes about 58 species. Fifteen species occur in Costa Rica, most of which also breed there. Herons frequent all sorts of aquatic habitats: along rivers and streams, in marshes and swamps, and along lake and ocean shorelines. They are, in general, highly successful birds, and some of them – for example, the GREEN HERON (Plate 24) – are among Costa Rica's most conspicuous and commonly seen water birds. Why some in the family are called herons and some egrets, well, it's a mystery; but egrets are usually all white and tend to have longer *nuptial plumes* – special, long feathers – than the darker-colored herons.

Most herons and egrets are easy to identify. They are the tallish birds standing upright and still in shallow water or along the shore, staring intently into the water. They have slender bodies, long necks (often coiled when perched or still, producing a short-necked, hunched appearance), long, pointed bills, and long legs with long toes. They range in height in Costa Rica from 0.3 to 1.3 m (1 to 4 ft). Most are attired in soft shades of gray, brown, blue, or green, and black and white. From afar most are not striking, but close-up, many are exquisitely marked with small colored patches of facial skin or broad areas of spots or streaks; the *tiger herons*, in particular, have strongly barred or streaked plumages. Some species during breeding seasons have a few very long feathers (nuptial plumes) trailing down their bodies from the head, neck, back, or chest. The sexes are generally alike in size and plumage, or nearly so. One exception to this general form is the BOAT-BILLED HERON (Plate 23), which, as its name implies, has an especially wide and thick bill.

Natural History
Ecology and Behavior

Herons and egrets walk about slowly and stealthily in shallow water and sometimes on land, searching for their prey, mostly small vertebrates, including fish, frogs, salamanders, and the occasional turtle, and small invertebrates like crabs. On land, they take mostly insects, but also other invertebrates and vertebrates such as small rodents. CATTLE EGRETS (Plate 24) have made a specialty of following grazing cattle and other large mammals, walking along and grabbing insects and small vertebrates that are flushed from their hiding places by the moving cattle. A typical pasture scene is a flock of these egrets intermixed among a cattle herd, with several of the white birds perched atop the unconcerned mammals. Many herons spend most of their foraging time as *sit-and-wait* predators, standing motionless in or adjacent to the water, waiting in ambush for unsuspecting prey to wander within striking distance. Then, in a flash, they shoot their long, pointed bills into the water to grab or spear the prey. They take anything edible that will fit into their mouths and down their throats, and then some. One particular heron that I recall grabbed a huge frog in its bill and spent the better part of a half hour trying to swallow it. Typically, the larger herons are easier to spot because they tend to stay out in the open while foraging and resting; smaller herons, easier prey for predators, tend to stay more hidden in dense vegetation in marshy areas. Most herons are day-active, but many of the subgroup known as *night herons* forage at least partly nocturnally. Also, the BOAT-BILLED HERON searches at night for prey along waterways. This bird's large bill may aid it in catching prey in lower light levels, in which precise spearing with a finer bill would be difficult. Most herons are social birds, roosting and breeding in colonies, but some, such as the tiger herons, are predominantly solitary.

Breeding

Many herons breed in monogamous pairs within breeding colonies of various sizes. A few species are solitary nesters and some are less monogamous than others. Herons are known for their elaborate courtship displays and ceremonies, which continue through pair formation and nest-building. Generally nests are constructed by the female of a pair out of sticks procured and presented to her by the male. Nests are placed in trees or reeds, or on the ground. Both sexes incubate the 3 to 7 eggs for 16 to 30 days, and both feed the kids for 35 to 50 days before the young can leave the nest and feed themselves. The young are *altricial* – born helpless; they are raised on regurgitated food from the parents. Many herons breed during wet seasons, but some do so all year.

Ecological Interactions

Herons and egrets often lay more eggs than the number of chicks they can feed. For instance, many lay 3 eggs when there is sufficient food around to feed only 2 chicks. This is contrary to our usual view of nature, which we regard as having adjusted animal behavior through evolution so that behaviors are finely tuned to avoid waste. Here's what biologists suspect goes on: females lay eggs 1 or 2 days apart, and start incubating before they finish laying all their eggs. The result is that chicks hatch at intervals of one or more days and so the chicks in a single nest are different ages, and so different sizes. In years of food shortage, the smallest chick dies because it cannot compete for food from the parents against its larger siblings, and also because, it has been discovered, the larger siblings attack it (behavior called *siblicide*). The habit of laying more eggs than can be reared as chicks may be an insurance game evolved by the birds to maximize their number of young; in many years, true, they waste the energy they invested to produce third eggs that have little future, but if food is plentiful, all 3 chicks survive and prosper. Apparently, the chance to produce 3 surviving offspring is worth the risk of investing in 3 eggs even though the future of one is very uncertain.

The CATTLE EGRET is a common, successful, medium-sized white heron that, until recently, was confined to the Old World, where it made its living following herds of large mammals. What is so interesting about this species is that, whereas many of the animals that have recently crossed oceans and spread rapidly into new continents have done so as a result of people's intentional or unintentional machinations, these egrets did it themselves. Apparently the first ones to reach the New World were from Africa. Perhaps blown off-course by a storm, they first landed in northern South America in about 1877. Finding the New World to its liking, during the next decades the species spread far and wide, finding abundant food where tropical forests were cleared for cattle grazing. Cattle Egrets have now colonized much of northern South America, Central America, all the major Caribbean islands, and eastern and central North America, as far as the southern USA. We must assume that they have Chicago and New York City in their sights.

Lore and Notes

The story of the *phoenix*, a bird that dies or is burned but then rises again from the ashes, is one of the best-known bird myths of the Western world. One version, from about 2800 years ago, has it that one phoenix arrives from Arabia every 500 years. When it is old, it builds a nest of spices in which to die. From the remains a young phoenix emerges, which carries its parent's bones to the sun. Some authorities believe that the phoenix was a heron; in fact, the Egyptian hieroglyph for the phoenix appears to be heron or egret.

Status

Some of Costa Rica's herons and egrets are fairly rare, but they are not considered threatened species because they are more abundant in other parts of their ranges, outside the country. Two species of concern, that some authorities consider near-threatened, are the FASCIATED TIGER-HERON, which ranges from Costa Rica to Argentina and Brazil, and the colorful but secretive CHESTNUT-BELLIED HERON (or AGAMI HERON), with a distribution from southern Mexico to northern South America.

Profiles

Boat-billed Heron, *Cochlearius cochlearius*, Plate 23a
Little Blue Heron, *Egretta caerulea*, Plate 23b
Tricolored Heron, *Egretta tricolor*, Plate 23c
Snowy Egret, *Egretta thula*, Plate 23d
Cattle Egret, *Bubulcus ibis*, Plate 24a
Great Egret, *Casmerodius albus*, Plate 24b
Bare-throated Tiger Heron, *Tigrisoma mexicanum*, Plate 24c
Green Heron, *Butorides striatus*, Plate 24d

4. Marsh and Stream Birds

Marsh and *stream birds* are small and medium-sized birds that are adapted to walk, feed, and breed in swamps, marshes, wet fields, and along streams. The chief characteristics permitting this lifestyle usually are long legs and very long toes that distribute the birds' weight, allowing them to walk among marsh plants and across floating vegetation without sinking. *Jacanas* (jah-KAH-nahs or hah-SAH-nahs; Family Jacanidae) are small and medium-sized birds with amazingly long toes and toenails that stalk about tropical marshes throughout the world. There are 8 species; only one occurs in Costa Rica, but it is found almost everywhere there is floating aquatic vegetation. The *rails* (Family Rallidae) are a large group of often secretive small and medium-sized swamp and dense vegetation birds, about 130 species strong. They inhabit most parts of the world save for polar regions. Fifteen species occur in Costa Rica, including rails, wood-rails, crakes, coots, and gallinules. Last, the SUNBITTERN (Plate 25), the single species comprising Family Eurypygidae, is a stocky, medium-sized bird of forested stream and riverbanks.

The NORTHERN JACANA (Plate 25), with incredibly long toes, has a drab brown and black body but a bright yellow bill and forehead. When their wings are spread during flight or displays, jacanas expose large patches of bright yellow, rendering them instantly conspicuous. Female jacanas are larger than males. GRAY-NECKED WOOD-RAILS (Plate 25) are brown, olive, and gray, with long necks, legs, and toes. Although most rails, like the wood-rail, are colored to blend into their surroundings, the PURPLE GALLINULE (Plate 25) is a strikingly colored bird, purple and green, with a reddish bill. Rails generally have short wings and tails. Males are often larger than females. SUNBITTERNS (Plate 25) are chicken-sized birds with long, thin bills, slender necks, and intricately patterned plumages of brown, black, white, and yellow. When a Sunbittern's wings are spread, the bars, and spots on its wings create a striking "sun" pattern.

Natural History
Ecology and Behavior
Jacanas are abundant birds of marshes, ponds, lakeshores, and wet fields. They walk along, often on top of lily pads and other floating plants, picking up insects, snails, small frogs and fish, and some vegetable matter such as seeds. Likewise, rails stalk through marshes, swamps, grassy shores, and wet grasslands, foraging for insects, small fish and frogs, bird eggs and chicks, and berries. Typically they move with a head-bobbing walk. Many rails are highly secretive, being heard but rarely seen moving about in marshes. PURPLE GALLINULES, brightly colored and less shy than many other rails, are usually easy to see as they forage singly or in small family groups. SUNBITTERNS are stream birds of the forest. Singly or in pairs they walk along the shores of rivers and streams, and hop about on mid-stream rocks, searching for food. With their long, sharp bill snapping forward and down, they take insects, crabs, frogs, small fish, and crayfish.

Breeding
NORTHERN JACANAS are one of 3 or 4 jacana species that employ *polyandrous* breeding, the rarest type of mating system among birds (see Close-Up, p. 182). In a breeding season, a female mates with several males, and the males then carry out most of the breeding chores. Males each defend small territories from other males, but each female has a larger territory that encompasses 2 to 4 male territories. Males build nests of floating, compacted aquatic vegetation. Following mating, the female lays 3 or 4 eggs in the nest, after which the male incubates them for 21 to 24 days and then cares for (leads and protects) the chicks. Young are dependent on the father for up to 3 to 4 months. Meanwhile, the female has mated with other males on her territory and provided each with a clutch of eggs to attend. (Predation on jacana nests is very common, PURPLE GALLINULES often being the culprits.) In rails such as wood-rails and gallinules, the sexes contribute more equally to the breeding effort. Male and female build well-hidden nests in dense vegetation, sometimes a meter or two (several feet) off the ground, or floating nests of aquatic plants. Both sexes incubate the 3 to 5 or more eggs for 2.5 to 4 weeks and care for the young for 7 or 8 weeks until they are independent. SUNBITTERN breeding is not well known. Apparently they are monogamous, with both sexes incubating the 2 eggs for about 4 weeks. Nests, of leaves, stems, moss, and mud, have been found 2 to 6 m (6 to 20 ft) up in tree branches overhanging watercourses.

Lore and Notes
Jacanas of Africa and Australia are also known as *lily-trotters* and *lotus-birds*. The word *jacana* is from a native Brazilian name for the bird.

Status
Although some of Costa Rica's rails are quite rare, they are not considered threatened or endangered because they are more numerous in other parts of their ranges. All four species profiled here are locally common or abundant, but the SUNBITTERN is declining in numbers as its forest habitats shrink in size.

Throughout the world, a number of rail species are threatened or already endangered; several rare species of the New World are Venezuela's PLAIN-FLANKED RAIL, Colombia's BOGOTA RAIL, and Brazil's RUFOUS-FACED CRAKE.

Profiles

Gray-necked Wood-rail, *Aramides cajanea*, Plate 25a
Purple Gallinule, *Porphryula martinica*, Plate 25b
Northern Jacana, *Jacana spinosa*, Plate 25c
Sunbittern, *Eurypyga helias*, Plate 25d

5. Ducks

Members of the Family Anatidae are universally recognized as *ducks*. They are water-associated birds that are distributed throughout the world in habitats ranging from open seas to high mountain lakes. The family includes about 150 species of ducks, geese, and swans. Although an abundant, diverse group throughout temperate regions of the globe, ducks, or *waterfowl*, (*wildfowl* to the British), have only limited representation in most tropical areas. About 15 species occur in Costa Rica, and only a fraction of those are local breeders; the remainder are migratory, only passing through or wintering in Central America. Only two ducks are profiled here (Plate 26), the MUSCOVY DUCK, a bird of streams and ponds in lowland forests, and the BLACK-BELLIED WHISTLING DUCK, which frequents freshwater marshes and ponds. Also duck-like in appearance and habits is the SUNGREBE (Plate 26), a fairly common but secretive stream and river bird, a member of a separate, very small family of birds, the Heliornithidae. The Sungrebe is the only member of this family in the New World, enjoying a broad distribution from Mexico southwards to Brazil.

Ducks vary quite a bit in size and coloring, but all share the same major traits: duck bills, webbed toes, short tails, and long, slim necks. Plumage color and patterning vary, but there is preponderance within the group of grays and browns, and black and white, although many species have at least small patches of bright color. In some species male and female look alike, but in others there is a high degree of difference between the sexes. The Muscovy Duck is large, chunky in appearance, mostly black with white patches on its wings, and with bare patches of skin on its face; males are much larger than females. Black-bellied Whistling Ducks are slender, medium-sized ducks, rust-colored with black bellies, and red bills and feet. The Sungrebe is a brownish-olive and white bird with bold black and white stripes on its head and neck. It is distinguishable from the duck family by its long tail, short legs, and long, straight, non-duckish bill.

Natural History
Ecology and Behavior

Ducks are birds of wetlands, spending most of their time in or near the water. Many of the typical ducks are divided into *divers* and *dabblers*. Diving ducks plunge underwater for their food; dabblers, such as mallards, pintail, widgeon, and teal take food from the surface of the water or, maximally, put their heads down into the water to reach food at shallow depths. When they reach underwater, their rear quarters tip up into the air, providing the typical response of frustrated birdwatchers when queried about what they see on the water through their binoculars – "nothing but duck butts." Ducks mostly eat aquatic plants or small fish, but some forage on land for seeds and other plant materials. The MUSCOVY

DUCK, for instance, in addition to eating small fish and seeds of aquatic plants, feeds on terrestrial foods including crops such as corn, and insects. BLACK-BEL-LIED WHISTLING DUCKS eat seeds, leaves, and small invertebrates such as insects. This duck spends relatively little time in the water; it grazes on land, usually at night. During the day it roosts on riverbanks, or in trees adjacent to the water. The SUNGREBE, a highy specialized water bird and a nimble swimmer, can vary its profile in the water, riding high or partly submerged, only its head and neck poking out from the water. Pairs establish territories along sections of stream or riverbank. They are consumers of insects, spiders, and small vertebrates such as frogs and lizards.

Breeding

Ducks place their nests on the ground in thick vegetation or in holes. Typically nests are lined with downy feathers that the female plucks from her own breast. In many of the ducks, females perform most of the breeding duties, including incubation of the 2 to 16 eggs and shepherding and protecting the ducklings. Some of these birds, however, particularly among the geese and swans, have life-long marriages during which male and female share equally in breeding duties. The young are *precocial*, able to run, swim and feed themselves soon after they hatch. Both MUSCOVY and BLACK-BELLIED WHISTLING DUCKS most often nest in cavities. Females, after mating, incubate eggs and raise ducklings themselves. SUNGREBES are monogamous, both sexes helping to build the stick nest that is hidden in thick vegetation, and to incubate the 2 to 4 eggs.

Lore and Notes

Ducks, geese and swans have been objects of people's attention since ancient times, chiefly as a food source. These birds typically have tasty flesh, are fairly large and so economical to hunt, and usually easier and less dangerous to catch than many other animals, particularly large mammals. Owing to their frequent use as food, several wild ducks and geese have been domesticated for thousands of years; Costa Rica's native MUSCOVY DUCK, in fact, in its domesticated form is a common farmyard inhabitant in several parts of the world. Wild ducks also adjust well to the proximity of people, to the point of taking food from them – a practice that surviving artworks show has been occurring for at least 2000 years. Hunting ducks and geese for sport is also a long-practiced tradition. As a consequence of these long interactions between ducks and people, and the research on these animals stimulated by their use in agriculture and sport, a large amount of scientific information has been collected on the group; many of the ducks and geese are among the most well known of birds. The close association between ducks and people has even led to a long contractual agreement between certain individual ducks and the Walt Disney Company.

Status

None of the Costa Rican ducks, neither the local breeders nor winter migrants, are currently threatened or endangered. A few species are now fairly rare in Costa Rica, but they are more abundant in other parts of their ranges. The MUSCOVY DUCK, because of hunting pressures and habitat destruction, has had its populations much reduced throughout its broad range in the Neotropics, so that it is now common only in restricted areas. When these ducks were more common, local hunters would tether a female to a tree and then kill males that came a-courting; with this method, up to 50 males could be lured to their deaths in a single day.

Profiles

Sungrebe, *Heliornis fulica*, Plate 26a
Black-bellied Whistling Duck, *Dendrocygna autumnalis*, Plate 26b
Muscovy Duck, *Cairina moschata*, Plate 26c

6. Shorebirds

Spotting *shorebirds* is usually a priority only for visitors to the Neotropics who are rabid birdwatchers. The reason for the usual lack of interest is that shorebirds are often very common, plain-looking brown birds that most people are familiar with from their beaches back home. Still, it is always a treat watching shorebirds in their tropical wintering areas as they forage in meadows, along streams, on mudflats, and especially on the coasts, as they run along beaches, parallel to the surf, picking up food. Some of the small ones, such as SANDERLINGS (Plate 27), as one biologist wrote, resemble amusing wind-up toys as they spend hours running up and down the beach, chasing, and then being chased by, the outgoing and incoming surf (J. Strauch 1983). Shorebirds are often conspicuous and let themselves be watched, as long as the watchers maintain some distance. When in large flying groups, shorebirds such as *sandpipers* provide some of the most compelling sights in bird-dom, as their flocks rise from sandbar or mudflat to fly low and fast over the surf, wheeling quickly and tightly in the air as if they were a single organism, or as if each individual's nervous system was joined to the others'.

Shorebirds are traditionally placed along with the gulls in the avian order Charadriiformes. They are global in distribution and considered to be hugely successful birds – the primary reason being that the sandy beaches and mudflats on which they forage usually teem with their food. There are several families, only three of which require mention. The sandpipers, Family Scolopacidae, are a worldwide group of approximately 85 species. About 30 species occur in Costa Rica, some being quite abundant during much of the year, yet they are all migrants – none breed in the country. The *plovers* (Family Charadriidae), with about 60 species, likewise have a worldwide distribution. Several species occur in Costa Rica, three of which breed there; the others are migrants from breeding sites to the north. Last, a single species of *thick-knee* occurs in Costa Rica and the rest of Central America, a member of the small Family Burhinidae; seven species are broadly distributed in the Old World, only two in the New.

All shorebirds, regardless of size, have a characteristic "look." They are usually drably colored birds (especially during the nonbreeding months), darker above, lighter below, with long, thin legs for wading through wet meadows, mud, sand, or surf. Depending on feeding habits, bill length varies from short to very long. Most of the Costa Rican sandpipers range from 15 to 48 cm (6 to 19 in) long. They are generally slender birds with straight or curved bills of various lengths. Plovers, 15 to 30 cm (6 to 12 in) long, are small to medium-sized, thick-necked shorebirds with short tails and straight, relatively thick bills. They are mostly shades of gray and brown but some have bold color patterns such as a broad white or dark band on the head or chest. The DOUBLE-STRIPED THICK-KNEE (Plate 26) is a large bird with an unusually large head, big yellow eyes (for night vision), long yellow legs, and knobby, thick "knees" that give the bird its name (actually, the "knees" correspond more to the ankle joint). The sexes look alike, or nearly so, in most of the shorebirds.

Natural History
Ecology and Behavior

Shorebirds typically are open-country birds, associated with coastlines and inland wetlands, grasslands, and pastures. Sandpipers, plovers, and thick-knees are all excellent flyers but they spend a lot of time on the ground, foraging and resting; when chased, they often seem to prefer running to flying away. Sandpipers pick their food up off the ground or use their bills to probe for it in mud or sand – they take insects and other small invertebrates, particularly crustaceans. They will also snatch bugs from the air as they walk and from the water's surface as they wade or swim. Larger, more land-dwelling shorebirds may also eat small reptiles and amphibians, and even small rodents; some of the plovers also eat seeds. The DOUBLE-STRIPED THICK-KNEE is unusual among shorebirds in that it spends days quietly in a sheltered spot, such as under a bush, becomes active at twilight, and forages nocturnally.

Many shorebirds, especially among the sandpipers, establish winter feeding territories along stretches of beach; they use the area for feeding for a few hours or for the day, defending it aggressively from other members of their species. Many of the sandpipers and plovers are gregarious birds, often seen in large groups, especially when they are travelling. Several species make long migrations over large expanses of open ocean, a good example being Costa Rica's rare AMERI-CAN (LESSER) GOLDEN-PLOVER, which flies in autumn over the Western Atlantic, some apparently nonstop from breeding grounds in northern Canada to Central and South America.

Breeding

Shorebirds breed in a variety of ways. Many species breed in monogamous pairs that defend small breeding territories. Others, however, practice *polyandry*, the least common type of mating system among vertebrate animals, in which some females have more than one mate in a single breeding season. This type of breeding is exemplified by the SPOTTED SANDPIPER (Plate 27). In this species, the normal sex roles of breeding birds are reversed: the female establishes a territory on a lakeshore that she defends against other females. More than one male settles within the territory, either at the same time or sequentially during a breeding season. After mating, the female lays a clutch of eggs for each male. The males incubate their clutches and care for the young. Females may help care for some of the broods of young provided that there are no more unmated males to try to attract to the territory.

Most shorebird nests are simply small depressions in the ground in which eggs are placed; some of these *scrapes* are lined with shells, pebbles, grass, or leaves. Sandpipers lay 2 to 4 eggs per clutch, which are incubated, depending on species, by the male alone, the female alone, or by both parents, for 18 to 21 days. Plovers lay 2 to 4 eggs, which are incubated by both sexes for 24 to 28 days. Thick-knees lay clutches of 1 to 3 eggs, which are incubated for 25 to 27 days by both male and female. Shorebird young are *precocial*, that is, soon after they hatch they are mobile, able to run from predators, and can feed themselves. Parents usually stay with the young to guard them at least until they can fly, perhaps 3 to 5 weeks after hatching.

Lore and Notes

The manner in which flocks of thousands of birds, particularly shorebirds, fly in such closely regimented order, executing abrupt maneuvers with precise coordination, such as when all individuals turn together in a split second in the same direction, has puzzled biologists and engendered some research. The questions include: What is the stimulus for the flock to turn – is it one individual within the flock, a "leader," from which all the others take their "orders" and follow into turns? Or is it some stimulus from outside the flock that all members respond to in the same way? And how are the turns coordinated? Everything from "thought transference" to electromagnetic communication among the flock members has been advanced as an explanation. After studying films of DUNLIN, a North American sandpiper, flying and turning in large flocks, one biologist has suggested that the method birds within these flocks use to coordinate their turns is similar to how the people in a chorusline know the precise moment to raise their legs in sequence or how "the wave" in a sports stadium is coordinated. That is, one bird, perhaps one that has detected some danger, like a predatory falcon, starts a turn, and the other birds, seeing the start of the flock's turning, can then anticipate when it is their turn to make the turn – the result being a quick wave of turning coursing through the flock.

Status

None of the plovers, sandpipers, or thick-knees of Costa Rica are threatened or endangered, although the thick-knee is scarce over parts of its range (CITES Appendix III listed for Guatemala). A major goal for conservation of shorebirds is the need to preserve critical migratory stopover points – pieces of habitat, sometimes fairly small, that hundreds of thousands of shorebirds settle into mid-way during their migrations to stock up on food. For instance, one famous small patch of coastal mudflats near Grays Harbor, Washington State, USA, is a popular, traditional stopover point for millions of shorebirds. Its destruction or use for any other activity could cause huge losses to the birds' populations. Fortunately, it has been deemed essential, and protected as part of a national wildlife refuge.

Profiles

Double-striped Thick-knee, *Burhinus bistriatus*, Plate 26d
Spotted Sandpiper, *Actitis macularia*, Plate 27a
Sanderling, *Calidris alba*, Plate 27b
Western Sandpiper, *Calidris mauri*, Plate 27c
Black-bellied Plover, *Pluvialis squatarola*, Plate 27d
Whimbrel, *Numenius phaeopus*, Plate 27e

7. Curassows and Quail

Large chicken-like birds strutting about the tropical forest floor or, somewhat to the surprise of visitors from temperate quarters, fluttering about in trees and running along high branches, are bound to be members of the *curassow* family. The family, Cracidae, contains not only the curassows, but their close relatives the *guans* and entertainingly named *chachalacas*. There are more than 40 species of *cracids*, which are limited in their distributions to warmer regions of the New World, most inhabiting moist forests at low and middle elevations. The curassow family is placed within the avian Order Galliformes, which also includes the pheasants, quail, bobwhite, and partridges (and which, for want of a better term, even professional ornithologists refer to technically as the "chicken-like birds").

Costa Rican curassows as a group range in length from 56 to 91 cm (20 to 36 in) – as large as small turkeys – and weigh up to 4 kg (9 lbs). They have long legs and long, heavy toes. Many have conspicuous crests. The colors of their bodies are generally drab – gray, brown, olive, or black and white; some appear glossy in the right light. They typically have small patches of bright coloring such as yellow, red, or orange on parts of their bills, cheeks, or on a hanging throat sac, or *dewlap*. Male GREAT CURASSOWS (Plate 28), for instance, although all black above and white below, have a bright yellow "knob" on the top of their bill. Within the group, males are larger than females; the sexes are generally similar in coloring, except for the curassows, in which females are drabber than males.

Natural History
Ecology and Behavior
The guans and curassows are birds of the forests, but the chachalacas prefer forest edge areas and even clearings – more open areas, in other words. The guans and chachalacas are mostly arboreal birds, staying high in the treetops as they pursue their diet of fruit, young leaves, and treebuds, and the occasional frog or large insect. For such large birds in trees, they locomote with surprising grace, running quickly and carefully along branches. One's attention is sometimes drawn to them when they jump and flutter upwards from branch to branch until they are sufficiently in the clear to take flight. While guans and chachalacas will occasionally come down to the forest floor to feed on fallen fruit, GREAT CURASSOWS are terrestrial birds, more in the tradition of turkeys and pheasants. They stalk about on the forest floor, seeking fruit, seeds, and bugs. Paired off during the breeding season, birds of this family typically are found at other times of the year in small flocks of 10 to 20 individuals. Chachalaca males provide some of the most characteristic background sounds of tropical American forests. In the evening and especially during the early morning, males in groups rhythmically give their very loud calls, described variously as "cha-cha-LAW-ka" or "cha-cha-lac."

Breeding
The curassows, guans, and chachalacas are monogamous breeders, the sexes sharing reproductive duties. Several of the species are known for producing loud whirring sounds with their wings during the breeding season, presumably during courtship displays. Male and female construct a simple, open nest of twigs and leaves, placed in vegetation or in a tree within several meters of the ground. Two to 4 eggs are incubated for 22 to 34 days. The young leave the nest soon after hatching to hide in the surrounding vegetation, where they are fed by the parents (in contrast to most of the chicken-like birds of the world, which feed themselves after hatching). Several days later, the fledglings can fly short distances. The family group remains together for a time, the male leading the family around the forest. Most breeding in Costa Rica takes place between March and June.

Ecological Interactions
In Central and South America, the curassows essentially take the ecological position of pheasants, which are only lightly represented in the Neotropics.

Status
A variety of factors converge to assure that the curassows will remain a problem group into the forseeable future. They are chiefly birds of the forests at a time when Neotropical forests are increasingly being cleared. They are desirable game birds, hunted by local people for food. In fact, as soon as new roads penetrate virgin forests in Central and South America, one of the first chores of settlers is to shoot curassows for their dinners. Unfortunately, curassows reproduce slowly,

raising only small broods each year. Exacerbating the problem, their nests are often placed low enough in trees and vegetation to make them vulnerable to a variety of predators, including people. In the face of these unrelenting pressures on their populations, curassows are among the birds thought most likely to survive in the future only in protected areas, such as national parks. In Costa Rica, none of the curassows are now endangered, but the CRESTED GUAN (Plate 28) and GREAT CURASSOW are becoming rather uncommon outside of protected places, and the BLACK GUAN (Plate 28), a bird of mountain forests, is considered to be near-threatened. Several guan species of South America are currently on lists of endangered species.

Profiles

Gray-headed Chachalaca, *Ortalis cinereiceps*, Plate 28a
Plain Chachalaca, *Ortalis vetula*, Plate 28b
Crested Guan, *Penelope purpurascens*, Plate 28c
Black Guan, *Chamaepetes unicolor*, Plate 28d
Great Curassow, *Crax rubra*, Plate 28e
Spotted-bellied Bobwhite, *Colinus leucopogon*, Plate 29a

8. Tinamous

The *tinamous* are an interesting group of secretive, chicken-like birds that are occasionally seen walking along forest trails. They apparently represent an ancient group of birds, most closely related not to chickens or pheasants but to the rheas of South America – large, flightless birds in the ostrich mold. The family, Tinamidae, with about 45 species, is confined in its distribution to the Neotropics, from Mexico to southern Chile and Argentina. Five species occur in Central America, Costa Rica being the only country having all of them. They inhabit a variety of environments, including grasslands and thickets, but most commonly they are forest birds.

Tinamous are medium-sized birds, 23 to 45 cm (9 to 18 in) long, chunky-bodied, with fairly long necks, small heads, and slender bills. They have short legs and very short tails. The back part of a tinamou's body sometimes appears higher than it should be, a consequence of a dense concentration of rump feathers. Tinamous are attired in understated, protective colors – browns, grays, and olives; often the plumage is marked with dark spots or bars. Male and female look alike, with females being a little larger than males.

Natural History
Ecology and Behavior

Except for the GREAT TINAMOU (Plate 29), which sleeps in trees, tinamous are among the most terrestrial of birds, foraging, sleeping, and breeding on the ground. They are very poor flyers, doing so only when highly alarmed by a predator or surprised, and then only for short distances. They are better at running along the ground, the mode of locomotion ecologists call *cursorial*. The tinamou diet consists chiefly of fruit and seeds, but they also take insects such as caterpillars, beetles, and ants, and occasionally, small vertebrates such as mice. Some South American species dig to feed on roots and termites. Tinamous avoid being eaten themselves primarily by often staying still, easily blending in with surrounding vegetation, and by walking slowly and cautiously through the forest. If approached closely, tinamous will fly upwards in a burst of loud wing-beating and fly usually less than 50 m (160 ft) to a new hiding spot in the undergrowth, often colliding with trees and branches as they go. Tinamous are known for their songs, which are loud, pure-tone, melodious whistles, and which are some of the most characteristic sounds of Neotropical forests.

Except during breeding, tinamous lead a solitary existence. They are considered secretive and, with their cryptic colors, elusive. It is common to hear them but not see them, or to see the rear of one, up ahead on the trail, disappearing into the underbrush.

Breeding

The tinamous employ some unusual mating systems, the most intriguing of which is a kind of *group polyandry* (polyandry being a system in which one female mates with several males during a breeding season). One or more females will mate with a male and lay clutches of eggs in the same nest, for the male to incubate and care for. The females then move on to repeat the process with other males of their choosing. Apparently in all tinamous the male incubates the eggs and leads and defends the young. Nests can hardly be called that; they are simply slight indentations in the ground, hidden in a thicket or at the base of a tree. Up to 12 eggs, deposited by one or more females, are placed in the nest. The male incubates for 19 or 20 days; when the eggs hatch, he leads the troop of tiny tinamous about, defending them from predators. From hatching, the young feed themselves.

Lore and Notes

Outside of protected areas, all tinamous are hunted extensively for food. Tinamou meat is considered tender and tasty, albeit a bit strange-looking; it has been described variously as greenish and transparent.

Status

The tinamous' camouflage coloring and secretive behavior must serve the birds well because, although hunted for food, tinamous presently are able to maintain healthy populations. None of the Central American species are considered vulnerable or threatened. Some of the tinamous are known to be able to move easily from old, uncut forest to *secondary*, recently cut, forest, demonstrating an impressive adaptability that should allow these birds to thrive even amid major habitat alterations such as deforestation. To be sure, some of the tinamous are in trouble, including especially the critically endangered MAGDALENA (RED-LEGGED) TINAMOU of Colombia and KALINOWSKI'S TINAMOU of Peru. Unfortunately, dependable information on many other tinamous is scarce, so it is very difficult to know their statuses accurately.

Profiles

Great Tinamou, *Tinamus major*, Plate 29b
Thicket Tinamou, *Crypturellus cinnamomeus*, Plate 29c
Slaty-breasted Tinamou, *Crypturellus boucardi*, Plate 29d

9. Vultures

Birds at the very pinnacle of their profession, eating dead animals, *vultures* are highly conspicuous and among the most frequently seen birds of rural Central America. That they feast on rotting flesh does not reduce the majesty of these large, soaring birds as they circle for hours high over field and forest. The family of American vultures, Cathartidae, has only seven species, all confined to the New World; several are abundant animals but one is close to extinction. They range from southern Canada to Tierra del Fuego, with several of the species sporting wide and overlapping distributions. Four species, the KING, BLACK, TURKEY (Plate 30), and LESSER YELLOW-HEADED VULTURES, occur in Costa Rica. The two largest members of the family are known as *condors*, the CALIFORNIA and ANDEAN CONDORS. Vultures are seen often above both open country and forested areas; the BLACK VULTURE, one of the most frequently encountered birds of tropical America, is very common around garbage dumps. Traditional classifications place the New World vulture family within the avian Order Falconiformes, with the hawks, eagles, and falcons, but some biologists believe the group is more closely related to the storks.

Central American vultures are large birds, from 60 to 80 cm (24 to 32 in) long, with wing spans to 1.8 m (6 ft). (The Andean Condor has a wing span of 3 m (10 ft)!). Vultures generally are black or brown, with hooked bills and curious, unfeathered heads whose bare skin is richly colored in red, yellow, or orange. Turkey Vultures, in fact, are named for their red heads, which remind people of turkey heads. The King Vulture, largest of the Costa Rican set, departs from the standard color scheme, having a white body, black rump and wing feathers, and multi-colored head. Male and female vultures look alike; males are slightly larger than females.

Natural History
Ecology and Behavior
Vultures are carrion eaters of the first order. Most soar during the day in groups, looking for and, in the case of TURKEY VULTURES, sniffing for, food. (Turkey Vultures can find carcasses in deep forest and also buried carcasses, strongly implicating smell, as opposed to vision, as the method of discovery.) They can move many miles daily in their search for dead animals. KING and BLACK VULTURES, supplementing their taste for carrion, also occasionally kill animals, usually newborn or those otherwise defenseless. Some of the vultures, especially the Black Vulture, also eat fruit. With their super eyesight, fine-tuned sense of smell, and ability to survey each day great expanses of habitat, vultures are, to paraphrase one biologist, amazingly good at locating dead animals. No mammal species specializes in carrion to the degree that vultures do, the reason being, most likely, that no mammal could search such large areas each day. That is, no mammal that ate only carrion could find enough food to survive.

King Vultures are usually seen in pairs or solitarily, as are Lesser Yellow-headed Vultures, but the other species are more social, roosting and foraging in groups of various sizes. Black Vultures, in particular, often congregate in large numbers at feeding places, and it is common to find a flock of them at any village dump. At small to medium-sized carcasses, there is a definite pecking order among the vultures: Black Vultures are dominant to Turkey Vultures, and can chase them away; several Black Vultures can even chase away a King Vulture, which is the bigger bird. However, in an area with plenty of food, all three species may feed together in temporary harmony (F.G. Stiles & D.H. Janzen 1983). When threatened, vultures may spit up partially-digested carrion, a strong defense against harassment if ever there was one.

Turkey Vultures form large, migratory flocks together with several species of large hawks, providing a common spectacle of hundreds of very large, soaring birds, circling upwards in *thermals*, columns of rising warm air, and gliding for long distances.

Breeding

Vultures are monogamous breeders. Both sexes incubate the 1 to 3 eggs, which are placed on the ground in protected places or on the floor of a cave or tree cavity. Eggs are incubated for 32 to 58 days; both sexes feed the young regurgitated carrion for 2 to 5 months until they can fly. Young vultures at the nest site very rarely become food for other animals, and it has been suggested that the odor of the birds and the site, awash as they are in badly decaying animal flesh, keep predators (and everything else) at bay. Nesting in Costa Rica occurs chiefly from November through March.

Ecological Interactions

Vultures are abundant and important scavengers around Neotropical towns and villages. Usefully, they help clean up garbage; expert observers have said they "perform at least as much of the Sanitation Department's chores as do its human members" (F.G. Stiles & D.H. Janzen 1983). Scavengers, or *detritus* feeders, are important parts of ecosystems, recycling energy and nutrients back into food webs. Although vultures are an integral part of these systems, most detritus is consumed by small arthropods (insects and the like) and such microorganisms as fungi and bacteria.

BLACK and TURKEY VULTURES roost communally, the two species often together. A common observation has been that once an individual finds a food source, other vultures arrive very rapidly to share the carcass. Biologists strongly suspect that the group roosting and feeding behavior of these birds are related, and that the former increases each individual's food-finding efficiency. In other words, a communal roost serves as an *information center* for finding food. Researchers believe that vultures may locate the probable position of the next day's food while soaring high in the late afternoon, before they return to the roost before sunset. In the morning, the ones that detected potential carcasses set out from the roost to locate the food, with others, less successful the previous day, following in the general direction. Thus, on different days, the birds take turns as leaders and followers, and all benefit from the communal roosting association. Recent research suggests that Black Vultures make more use of roosts as information centers than do Turkey Vultures.

Lore and Notes

Being such large and conspicuous birds, and being carrion-eaters associated with death, guaranteed that vultures would figure prominently in the art and culture of most civilizations. Indeed, descriptions and pictorial renderings of vultures are found in the remains of early Iranian, Mesopotamian, and Egyptian civilizations. In some cases, they are thought to be symbols of death. However, some good was thought to come from vultures; for instance, their bile was considered a top curative agent in ancient Egypt. Vultures were sacred to Mut, the Egyptian goddess of maternity; having them close by was reputed to ease childbirth. Vultures have also played the role of undertaker in past cultures and still do, to this day. In parts of India, Tibet, and Mongolia, dead people are laid out to be disposed of by vultures.

The ancient Mayans of Mexico called the KING VULTURE "Oc," including it frequently in their artworks. Vulture feathers were used in Mayan headdresses.

Mayans apparently believed that vultures, when near death, changed into armadillos; the proof being that both were "bald."

The Mayan legend of how the vulture came to be black and bald and to feed on carrion goes like this: In the old days, vultures were actually handsome, white birds with feathered heads, which ate only the finest fresh meat; they had an ideal life. One day, the vulture family, out soaring in the sun, spied a feast laid out on banquet tables in a forest clearing. They swooped down and ate the splendid food. Unfortunately for the vultures, the food had been set out by nobles as an offering to the gods. The nobles schemed to punish the unknown culprits. They set out another feast in the clearing and hid behind trees with their witch doctors. When the vultures returned for another meal, the nobles and witch doctors raced out from the trees and threw magic powder on the birds. The vultures, in their panic to escape the people, flew straight up and got too close to the sun, scorching their heads, causing their feathers to fall out. In the clouds, the magic powder turned their white plumage to black. When they returned to earth, the Great Spirit ruled that for their thievery, from that day forward, vultures would eat only carrion (A.L. Bowes 1964).

Status

The four Central American vultures are all somewhat common to very common birds; none are threatened. The only New World vulture in dire trouble is the CALIFORNIA CONDOR (CITES Appendix I and USA ESA listed), which for a while was extinct in the wild. The main causes of their decline in the 20th century were: hunting (they were persecuted especially because ranchers believed they ate newborn cattle and other domesticated animals); their ingestion of poisonous lead shot from the carcasses they fed on; and the thinning of their eggshells owing to the accumulation of organochlorine pesticides (DDT) in their bodies. The last eight free-ranging specimens were caught during the mid-1980s in their southern Californian haunts for use in captive breeding programs. The total captive population is now more than 100 individuals, and several have been released back into the wild in California and Arizona.

Profiles

Turkey Vulture, *Cathartes aura*, Plate 30a
Black Vulture, *Coragyps atratus*, Plate 30b
King Vulture, *Sarcoramphus papa*, Plate 30c

10. Raptors

Raptor is another name for *bird-of-prey*, birds that make their living hunting, killing, and eating other animals, usually other vertebrates. When one hears the term raptor, one usually thinks of soaring hawks that swoop to catch rodents, and of speedy, streamlined falcons that snatch small birds out of the air. Although these *are* common forms of raptors, the families of these birds are large, the members' behavior, diverse. The two main raptor families are the Accipitridae, containing the *hawks, kites* and *eagles*, and the Falconidae, including the *true falcons, forest-falcons,* and *caracaras*. The reasons for classifying the two raptor groups separately mainly have to do with differences in skeletal anatomy and hence, suspected differences in evolutionary history. (*Owls*, nocturnal birds-of-prey, can also be considered raptors; p. 134) Raptors are common and conspicuous animals in Costa Rica and, generally, in the Neotropics. Many are birds of open areas, above which they soar during the day, using the currents of heated air that rise from the sun-warmed ground to support and propel them as they search for meals. But raptors are found in all types of habitats, including within woodlands and closed forests.

The *accipitrids* are a worldwide group of about 200 species; they occur everywhere but Antarctica. Costa Rica is home to 35 species, some of them migratory: 21 hawks, 8 kites, 6 eagles and hawk-eagles. *Falconids* likewise are worldwide in their distribution. There are about 60 species, 13 occurring in Costa Rica. Some falcons have very broad distributions, with the PEREGRINE FALCON found almost everywhere, that is, its distribution is *cosmopolitan*. Peregrines may have the most extensive natural distribution of any bird.

Raptors vary considerably in size and in patterns of their generally subdued color schemes, but all are similar in overall form – we know them when we see them. They are fierce-looking birds with strong feet, hooked, sharp claws, or *talons*, and strong, hooked and pointed bills. Accipitrids vary in size in Costa Rica from a 20-cm-long (8 in) hawk to 1 m-long (40 in) eagles. Females are usually larger than males, in some species noticeably so. Most raptors are variations of gray, brown, black, and white, usually with brown or black spots, streaks, or bars on various parts of their bodies. The plumages of these birds are actually quite beautiful when viewed close-up, which, unfortunately, is difficult to do. Males and females are usually alike in color pattern. Juvenile raptors often spend several years in *subadult* plumages that differ in pattern from those of adults. Many falcons can be distinguished from hawks by their long, pointed wings, which allow the rapid, acrobatic flight for which these birds are justifiably famous. The falcons known as *caracaras* have distinctively long legs and unfeathered facial skin.

Natural History
Ecology and Behavior

Raptors are meat-eaters. Most hunt and eat live prey; the caracaras have a reputation as carrion eaters, but they will also take any slow-moving prey they stumble across. Raptors usually hunt alone, although, when mated, the mate is often close by. Hawks, kites, and eagles take mainly vertebrate animals, including some larger items such as monkeys, sloths, and birds up to the size of small vultures. Prey is snatched with talons first, and then killed and ripped apart with the bill. Some invertebrate prey is also taken. One species, the SNAIL KITE, specializes almost completely on one kind of freshwater marsh snail, which before eating it daintily removes from the shell with its long, pointed bill.

Falcons are best known for their remarkable eyesight and fast, aerial pursuit and capture of flying birds – they are "birdhawks." Thus, the small AMERICAN KESTREL, a telephone wire bird familiar to many people, is a falcon that formerly was known as the Sparrowhawk; the MERLIN, a slightly larger falcon, was known as the Pigeonhawk. Both of these falcons breed in North America, with some populations migrating south to winter in Central and South America. Most people are familiar with stories of PEREGRINE FALCONS diving through the atmosphere (*stooping*, defined as diving vertically from height to gain speed and force) at speeds approaching 320 kph (200 mph) to stun, grab, or knock from the sky an unsuspecting bird. But some falcons eat more rodents than birds, and some even take insects. One species specializes on taking bats on the wing at dawn and dusk. Forest-falcons are just that, falcons of the inner forest. They perch motionless for long periods on tree branches, waiting to ambush prey like birds and lizards. The LAUGHING FALCON (Plate 31) is a bird of open fields and forest edge that specializes on snakes. It perches until it spots a likely candidate for dinner, then swoops down fast and hits powerfully, grabbing the reptile and immediately biting off the head – a smart move because this falcon takes even highly poisonous prey such as coral snakes (p. 84). It then flies off to a high perch to feast on the headless serpent. Caracaras are common, if slower-than-typical falcons; less agile flyers than their true-falcon cousins, they are often seen in groups along rivers, at forest edges, and along roads.

Many raptors are territorial, a solitary individual or a breeding pair defending an area for feeding and, during the breeding season, for reproduction. Displays that advertise a territory and may be used in courtship consist of spectacular aerial twists, loops, and other acrobatic maneuvers. Although many raptors are common birds, typically they exist at relatively low densities, as is the case for all *top predators* (a predator at the pinnacle of the food chain, preyed upon by no animal). That is, there usually is only enough food to support one or two of a species in a given area. For example, a typical density for a small raptor species, perhaps one that feeds on mice and small lizards, is one individual per sq kilometer. A large eagle that feeds on monkeys may be spaced so that a usual density is one individual per thousand sq kilometers.

Breeding

Hawk and eagle nests are constructed of sticks that both sexes place in a tree or on a rock ledge. Some nests are lined with leaves. The female only incubates the 1 to 6 eggs (only 1 or 2 in the larger species) for 28 to 49 days and gives food to the nestlings. The male frets about and hunts, bringing food to the nest for the female and for her to provide to the nestlings. Both sexes feed the young when they get a bit older; they can fly at 28 to 120 days of age, depending on species size. After fledging, the young remain with the parents for several more weeks or months until they can hunt on their own. Falcon breeding is similar. Falcons nest in vegetation, in a rock cavity, or on a ledge; some make a stick nest, others apparently make no construction. Incubation is from 25 to 35 days, performed only by the female in most of the falcons, but by both sexes in the caracaras. In most falcons, the male hunts for and feeds the female during the egg-laying, incubation, and early nestling periods. Male and female feed nestlings, which fledge after 25 to 49 days in the nest. The parents continue to feed the youngsters for several weeks after fledging until they are proficient hunters.

Ecological Interactions

A common sight in Costa Rica in spring (March to April) and autumn (late September to November) is large mixed-species flocks of soaring migrant hawks and TURKEY VULTURES (Plate 30). These birds breed in North America but winter in South America. The most abundant hawks in the flocks are SWAINSON'S and BROAD-WINGED HAWKS (Plate 33), which breed, respectively, in western and eastern North America. In Costa Rica a flock can include many hundreds of birds. The flocks move over long distances in spurts by circling higher and higher on rising warm air currents, then gliding in the direction of the migration. Gradually losing altitude in their glides, they again seek *thermals* to gain height, gliding again when they reach a good altitude. The process is repeated for hours on end, the hawks having to expend very little energy flapping their wings; the air currents and the shapes of their wings do most of the work. In the evening, the flocks settle into trees to roost for the night. Such flocks on long-distance migrations need to feed *en route*. A problem for the migrating hawks, about which little is known, is that they must compete for food with the resident, local hawks. Some of the migrants probably share prey with the local residents, but others apparently shift their diets to eat what is easily available. For instance, migrating Swainson's Hawks have been found in groups of up to 400 individuals, congregating where there are swarms of grasshoppers and beetles. They may therefore eat more insects during their migrations than they would in their northern breeding areas.

The hunting behavior of falcons has over evolutionary time shaped the behavior of their prey animals. Falcons hit perched or flying birds with their talons, stunning the prey and sometimes killing it outright. An individual bird caught unawares has little chance of escaping the rapid, acrobatic falcons. But birds in groups have two defenses. First, each individual in a group benefits because the group, with so many eyes and ears, is more likely to spot a falcon at a distance than is a lone individual, thus providing all in the group with opportunities to watch the predator as it approaches and so evade it. This sort of anti-predation advantage may be why some animals stay in groups. Second, some flocks of small birds, such as starlings, which usually fly in loose formations, immediately tighten their formation upon detecting a flying falcon. The effect is to decrease the distance between each bird, so much so that a falcon flying into the group at a fast speed and trying to take an individual risks injuring itself – the "block" of starlings is almost a solid wall of bird. Biologists believe that the flock tightens when a falcon is detected because the behavior reduces the likelihood of an attack.

Lore and Notes

Large, predatory raptors have doubtless always attracted people's attention, respect, and awe. Wherever eagles occur, they are chronicled in the history of civilizations. Early Anglo-Saxons were known to hang an eagle on the gate of any city they conquered. Some North American Indian tribes and also Australian Aboriginal peoples deified large hawks or eagles. Several states have used likenesses of eagles as national symbols, among them Turkey, Austria, Germany, Poland, Russia, and Mexico. Eagles reside on the robes of British royalty and one of their kind, a fish-eater, was chosen as the emblem of the USA (although, as most USA schoolchildren know, Benjamin Franklin would have preferred that symbol to be the Wild Turkey.) People have had a close relationship with falcons for thousands of years. Falconry, in which captive falcons are trained to hunt and kill game at a person's command, is one of the oldest sports, with evidence of it being practiced in China 4000 years ago and in Iran 3700 years ago. Perhaps the oldest known book on a sport is *The Art of Falconry*, written by the King of Sicily in 1248. Falconry reached its pinnacle during medieval times in Europe, when a nobleman's falcons were apparently considered among his most valued possessions. The Crested Caracara (Plate 31), a type of falcon, is depicted on the national emblem of Mexico.

Status

Several of Costa Rica's hawks and falcons are considered threatened or endangered, such as the HARPY EAGLE (CITES Appendix I and USA ESA listed), CRESTED EAGLE and ORANGE-BREASTED FALCON (the latter two being CITES Appendix II listed, as are all hawks, kites, eagles and falcons); all of these were formerly much more common in Costa Rica and are now quite rare. Harpy Eagles are almost extinct in the country owing to hunting and deforestation, and Orange-breasted Falcons may now be gone entirely (no reliable sightings in 30 years). Many of these large raptors enjoy extensive distributions external to the country, often ranging from Mexico to northern or central South America, and are more numerous in other regions. The RED-THROATED CARACARA formerly was a fairly abundant resident of Costa Rica, but now is rare in most areas. On the other hand, the YELLOW-HEADED CARACARA (Plate 31), first noticed in Costa Rica in 1973, has been increasing in numbers and expanding its range. The SNAIL KITE, which eats only freshwater apple snails, is uncommon in many parts of its range, including most of Costa Rica, owing to destruction of its marsh habitats; it is also rare in Florida, the only part of the USA where it occurs (it is known there as the EVERGLADES KITE and is considered endangered, USA ESA listed). Some hawks adapt well to peoples' habitat alterations. A case in point is the common ROAD-SIDE HAWK (Plate 33). It prefers open habitats and, especially, roadsides. It has expanded its range and numbers in Costa Rica with deforestation and road-building in areas that previously were large tracts of inaccessible closed forest. Conservation measures aimed at raptors are bound to be difficult to formulate and enforce because the birds are often persecuted for a number of reasons (hunting, pet and feather trade, ranchers protecting livestock) and they roam very large areas. Also, some breed and winter on different continents, and thus need to be protected in all parts of their ranges, including along migration routes. Further complicating population assessments and conservation proposals, there are still plenty of Neotropical raptor species about which very little is known. For example, for the approximately 80 species of raptors that breed primarily in Central and South America (excluding the vultures), breeding behavior has not been described for 27 species, nests are unknown for 19 species, as is the typical prey taken by 6 species.

Profiles

Crested Caracara, *Polyborus plancus*, Plate 31a
Yellow-headed Caracara, *Milvago chimachima*, Plate 31b
Laughing Falcon, *Herpetotheres cachinnans*, Plate 31c
Collared Forest Falcon, *Micrastur semitorquatus*, Plate 31d
American Swallow-tailed Kite, *Elanoides forficatus*, Plate 32a
Gray-headed Kite, *Leptodon cayanensis*, Plate 32b
Common Black Hawk, *Buteogallus anthracinus*, Plate 32c
White Hawk, *Leucopternis albicollis*, Plate 32d
Roadside Hawk, *Buteo magnirostris*, Plate 33a
Osprey, *Pandion haliatus*, Plate 33b
Broad-winged Hawk, *Buteo platypterus*, Plate 33c
Swainson's Hawk, *Buteo swainsoni*, Plate 33d

11. Pigeons and Doves

The *pigeon* family is a highly successful group, represented, often in large numbers, almost everywhere on dry land, save for Antarctica and some oceanic islands. Their continued ecological success must be viewed as at least somewhat surprising, because pigeons are largely defenseless creatures and quite edible, regarded as a tasty entree by human and an array of nonhuman predators. The family, Columbidae, includes approximately 250 species, 22 of which occur in Costa Rica. They inhabit almost all kinds of habitats, from semi-deserts to tropical moist forests, to high-elevation mountainsides. Smaller species generally are called *doves*, larger ones, pigeons, but there is a good amount of overlap in name assignments.

All pigeons are generally recognized as such by almost everyone, a legacy of people's familiarity with domestic and feral pigeons. Even small children in zoos, upon encountering an exotic, colorful dove will determine it to be "some kind of pigeon." Pigeons worldwide vary in size from the dimensions of a sparrow to those of a small turkey; Costa Rica's range from 15 cm-long (6 in) ground-doves to the 35 cm (14 in) BAND-TAILED PIGEON (Plate 34). Doves and pigeons are plump-looking birds with compact bodies, short necks, and small heads. Legs are usually fairly short, except in the ground-dwelling species. Bills are small, straight, and slender. Typically there is a conspicuous patch of naked skin, or *cere*, at the base of the bill, over the nostrils. Although many of the Old World pigeons are easily among the most gaily colored of birds (Asian *fruit doves,* for instance), the New World varieties generally color their soft, dense plumages with understated grays and browns, although a few also have bold patterns of black lines or spots. Many have splotches of iridescence, especially on necks and wings. In the majority of Central American species, male and female are generally alike in size and color, although females are often a bit duller than the males.

Natural History
Ecology and Behavior
Most of the pigeons are at least partly arboreal, but some spend their time in and around cliffs, and still others are primarily ground-dwellers. They eat seeds, ripe and unripe fruit, berries, and the occasional insect, snail, or other small invertebrate. Even those species that spend a lot of time in trees often forage on the ground, moving along the leaf-strewn forest floor, for example, with the head-bobbing walk characteristic of their kind. Owing to their small, weak bills, they eat only what they can swallow whole; "chewing" is accomplished in the *gizzard*, a muscular portion of the stomach in which food is mashed against small pebbles that are eaten by pigeons expressly for this purpose. Pigeons typically are strong, rapid flyers, which, in essence, along with their cryptic color patterns, provide their only defenses against predation. Most pigeons are gregarious to some degree, staying in groups during the nonbreeding portion of the year; some gather into large flocks. Visitors to the Neotropics from North America often are struck by the relative scarcity of sparrows; it is in large part the pigeons of the region that ecologically "replace" sparrows as predominant seed-eaters.

Breeding
Pigeons are monogamous breeders. Some breed solitarily, others in colonies of various sizes. Nests are shallow, open affairs of woven twigs, plant stems, and roots, placed on the ground, on rock ledges, or in shrubs or trees. Reproductive duties are shared by male and female. This includes nest-building, incubating the 1 or 2 eggs, and feeding the young, which they do by regurgitating food into the nestlings' mouths. All pigeons, male and female, feed their young *pigeon milk*, a nutritious fluid produced in the *crop*, an enlargement of the esophagus used for food storage. During the first few days of life, nestlings receive 100% pigeon milk but, as they grow older, they are fed an increasing proportion of regurgitated solid food. Incubation time ranges from 11 to 28 days, depending on species size. Nestlings spend from 11 to 36 days in the nest. Parent pigeons of some species give *distraction displays* when potential predators approach their eggs or young;

they feign injury as they move away from the nest, luring the predator away. Most nesting occurs within the period from March through August, although some species breed year round.

Ecological Interactions

The great success of the pigeon family – a worldwide distribution, robust populations, the widespread range and enormous numbers of rock doves (wild, domestic pigeons) – is puzzling to ecologists. At first glance, pigeons have little to recommend them as the fierce competitors any hugely successful group needs to be. They have weak bills and therefore are rather defenseless during fights and ineffectual when trying to stave off nest predators. They are hunted by people for food. In several parts of the world they compete for seeds and fruit with parrots, birds with formidable bills, yet pigeons thrive in these regions and have spread to many more that are parrot-less. To what do pigeons owe their success? First, to reproductive advantage. For birds of their sizes, they have relatively short incubation and nestling periods; consequently, nests are exposed to predators for relatively brief periods and, when nests fail, parents have adequate time to nest again before the season ends. Some species breed more than once per year. Also, the ability of both sexes to produce pigeon milk to feed young may be an advantage over having to forage for particular foods for the young. Second, their ability to capitalize on human alterations of the environment points to a high degree of hardiness and adaptability, valuable traits in a world in which people make changes to habitats faster than most organisms can respond with evolutionary changes of their own.

A general pattern within the pigeon group is that smaller pigeons are usually cryptically colored, whereas larger ones are more often brightly-colored. The reason probably has to do with predation pressures: large pigeons are quite a bit safer from such predators as hawks and falcons, and thus have less need of camouflage.

Lore and Notes

Preparation: Singe, clean, draw and stuff 4 squab. Butter well and place in a preheated 180°C(350°F) oven and roast for 30 to 45 minutes or until tender. Salt and pepper to taste and baste every 5 minutes with drippings from the pan. Serve on rice. Serves 4.

Although many pigeons today are very successul animals, some species met extinction within the recent past. There are two particularly famous cases. The DODO was a large, flightless pigeon, the size of a turkey, with a large head and strong, robust bill and feet. Dodos lived, until the 17th century, on the island of Mauritius, in the Indian Ocean, east of Madagascar. Reported to be clumsy and stupid (hence the expression, "dumb as a dodo"), but probably just unfamiliar with and unafraid of predatory animals, such as people, they were killed in thousands by sailors who stopped at the island to stock their ships with food. This caused population numbers to plunge; the birds were then finished off by the pigs, monkeys, and cats introduced by people to the previously predator-free island – animals that ate the Dodos' eggs and young. The only stuffed Dodo in existence was destroyed by fire in Oxford, England, in 1755.

North America's PASSENGER PIGEON, a medium-sized, long-tailed member of the family, suffered extinction because of overhunting and because of its habits of roosting, breeding, and migrating in huge flocks. People were able to kill many thousands of them at a time on the Great Plains in the central part of the USA, shipping the bodies to markets and restaurants in large cities through the mid-

1800s. It is estimated that when Europeans first settled in the New World, there were 3 billion Passenger Pigeons, a population size perhaps never equalled by any other bird, and that they may have accounted for up to 25% or more of the birds in what is now the USA. It took only a bit more than 100 years to kill them all; the last one died in the Cincinnati Zoo in 1914.

The common ROCK DOVE, with which everyone who has visited a city or town is familiar, is a native of the Old World. Domesticated for thousands of years and transported around the world by people, feral populations have colonized all settled and many unsettled areas of the Earth. In the wild, they breed and roost in cliffs and caves. In several large cities of North America, aside from creating problems in parks, plazas, and buildings, pigeons have become the staple prey of Peregrine Falcons. The falcons have been introduced to cities by people seeking to reestablish populations in areas from which they have disappeared. A common if gruesome sight these days for visitors to the observatory at the Sears Tower building in Chicago, for instance, is a Peregrine perched on one of the building's nearby 90th floor corner setbacks, pulling apart its pigeon dinner.

Status

None of the pigeon species that occur in Costa Rica are currently threatened. Several New World pigeons in other regions, however, are now endangered, some critically so. Among the most endangered are the RING-TAILED WOOD PIGEON of Jamaica, the PLAIN PIGEON of the Caribbean, the BLUE-EYED and PURPLE-WINGED GROUND DOVES of Brazil and Argentina, the VERACRUZ QUAIL-DOVE of Mexico, and the BLUE-HEADED QUAIL-DOVE of Cuba. The SOCORRO DOVE, which was endemic to some small islands off Mexico's Pacific coast, was last seen in the wild in the 1950s. It was a victim of human settlement of the islands, and of the cats people brought along. Today, only about 200 of the doves exist, all in captivity.

Profiles

Band-tailed Pigeon, *Columba fasciata*, Plate 34a
Red-billed Pigeon, *Columba flavirostris*, Plate 34b
Short-billed Pigeon, *Columba nigrirostris*, Plate 34c
Blue Ground Dove, *Claravis pretiosa*, Plate 34d
Ruddy Ground-dove, *Columbina talpacoti*, Plate 34e
Common Ground-dove, *Columbina passerina*, Plate 35a
Inca Dove, *Columbina inca*, Plate 35b
White-tipped Dove, *Leptotila verreauxi*, Plate 35c
White-winged Dove, *Zenaida asiatica*, Plate 35d
Ruddy Quail-dove, *Geotrygon montana*, Plate 35e

12. Parrots

Everyone knows *parrots* as caged pets, so discovering them for the first time in their natural surroundings is often a strange but somehow familiar experience (like a dog-owner's first sighting of a wild coyote): one has knowledge and expectations of the birds' behavior and antics in captivity, but how do they act in the wild? Along with toucans, parrots are probably the birds most commonly symbolic of the tropics. The 300+ parrot species that comprise the Family Psittacidae (the P is silent; refer to parrots as *psittacids* to impress your friends and tourguides!) are globally distributed across the tropics, with some species extending into subtropical and even temperate zone areas, and with a particularly diverse and abundant presence in the Neotropical and Australian regions. Ornithologists divide parrots by size: *parrotlets* are small birds (as small as 10 cm, or 4 in) with short tails; *parakeets* are also small, with long or short tails; *parrots* are medium-sized, usually with short tails; and *macaws* are large (up to 1 m, or 40 in) and long-tailed.

Consistent in form and appearance, all parrots are easily recognized as such. They share a group of traits that set them distinctively apart from all other birds. Their typically short neck and compact body yield a form variously described as stocky, chunky, or bulky. All possess a short, hooked, bill with a hinge on the upper part that permits great mobility and leverage during feeding. Finally, their legs are short and their feet, with two toes projecting forward and two back, are adapted for powerful grasping and a high degree of dexterity – more so than any other bird. The basic parrot color scheme is green, but some species, such as a few of the macaws, depart from basic in spectacular fashion, with gaudy blues, reds, and yellows. Green parrots feeding quietly amid a tree's high foliage can be difficult to see, even for experienced bird-watchers. Parrots in Central America are most numerous in forested lowland areas. Best views are commonly obtained when flocks fly noisily overhead, when they depart feeding trees, or when a flock is located loafing and squabbling the afternoon away in an isolated, open tree.

Natural History
Ecology and Behavior
Parrots are incredibly noisy, highly social seed and fruit eaters. Some species seem to give their assortment of harsh, screeching squawks during much of the day, whereas others are fairly quiet while feeding. During early mornings and late afternoons, raucous, squawking flocks of parrots characteristically take flight explosively from trees, heading in mornings for feeding areas and later for night roosts, and these are usually the best sighting times. Parrots are almost always encountered in flocks of 4 or more, and groups of 30+ macaws or 50+ smaller parrots are common. Flocks are usually groups of mated pairs and, with brief observation of behavior, married pairs are often noticeable. Flocks move about seeking fruits and flowers in forests, parkland, and agricultural areas. In flight, parrots are easily identified by their family-specific silhouette: thick bodies and usually long tails, with short, relatively slowly-beating wings. Parrots generally are not considered strong flyers, but are certainly fast over the short run. Most do not need to undertake long-distance flights; they are fairly sedentary in their habits, with some regular movements as they follow the seasonal geographic progressions of fruit ripening and flower blossoming.

Parrots use their special locomotory talent to clamber methodically through trees in search of fruits and flowers, using their powerful feet to grasp branches and their bills as, essentially, a third foot. Just as caged parrots, they will hang at odd angles and even upside down, the better to reach some delicious morsel. Parrot feet also function as hands, delicately manipulating food and bringing it to the bill. Parrots feed mostly on fruits and nuts, buds of leaves and flowers, and on flower parts and nectar. They are usually considered frugivores, but careful study reveals that when they attack fruit, it is usually to get at the seeds within. The powerful bill slices open fruit and crushes seeds. As one bird book colorfully put it, "adapted for opening hard nuts, biting chunks out of fruit, and grinding small seeds into meal, the short, thick, hooked parrot bill combines the destructive powers of an ice pick (the sharp-pointed upper mandible), a chisel (the sharp-edged lower mandible), a file (ridged inner surface of the upper mandible), and a vise" (F.G. Stiles & A.F. Skutch 1989). Thick, muscular parrot tongues are also specialized for feeding, used to scoop out pulp from fruit and nectar from flowers.

Breeding

In all of the Costa Rican parrots, the sexes are very similar or identical in appearance; breeding is monogamous and pairing is often for life. Nesting is carried out during the dry season and, for some, into the early wet season. Most species breed in cavities in dead trees, although a few build nests. Macaw nests are almost always placed 30 m (100 ft) or more above the ground. A female parrot lays 2 to 8 eggs, which she incubates alone for 17 to 35 days while being periodically fed regurgitated food by her mate. The helpless young of small parrots are nest-bound for 3 to 4 weeks, those of the huge macaws, 3 to 4 months. Both parents feed nestlings and fledglings.

Ecological Interactions

Many fruit-eating birds are fruit seed dispersers (see Close-Up, p. 179), but apparently not so parrots. Their strong bills crush seeds, and the contents are digested. For example, one ORANGED-CHINNED PARAKEET (Plate 37) that was examined after feeding all morning at a fig tree in Costa Rica's Santa Rosa National Park had in its digestive tract about 3500 fig seeds, almost all of which were broken, cracked, or already partially digested. Therefore, the main ecological interaction between parrots and at least some fruit trees is that of seed predator. Because parrots eat fruit and seeds, they are attracted to farms and orchards and in some areas are considered agricultural pests, with implications for their future populations (see below). Macaws and other parrots often congregate at *licks*, exposed riverbank or streamside clay deposits. The clay that is eaten may help detoxify harmful compounds that are consumed in their seed, fruit and leaf diet, or may supply essential minerals that are not provided by a vegetarian diet. Some ecotour destinations are based on lick locations, e.g., in Peru, where visitors reliably find parrots to watch at traditional clay licks.

Lore and Notes

Parrots have been captured for people's pleasure as pets for thousands of years; Greek records exist from 400 BC describing parrot pets. The fascination stems from the birds' bright coloring, their ability to imitate human speech and other sounds, their individualistic personalities (captive parrots definitely like some people while disliking others), and their long lifespans (up to 80 years in captivity). Likewise, parrots have been hunted and killed for food and to protect crops for thousands of years. Some Peruvian Inca pottery shows scenes of parrots eating corn and being scared away from crops. Historically, people have also killed parrots to protect crops – Charles Darwin noted that in Uruguay in the early 1800s, thousands of parakeets were killed to prevent crop damage. Macaws, the largest parrots, are thought to have been raised in the past for food in the West Indies, and macaw feathers were used as ornaments and had ceremonial functions.

Status

About 90 parrot species are vulnerable, threatened, or endangered worldwide, but only two of the 16 species that occur in Costa Rica are currently endangered. The GREAT GREEN (or MILITARY) MACAW (CITES Appendix I listed) has been reduced in the country to probably less than 50 breeding pairs, but the species is more numerous in other parts of its range in Central and northern South America. The ranges and abundances of some others, such as the SCARLET MACAW (Plate 36; CITES Appendix I listed), have been severely reduced during the past 100 years, primarily owing to destruction of forests. Whereas during the early years of this century this macaw was common throughout lowland areas, now it is almost absent from the Caribbean side of the country. Many Costa Rican parrot species still enjoy healthy populations and are frequently seen. Unfortunately, however, parrots are subject to three powerful forces that, in combination, take heavy tolls on their numbers: parrots are primarily forest birds, and forests are increasingly under attack by farmers and developers; parrots are considered agricultural pests by farmers and orchardists owing to their seed and fruit eating, and are persecuted for this reason; and parrots are among the world's most popular cage birds. Several Costa Rican species – Scarlet Macaws, YELLOW-NAPED PARROTS, MEALY PARROTS (Plate 36) – are particularly prized as pets, and nests of these parrots are often robbed of young for local sale as pets or to international dealers. Without fast, additional protections, many Central American parrots will probably soon be threatened.

Profiles

Scarlet Macaw, *Ara macao*, Plate 36a
Mealy Parrot, *Amazona farinosa*, Plate 36b
Red-lored Parrot, *Amazona autumnalis*, Plate 36c
Yellow-naped Parrot, *Amazona auropalliata*, Plate 36d
White-fronted Parrot, *Amazona albifrons*, Plate 37a
White-crowned Parrot, *Pionus senilis*, Plate 37b
Brown-hooded Parrot, *Pionopsitta haematotis*, Plate 37c
Orange-fronted Parakeet, *Aratinga canicularis*, Plate 37d
Orange-chinned Parakeet, *Brotogeris jugularis*, Plate 37e

13. Cuckoos and Anis

Many of the *cuckoos* and *anis* (AH-neez) are physically rather plain but behaviorally rather extraordinary: as a group they employ some of the most bizarre breeding practices known among birds. Cuckoos and anis are both included in the cuckoo family, Cuculidae, which, with a total of about 130 species, enjoys a worldwide distribution in temperate areas and the tropics. Eleven species occur in Costa Rica. Cuckoos are mainly shy, solitary birds of forests, woodlands, and dense thickets. Anis are the opposite; gregarious animals that spend their time in small flocks in savannas, brushy scrub, and other open areas, particularly around human habitations. Anis are among those birds that make one wonder where they perched before the advent of fences. A notable *cuculid* relative of the cuckoos and anis is a common ground bird of scrub desert areas of Mexico and southwestern USA, the GREATER ROADRUNNER of cartoon fame.

Most cuckoos are medium-sized, slender, long-tailed birds. Male and female mostly look alike, attired in plain browns, tans, and grays, often with streaked or spotted patches. Several have alternating white and black bands on their tail undersides. (Many cuckoos of the Old World are more colorful.) They have short legs and bills that curve downwards at the end. Anis are conspicuous medium-sized birds, glossy black all over, with iridescent sheens particularly on the head, neck and breast. Their bills are exceptionally large, with humped or crested upper parts.

Natural History
Ecology and Behavior
Most of the cuckoos are arboreal. They eat insects, apparently having a special fondness for caterpillars. They even safely consume hairy caterpillars, which are avoided by most potential predators because they taste bad or contain sickness-causing noxious compounds. Cuckoos have been observed to snip off one end of the hairy thing, squeeze the body in the bill until the noxious entrails fall out, then swallow the harmless remainder. A few cuckoos, such as Costa Rica's infrequently seen PHEASANT CUCKOO, are ground-dwellers, eating insects but also vertebrates such as small lizards and snakes. These large cuckoos typically follow army ant swarms, picking off prey that rushes from cover to evade the ant hordes.

The highly social anis forage in groups, usually on the ground. Frequently they feed around cattle, grabbing the insects that are flushed out of hiding places by the grazing mammals. They eat mostly bugs, but also a bit of fruit. Anis live in groups of 8 to 25 individuals, each group containing 2 to 8 adults and several juveniles. Each group defends a territory from other groups throughout the year. The flock both feeds and breeds within its territory.

Breeding
Cuckoos are known in most parts of the world for being *brood parasites*: they build no nests of their own, and the females lay their eggs in the nests of other species. These other birds often raise the young cuckoos as their own offspring, usually to the significant detriment of their own, often smaller, young. About 50 of the 130 members of the family are brood parasites. Only two of the Costa Rican species, STRIPED (Plate 38) and PHEASANT CUCKOOS, breed in this manner. The rest of them are somewhat typically monogamous breeders. The male feeds the female in courtship, especially during her egg-laying period. Both sexes build the plain platform nest that is made of twigs and leaves and placed in a tree or shrub. Both sexes incubate the 2 to 6 eggs for about 10 days, and both parents feed the young. In several species, the young hop out of the nest before they have been flight-certified, to spend the several days before they can fly flopping around in the vegetation near the nest, being fed by their parents.

Anis, consistent with their highly social ways, are *communal breeders*. In the most extreme form, all the individuals within the group contribute to a single nest, several females laying eggs in it; up to 29 eggs in one nest have been noted. Many individuals help build the stick nest and feed the young. Although at first glance it would seem as if all benefit by having the group breed together, females contributing eggs to a common nest which all build, defend and tend, actually it is the dominant male and female within each group that gain most. Their eggs go in the nest last, on top of the others that sometimes become buried. Also, some females roll others' eggs out of the nest before they lay their own; thus, it pays to lay last. In some species, several nests are built by pairs within the group's territory. Ani breeding in Costa Rica occurs during the wet season, when bugs are most abundant.

Lore and Notes
The name *cuckoo* comes from the calls made by a common member of the family, the EUROPEAN CUCKOO. Many of the parasitic cuckoos lay their eggs in the nests of *host* species that are much smaller than they are. The result is that the host parents often end up bringing food to the nest to feed cuckoo nestlings that are not only much larger than their own offspring (which cannot compete for

food against the larger cuckoos and starve), but that are often larger than the parents themselves – a phenomenon that provides a never-ending stream of striking photographs in biology books.

The Mayan folk tale about how the Ani came to have only black feathers is a sad one. It seems the Ani in the past was bright pink. She was very proud of her young nestlings, so when her friend the hawk said he was going off to feed, mother Ani, exaggerating, told him to be sure to avoid the nest of beautiful young birds that was her own. The hawk tried, but when he spied a nest of runty-looking, ugly little birds, he judged that they could not be the fine-looking youngsters described by the Ani, so he ate them. When the Ani found out what her incorrect description had cost her, she put on black feathers to mourn, and all anis ever since have worn black mourning plumage (A.L. Bowes 1964).

Status

Of the 11 cuckoos or anis occurring in Costa Rica, only one, the COCOS CUCKOO is considered vulnerable. The reason is that it is endemic to Cocos Island, which is in the Pacific some 800 km (500 miles) from the mainland. Although the precise population size is unknown, species confined to a single small place are always vulnerable, because a single catastrophe there could exterminate the species. Another Costa Rican species, the STRIPED CUCKOO (Plate 38), actually has been expanding its range within the country, it being a species that does well in the forest edge, thicket, and open areas that increasingly are created through deforestation. Two species of New World cuckoos appear to be threatened: the RUFOUS-BREASTED CUCKOO, endemic to the island of Hispaniola, and the BANDED GROUND-CUCKOO of Ecuador and Colombia.

Profiles

Striped Cuckoo, *Tapera naevia*, Plate 38a
Squirrel Cuckoo, *Piaya cayana*, Plate 38b
Smooth-billed Ani, *Crotophaga ani*, Plate 38c
Groove-billed Ani, *Crotophaga sulcirostris*, Plate 38d

14. Owls

Although some *owls* are common Costa Rican birds, they are considered here only briefly because most are active only at night and so are rarely seen. But there are a few exceptions. Most owls are members of the Family Strigidae, a worldwide group of about 120 species that lacks representation only in Antarctica and remote oceanic islands. Owls are particularly diverse in the tropics and subtropics; Costa Rica has about 15 species. Most people can always identify owls because of several distinctive features. All have large heads with forward-facing eyes, small, hooked bills, plumpish bodies and sharp, hooked claws. Most have short legs and short tails. Owls are clad mostly in mixtures of gray, brown, and black, the result being that they usually are highly camouflaged against a variety of backgrounds. They have very soft feathers. Most are medium-sized birds, but the group includes species that range in length from 15 to 75 cm (6 to 30 in). Males and females generally look alike, although females are a bit larger.

Natural History
Ecology and Behavior

In general, owls occupy a variety of habitats: forests, clearings, fields, grasslands, mountains, marshes. They are considered to be the nocturnal equivalents of the day-active birds-of-prey – the hawks, eagles, and falcons. Most owls hunt at night, taking prey such as small mammals, birds (including smaller owls), and reptiles; smaller owls specialize on insects, earthworms, and other small invertebrates. But some owls hunt at twilight (*crepuscular* activity) and sometimes during the day, including the SPECTACLED OWL and FERRUGINOUS PYGMY-OWL (Plate 39). Owls hunt by sight and by sound. Their vision is very good in low light, the amount given off by moonlight, for instance; and their hearing is remarkable. They can hear sounds that are much lower in sound intensity (softer) than most other birds, and their ears are positioned on their heads asymmetrically, the better for localizing sounds in space. This means that owls in the darkness can, for example, actually hear small rodents moving about on the forest floor, quickly locate the source of the sound, then swoop and grab. Additionally, owing to their soft, loose feathers, owls' flight is essentially silent, permitting prey little chance of hearing their approach. Owls swallow small prey whole, then instead of digesting or passing the hard bits, they regurgitate bones, feathers, and fur in compact *owl pellets*. These are often found beneath trees or rocks where owls perch and they can be interesting to pull apart to see what an owl has been dining on.

Breeding

Most owls are monogamous breeders. They do not build nests themselves, but either take over nests abandoned by other birds or nest in cavities such as tree or rock holes. Incubation of the 1 to 10 or more eggs (often 2 to 4) is usually conducted by the female alone for 4 to 5 weeks, but she is fed by her mate. Upon hatching, the female broods the young while the male hunts and brings meals. Young fledge after 4 to 6 weeks in the nest.

Lore and Notes

The forward-facing eyes of owls are a trait shared with only a few other animals: humans, most other primates, and to a degree, the cats. Eyes arranged in this way allow for almost complete binocular vision (one eye sees the same thing as the other), a prerequisite for good depth perception, which, in turn, is important for quickly judging distances when catching prey. On the other hand, owl eyes cannot move much, so owls swivel their heads to look left or right.

Owls have a reputation for fierce, aggressive defense of their young; many a human who ventured too near an owl nest has been attacked and had damage done!

Status

Owls in Central America are threatened primarily by forest clearing. The only Costa Rican species that is considered near-threatened is the small UNSPOTTED SAW-WHET OWL, which occurs only in high forested areas and about which little is known. Most currently threatened owls are Old World species. Trade in owls is severely restricted; the group as a whole is CITES Appendix II listed.

Profiles

Spectacled Owl, *Pulsatrix perspicillata*, Plate 39a
Pacific Screech-owl, *Otus cooperi*, Plate 39b
Ferruginous Pygmy-owl, *Glaucidium brasilianum*, Plate 39c

15. Goatsuckers

Members of the family of birds known as the *goatsuckers*, or Caprimulgidae, do not actually suck the milk of goats, as legend has it, but they do possess one of the most fanciful of bird names. The *caprimulgids* are a group of about 70 species spread over most of the world's land masses, with the exceptions of northern North America and northern Eurasia, southern South America, and New Zealand. Their closest relatives are probably the owls, and some recent classification schemes place the two in the same avian order. Nine species occur in Costa Rica. One of them, the PAURAQUE (POWR-ah-kay; Plate 39) is an extremely common bird in many regions of the country and the most abundant caprimulgid of Central America. Pauraques, like most caprimulgids, inhabit open areas such as grassland and farmland, thickets, parkland, and forest edge areas.

Goatsuckers have a very characteristic appearance. In the New World most range from 16 to 32 cm (6 to 12 in) in length. They have long, pointed wings, medium or long tails, and big eyes. Their small, stubby bills enclose big, wide mouths that they open in flight to scoop up flying insects. Many species have bristles around the mouth area. With their short legs and weak feet, they are poor walkers – flying is their usual mode of locomotion. The plumage of these birds is uniformly cryptic: mottled, spotted, and barred mixtures of browns, grays, tans, and black. They often have white patches on their wings or tails that can be seen only in flight.

Natural History
Ecology and Behavior
Most caprimulgids are night-active birds, with some, such as the COMMON NIGHTHAWK (familiar to North Americans) and LESSER NIGHTHAWK (Plate 39), becoming active at twilight (*crepuscular* is the term ecologists use for such a habit). They feed on insects, which they catch on the wing, either with repeated forays from perched locations on the ground or on tree branches, or, as is the case with Common and Lesser Nighthawks, with continuous, often circling flight. Caprimulgids usually gather at night near bright lights to feast on the light-drawn insects. Most of these birds are not seen during the day unless they are accidentally flushed from their roosting spots, which are either on the ground or on tree branches on which they perch sideways. Because of their camouflage coloring, they are almost impossible to see when perched.

Breeding
Goatsuckers breed monogamously. No nest is built. Rather, the female lays her 1 or 2 eggs on the ground, perhaps in a small depression in the soil under the branches of a tree, or on a rock or sandbar. Around human developments, they are known for placing their eggs on bare, gravelly rooftops. Either the female alone or both sexes incubate (both in the PAURAQUE) for 18 to 20 days, and both parents feed insects to the young. Goatsuckers engage in *broken-wing displays* if their nest is approached by a predator or a person, which distracts a predator's attention. They flop about on the ground, often with one or both wings held out as if injured, making gargling or hissing sounds, all the while moving away from the nest.

Lore and Notes
Americans tend to call this group either goatsuckers or *nighthawks*, whereas Europeans prefer *nightjars*.

One of the goatsucker family, North America's COMMON POORWILL, may be the only bird known actually to hibernate, as some mammals do, during very cold weather. During their dormant state, poorwills save energy by reducing their metabolic rate and their body temperature, the latter by about 22°C (40°F).

Status

None of the Costa Rican goatsuckers are threatened. In the New World, the WHITE-WINGED NIGHTJAR of Brazil and the USA's PUERTO RICAN NIGHTJAR (USA ESA listed) occur in very limited areas and are endangered. The former is known from only a few old specimens and a few modern sightings in Central Brazil. Little is known about the bird, but the area of modern sightings falls within a national park, offering some hope for its survival. The Puerto Rican Nightjar occupies dry forest areas of southwestern Puerto Rico; only several hundred pairs remain.

Profiles

Pauraque, *Nyctidromus albicollis*, Plate 39d
Lesser Nighthawk, *Chordeiles acutipennis*, Plate 39e

16. Swifts and Swallows

Swifts and *swallows*, although not closely related, are remarkably similar in appearance and habit. Most famously, they pursue the same feeding technique – catching insects on the wing during long periods of sustained flight. The swallows (Family Hirundinidae) are a passerine group, 80 species strong, with a worldwide distribution. Twelve species occur in Costa Rica, but several are present only as over-winter migrants from more northerly breeding areas (for instance, PURPLE MARTIN and TREE, BANK, BARN (Plate 40), and CLIFF SWALLOWS). Swallows are small, streamlined birds, 11.5 to 21.5 cm (4.5 to 8.5 in) in length, with short necks, bills, and legs. They have long, pointed wings and forked tails, plainly adapted for sailing through the air with high maneuverability. Some are covered in shades of blue, green, or violet, but many are gray or brown. The sexes look alike.

Swifts, although superficially resembling swallows, are actually only distantly related; they are not even classified with the passerines. The 80 or so species of swifts (Family Apodidae) are, in fact, most closely related to hummingbirds. Eleven species are found in Costa Rica, some albeit rarely. Swifts, like swallows, are slender, streamlined birds, with long, pointed wings. They are 9 to 25 cm (3.5 to 10 in) long and have very short legs, short tails or long, forked tails, and very small bills. Swifts' tails are stiffened to support the birds as they cling to vertical surfaces. The sexes look alike: sooty-gray or brown, with white, grayish, or reddish rumps or flanks. Many are glossily iridescent.

Natural History
Ecology and Behavior

Among the birds, swifts and swallows represent pinnacles of flying prowess and aerial insectivory. It seems as if swifts and swallows fly all day, circling low over water or land, or flying in erratic patterns high overhead, snatching insects from the air. Perpetual flight was in the past so much the popular impression of swifts that it was actually thought that they never landed – that they essentially remained flying throughout most of their lives (indeed, it was long ago believed that they lacked feet; hence the family name, Apodidae, literally, *without feet*). They do land, however, although not often. When they do, they use their clawed feet and stiff tail to cling to and brace themselves against vertical structures. They almost never land on the ground, having trouble launching themselves back into the air from horizontal surfaces. A swift spends more time airborne than any other type of bird, regularly flying all night, and even copulating while in the air (a tricky affair, apparently: male and female are partially in freefall during this activity). Swifts are also aptly named, as they are among the fastest flyers on record.

Swallows also take insects on the wing as they fly back and forth over water and open areas. Some also eat berries. Not quite the terra-phobes that swifts are, swallows land more often, often resting during the hottest parts of the day. Directly after dawn, however, and at dusk, swallows are always airborne.

Breeding
All swallows are monogamous, many species breeding in dense colonies of several to several thousand nesting pairs. Nests are constructed of plant pieces placed in a tree cavity, burrow, or building, or, alternatively, consist of a mud cup attached to a vertical surface such as a cliff. Both sexes or the female alone incubate the 3 to 7 eggs for 13 to 16 days. Both parents feed nestlings, for 18 to 28 days, until they fledge. Swifts are monogamous and most are colonial breeders, but some species nest solitarily. The sexes share breeding chores. Nests consist of plant pieces, twigs, and feathers glued together with the birds' saliva. One to 6 eggs are incubated for 16 to 28 days, with young fledging at 25 to 65 days of age. Most breeding is accomplished from March to August.

Ecological Interactions
Swallows, small, vulnerable light-weights, are often under competitive pressure for breeding space from other hole-nesting species. Starlings and some sparrows, for instance, sometimes try to take over nests built by swallows and, indeed, such nest usurpation appears to be chief cause for the serious decline in numbers of the GOLDEN SWALLOW in Jamaica.

Some swallows, such as CLIFF SWALLOWS, locate their colonies near to or actually surrounding the cliff-situated nests of large hawks (predatory birds that take mostly rodents), basking in the protection afforded by having a nest close to a fearsome predator.

Because swifts and swallows depend each day on capturing enough insects, their daily habits are largely tied to the prevailing weather. Flying insects are thick in the atmosphere on warm, sunny days, but relatively scarce on cold, wet ones. Therefore, on good days, swallows, for instance, can catch their fill of bugs in only a few hours of flying, virtually anywhere. But on cool, wet days, they may need to forage all day to find enough food, and they tend to do so over water or low to the ground, where under such conditions bugs are more available.

Lore and Notes
Swallows have a long history of beneficial association with people. In the New World, owing to their insect-eating habits, they have been popular with people going back to the time of the ancient Mayan civilization. Mayans, it is believed, respected and welcomed swallows because they reduced insect damage to crops. In fact Cozumel (the word refers to swallows), off Mexico's Yucatán Peninsula, is the Island of Swallows. People's alterations of natural habitats, harmful to so many species, are often helpful to swallows, which adopt buildings, bridges, road culverts, roadbanks, and quarry walls as nesting areas. BARN SWALLOWS have for the most part given up nesting in anything other than human-crafted structures. The result of this close association is that, going back as far as ancient Rome, swal-

lows have been considered good luck. Superstitions attached to the relationship abound; for example, it is said that the cows of a farmer who destroys a swallow's nest will give bloody milk. Arrival of the first migratory Barn Swallows in Europe is considered a welcoming sign of approaching spring, as is the arrival of CLIFF SWALLOWS at some of California's old Spanish missions.

Status

None of the swifts or swallows that breed or winter in Central America are threatened. A few Old World species, from Africa and Asia, are known to be quite rare and are considered threatened; for some others, so little is known that we are uncertain of their populations' sizes or vulnerabilities.

Profiles

White-collared Swift, *Streptoprocne zonaris*, Plate 40a
Gray-rumped Swift, *Chaetura cinereiventris*, Plate 40b
Barn Swallow, *Hirundo rustica*, Plate 40c
Southern Rough-winged Swallow, *Stelgidopteryx ruficollis*, Plate 40d
Blue and White Swallow, *Notiochelidon cyanoleuca*, Plate 41a
Mangrove Swallow, *Tachycineta albilinea*, Plate 41b

17. Hummingbirds

Hummingbirds are birds of extremes. They are among the most recognized kinds of birds, the smallest of birds, and undoubtedly among the most beautiful, albeit on a minute scale; fittingly, much of their biology is nothing short of amazing. Limited to the New World, the hummingbird family, Trochilidae, contains about 330 species, 50+ of which occur in Costa Rica. The variety of forms encompassed by the family, not to mention the brilliant iridescence of most of its members, is indicated in the names attached to some of the different subgroups: in addition to the hummingbirds proper, there are the *emeralds, sapphires, sunangels, sunbeams, comets, metaltails, fairies, woodstars, woodnymphs, pufflegs, sabrewings, thorntails, thornbills,* and *lancebills.* Hummingbirds occupy a broad array of habitat types, from exposed high mountainsides at 4000 m (13,000 ft) to mid-elevation arid areas to sea level tropical forests and mangrove swamps, as long as there are nectar-filled flowers to provide necessary nourishment.

Almost everyone can identify hummingbirds (call them *hummers* to sound like an expert), being familiar with their general appearance and behavior: very small birds, usually gorgeously clad in iridescent metallic greens, reds, violets, and blues, that whiz by us at high speeds, with the smallest among them resembling nothing so much as large flying insects.

Most hummers are in the range of only 6 to 13 cm (2.5 to 5 in) long, although a few of the larger kinds reach 20 cm (8 in), and they tip the scales at an almost imperceptibly low 2 to 9 g (most being 3 to 6 g) – the weight of a large paper-clip! Bill length and shape varies extensively among species, each bill closely adapted to the precise type of flowers from which a species delicately draws its liquid food. Males are usually more colorful than females, and many of them have *gorgets*, bright, glittering throat patches in red, blue, green, or violet. Not all hummers are so vividly outfitted; one group, called *hermits* (because of their solitary ways), are known for dull, greenish-brown and gray plumages. Hummers have tiny legs and feet; in fact, in some classifications they are included with the swifts in the avian order Apodiformes, meaning *those without feet.*

Natural History
Ecology and Behavior

Owing to their many anatomical, behavioral, and ecological specializations, hummingbirds have long attracted the research attention of biologists; the result is that we know quite a bit about them. A hefty fraction of the best studies have taken place in Costa Rica. These highly active, entertaining-to-watch birds are most often studied for one of four aspects of their biology:

1 flying ability
2 metabolism
3 feeding ecology
4 aggressive defense of food resources.

(1) Hummers are capable of very rapid, finely-controlled, acrobatic flight, more so than any other kind of bird. The bones of their wings have been modified through their evolutionary history to allow for perfect, stationary hovering flight and also for the unique ability to fly *backwards*. Their wings vibrate in a figure eight-like wingstroke at a speed beyond our ability to see each stroke – up to 80 times per second. Because people usually see hummers only during the birds' foraging trips, they often appear never to land, remaining airborne as they zip from flower to flower, hovering briefly to probe and feed at each. But they do perch every now and again, providing opportunities to get good looks at them.

(2) Hummingbirds have very fast metabolisms, a necessary condition for small, warm-blooded animals. To pump enough oxygen and nutrient-delivering blood around their little bodies, their hearts beat up to 10 times faster than human hearts – 600 to 1000 times per minute. To obtain sufficient energy to fuel their high metabolism, hummingbirds must eat many times each day. Quick starvation results from an inability to feed regularly. At night, when they are inactive, they burn much of their available energy reserves and on cold nights, if not for special mechanisms, they would surely starve to death. The chief method to avoid energy depletion on cold nights is to enter into a sleep-like state of *torpor*, during which the body's temperature is lowered to just above that of the outside world, from 17 to 28°C (30 to 50°F) below their daytime operating temperatures, saving them enormous amounts of energy. In effect, they put the thermostat down and hibernate overnight.

(3) All hummingbirds are *nectarivores* – they get most of their nourishment from consuming nectar from flowers. They have long, thin bills and specialized tongues to lick nectar from long, thin flower tubes, which they do while hovering. Because nectar is mostly a sugar and water solution, hummingbirds need to obtain additional nutrients, such as proteins, from other sources. Toward this end they also eat the odd insect or spider, which they catch in the air or pluck off spider webs. Some ornithologists believe that insects constitute a larger proportion of hummingbird diets than is generally believed, some going so far as to suggest that some species visit flowers more often to catch bugs there than to gather nectar. Recent research in Costa Rica shows that hummers with strongly curved bills (adapted to feed from curved flower nectar tubes) obtain their protein from spider webs, hovering while they glean spiders and bugs from the webs; whereas those with straight bills tend to obtain their protein in "flycatching" mode – via aerial capture of flying wasps and flies. The difference makes sense: flycatching with a long, sharply curved bill, we may assume, would be quite difficult.

(4) Many hummers are highly aggressive birds, energetically defending individual flowers or feeding territories from all other hummingbirds, regardless of species. Not all are territorial, however. Some are *trapline* feeders, repeatedly following a regular route around a section of their habitat, checking the same flowers for nectar, which the flowers replenish at intervals. Some traplines cover as much as a kilometer (0.6 miles) of habitat. Whether birds defend territories depends usually on whether it is an economically attractive option. If the costs of defense (including forcefully evicting intruders), in terms of the amount of energy expended, exceed the amount that can be gained from feeding on the territory, or if nectar-producing flowers are super-abundant in the environment, providing sufficient food for all, then owning and defending a territory is not worthwhile.

Predators on hummingbirds include small, agile hawks and falcons and also frogs and large insects, such as praying mantises, that ambush the small birds as they feed at flowers. Another hazard is large spider webs, from which sometimes they cannot extricate themselves.

Breeding

Hummingbirds are polygamous breeders in which females do almost all the work. In some species, a male in his territory advertises for females by singing squeaky songs. A female enters the territory and, following courtship displays, mates. Afterwards, she leaves the territory to nest on her own. Other species are *lek breeders*. In these systems, males gather at traditional, communal mating sites called leks. For instance, a lek may be in a cleared spot in the forest undergrowth. Each of 3 to 25 males has a small mating territory in the lek, perhaps just a perch on a flower. The males spend hours there each day during the breeding season, advertising for females. Females enter a lek, assess the displaying males, and choose ones to mate with. A male might spend months at the lek, but only have one 15-minute mating interaction with a female; other males may mate with many females in a season. After mating, females leave the lek or territory and build their nests, which are cup-like and made of plant parts, mosses, lichens, feathers, animal hairs, and spider webs. Nests are placed in the small branches of trees, often attached with spider web. The female lays 2 eggs, incubates them for 15 to 19 days, and feeds regurgitated nectar and insects to her young for 20 to 26 days, until they fledge. Hummers may be found breeding at any time of year, depending on species and geography. Breeding in a particular area often occurs when flowers are most abundant.

Ecological Interactions

The relationship between hummingbirds (nectar consumers) and the flowering plants from which they feed (nectar producers) is mutually beneficial. The birds obtain a high-energy food that is easy to locate and always available because various flowering plant species, as well as groups of flowers on the same plant, open and produce nectar at different times. The flowering plants, in turn, use the tiny birds as other plants use bees – as pollinators. The nectar is produced and released into the part of flower the hummer feeds from for the sole reason of attracting the birds so that they may accidentally rub up against other parts of the flower (*anthers*) that contain pollen grains. These grains are actually reproductive spores that the flower very much "wants" the bird to pick up on its body and transfer to other plants of the same species during its subsequent foraging, thereby achieving for the flower *cross-pollination* – breeding with another member of its species (many plants also have the ability to pollinate themselves). Flowers that are specialized for hummingbird pollination place nectar in long, thin tubes that fit the shape of the birds' bills and also protect the nectar from foraging insects. Hummingbird-pollinated plants often have red, pink, or orange flowers, colors which render them easily detectable to the birds but, owing to peculiarities of their vision, indistinguishable from the background environment to insects. Furthermore, these flowers are often odorless because birds use color vision and not smell to find them (whereas nectar-eating insects, which the plants want to discourage, use odor to find flowers).

Interlopers in this mutualistic interaction are a group of pollen-eating mite species. Mites are miniscule arthropods, allied with the spiders and ticks. Some mites may spend their lives on a single plant, feeding and reproducing, but others, perhaps searching for mates or new sites to colonize, try to reach other plants. Walking to another plant for such a small animal is almost out of the question. What to do? The mites jump onto the bills of hummingbirds when the birds visit flowers and become hitchhikers on the bird, usually holing up in their nostrils. The passengers leap off the bird's bill during a subsequent visit to a plant of the same species that they left, necessary because the mites are specialized for certain plants. Recent research in Costa Rica suggests that the passenger mites monitor the scents of flowers to identify the correct type, to know when to get off the bus.

Lore and Notes

Intriguingly, some hummingbirds are as curious about us as we are of them. A common occurrence while following a trail is to be closely approached by a passing hummingbird, which stops in mid-air to size up the large primate, darts this way and that to view the intruder from all angles, then, its curiosity apparently satisfied, zips off into the forest.

Hummingbirds, as one might expect, have been the object of considerable myth and legend. The Mayan tale of how hummingbirds became so bright and beautiful is that, way back, the Great Spirit created the hummingbird as a tiny, plain-looking, delicate bird with exceptional flying prowess. The plain hummingbird was nonetheless happy with its existence, and privileged to be the only bird permitted to drink the nectar of pretty flowers. When the drably attired hummer planned her marriage, all the other birds of the kingdom, including the motmot and oriole, donated colorful feathers, so that the hummer's bridal gown was glittering and showy. The Great Spirit, pleased with the hummingbird and her gown, ruled that she could wear it forever (A.L. Bowes 1964).

The Aztecs also took note of hummers, adorning their ceremonial clothes with the birds' gaudy, metallic feathers. Several groups of Indians used these feathers in their wedding ornaments. Hummingbird bodies have a long mythical history in Latin America of being imbued with potent powers as love charms. Having a dead hummer in the hand or pocket is thought by some even today to be a sure way to appear irresistible to a member of the opposite sex. Even powdered hummingbird is sold for this purpose.

Status

At least 25 species of hummers are currently threatened or considered vulnerable to threat. Several are endangered, including the ESMERALDAS WOODSTAR of Ecuador, the LITTLE WOODSTAR of Ecuador and Peru, the HONDURAN EMERALD of Honduras, the TURQUOISE-THROATED PUFFLEG of Colombia, the BLACK-BREASTED PUFFLEG of Ecuador, and the SHORT-CRESTED COQUETTE of

Mexico. Of the Costa Rican species, the MAGENTA-THROATED HUMMINGBIRD (Plate 43) is considered near-threatened, and the MANGROVE HUMMINGBIRD, owing to the continued destruction of its breeding habitat in Pacific coast mangrove swamps, is considered vulnerable to threat. The latter species occurs only in Costa Rica, and only in remaining, fragmented mangrove habitat. There is always danger to a species when all its living members are included in a single population within a relatively small area; a single catastrophic event could eliminate the species. Several other Costa Rican species are very uncommon in the country, but are more abundant in other parts of their ranges. All hummers are CITES Appendix II listed.

Profiles

Green Hermit, *Phaethornis guy*, Plate 41c
Long-tailed Hermit, *Phaethornis superciliosus*, Plate 41d
Little Hermit, *Phaethornis longuemareus*, Plate 41e
Crowned Woodnymph, *Thalurania colombica (furcata)*, Plate 42a
Steely-vented Hummingbird, *Amazilia saucerrottei*, Plate 42b
Cinnamon Hummingbird, *Amazilia rutila*, Plate 42c
Rufous-tailed Hummingbird, *Amazilia tzacatl*, Plate 42d
Striped-tailed Hummingbird, *Eupherusa eximia*, Plate 42e
Purple-throated Mountain-gem, *Lampornis calolaema*, Plate 43a
Violet Sabrewing, *Campylopterus hemileucurus*, Plate 43b
Green Violet-ear, *Colibri thalassinus*, Plate 43c
Green-crowned Brilliant, *Heliodoxa jacula*, Plate 43d
Magenta-throated Hummingbird, *Calliphlox bryantae*, Plate 43e

18. Trogons

Although not as familiar to most people as other gaudy birds such as toucans and parrots, *trogons* are generally regarded by wildlife enthusiasts as among the globe's most visually striking, glamorous of birds; as such, visitors to Costa Rica should try hard not to miss them. The trogon family, Trogonidae, inhabits tropical and semi-tropical regions in the Neotropics, Africa, and southern Asia. It consists of about 40 species of colorful, medium-sized birds with compact bodies, short necks and short "chicken-like" bills. Considering that trogons are distributed over three widely separated geographic regions, it is striking that the family's body plan and plumage pattern are so uniform. Male trogons are rather consistently described as having metallic or glittering green, blue, or violet heads and chests, with deeply contrasting bright red, yellow, or orange underparts. Females are duller in color, usually with brown or gray heads, but share the males' brightly colored breasts and bellies. The characteristic trogon tail is long and squared-off, with horizontal black and white stripes on the underside. Trogons usually sit erect with their distinctive tails pointing straight to the ground.

One trogon stands out from the flock: the regal-looking RESPLENDENT QUETZAL (Plate 44). Famously described as "the most spectacular bird in the New World," the quetzal generally resembles other trogons, but the male's emerald-green head is topped by a ridged crest of green feathers and, truly ostentatiously, long green plumes extend half a meter (18 in) or more past the end of the male's typical trogon tail. Seeing a male quetzal gracefully swooping low through a forest, its long, trailing plumes flashing by, is frequently mentioned by bird lovers as a supreme experience.

Natural History
Ecology and Behavior

Although trogons are distributed throughout many Neotropical forests, they are not limited to warm areas: some species, such as the quetzal, inhabit cool cloud forests at elevations up to 3000 m (10,000 ft). One species, the ELEGANT TROGON, ranges northward into southern Arizona (USA). Trogons are generally observed either solitarily or in pairs, and occasionally in small family groups. In spite of their distinctive calls (typically a *cow-cow-cow* call that is one of a tropical forest's characteristic sounds) and brilliant plumages, trogons can be difficult to locate and even to see clearly when spotted perched on a tree branch. This is because, just like green parrots, partly green trogons easily meld into dark green overhead foliage. (Some biologists, in fact, suspect that the flashy hues of forest birds such as trogons, so glaring and conspicuous when the birds are viewed in the open, might actually appear as dull and inconspicuous to potential predators within the dark confines of closed forests.) Trogon behavior is not much help because typically these birds perch for long periods with little moving or vocalizing, the better presumably to keep them off some predator's dinner plans. Trogons are best seen, therefore, when flying. This often occurs in sudden bursts as they flip off the branches on which a moment before they sat motionless, and sally out in undulatory, short flights to snatch succulent insects. Trogons can thus be considered *sit-and-wait* predators. They also swoop to grab small lizards, frogs, and snails. Trogons are also partial frugivores, taking small fruits from trees while hovering. Quetzals in Costa Rica are particularly fond of wild figs and avocados (they regurgitate the large seeds, dispersing them).

Breeding

Trogons usually breed from March through June. They nest in cavities in dead trees or in structures high up in trees, such as termite or wasp nests (they have been observed "taking over" a wasp nest, carving a nest hole in it and, adding insult to injury, feasting daily on the wasps during nesting!). Generally the trogon female incubates her 2 or 3 eggs overnight and the male takes over during the day. Incubation is 17 to 19 days. Young are tended by both parents; fledging is at 14 to 30 days. Quetzal nest holes generally are about 10 m (33 ft) high in trees. Both sexes share nest duties and apparently divide each day into two shifts each at the nest. Quetzals are known to defend exclusive territories around their nest tree that average about 700 m (2300 ft) in diameter.

Lore and Notes

Most trogon lore concentrates, as might be expected, on the RESPLENDENT QUETZAL, which is thought to have been revered by, or even sacred to, local peoples going back to ancient Mayan and Incan times. One legend of indigenous Guatemalans is that the quetzal received its showy plumage during the European conquest of the Americas: "After a particularly gruesome battle, huge flocks of quetzals (which were then only green) flew down to keep a watch over dead Mayans, thus staining their breasts red" (C.M. Perrins 1985). Another story is that the Great Spirit of the Mayans decided one day to choose a king of the birds. The various species competed, showing off their beauty, intelligence, strength, knowledge, or artistry. The quetzal initially held back because, although he was ambitious and proud, his plumage was quite plain. An idea came to the quetzal. He convinced his friend, the roadrunner, to lend him some elegant feathers (promising untruthfully to return them later) and, with the new, long, showy tail feathers, was appointed king of the birds (A.L. Bowes 1964). Mayans used the long quetzal tail plumes for ceremonial head-dresses, feather capes, and artwork. The chief god of the Mayans was *Kukulcan* and the chief god of the Toltecs was *Quetzalcoatl*, both meaning "The Plumed Serpent."

Status

Most of the 10 trogon species that occur in Costa Rica are fairly common forest residents, although some range over relatively small, local areas. One, BAIRD'S TROGON, is thought to be near-threatened. The RESPLENDENT QUETZAL is considered by some authorities to be endangered (CITES Appendix I and USA ESA listed) throughout Central America primarily owing to destruction of its favored cloud forest habitat. Large tracts of cloud forest continue to be cleared for cattle pasture, agriculture, and logging, especially below 2000 m (6500 ft). Another factor threatening quetzal populations is that local people illegally hunt them with rifles, blowguns, and traps for trade in skins, feathers, and live birds. Because of the quetzal's special prominence as the national bird of Guatemala (depicted on its state seal and on its currency) and as a particularly gorgeous poster animal for conservation efforts, several special reserves have been established for the bird in Guatemala, and quetzals are specially protected in Costa Rica's Poás Volcano, Braulio Carrillo, and Chirripó National Parks and the Monteverde Cloud Forest Reserve. A system of cloud forest reserves stretching from Mexico to Panama is required for complete protection of the quetzal and other higher elevation Central American trogons. Northern Mexico's EARED TROGON also appears on lists of threatened species.

Profiles

Resplendent Quetzal, *Pharomachrus mocinno*, Plate 44a
Slaty-tailed Trogon, *Trogon massena*, Plate 44b
Violaceous Trogon, *Trogon violaceus*, Plate 44c
Black-throated Trogon, *Trogon rufus*, Plate 44d
Black-headed Trogon, *Trogon melanocephalus*, Plate 44e

19. Jacamars and Puffbirds

Two interesting, closely related families of insect eaters, each represented in Costa Rica by only a few species, are the *jacamars* and *puffbirds*. The jacamar family (Galbulidae) includes 16 species, all Neotropical in distribution, and the puffbirds (Family Bucconidae) about 30 species, similarly limited in distribution. Both kinds of birds are typically forest dwellers, usually in warmer, lowland areas. Jacamars are often described by bird experts as resembling glittering, iridescent hummingbirds enlarged to the size of starlings or robins. They are fairly slender, small to medium-sized birds (15 to 31 cm, 6 to 12 in, long), metallic green above and brownish or reddish below, with very long, fine, pointed bills. Most puffbirds are smaller (15 to 24 cm, 6 to 9 in), with distinctively large heads, stout bills with hooked ends, heavy-looking bodies, and loose plumage that produces a chubby, puffy appearance. Puffbirds are not glamorously colored as are the jacamars, being covered in more subdued browns, grays, and whites.

Natural History
Ecology and Behavior

Jacamars are often seen along rivers and in forests and forest clearings, whereas puffbirds are chiefly forest birds. Both eat insects and hunt in the same way. They perch quietly on tree limbs and, spotting a flying insect, dart out suddenly to overtake and snatch it in mid-air, flycatcher-fashion. Jacamars are renowned for their vital, "charged" personality and lifestyle: they sit quietly waiting for a meal to happen by, but they do so very alertly, snapping their heads this way and that as they scan for moving insects. After these birds grab an insect, such as a large butterfly, they often return to their perch, and proceed manically to beat the insect against the perch until wings fall off and the body alone can be swallowed. The jacamar's long, elegant bill may aid the birds in tightly grasping a butterfly's body while its wings flap violently as it attempts escape, and also in holding wasps and other stinging insects at safe distances from vulnerable parts of its body. Other common diet items are beetles, bees and dragonflies.

Jacamars are usually encountered singly. Some of the puffbirds, in contrast, are quite the little socialites. *Nunbirds*, for instance, congregate in groups of up to 10, and are often observed perched in a row on a branch or telephone wire, all clamorously vocalizing with loud, ringing calls. Like jacamars, puffbirds sit quietly until they detect a bug, then zip out and grab it. Puffbirds take insects on the wing and, from leaves, such other delicacies as spiders and small frogs and lizards.

Breeding
Jacamars nest in short burrows that they dig in steep hillsides or in river or stream banks. Both parents incubate the 2 to 4 eggs, for a total of 20 to 22 days. Young are fed insects by the parents for 19 to 26 days before fledging. Not much is known about breeding of puffbirds, but some of them nest in burrows on the forest floor and some in burrows in arboreal termite nests.

Ecological Interactions
Nunbirds have been observed following groups of monkeys, catching insects that are flushed out from hiding places as the monkeys move.

Lore and Notes
A jacamar is among "the most exciting birds to meet, as it seems to be even more highly charged with energy than most feathered creatures; it gives the impression of being electrified with high voltage ... Between forays they rest, incessantly turning their heads as they keep a sharp watch for prey...." (A.F. Skutch 1963)

"Puffbirds of several kinds have frequently been called 'stupid' ('bobo') because, fearless of man in regions where they have had little experience of him, they often remain perching quietly while one approaches fairly close to them. But this appearance of dull apathy is most deceptive. One need only attempt to study the (puffbird) at its subterranean burrows, using all one's ingenuity to overcome its distrust, to realize what a keen-sighted, wary creature it can be." (A.F. Skutch 1958)

Status
Only two jacamars occur in Costa Rica, the RUFOUS-TAILED JACAMAR (Plate 45), which is fairly common in some areas, and the GREAT JACAMAR, which is rare; neither, however, is considered threatened. Two other family members, COPPERY-CHESTED and THREE-TOED JACAMARS, which occur in Brazil, Colombia, and Ecuador, are now threatened. Of the puffbirds, only one species, known as the LANCEOLATED MONKLET, is in trouble – now considered near-threatened.

Profiles
Rufous-tailed Jacamar, *Galbula ruficauda*, Plate 45a
White-necked Puffbird, *Bucco macrorhynchos*, Plate 45b

White-fronted Nunbird, *Monasa morphoeus*, Plate 45c
White-whiskered Puffbird, *Malacoptila panamensis*, Plate 45d

20. Kingfishers

Kingfishers are handsome, bright birds most often encountered along rivers and streams or along the seashore. Classified with the motmots in the Order Coraciiformes, the approximately 90 kingfisher species are grouped in 3 families and range throughout the tropics, with a few of them pushing deeply northward and southward into temperate areas. Only 6 kingfisher species, all in the Family Cerylidae, reside in the New World and all 6 are found in Costa Rica (one is migratory from North America). They differ in size (see below), from 12 to 40 cm (5 to 16 in), but all are of a similar form: large heads with very long, robust, straight bills, short necks, short legs, and, for some, highly noticeable crests. The kingfisher color scheme in the New World is also fairly standardized: dark green or blue-gray above, white and/or chestnut-orange below.

Natural History
Ecology and Behavior
New World kingfishers, as the name suggests, are all mainly fish eaters (that is, they are *piscivores*). Usually seen hunting alone, they sit quietly, attentively on a low perch – a tree branch over the water, a bridge spanning a stream – while scanning the water below. When they locate suitable prey, they swoop and dive, plunging head-first into the water (to depths up to 60 cm, or 24 in) to seize it. If successful, they quickly emerge from the water, return to the perch, beat the fish against the perch to stun it, then swallow it whole, head first. Thus, kingfishers are sit-and-wait predators of the waterways. They will also, when they see movement below the water, hover over a particular spot before diving in. BELTED KINGFISHERS (Plate 46), migrants that breed to the north and only winter in Costa Rica, commonly fly out 500 m (a quarter mile) or more from a lake's shore to hover 3 to 15 m (10 to 50 ft) above the water, searching for fish. Kingfisher diets are occasionally supplemented with tadpoles and insects. Kingfishers fly fast and purposefully, usually in straight and level flight, from one perch to another; often they are seen only as flashes of blue or green darting along waterways.

Kingfishers are highly territorial, aggressively defending their territories from other members of their species with noisy, chattering vocalizations, chasing, and fighting. They inhabit mostly lowland forests and waterways, but some range up to elevations of 2500 m (8000 ft).

Breeding
Kingfishers are monogamous breeders that nest in holes. Both members of the pair help defend the territory in which the nest is located, and both take turns digging the 0.75 to 1.5 m (2 to 5 ft) long nest burrow into the soft earth of a river or stream bank. Both parents incubate the 3 to 8 eggs, up to 24 hours at a stretch, for a total of 19 to 26 days. The young are fed increasingly large fish by both parents until they fledge at 25 to 38 days old. Fledglings continue to be fed by the parents for up to 10 weeks. At some point after they are independent, the parents expel the young from the territory. Many juvenile kingfishers apparently die during their first attempts at diving for food. Some have been seen first "practicing" predation by capturing floating leaves and sticks.

Ecological Interactions

Costa Rican kingfishers can be arranged quite nicely by size order, from the largest, the RINGED KINGFISHER (Plate 46), to the smallest, the 12.5 cm (5 in) long AMERICAN PYGMY KINGFISHER (Plate 46). The size order is not accidental. Ecologists believe that such graded variation in size allows all the different kingfisher species to coexist in the same places because, although they are so alike in habits and, especially, in the kinds of foods they eat, they actually avoid serious competition by specializing on eating fish of different sizes. Ringed Kingfishers eat large fish, BELTEDS eat slightly smaller fish, and Pygmys eat tiny fish, tadpoles, and insects. Costa Rica's four species of green kingfishers (the largest is about twice the weight of the second largest, 4 times the weight of the next largest, and 8 times the weight of the smallest) probably all evolved from a single green ancestor. Intriguingly, the larger the species of kingfisher, the higher is the average perch height above the water from which it hunts – from 1.4 m (4 ft) for the smallest species to about 10 m (32 ft) for the largest.

Lore and Notes

Kingfishers are the subject of a particularly rich mythology, a sign of the bird's conspicuousness and its association with water throughout history. In some parts of the world, kingfishers are associated with the biblical Great Flood. It is said that survivors of the flood had no fire and so the kingfisher was chosen to steal fire from the gods. The bird was successful, but during the theft, burned his chest, resulting in the chestnut-orange coloring we see today. According to the ancient Greeks, Zeus was jealous of Alcyone's power over the wind and waves and so killed her husband by destroying his ship with thunder and lightning. "In her grief, Alcyone threw herself into the sea to join her husband, and they both turned immediately into kingfishers. The power that sailors attributed to Alcyone was passed on to the Halcyon Bird, the kingfisher, which was credited with protecting sailors and calming storms" (D. Boag 1982). Halcyon birds were thought to nest 7 days before and 7 days after the winter solstice and these days of peace and calm, necessary to rear young, were referred to as *halcyon* days.

Status

All Costa Rican kingfishers are moderately to very abundant; none are considered threatened. Some breed quite well in the vicinity of human settlements. Eleven species of kingfishers currently reside on lists of vulnerable or threatened animals, but they are Old World in their distributions, most from Polynesia and the Philippines.

Profiles

Ringed Kingfisher, *Ceryle torquata*, Plate 46a
Belted Kingfisher, *Ceryle alcyon*, Plate 46b
Amazon Kingfisher, *Chloroceryle amazona*, Plate 46c
Green Kingfisher, *Chloroceryle americana*, Plate 46d
American Pygmy Kingfisher, *Chloroceryle aene*, Plate 46e

21. Motmots

Motmots – beautiful kingfisher relatives with several distinctive features and a ridiculous name. The name probably originates with the BLUE-CROWNED MOTMOT (Plate 47), whose common call is *whoot-whoot, whoot-whoot*. Family Momotidae includes only 9 species, all limited geographically to the Neotropics. Motmots are mainly residents of low-altitude forests, but occur in other habitats also, such as orchards, tree-lined plantations, suburban parks, and some drier scrub areas. Motmots are colorful, slender, small to medium-sized birds, 18 to 48 cm (7 to 19 in) long. They have fairly long, broad, bills downcurved at the end, with serrated edges, adapted to grab and hold their animal prey. Their most peculiar feature, however, is their tail. In most motmots, two central feathers of the tail grow much longer than others. Soon, feather barbs near the end of these two feathers drop off, either from the bird's preening or from brushing against tree branches, resulting in short lengths of barbless vane and, below this area, in what is commonly described as a *racquet head* appearance of the feather ends. If you get a sufficiently close look, you will discover that motmots are among the most handsome, visually stunning of Central American birds, with their bodies of blended shades of green, black masks and, in some, brilliant patches of blue on their heads. A close look through binoculars at a TURQUOISE-BROWED MOTMOT (Plate 47), in particular, will be unforgettable.

Natural History
Ecology and Behavior
Motmots are predators on insects (particularly beetles, butterflies, dragonflies, and cicadas), spiders, and small frogs, lizards and snakes, which they snatch in the air, off leaves, and from the ground. Typically they perch quietly on tree branches or on telephone wires or fences, sometimes idly swinging their long tails back and forth, until they spy a suitable meal. They then dart quickly, seize the prey, and ferry it back to the perch for munching. If the item is large or struggling – a big beetle, a lizard – the hungry motmot will hold it tight in its serrated bill and whack it noisily against the perch before swallowing it. Motmots are also frugivores, eating small fruits, up to the size of plums, which they collect from trees while hovering. Motmots are never observed in flocks. They are seen either solitarily or in pairs, and may remain in pairs throughout the year (although the sexes may separate during the day to feed). An unusual feature of their behavior is that motmots are usually active well into the twilight, going to sleep later than do most birds.

Male and female motmots are alike in size and coloring. Some courtship activities have been observed, with motmots calling back and forth high up in the trees, and sometimes holding bits of green leaves in their bills. Motmots are burrow nesters, like their kingfisher cousins. Both male and female dig the burrow, often placed in the vertical bank of a river or roadside. Tunnels up to 4 m (13 ft) long have been uncovered, but most are on the order of 1.5 m (5 ft). Both parents incubate the 2 to 4 eggs. Young are fed and brooded by male and female for 24 to 30 days, at the end of which the juvenile motmots are well-feathered and able to fly from the burrow entrance.

Lore and Notes
"In the wet Caribbean forests of southern Central America, the hollow hooting of RUFOUS MOTMOTS (Plate 47) ('hoohoo' or 'hoohoohoo') is one of the characteristic dawn sounds. Until traced to their source – which may take long – the deep, soft, scarcely birdlike notes create an atmosphere of unfathomable mystery. It is easy to imagine that the ghosts of the vanished aborigines are calling to each other through the dripping woodland." (A.F. Skutch 1971)

"The curious racket-tailed motmots have what I call the most velvety of all bird notes. It is usually a single short *oot*, pitched about five tones below where one can whistle. . . . Most of the natives have sound-names for motmots, and the Maya Indians of Yucatán call the brilliant (Turquoise-browed Motmot) "Toh," and, as an appreciation of the interest, he has come to nest and roost familiarly in the age-long deserted ruins of their former glory." (L.A. Fuertes 1914)

One Mayan legend explains both how motmot tails came to have racket ends and why motmots are burrow nesters. The motmot, with his brilliant coloring and long tail, considered himself a bit above other, less regal-looking birds. When a large storm was brewing and all the birds set to work to prepare to weather the storm and survive, building dams and storing fruits and seeds, the motmot, too pretty and important to be bothered with work, hid in the brush and went to sleep. He did not notice that his long tail stuck out into a trail, where working birds frequently stepped on it, causing barbs to fall out. The storm never materialized and, later, as all the birds gathered to preen in relief, they laughed at the motmot's ruined tail. The embarrassed motmot fled into the dark forest, dug a burrow, and became an underground recluse (A.L. Bowes 1964).

Status

Two motmots – TODY and KEEL-BILLED MOTMOTS – are rare in Costa Rica, but are not considered formally endangered owing to their greater abundance in other parts of their ranges. The Keel-bill is on some lists of threatened species, chiefly because its extremely patchy distribution is not understood. That is, Keel-bills have an extensive range within Central America but they are common only in small, isolated areas within that range, in Mexico, Belize, Guatemala, Nicaragua, and Costa Rica. Costa Rica's protected areas do not include much of the Keel-bill's lowland habitat, but several parks in Belize and Honduras do.

Profiles

Rufous Motmot, *Baryphthengus martii*, Plate 47a
Blue-crowned Motmot, *Momotus momota*, Plate 47b
Broad-billed Motmot, *Electron platyrhynchum*, Plate 47c
Turquoise-browed Motmot, *Eumomota superciliosa*, Plate 47d

22. Woodpeckers

We are all familiar with *woodpeckers*, at least in name and in their cartoon incarnations. These are industrious, highly specialized birds of the forest – where there are trees in the world, there are woodpeckers (excepting only Australia, the polar regions, and some island nations). The group, encompassing 200+ species, from the 9-cm (3.5-in) *piculets* to large woodpeckers up to 50 cm (20 in) long, is contained in the Family Picidae, placed, along with the toucans, in the Order Piciformes. Sixteen species of various sizes occur in Costa Rica (one, the YELLOW-BELLIED SAPSUCKER, is a North American migrant, present only during winter) and they occupy diverse habitats and employ various feeding methods. Small and medium-sized birds, woodpeckers have strong, straight, chisel-like bills, very long tongues that are barbed and often sticky-coated, and toes that spread widely, firmly anchoring the birds to tree trunks and branches. They come in various shades of olive-green, brown, and black and white, usually with small but conspicuous head or neck patches of red or yellow. Some have red or brown crests. A few woodpeckers are actually quite showy, and some have striking black and white stripes on chest or back. The sexes usually look alike. Because of the tapping sounds they produce as they butt their bills against trees and wooden structures, and owing to their characteristic stance – braced upright on vertical tree trunks – woodpeckers often attract our notice and so are frequently observed forest-dwellers.

Natural History
Ecology and Behavior
Woodpeckers are associated with trees and are adapted to cling to a tree's bark and to move lightly over its surface, searching for insects; they also drill holes in bark and wood into which they insert their long tongues, probing for hidden bugs. They usually move up tree trunks in short steps, using their stiff tail as a prop, or third foot. Woodpeckers eat many kinds of insects that they locate on or in trees, including larval ones. They also are not above a bit of flycatching, taking insects on the wing, and many supplement their diets with fruits, nuts, and nectar. Members of the genus *Melanerpes*, in particular, which includes the HOFFMAN'S and RED-CROWNED WOODPECKERS (Plate 48), also eat a lot of fruit. A few species have ants as a dietary staple. The *sapsuckers*, a type of woodpecker, use their bills to drill small holes in trees that fill with sap, which is then eaten. Some woodpeckers also forage on the ground.

Woodpeckers are monogamous, and some live in large family groups. Tropical woodpeckers usually remain paired throughout the year. They sleep and nest in cavities that they excavate in trees. Woodpeckers hit trees with their bills for three very different reasons: for drilling bark to get at insect food; for excavating holes for roosting and nesting; and for *drumming*, sending communication signals to other woodpeckers. Thus, one never knows upon first hearing the characteristic drumming sound whether the bird in question is feeding, signalling, or carving a new home. Woodpeckers typically weave up and down as they fly (*undulatory* flight), a behavior suited to make it more difficult for predators to track the birds' movements.

Breeding
A mated male and female woodpecker carve a nesting hole in a tree. Sometimes they line the cavity with wood chips. Both sexes incubate the 2 to 4 eggs for 11 to 18 days, males typically taking the entire night shift. Young are fed by both parents for 20 to 35 days until they fledge. Juveniles probably remain with the parents for several months more, or longer in those species in which families of up to 20 individuals associate throughout the year. Most Costa Rican woodpeckers breed from February to July.

Ecological Interactions
The different woodpecker species that live in one region usually are graded in size. There are small (for instance, the OLIVACEOUS PICULET; Plate 48), medium (RED-CROWNED WOODPECKER), and large (PALE-BILLED WOODPECKER; Plate 49) species. The size differences permit coexistence in the same area of such ecologically similar species because birds of various sizes specialize on different foods, thereby reducing negative effects of competition. When there are two or more woodpecker species of about the same size inhabiting the same place, it always appears to be the case that the potential competitors forage in different ways, or for different items – again, eliminating competition that could drive one of the species to extinction in the region over which they overlap.

Woodpeckers as a group have both beneficial and harmful effects on forests. On the one hand, they damage living, dying, and dead trees with their excavations and drilling, but on the other, they consume great quantities of insects, such as tree borers, that can themselves significantly damage forests. Because other birds use tree holes for roosting and/or nesting, but do not necessarily or cannot dig holes themselves, sometimes the carpenter-like woodpeckers end up doing the work for them. Many species occupy deserted woodpecker holes. More sinisterly, some birds "parasitize" the woodpecker's work by stealing holes. For instance, COLLARED ARACARIS (Plate 49), medium-sized toucans, have been observed evicting PALE-BILLED WOODPECKERS from their nest holes.

Lore and Notes

In ancient Roman mythology, Saturn's son, Picus, was a god of the forests. The sorceress Circe, attracted to the handsome Picus, courted him, but was rejected. In her wrath, she transformed Picus into a woodpecker, providing the basis for the woodpecker family's name, Picidae. The Mayans of ancient America thought that the woodpecker was a lucky bird, possessor of a lucky green stone that it kept under its wing. The legend was that the luck would be transferred to any person who could find a woodpecker hole and cover it. The bird would excavate a new hole, but that one, too, should be covered. After nine excavations, the woodpecker would drop the charm, allowing the person to claim it. During the Mayan civilization, presumably, there were quite a few highly frustrated woodpeckers.

Woodpeckers damage trees and buildings and also eat fruit from gardens and orchards (especially cherries, apples, pears, and raspberries) and so in some parts of the tropics are considered significant pests and treated as such. The HISPANIOLAN WOODPECKER was routinely killed in the Dominican Republic because of its habits of carving holes in royal palms and boring into woody cacao pods to eat the inner pulp and insects. And, of course, we cannot fail to mention the lovesick NORTHERN FLICKER (a type of woodpecker) in Florida (USA) that continually drilled holes in what the bird must have thought was soft wood, but what was actually the hardened foam protective covering of the about-to-be-launched Space Shuttle's nose cone. The space ship was delayed for several days while ornithologists and technicians figured out how to move the troublesome bird from the area.

Status

None of Costa Rica's woodpeckers are presently threatened, but several species are noticeably declining as forests continue to be cut. Several woodpeckers appear on lists of endangered animals, including the HELMETED WOODPECKER of South America and the RED-COCKADED WOODPECKER (USA ESA listed) of the southeastern USA. Two of the largest woodpeckers, which survived until several decades ago, are now probably extinct: The USA's IVORY-BILLED WOODPECKER, a victim of the destruction of its old growth river forest habitat, and Mexico's IMPERIAL WOODPECKER, which, at 58 cm (22 in) long, was the largest member of the family.

Profiles

Olivaceous Piculet, *Picumnus olivaceus*, Plate 48a
Hoffman's Woodpecker, *Melanerpes hoffmannii*, Plate 48b
Red-crowned Woodpecker, *Melanerpes rubricapillus*, Plate 48c
Black-cheeked Woodpecker, *Melanerpes pucherani*, Plate 48d
Lineated Woodpecker, *Dryocopus lineatus*, Plate 49a
Pale-billed Woodpecker, *Campephilus guatemalensis*, Plate 49b

23. Toucans

Spectacular. No other word fits them – *toucans* are spectacular animals. Their shape, brilliant coloring, and tropical quintessence make them one of the most popular "poster animals" for the tropical forests of the Americas and one most visitors want to see. It's hardly surprising, therefore, that the logos of several conservation organizations and tour companies feature toucans. The toucan family, Ramphastidae, is classified with the woodpeckers, and contains about 40 species – the toucans and the usually smaller *toucanets* and *aracaris* (AH-rah-SAH-reez); all are restricted to the American tropics. Six species occur in Costa Rica.

The first sighting of toucans in the wild is always exhilarating – the large size of the bird, the bright colors, the enormous, almost cartoonish bill. Toucans are usually first noticed flying from treetop to treetop in small groups. Your eyes immediately lock onto the flight silhouette; something is different here! As one observer put it, it looks as if the bird is following its own bill in flight (J.C. Kricher 1989). The effect of the bill seeming to lead the bird is that toucans appear unbalanced while flying. The bird's most distinguishing feature – its colorful, disproportionately large bill – is actually light, mostly hollow, and used for cutting down and manipulating the diet staple, tree fruit.

Natural History
Ecology and Behavior

Toucans are gregarious forest birds, usually observed in flocks of 3 to 12. They follow each other in *strings* from one tree to another, usually staying in the high canopy (a toucan only occasionally flies down to feed at shrubs, or to pluck a snake or a lizard from the forest floor). The birds are playful, grasping each other's bills in apparent contests, and tossing fruit to each other. Toucans are primarily fruit-eaters, preferring the darkest, so ripest, fruit. Their long bill allows them to perch on heavier, stable branches and reach a distance for hanging fruits. They snip the fruit off, hold it at the tip of the bill, and then, with a forward flip of the head, toss the fruit into the air and into their throats. (Seems, we humans think, an inefficient eating method, but the toucans do quite nicely with it.) Toucans also increase their protein intake by consuming the occasional insect, spider, or small reptile, or even bird eggs or nestlings. (I will never forget my surprise when I lifted my binoculars to a toucan high up in an Argentine tree and watched it snatch in its bill a big black tarantula, then hit its bill against a heavy branch, the better to knock the spider senseless, then gulp it down.) Sometimes individual fruit trees are defended by a mated toucan pair from other toucans or from other frugivorous birds – defended by threat displays and even, against other toucans, by bill clashes. CHESTNUT-MANDIBLED TOUCANS (Plate 50), the largest in Costa Rica, may "parasitize" the slightly smaller KEEL-BILLED TOUCAN (Plate 50): the larger bird follows the smaller, then chases the smaller away after it succeeds at locating a fruit-filled tree.

Breeding

Breeding is during the dry season. Toucans nest (and some sleep) in tree cavities, either natural ones or those hollowed out by woodpeckers, in either live or dead trees. Nests can be any height above the ground, up to 30 m (100 ft) or more. Both sexes incubate and feed the 2 to 4 young. Toucans are apparently monogamous. Some species, such as the COLLARED ARACARI (Plate 49), seem to breed cooperatively; that is, other family members, in addition to the mother and father, help raise the young in a single nest.

Ecological Interactions

Small fruit seeds pass unharmed through toucan digestive tracts and large seeds are regurgitated, also unharmed. Thus, these frugivores aid in the dispersal of tree seeds, and, together with other fruit-eaters, are responsible for the positions of some forest trees. In other words, many forest trees grow not where a parent tree drops its seeds, but where frugivorous birds do so (see Close-Up, p. 179).

Lore and Notes

Toucans are commonly known in many areas of the Neotropics as "Dios te de," (God gives it to you), apparently because the three-syllable call of the CHESTNUT-MANDIBLED TOUCAN sounds like this expression. Toucan feathers have long been used as ornaments. Alfred Russell Wallace, co-formulator with Darwin of the theory of evolution, visited South America from 1848 to 1852, noting in his journals that dancers in Brazilian villages commonly wore hats with red and yellow toucan feathers.

Status

Toucans are common residents in the various regions in which they occur, except where there is extensive deforestation. None of the family are currently threatened in Costa Rica. Some toucans, e.g., the CHESTNUT-MANDIBLED, have suffered substantial population declines in heavily deforested areas of Central America, for instance, in some regions of Panama. Also, some toucan species may be scarce locally due to hunting. Several toucans, including the KEEL-BILLED, are CITES listed but, rather than being immediately threatened, they are listed because they are considered "look-alikes" of threatened species, and so they need to be monitored during international trade.

Profiles

Collared Aracari, *Pteroglossus torquatus*, Plate 49c
Fiery-billed Aracari, *Pteroglossus frantzii*, Plate 49d
Keel-billed Toucan, *Ramphastos sulfuratus*, Plate 50a
Chestnut-mandibled Toucan, *Ramphastos swainsonii*, Plate 50b
Emerald Toucanet, *Aulacorhynchus prasinus*, Plate 50c

All of the bird families considered below are of *passerine*, or *perching*, birds, contained within the Order Passeriformes (see p. 100).

---

24. Woodcreepers

Woodcreepers are small and medium-sized brown birds that pursue a mostly arboreal lifestyle. The family, Dendrocolaptidae, consists of about 50 species, all tree-climbing birds of Central and South America. They are common in wet forest at low and moderate elevations, but also at the forest edge and in semi-open areas. In contrast to many other groups, the woodcreepers, including the 16 species that occur in Costa Rica, are fairly uniform in size, plumage colors, and natural history. Most are slender birds, 20 to 36 cm (8 to 14 in) in length. The sexes look alike, with plumages mostly of various shades of brown, chestnut, or tan. Many have white patches of varying dimension on breast, head, or back; and most have some spotting, streaking, or banding, particularly on the chest. Woodcreepers resemble woodpeckers to some extent, with longish bills (some strongly curved downwards) and stiff tails that they use to brace themselves against tree trunks.

Owing to their physical similarities, the various woodcreepers are often difficult to tell apart, even for experienced birdwatchers. Body size, bill size and shape, and type of streaking are used to distinguish members of the group.

Natural History

Ecology and Behavior
Woodcreepers feed by moving upwards on tree trunks and also horizontally along branches, peering under bark and into moss clumps and epiphytes, using their long bills to probe and snatch prey in tight nooks and crannies. Unlike woodpeckers, they do not dig holes in search of prey. The foraging technique is quite standardized: a woodcreeper flies to the base of a tree and then spirals up the trunk, using its stiff, spiny tail as a third foot to brace itself in a vertical posture against the tree; it checks for prey as it climbs. At the top, the bird flies down to the base of the next tree, and repeats the process. The group is primarily *insectivorous*, but also takes spiders as well as small lizards and amphibians. Many woodcreepers are frequent participants, with antbirds, tanagers, and motmots, among others, in *mixed-species flocks* (see p. 157) that follow swarms of army ants, taking prey that rush out from hiding places to avoid the voracious ants. Woodcreepers are most often observed singly or in pairs, but occasionally in small family groups. They roost in tree crevices or holes.

Breeding
Most Costa Rican woodcreepers breed from March through July. Some practice standard monogamy, with the sexes equally sharing nesting chores, but in some, apparently no real pair-bonds are established and, after mating, females nest alone. Nests are usually tree crevices or holes, but sometimes are established in arboreal termite nests. Parents line nests with wood chips. The 2 or 3 eggs are incubated for 17 to 21 days and young fledge 18 to 24 days after hatching.

Ecological Interactions
Quite often, a large number of woodcreeper species coexist in the same local area. The food items they take and their foraging methods are quite similar – which ordinarily should engender much harmful competition among the birds and lead to elimination of the weaker competitors. But the species apparently avoid much direct competition by having sufficiently different body sizes and bill sizes and shapes to support specialization on slightly different prey and foraging on slightly different parts of trees.

Lore and Notes
Some woodcreepers have reputations for being extremely aggressive toward other species, for instance, for harassing and evicting roosting or nesting woodpeckers from tree cavities.

Status
Many woodcreepers are quite abundant in Costa Rica. A few species are uncommon within the country, but are not threatened because they are more abundant in other parts of their ranges. One Brazilian species with low population numbers, the MOUSTACHED WOODCREEPER, is considered vulnerable to threat.

Profiles
Wedge-billed Woodcreeper, *Glyphorhynchus spirurus*, Plate 51a
Olivaceous Woodcreeper, *Sittasomus griseicapillus*, Plate 51b

Streaked-headed Woodcreeper, *Lepidocolaptes souleyetii*, Plate 51c
Barred Woodcreeper, *Dendrocolaptes certhia*, Plate 51d

25. Antbirds

Antbirds are small and medium-sized, rather drably attired inhabitants of the lower parts of the forest that have intriguing feeding behavior; unfortunately, owing to their behavior, they are difficult to observe. Antbirds (Family Formicariidae) are active passerines, about 250 species strong, which are confined chiefly to the warm forests and thickets of the Neotropics. The family name refers to the feeding behavior of some of the species, which regularly follow ant swarms, snatching small creatures that leave their hiding places to avoid the predatory ants.

Antbirds range in size from 8 to 36 cm (3 to 14 in). The smallest are the *antwrens* and *antvireos*, whereas the ones known formally as *antbirds* are mid-sized, and the largest are *antshrikes* and *antthrushes*. In fine detail, these birds are quite varied in appearance and some are boldly patterned, but males mostly appear in understated shades of dark gray, brown, or black, with varying amounts of white on backs, shoulders, or wings. A few species are black and white striped. Female plumage is likewise dull, generally olive, brown, or chestnut. Both sexes in some species have red eyes surrounded by patches of bare skin that are bright blue or other colors.

Natural History
Ecology and Behavior
Antbirds are mostly found at the lower levels of the forest or on the forest floor – they are shade dwellers. Most species practice insectivory, although some of the larger ones also eat fruit or small lizards, snakes, and frogs. Some are ant-followers, feeding in mixed-species flocks that follow army ants (see below), but others are ground and foliage gleaners, many rummaging around on the ground through the leaf litter, tossing dead leaves aside with their bills as they search for insects. When those that follow ants for a living breed, they temporarily cease ant following and establish and defend breeding territories. In some species, family groups remain together, male offspring staying with the parents, even after acquiring mates.

Breeding
Many antbirds appear to mate for life. Courtship feeding occurs in some of these birds, males passing food to females prior to mating. Many antbirds build cup nests out of pieces of plants that they weave together. Nests are usually placed in a fork of branches low in a tree or shrub. Some nest in tree cavities. Male and female share nest-building duty, as well as incubation of the 2 to 3 eggs and feeding insects to the young. Incubation is 14 to 20 days and young remain in the nest for 9 to 18 days. Most antbird breeding is accomplished from March to August.

Ecological Interactions
Antbirds are participants in two related ecological interactions that facilitate feeding. Some antbirds are "professional" *ant followers* (that is, they do it all the time), such as Costa Rica's BICOLORED ANTBIRD (Plate 52), and some follow army ant swarms occasionally. Because these birds usually refrain from eating the ants – a high formic acid content makes these insects unpalatable to most – but simply

follow swarms of ants, using them to scare food out into the open as hunters use beaters to flush animals from hiding spots, this interaction between birds and bugs is a *commensalism*: one population benefits and the other, the ants, is essentially unaffected by it. Army ant swarms, consisting of from 50,000 to a million tiny carnivores, generally advance across the forest floor with a front that is 3 to 15 m (10 to 50 ft) wide, driving out all animals they encounter; the ants get some and the birds get many of the others.

A second phenomenon, *mixed species flocks* of foragers that roam large territories within the forest, is suspected of being a strong *mutualistic* interaction, in which all participants benefit. Interestingly, we are not sure in this case precisely what those benefits are, but many bird species throughout the tropics participate in such feeding flocks, so benefits to all there must be. Some of the flocks follow army ants, but others do not. Antbirds are regular members of these feeding flocks, with some South American species even appearing to be regular flock "leaders." Other birds join the feeding assemblages occasionally, or for parts of a day – tanagers (frequently), motmots, cuckoos, woodcreepers, ovenbirds. Sometimes upwards of 50 different species are observed moving in a single flock. Individuals tend to remain with the same flock for a year or more, breeding within the flock's territory. These flocks move through forests at a reported typical speed of about 1 km (0.6 miles) every 3 hours, although not in a straight line. A common experience of visitors to tropical forests is that, as they walk along a trail, very few birds are noticed. Suddenly, from nowhere, a large flock appears, birds of many species are everywhere, calling, foraging, fluttering around, flying, moving; then, in a few moments, just as suddenly, they are gone, passed on, and the quiet calm returns.

As you might expect, to avoid direct competition, the various species within a flock will specialize on feeding in particular places with respect to the flock; in fact, on close examination, the feeding flocks appear to be tightly structured. Some species always forage on or next to the ground, others on trees at 2, 5 or 10 m (6, 15, 30 ft) up. Some explore live leaves for bugs, others specialize on dead leaves. Some might make constant, short sallies, flycatching. One species might always be at the flock's center, another typically at the flock periphery. Some birds concentrate on catching prey that flushes in response to the flock's whirlwind arrival, while others search the leaf litter. Notice the advantage of this arrangement for an individual bird, as opposed to its joining a single-species flock: because feeding behavior is usually the same for all members of a species, in a single-species flock an individual needs to compete continually for the same food in the same part of the forest using the same feeding method.

What are the possible benefits of foraging in large flocks of diverse species? First, there is always safety in numbers – more birds means more eyes and ears available to detect dangerous predators, such as falcons or snakes. Also, some of the flock members (often shrike-tanagers and antshrikes), in shifts, seem to serve as *sentinels*, feeding less, keeping alert for danger, and giving alarm calls when predators are detected. It has been noted that some of the flock participants that feed on the forest floor will not even put their head down into the leaf litter unless sentinels are posted. Further, should a predator strike, the likelihood of any one individual flock member being taken is small. Second, there must be some feeding advantage that results from the moving, mixed-species flock – probably the propensity of the rapidly moving flock to flush insects from hiding places, thus making them easier to find for all.

Lore and Notes

The strange compound names of these birds, such as antwrens, antshrikes, antthrushes, apparently arose because naturalists from outside of the Neotropics who named them could not ascertain local names or believed that local peoples had no names for these species. Although the birds do not resemble, for example, wrens, shrikes, or thrushes, they were so designated owing to their relative sizes.

Status

None of the Costa Rican antbirds are presently considered threatened, and many are very common, if difficult to see, residents of various forest areas. About 30 species within the Family Formicariidae, mostly Brazilian, are classed as vulnerable to threat, or are already threatened or endangered.

Profiles

Barred Antshrike, *Thamnophilus doliatus*, Plate 52a
Bicolored Antbird, *Gymnopithys leucaspis*, Plate 52b
Black-faced Antthrush, *Formicarius analis*, Plate 52c
Dotted-winged Antwren, *Microrhopias quixensis*, Plate 52d

26. Manakins

The *manakins*, Family Pipridae, are a Neotropical group of about 60 species of small, compact, stocky passerine birds, 9 to 19 cm (3.5 to 7.5 in) long, with short tails and bills, and two attention-grabbing features: brightly colored plumages and perhaps the most elaborate courtship displays among birds. Some male manakins are outstandingly beautiful, predominantly glossy black but with brilliant patches of bright orange-red, yellow, or blue on their heads and/or throats. Some have deep blue on their undersides and/or backs. The exotic appearance of male manakins is sometimes enhanced by long, streamer-like tails, up to twice the length of the body, produced by the elongation of two of the central tail feathers. Females, in contrast, are duller and less ornate, usually shades of yellowish olive green or gray. To accompany the bird's courtship displays, the wing feathers of some species, when moved in certain ways, make whirring or snapping sounds.

Natural History
Ecology and Behavior

Manakins are highly active forest birds, chiefly of warmer, lowland areas, although some range up into cloud forests. Residents of the forest understory, they eat mostly small fruits, which they pluck from bushes and trees while in flight, and they also take insects from the foliage. Manakins are fairly social animals when it comes to feeding and other daily activities, but males and females do not pair. They employ a non-monogamous mating system and, in fact, most of our knowledge about manakin behavior concerns their breeding behavior – how females choose males with which to mate and, in particular, male courting techniques. To use the ornithological jargon, manakins are *promiscuous* breeders. No pair-bonds are formed between males and females. Males mate with more than one female and females probably do the same. After mating, females build nests and rear young by themselves. Males, singly or in pairs, during the breeding season stake out display sites on tree branches, in bushes, or on cleared patches of the forest floor, and then spend considerable amounts of time giving lively vocal and visual displays, trying to attract females. An area that contains several of these performance sites is called a *lek*, and thus manakins, along with other birds such as some grouse, some cotingas, and some hummingbirds, are *lekking* breeders.

At the lek, male manakins *dance*, performing elaborate, repetitive, amazingly rapid and acrobatic movements, sometimes making short up and down flights, sometimes rapid slides, twists, and turn-arounds, sometimes hanging upside down on the tree branch while turning rapidly from side to side and making snapping sounds with their wings. The details of a male's dance are *species specific*, that is, different species dance in different ways. Females, attracted to leks by the sounds of male displays and by their memories of lek locations – the same traditional forest sites are used from one year to the next – examine the energetically performing males with a critical eye and then choose the ones they want to mate with, sometimes making the rounds several times before deciding. In a few species, such as the LONG-TAILED MANAKIN (Plate 53), two and sometimes three males (*duos* and *trios*) join together in a coordinated dance on the same perch. Long-tails in their dance alternate *leapfrog hops* with bouts of slow, *butterfly* flight, and the males jointly give a synchronous call that sounds like "toledo" up to 19 times per minute. A duo may give up to 5000 "toledos" in a single day, apparently alerting passing females that the males are ready to display and mate. In these curious cases, one male is dominant, one subordinate, and only the dominant of the pair eventually gets to mate with interested females. Why the subordinate male appears to help the dominant one obtain matings (are they closely related? Do subordinate males stand to inherit display sites when the dominants die? Do subordinates achieve "stolen" matings with females when the dominants are temporarily distracted?), why the manakins dance at all, and on what basis females choose particular males to become the fathers of their young, are all areas of continuing scientific inquiry; and Costa Rica's LONG-TAILED MANAKIN is a frequent study subject.

Breeding

Most manakins in Costa Rica breed within the interval from February to July, although some breed in both wet (May to November) and dry (December to April) seasons. Males take no part in nesting. The female builds a shallow cup nest that she weaves into a fork of tree branches, 1 to 15 m (3 to 50 ft) off the ground. She incubates the 1 to 2 eggs for 17 to 20 days, and rears the nestlings herself, bringing them fruit and insects, for 13 to 20 days.

Ecological Interactions

Largely frugivorous, manakins are important seed dispersers of the fruit tree species from which they feed. The cozy relationships between fruit trees and the birds that feed on them are explored in the Close-Up on p. 179.

Manakins, like most birds that use open, cup-like nests, often suffer very high rates of nest destruction. In one small study, only about 7% of eggs survived the incubation stage and hatched. Most nests were lost to predators, for which the suspect list is quite lengthy: ground-dwelling as well as arboreal snakes, birds such as motmots, puffbirds, toucans, and magpie-jays, large arboreal lizards, and mammals such as opossums, capuchin monkeys, kinkajous, and coati.

Lore and Notes

Colorful manakin feathers were often used by the indigenous peoples of Central and South America for ornamental purposes, especially for clothing and masks used during dances and solemn festivals.

Status

None of the Costa Rican manakins are currently considered to be threatened. One species is fairly rare and is classified as near-threatened – the GRAY-HEADED MANAKIN. Several South American species possibly face more trouble, including the threatened GOLDEN-CROWNED MANAKIN of Brazil and the BLACK-CAPPED MANAKIN of Argentina and Brazil.

Profiles

White-collared Manakin, *Manacus candei*, Plate 53a
Long-tailed Manakin, *Chiroxiphia linearis*, Plate 53b
Red-capped Manakin, *Pipra mentalis*, Plate 53c
White-ruffed Manakin, *Corapipo leucorrhoa*, Plate 53d

27. Cotingas

Owing to their variety of shapes, sizes, ecologies, and breeding systems, as well as to their flashy coloring, *cotingas* are usually considered to be among the Neotropic's glamour birds. The family, Cotingidae, is closely allied with the *manakins* and contains 65 species that live primarily in lowland tropical forests. All observers of these birds stress the group's diversity. The cotingas include tiny, warbler-sized birds and large, crow-sized birds (in fact, the group contains both some of the smallest and largest passerine birds); fruit-and-insect eaters but also some that eat only fruit (which among birds is uncommon); species in which the sexes look alike and many in which males are spectacularly attired in bright spectral colors but females are plain; territorial species that breed monogamously and *lekking* species that breed *promiscuously* (see below); and, without doubt, some of the strangest looking birds of the forests.

Among the 10 or so Costa Rican cotingas are *pihas, bellbirds, typical cotingas, umbrellabirds,* and *fruitcrows,* the last two being quite large. Perhaps the only generalizations that apply to these birds is that all have short legs and relatively short, rather wide bills, the better to swallow fruits. Males of some of the group are quite ornate, with patches of gaudy plumage in unusual colors. For instance, some of the typical cotingas are lustrous blue and deep purple, and some are all white; others are wholly black, or green and yellow, or largely red or orange or gray. The PURPLE-THROATED FRUITCROW male (Plate 54) is all-black with a purple throat. The THREE-WATTLED BELLBIRD (Plate 54) male is brown but has a shiny white head. This group also includes birds with unusual ornaments – fleshy wattles, patches of brightly colored bare skin, or flashy crests. The male BARE-NECKED UMBRELLABIRD, largely black, has both a large red throat sac that is inflated during displays and an umbrella-shaped black crest; the male Three-wattled Bellbird has attached to its bill area three hanging, worm-like, darkly colored wattles that are shown during displays.

Natural History

Ecology and Behavior

Cotingas primarily inhabit the high canopy of the forest. They are fruit specialists, a feature of their natural history that has engendered much study. They eat small and medium-sized fruits that they take off trees, often while hovering. Some cotingas, such as the fruitcrows and pihas, supplement the heavily frugivorous diet with insects taken from the treetop foliage, but others, particularly the bellbirds, feed exclusively on fruit. Fruit-eating creates both problems and benefits (as detailed in the Close-Up, p. 179); one consequence is that when young are fed only fruit, as in the bellbirds, the nestling period can be unusually long because rapidly growing nestlings require protein that an all-fruit diet provides at only a low rate.

Some cotingas pair up, defend territories, and breed conventionally in apparent monogamy. But others, such as umbrellabirds and bellbirds, are *lekking* species, in which males individually stake out display trees and repeatedly perform vocal and visual displays to attract females. Females enter display areas (*leks*), assess the jumping and calling males, and choose the ones they wish to mate with. In the THREE-WATTLED BELLBIRD, for instance, males at the lek give the loud, bell-like *bock* call (which is heard clearly at least a kilometer away) and other calls and flight displays, jumping displays, and a special *changing place* display. In the latter, a male that has managed to attract a female to his display perch jumps over her, displaces her, then leans close to her and utters calls (sweet nothings?) quietly into her ear. Male bellbirds that own a display perch in the lek spend during the breeding season up to 80% to 90% of their daylight hours there, trying to attract females. With this type of breeding, females leave after mating and then nest and rear young alone.

Breeding
Most Costa Rican cotingas breed from March through July or August, although complete information is not yet available for all species. Some are *altitudinal migrants*, breeding in higher-elevation forests but spending the "off" season in lowland forests. Nests, usually placed in trees or bushes, are generally small, open, and inconspicuous, some nest cups being made of loosely arranged twigs, some of mud, and some of pieces of plants. Many species lay only a single egg, some 1 or 2 eggs. Incubation is 17 to 28 days and the nestling period is 21 to 44 days, both stages quite long for passerine birds.

Ecological Interactions
Because of the cotingas' feeding specialization on fruit, they are considered to be major dispersers of tree seeds. Owing to their high-canopy habits, the precise fruits cotingas go after often are difficult to determine. They are believed to feed heavily at palms, laurels, and incense trees, and also at, among others, members of the blackberry/raspberry family.

Status
Four Costa Rican cotingas are threatened: the YELLOW-BILLED and TURQUOISE COTINGAS, THREE-WATTLED BELLBIRD, and BARE-NECKED UMBRELLABIRD. The last is sparsely distributed in several localized areas scattered throughout its range (Costa Rica and Panama) and, often, only a few individuals can be found where it does occur. Leks that have been discovered have contained only 3 to 6 displaying males. The prime threat to umbrellabirds is deforestation, and a particular problem for this species, an altitudinal migrant, is that to live its life it requires both highland forest breeding habitat and lowland forest wintering habitat. Thus, for the bird to prosper, both types of forests in a single area, together with connecting forest corridors, must be preserved. These umbrellabirds are found in, and so protected by, Rincón de la Vieja National Park (breeding habitat), Monteverde Cloud Forest Reserve (breeding), La Selva Biological Reserve (wintering), Braulio Carrillo National Park (breeding), Hitoy Cerere Biological Reserve, and La Amistad International Park, on the Panamanian border. More research is

needed on identifying the locations of umbrellabirds throughout the year before specific conservation plans can be crafted.

The YELLOW-BILLED COTINGA, all white except for the bill, found in coastal mangrove and lowland forest along the Pacific coast, has been little-studied, so there is scant information on it. Mangroves appear to be its main breeding habitat, but mangrove areas in Costa Rica are increasingly under threat. These areas are not widely protected – even though there are laws prohibiting their being cut, mangroves are taken for fuel. Carara Biological Reserve and Corcovado National Park protect some needed habitat, and the bird occurs in these parks. For this species to survive, some of the mangrove areas around the Golfo Dulce will probably have to be protected.

The smallest cotinga, the 7.5-cm (3-in) KINGLET CALYPTURA of southeastern Brazil, is either endangered or extinct. There are a few museum specimens taken in the 1800s from near Rio de Janeiro, but no one this century has reported a live sighting of the bird.

Profiles

Rufous Piha, *Lipaugus unirufus*, Plate 54a
Three-wattled Bellbird, *Procnias tricarunculata*, Plate 54b
Purple-throated Fruitcrow, *Querula purpurata*, Plate 54c
Snowy Cotinga, *Carpodectes nitidus*, Plate 54d
Masked Tityra, *Tityra semifasciata*, Plate 55a

28. American Flycatchers

The *American flycatchers* comprise a huge group of passerine birds that is broadly distributed over most habitats from Alaska and northern Canada to the southern tip of South America. The flycatcher family, Tyrannidae, is considered among the most diverse of avian groups. With about 380 species, flycatchers usually contribute a hefty percentage of the avian biodiversity in every locale. For instance, it has been calculated that flycatchers make up fully one tenth of the land bird species in South America, and perhaps one-quarter of Argentinian species. Even in relatively tiny Costa Rica, the group is represented by a healthy contingent of about 75 species.

Flycatchers range in length from 6.5 to 30 cm (2.5 to 12 in). At the smallest extreme are some of the world's tiniest birds, weighing, it is difficult to believe, only some 7 g (1/4 oz). Bills are usually broad and flat, the better to snatch flying bugs from the air. Tail length is variable, but some species have very long, forked tails, which probably aid the birds in their rapid, acrobatic, insect-catching maneuvers. Most flycatchers are dully turned out in shades of gray, brown, and olive-green; many species have some yellow in their plumage, and a relatively few are quite flashily attired in, for example, bright expanses of red or vermilion. One set of frequently seen flycatchers, the best known of which is the GREAT KISKADEE (Plate 55), share a common, bright color scheme, with yellow chests and bellies, and black and white striped heads. A great many of the smaller, drabber flycatchers, clad in olives and browns, are extremely difficult to tell apart in the field, even for experienced birdwatchers. Flycatcher sexes are usually similar in size and coloring.

Natural History
Ecology and Behavior

Flycatchers are common over a large array of different habitat types, from mountainsides high in the Andes and in Costa Rica's Cordillera de Talamanca, to lowland moist forests, to treeless plains and grasslands, to marshes and mangrove swamps; they are especially prevalent in rainforests. As their name implies, most flycatchers are insectivores, obtaining most of their food by employing the classic flycatching technique: they perch motionless on tree or shrub branches or on fences or telephone wires, then dart out in short, swift flights to snatch from the air insects foolhardy enough to enter their field of vision; they then return time and again to the same perch to repeat the process. Many flycatchers also take insects from foliage as they fly through vegetation, and many supplement their diets with berries and seeds. Some of the larger flycatchers will also take small frogs and lizards, and some, such as the GREAT KISKADEE, consider small fish and tadpoles delicacies to be plucked from shallow edges of lakes and rivers. A few, such as the OCHRE-BELLIED FLYCATCHER (Plate 57), have ceded flycatching to their relatives and eat only fruit. Almost all of the relatively few flycatchers that have been studied inhabit exclusive territories that mated pairs defend for all or part of the year.

Breeding

Flycatchers are mainly monogamous. Some forest-dwelling species, however, breed *promiscuously*: groups of males call and display repeatedly at traditional courting sites called *leks*, attracting females that approach for mating but then depart to nest and raise young by themselves. Many flycatchers are known for spectacular courtship displays, males showing off to females by engaging in aerial acrobatics, including flips and somersaults. In monogamous species, males may help the females build nests. Some build cup nests, roofed nests, or globular hanging nests placed in trees or shrubs, others construct mud nests that they attach to vertical surfaces such as rock walls, and some nest in holes in trees or rocks. Tropical flycatchers generally lay 2 eggs that are incubated by the female only for 12 to 23 days; nestlings fledge when 14 to 28 days old.

Ecological Interactions

Some flycatchers show marked alterations in their lifestyles as seasons, locations, and feeding opportunities change. Such ongoing capacity for versatile behavior in response to changing environments is considered a chief underlying cause of the group's great ecological success. An excellent example is the EASTERN KINGBIRD'S drastic changes in behavior between summer and winter. Breeding during summer in North America, these flycatchers are extremely aggressive in defending their territories from birds and other animals, and they feed exclusively at that time on insects. But a change comes over the birds during the winter, as they idle away the months in South America's Amazon Basin. There, Eastern Kingbirds congregate in large, nonterritorial flocks with apparently nomadic existences, and they eat mostly fruit.

Some small flycatchers, known as *tody flycatchers* (for example, Plate 57), construct large, hanging, woven, or "felted," nests that take up to a month or more to build. These nests tend to hang from slender vines or weak tree branches, which provides a degree of safety from climbing nest predators such as snakes and small mammals. Often, however, such efforts are ineffective – nest predation rates are quite high. In response, some of the tody flycatchers purposefully build their nests near to colonies of stinging bees, apparently seeking additional protection from predators.

Lore and Notes

Of all the groups of birds, it is probably among the flycatchers that the most undiscovered species remain. This distinction is owing to the group's great diversity, its penetration into essentially all terrestrial habitats, and the inconspicuousness of many of its members. In fact, as people reach previously inaccessible locations – hidden valleys, cloud-draped mountain plateaus – in the remotest parts of South America, previously unknown flycatchers are indeed sighted. One new species was first identified in 1976 in northern Peru, and another, weighing only 7 g (¼ oz), was found in southern Peru in 1981. Two more new species were first described in the scientific literature in 1997.

Status

The COCOS FLYCATCHER is endemic to Costa Rica's Cocos Island and is now considered vulnerable to threat, as is the country's TAWNY-CHESTED FLY-CATCHER. No other Central American flycatchers are known to be in trouble. At least 6 South American species are presently endangered, including especially the very rare ASH-BREASTED TIT-TYRANT, which is confined to small, wooded patches of Peru and adjacent Bolivia.

Profiles

Tropical Kingbird, *Tyrannus melancholicus*, Plate 55b
Great Kiskadee, *Pitangus sulphuratus*, Plate 55c
Boat-billed Flycatcher, *Megarhynchus pitangua*, Plate 55d
Social Flycatcher, *Myiozetetes similis*, Plate 56a
Gray-capped Flycatcher, *Myiozetetes granadensis*, Plate 56b
Brown-crested Flycatcher, *Myiarchus tyrannulus*, Plate 56c
Dusky-capped Flycatcher, *Myiarchus tuberculifer*, Plate 56d
Ochre-bellied Flycatcher, *Mionectes oleagineus*, Plate 57a
Common Tody Flycatcher, *Todirostrum cinereum*, Plate 57b
Scissor-tailed Flycatcher, *Tyrannus forficatus*, Plate 57c
Long-tailed Tyrant, *Colonia colonus*, Plate 57d

29. Wrens

Wrens are small brownish passerines with an active, snappish manner and, characteristically, upraised tails. The approximately 60 wren species comprise the family Troglodytidae, a group for the most part confined in distribution to the Western Hemisphere. Among other traits, wrens are renowned for their singing ability, vocal duets, and nesting behavior. They range in length from 10 to 20 cm (4 to 8 in) and usually appear mainly in shades of brown or reddish brown, with smaller bits of tan, gray, black, and white. Some of these birds are tiny, weighing in at less than 15 g, or half an ounce. Wings and tails are frequently embellished with finely barred patterns. Wrens have rather broad, short wings and owing to this, are considered poor flyers. The sexes look alike. Wren's tails may be the group's most distinguishing feature, much of the time being held stiffly upright, at military attention. Tails are waved back and forth during displays, both those for courtship and aggression.

Natural History
Ecology and Behavior

Wrens are cryptically colored and fairly secretive in their habits as they flip, flutter, hop, and poke around the low levels of the forest, and through thickets, grasslands, and marshes, searching for insects. They are completely *insectivorous* or nearly so. Often spending the year living in pairs, they defend territories in which during the breeding season they will nest. Some of the larger wrens, such as the RUFOUS-NAPED WREN (Plate 58), spend their days in small family flocks, and, owing to their size, are a bit bolder in their movements. After they have been used for breeding, wrens will use their nests as roosting places – or "dormitories," as one researcher puts it. The vocalizations of wrens have been studied extensively. A pair will call back and forth as they lose sight of each other while foraging in thickets, keeping in contact. In some species, mated pairs sing some of the bird world's most complex duets, male and female rapidly alternating in giving parts of one song (as we think of it), so rapidly and expertly that it actually sounds as if one individual utters the entire sequence. Such duets probably function as "keep-out" signals, warning away from the pair's territory other members of the species, and in maintaining the pair-bond between mated birds. Other wrens, such as the WINTER WREN, have amazingly complex songs, long trains of notes in varied sequences up to 10 seconds or more in duration; researchers place these vocalizations at the very pinnacle of bird song complexity.

Breeding

The wrens of Central America are mainly monogamous, but some breed *cooperatively*, with members of the small family group helping out at the single nest of the parents. Nests, generally of woven grass, are placed in vegetation or in tree cavities. They are small but elaborate nests, roofed, with inconspicuous side entrances. Intriguingly, in some species the male builds many more nests on his territory than his mate (or mates, in polygynous species) can use, apparently as a courtship signal, perhaps as an inducement for a female to stay and mate. Only the female incubates the 2 to 5 eggs, for 13 to 19 days. Sometimes she is fed by the male during this period. Nestlings are fed by both parents for 14 to 19 days, until fledging. Most wren breeding in Costa Rica occurs from March to August.

Ecological Interactions

Some wrens, including the RUFOUS-NAPED, enjoy a commensal relationship with ants. They often place their nests in cactus or acacia plants that serve as residences for ant colonies. The ants do not bother the birds and *vice versa*, yet the birds' nests bask in the ants' formidable protective powers against such possible egg and nestling predators as snakes and small mammals.

Lore and Notes

The HOUSE WREN (Plate 58) has all but abandoned breeding in its forgotten natural haunts and now, quite profitably, associates itself with people. These birds root about near and in human settlements, looking for insects. Nests are often placed in crannies and crevices within buildings or other structures. (Many wrens nest in naturally occurring cavities, hence the family name, Troglodytidae, or *cave dweller*.) The bird has been so successful living with people that it is quite common throughout its range, from Canada to the southern tip of South America.

Status

Most of the 20 or so wren species that occur in Costa Rica are fairly or very abundant; none are threatened. A few Mexican species are considered vulnerable to threat, owing to small and/or declining populations. Only a few wrens are known to be endangered: Cuba's ZAPATA WREN and Colombia's APOLINAR'S and NICE-FORO'S WRENS.

Profiles

Rufous-naped Wren, *Campylorhynchus rufinucha*, Plate 58a
Banded-backed Wren, *Campylorhynchus zonatus*, Plate 58b
Gray-breasted Wood-wren, *Henicorhina leucophrys*, Plate 58c
White-breasted Wood-wren, *Henicorhina leucosticta*, Plate 58d
House Wren, *Troglodytes aedon*, Plate 58e

30. Thrushes

The more than 300 species of *thrushes* inhabit most terrestrial regions of the world and include some of the most familiar park and garden birds. The family, Turdidae, has few defining, common features that set all its members apart from other groups, as perhaps could be expected; so large an assemblage of species is sure to include a significant amount of variation in appearance, ecology, and behavior. Thrushes as a group are tremendously successful birds, especially when they have adapted to living near humans and benefitting from their environmental modifications. Most obviously, on five continents, a thrush is among the most common and recognizable garden birds, including North America's AMERICAN ROBIN, Europe's REDWING and BLACKBIRD, and Central America's CLAY-COLORED ROBIN (Plate 59). Thrushes of the Western Hemisphere are slender-billed birds that range from 12.5 to 31 cm (5 to 12 in) in length. Generally they are not brightly colored; instead, they come in drab browns, grays, brown-reds, olive, and black and white. The sexes are very similar in appearance. During their first year of life, young thrushes are clad in distinctively spotted plumages.

Natural History
Ecology and Behavior

Among the thrushes are species that employ a variety of feeding methods and that take several different food types. Many eat fruits, some are primarily *insectivorous*, and most are at least moderately *omnivorous*. Although arboreal birds, many thrushes frequently forage on the ground for insects, other arthropods, and, a particular favorite, delicious earthworms. The thrushes associated with gardens and lawns in Costa Rica usually forage like the familiar thrushes from North America or Europe – they hop and walk along the ground, stopping at intervals, cocking their heads to peer downwards. These birds are residents of many kinds of habitats – forest edge, clearings, and other open areas such as shrub areas and grasslands, gardens, parks, suburban lawns, and agricultural areas. Many thrushes are quite social, spending their time during the nonbreeding season in flocks of the same species, feeding and roosting together. Some of the tropical thrushes make seasonal migrations from higher to lower elevations, following abundant food supplies.

Breeding

Thrushes breed monogamously, male and female together defending exclusive territories during the breeding season; pairs may associate year round. Nests, usually built by the female and placed in tree branches, shrubs, or crevices, are cup-shaped, made of grass, moss, and like materials, and often lined with mud. Two to 6 eggs (usually 2 or 3) are incubated by the female only for 12 to 14 days. Young are fed by both parents for 12 to 16 days prior to fledging. Most breeding occurs within the period from March through July.

Lore and Notes

English colonists in the New World gave the AMERICAN ROBIN, a thrush, its name because it resembled England's common ROBIN – both birds have reddish breasts. The New World bird, however, is more closely related to Europe's BLACK-BIRD, also a common garden bird and a true thrush. Not content with incorrectly labeling birds that were new to them with English names, British settlers around the world, homesick, it is thought, imported birds from the British Isles to their new domains so that familiar birds would surround their new homes. The effects on native birds were often disastrous, and European thrushes such as the SONG THRUSH and BLACKBIRD, among many other birds, are now naturalized, dominant citizens of, for instance, Australia and New Zealand.

Status

Although several thrushes in many different parts of the world are vulnerable to threat or are now considered threatened, none of the 11 species that breed in Costa Rica are in imminent danger. One, the BLACK-FACED SOLITAIRE (Plate 59), has suffered recent population declines in accessible areas, probably owing to poaching of the bird for the pet trade: these birds are famous in Costa Rica owing to their superior singing abilities.

Profiles

Sooty Robin, *Turdus nigrescens*, Plate 59a
Clay-colored Robin, *Turdus grayi*, Plate 59b
Black-faced Solitaire, *Myadestes melanops*, Plate 59c

31. Jays and Silky-flycatchers

Jays are members of the Corvidae, a passerine family of a hundred or so species that occurs just about everywhere in the world – or, as ecologists would say, corvid distribution is *cosmopolitan*. The group includes the *crows, ravens,* and *magpies.* Although on many continents birds of open habitats, jays of the Neotropics are primarily woodland or forest birds. Jays, aside from being strikingly handsome birds, are known for their versatility, adaptability, and for their seeming intelligence; in several ways, the group is considered by ornithologists to be the most highly developed of birds. They are also usually quite noisy.

Members of the family range in length from 20 to 71 cm (8 to 28 in), many near the higher end – large for passerine birds. *Corvids* have robust, fairly long bills and strong legs and feet. Many corvids (crows, ravens, rooks, jackdaws) are all or mostly black, but the jays are different, being attired in bright blues, purples, greens, yellows, and white. American jays tend to be blue, and many have conspicuous crests (like North America's BLUE JAY and STELLER'S JAY). Costa Rica's BROWN JAY (Plate 60) is an exception among Neotropical jays, being plain brown and white and crest-less; owing to this, even researchers that work with the bird affectionately refer to it as the most homely of the group. In corvids, the sexes generally look alike. The COMMON RAVEN is the largest passerine bird, but although its range encompasses several continents, it does not extend to Costa Rica.

The LONG-TAILED SILKY-FLYCATCHER (Plate 60) is in a small family (Ptilogonatidae) separate from the jays; two of four species occur in Costa Rica.

Natural History
Ecology and Behavior

Jays eat a large variety of foods (and try to eat many others) and so are considered *omnivores*. They feed on the ground, but also in trees, taking bird eggs and nestlings, carrion, insects (including some in flight), and fruits and nuts. Bright and versatile, they are quick to take advantage of new food sources and to find food in agricultural and other human-altered environments. Jays use their feet to hold food down while tearing it with their bills. Hiding food for later consumption, *caching*, is practiced widely by the group.

Corvids are usually quite social, Costa Rican jays being no exception. Both WHITE-THROATED MAGPIE-JAYS and BROWN JAYS (Plate 60) remain all year in small groups of relatives, 5 to 10 individuals strong, that forage together within a restricted area, or *home range*, and at the appropriate time, breed together on a group-defended territory. Both species prefer to inhabit more open wooded areas, forest edges, fields, plantations, and habitat along waterways and near human settlements. Jays are raucous and noisy, giving varieties of harsh, grating, loud calls (some that sound like *jay*) as the foraging flock straggles from tree to tree.

Breeding

Both WHITE-THROATED MAGPIE-JAYS and BROWN JAYS breed cooperatively. Generally the oldest pair in the group breeds and the other members serve only as *helpers*, assisting in nest construction and feeding the young. Courtship feeding is common, the male feeding the female before and during incubation, which she performs alone. Bulky, open nests, constructed primarily of twigs, are placed in trees or rock crevices. Two to 7 eggs are incubated for 16 to 21 days, the young then being fed in the nest by parents and helpers for 20 to 24 days. Most breeding is accomplished from February through June.

Ecological Interactions

Jays and other corvids are often scavengers. Other carrion-eating birds exist, such as vultures, but jays and crows and their relatives contribute a good deal to breaking down dead animals so that the nutrients bound up in them are recycled into food webs. (And where there are roads, civic-minded corvids assist highway departments in keeping them clear of automobile-killed animals.)

Corvids' omnivory also drives them to be predators on bird nests – generally on species that are smaller than they are, of which there are many. Jays, crows and magpies tear up nests and eat eggs and nestlings. They are considered to be responsible for a significant percentage of the nest predation on many songbird species, particularly those with open-cup nests.

Owing to their seed caching behavior, jays are important to trees as dispersal agents. In the USA, for example, the BLUE JAY'S acorn-burying habit must surely result in the maintenance and spread of oak forests.

Lore and Notes

Although considered by many to be among the most intelligent of birds, and by ornithologists as among the most highly evolved, corvid folklore is rife with tales of crows, ravens and magpies as symbols of ill-omen. This undoubtedly traces to the group's frequent all-black plumage and habit of eating carrion, both sinister traits. Ravens, in particular, have long been associated in many Northern cultures with evil or death, although these large, powerful birds also figure more benignly in Nordic and Middle Eastern mythology. Several groups of indigenous peoples of northwestern North America consider the COMMON RAVEN sacred and sometimes, indeed, as a god.

Status

Some of the five jays that occur in Costa Rica are fairly rare, but none are considered threatened. Many corvids adjust well to people's activities, indeed often expanding their ranges when they can feed on agricultural crops. Four corvids are endangered: two species endemic to small regions of Mexico and two Pacific island species – the HAWAIIAN and MARIANA CROWS (both USA ESA listed).

Profiles

White-throated Magpie-jay, *Calocitta formosa*, Plate 60a
Brown Jay, *Cyanocorax morio*, Plate 60b
Azure-hooded Jay, *Cyanolyca cucullata*, Plate 60c
Long-tailed Silky-flycatcher, *Ptilogonys caudatus*, Plate 60d

32. Warblers and Other Small, Flitting Birds

Birdwatchers and perhaps other users of this book realize that there are a large number of tiny birds that flit about trees, shrubs, thickets, and grasslands, birds that go by such names as *vireo, warbler, gnatcatcher, yellowthroat, redstart*. For good reasons, these birds are treated here only lightly. Owing to their sizes and agile natures, they are often difficult to identify, even for journeymen birdwatchers. Although they are beautiful little birds, even experienced birders sometimes despair of trying to differentiate the various species. Also, American warblers are common birds of North America, and so are not in any way exotic to travellers from that continent. In fact, many of the warblers seen in Costa Rica, particularly from November through March, are breeders from North America, escaping the northern cold to winter in the tropics. Warblers are also more important birds in North than in Central America, in the sense that they are often so diverse and numerous in many northern forest habitats that, as a group, they make up more of the birdlife than all other birds combined. But for our purposes here, brief descriptions of a few of these birds will suffice. When one's interest is sufficiently peaked by these tiny birds to warrant further exploration, it is time to consider oneself a birdwatcher and to invest in a professional field guide!

Warblers, gnatcatchers, and the BANANAQUIT (Plate 62) are very small birds that flit and move jauntily about in trees, shrubs, and gardens, for the most part searching for or pursuing their dietary staple, insects. American warblers (Subfamily Parulinae, classified with the sparrows and tanagers in Family Emberizidae), also known as *wood warblers*, are a group of approximately 110 species, with wide distributions over the New World's forests, fields, marshes, and gardens. About 50 species occur in Costa Rica, many of them seasonal migrants from North American breeding sites. Warblers are brightly colored, predominantly yellow or greenish, often mixed with varying amounts of gray, black and white; a few have even more color, with patches of red, orange or blue. Gnatcatchers are members of a large, primarily Old World family, Sylviidae. There are 11 gnatcatcher species, tiny gray birds that flit about in wooded and forest edge areas; 2 species occur in Costa Rica. The Bananaquit, which is either lumped into the war-

bler group or is the only member of its own subfamily, Coerebinae (its classifica-
tion is controversial), is a tiny yellow and olive/grayish bird with a broad
Neotropical distribution: from southern Mexico and the Caribbean to northern
Argentina.

Natural History
Ecology and Behavior
These birds are commonly found in a variety of natural habitats and in gardens
and plantations. They forage in lively fashion mainly for insects and spiders;
many also pierce berries to drink juice and some partake of nectar from flowers.
Several species, such as the BUFF-RUMPED WARBLER and TROPICAL GNAT-
CATCHER (Plates 61, 62), energetically move their tails up and down or side-to-
side as they forage. Many warblers typically join *mixed species feeding flocks* (see p.
157) with other small songbirds such as honeycreepers and tanagers. Warblers
generally are territorial birds: either during the breeding season (in migratory
species) or year-round (in nonmigratory, purely tropical, species) a male and a
female defend a piece of real estate from other members of the species. Some tropical warblers and the Tropical Gnatcatcher remain paired throughout the year. For
the most part, warblers that remain all year in the tropics reside at middle and
high elevations, whereas migratory warblers are found at a variety of elevations.
Unusual among birds, BANANAQUITS build not only breeding nests, but also
lighter, domed *dormitory* nests, which they sleep in individually.

Breeding
Warblers, gnatcatchers, and the BANANAQUIT are monogamous, but partners do
not necessarily make equal contributions to breeding efforts. Warblers build open
cup or roofed nests in trees or bushes, but sometimes on the ground. Often the
female alone builds the nest and incubates the 2 to 3 eggs for 14 to 17 days; the
male may feed his incubating mate. Young fledge after 8 to 15 days in the nest.
Gnatcatchers build cup nests several meters up in trees, weaving together vegetation, moss, and spider web. Both sexes build the nest, incubate the 2 to 3 eggs for
13 to 15 days, and feed chicks, which fledge 11 to 14 days after hatching. Both
Bananaquit sexes build the round, domed, breeding nest. Only the female incubates the 2 to 3 eggs, for 12 to 13 days. Both parents feed the chicks in the nest
for 17 to 19 days by regurgitating food to them.

Ecological Interactions
For many years, North American scientists interested in warblers and many other
songbirds concentrated their research on the birds' ecology and behavior during
breeding, essentially ignoring the fact that the birds spent half of each year wintering in the tropics, many of them in Central America. Now, with the realization
that the birds' biology during the nonbreeding season is also important for understanding their lives, their ecology and behavior during the winter have become
areas of intense interest. Being addressed in research studies are such questions as:
are species that are territorial during breeding also territorial on their wintering
grounds, and if so, in what way? Do individual birds return to the same spot in
the tropics each year in winter as they do for nesting during the North American
spring? Do migratory birds compete for food on their wintering grounds with
those species that remain all year in the tropics? Are the highly colored plumages
of many migratory birds more of use in signalling to other birds on the breeding
or wintering grounds?

Status

No warblers or gnatcatchers that occur in Costa Rica are known to be threatened. Three notable warblers now in trouble (all are USA ESA listed) are KIRTLAND'S WARBLER, which breeds in the USA (Michigan) and winters in the Bahamas, SEMPER'S WARBLER, which occurs only on the Caribbean island of St. Lucia, and BACHMAN'S WARBLER, which breeds in southeastern USA and winters in Cuba. Kirtland's Warbler, which nests only in stands of young Jack-pine trees, has been victimized by its own specialization on one type of breeding habitat combined with a shrinking availability of that habitat, by destruction of its wintering habitat, and by BROWN-HEADED COWBIRDS, which lay their eggs in the nests of warblers and other species, reducing their reproductive success (see p. 173). It is suspected that mongooses, which were introduced to St. Lucia by people and which are predators on bird nests, play a major role in endangering Semper's Warbler, which nests on or near the ground. Several other American warbler species are probably now at risk, but there is at present insufficient information about their populations to judge their statuses with any certainty.

Profiles

Buff-rumped Warbler, *Phaeothlypis fulvicauda*, Plate 61a
Three-striped Warbler, *Basileuterus tristriatus*, Plate 61b
Chestnut-sided Warbler, *Dendroica pensylvanica*, Plate 61c
Tennessee Warbler, *Vermivora peregrina*, Plate 61d
Slate-throated Redstart, *Myioborus miniatus*, Plate 61e
Bananaquit, *Coereba flaveola*, Plate 62a
Tropical Gnatcatcher, *Polioptila plumbea*, Plate 62b

33. Blackbirds and Orioles

Diversity is the key to comprehending the American orioles and blackbirds. The passerine subfamily Icterinae includes about 95 species, which partition neatly into very different groups called *blackbirds, caciques (kah-SEE-kays), cowbirds, grackles, meadowlarks, orioles,* and *oropendolas*; they vary extensively in size, coloring, ecology, and behavior. These *icterines* are highly successful and conspicuous birds throughout their range, which encompasses all of North, Central, and South America. Distinguishing this varied assemblage from other birds are a jaunty deportment and a particular feeding method not widely used by other birds, known as *gaping* – a bird places its closed bill into crevices or under leaves, rocks or other objects, then forces the bill open, exposing the previously hidden space to its prying eyes and hunger. Most icterines are tropical in distribution and about 20 species, a few of which are seasonal migrants from the north, occur in Costa Rica. The icterine group inhabits marshes and almost all types of terrestrial habitats, and occupies warm lowland areas, middle elevations, as well as colder, mountainous regions. Many of these birds have adapted well to human settlements and are common denizens of gardens, parks, and urban and agricultural areas. The wide ranges of sizes, shapes, colors, mating systems, and breeding behaviors of these birds attract frequent interest from avian researchers.

Grackles, common in city areas, are primarily black birds with slender bills and, usually, long tails. Blackbirds are often marsh-dwellers (the term "blackbirds" is also sometimes used as a synonym for the entire icterine group, as in "the New World Blackbirds"). Orioles are small, bright, often exquisitely marked birds in yellow or orange mixed with black and white, whose preferred habitat is forest.

Meadowlarks are yellow, black, and brown grassland birds. Oropendolas are spectacular, larger birds of tropical forests and woodlands that often breed in colonies. Caciques, which also breed in colonies, are smaller, sleeker black birds, frequently with red or yellow rumps and yellow bills. Finally, cowbirds, usually quite inconspicuous in various shades of brown and black, have a dark family (or subfamily) secret – they are *brood parasites*.

Icterines range in length from 15 to 56 cm (6 to 22 in) – medium to fairly large-sized birds. Bills are usually sharply pointed and conical. Black is the predominant plumage color in the group, but many combine black with bright reds, yellows, or oranges. In some species, the sexes are alike (particularly in the tropical species), but in others, females look very different from males, often more cryptically outfitted in browns, grays, or streaked plumage. Pronounced size differences between the sexes, females being smaller, are common; male oropendolas, for instance, may weigh twice as much as females. Bills and eyes are sometimes brightly colored.

Natural History
Ecology and Behavior
Icterines occur in all sorts of habitat types – woodlands, thickets, grassland, marshes, forest edges, and the higher levels of closed forests – but they are especially prevalent in more open areas. Their regular occupation of marshes has always been viewed as interesting, as they are not obviously adapted for living in aquatic environments – they do not have webbed feet, for example, nor are they able to float or dive. They eat a wide variety of foods including insects and other small animals, fruit and seeds. Some are fairly omnivorous, as befitting birds that frequently become scavengers in urban and suburban settings. A common feature of the group is that seed-eaters (granivores) during the nonbreeding periods become insectivorous during breeding, and feed insects to the young. Gaping for food is frequent and will be seen repeatedly if one observes these birds for any length of time. Orioles and caciques join in mixed-species foraging flocks; in a single fruit tree one may see two or more oriole species feeding with several species of tanagers, honeycreepers, and others. Caciques often associate with oropendolas, fruitcrows, and other birds in foraging flocks. Outside of the breeding season, icterines, particularly the blackbirds and grackles, typically gather in large, sometimes enormous, flocks that can cause damage to roosting areas and agricultural crops.

Breeding
Icterine species pursue a variety of breeding strategies. Some, such as the orioles, breed in classically monogamous pairs, male and female defending a large territory in which the hanging pouch nest is situated. But others, including many caciques and the oropendolas, nest in colonies. The members of an oropendola colony weave large, bag-like or pouch-like nests that hang from the ends of tree branches, many on the same tree. In a rare form of non-monogamous breeding, 3 to 10 male MONTEZUMA'S OROPENDOLAS (Plate 63) establish a colony in a tree (often an isolated one) and defend a group of 10 to 30 females that will mate and nest in the colony. The males engage in fighting and aggressive displays, competing among themselves to mate with the females. Detailed observations in Costa Rica showed that the most dominant males (the *alpha* animals) in each colony, usually heavier males, obtained up to 90% of all matings, and therefore, were the fathers of most of the colony's young. Caciques, also with pouch-like nests, breed either solitarily in the forest or in colonies. In one study it was noted

that each cacique in a colony tries to locate its nest toward the center of the colony, presumably because there is less of a chance of suffering nest predation at the colony's center. Perhaps most intriguing to scientists that study mating systems is that some very closely related icterine species have very different mating systems and breeding behaviors.

Icterine nests range from hanging pouches woven from grasses and other plant materials to open cups lined with mud to roofed nests built on the ground, hidden in meadow grass. Nests are almost always built by females. The female also incubates the 2 to 3 eggs, for 11 to 14 days, while the male guards the nest. Nestlings are fed for 10 to 30 days either by both parents (monogamous species) or primarily by the female (polygamous species).

Most of the cowbirds are brood parasites, building no nests themselves. Rather, females, after mating with one or more males, lay their eggs, up to 14 or more per season, in the nests of other species – other icterines as well as other birds – and let "host" species raise their young (see below).

Ecological Interactions

Breeding colonies of caciques and oropendolas are often located in trees that contain or are near large bee or wasp nests. The wasps or bees swarm in large numbers around the birds' nests. Apparently the birds benefit from this close association because the aggressiveness the stinging insects show toward animals that try to raid the birds' hanging nests offers a measure of protection.

As are many cuckoo species, especially those of the Old World, 5 of the 6 species of cowbirds are brood parasites – including North America's BROWN-HEADED COWBIRD and Costa Rica's GIANT and BRONZED COWBIRDS (Plate 64). In these species, a female, the parasite, lays eggs in the nests of other species, the hosts, and her young are raised by the foster parents. Some of the cowbirds specialize on icterine hosts – the Giant Cowbird parasitizes only caciques and oropendolas. Some host species have evolved the abilities to recognize cowbird eggs and eject them from their nests, but others have not. The cowbirds benefit from the interaction by being freed from defending a nesting territory and from nest-building and tending chores – what must amount to significant savings of energy and also decreased exposure to predators. The host species suffer reproductive harm because a female cowbird often ejects a host egg when she lays her own (when the nest is left unguarded). Also, more often than not, the cowbird's young are larger than the host's own, and are thus able to out-compete them for food brought to the nest by the adult birds. The host's own young often starve or are significantly weakened. Because of these harmful effects, the very successful cowbirds are believed to be responsible for severe population declines in North America of several species of small passerine birds. Because one population in these interactions benefits and one is harmed, the relationships between cowbirds and their hosts is parasitic – social parasitism in this case. How can brood parasitic behavior arise? Evolutionary biologists posit that one way would be if, long ago, some female cowbirds that built nests had their nests destroyed mid-way through their laying period. With an egg to lay but no nest in which to place it, females in this situation may have deposited the eggs in the nests of other species, which subsquently raised the cowbird young.

Status

The icterine group includes some of the most abundant birds of the Western Hemisphere, such as RED-WINGED BLACKBIRDS and COMMON GRACKLES. Of the Costa Rican icterines, only the YELLOW-TAILED ORIOLE bears close monitoring: its populations have been severely reduced because it is hunted as a prized cage bird. Also, the NICARAGUAN GRACKLE in Costa Rica is considered by some to be near-threatened. Several icterines are currently endangered: Puerto Rico's YELLOW-SHOULDERED BLACKBIRD (USA ESA listed), Brazil's FORBE'S BLACK-BIRD, and Martinique's MARTINIQUE ORIOLE. A few others in South America are threatened from combinations of habitat destruction, brood parasitism, and the pet trade.

Profiles

Streak-backed Oriole, *Icterus pustulatus*, Plate 62c
Baltimore Oriole, *Icterus galbula*, Plate 62d
Montezuma's Oropendola, *Psarocolius montezuma*, Plate 63a
Chestnut-headed Oropendola. *Psarocolius wagleri*, Plate 63b
Scarlet-rumped Cacique, *Cacicus uropygialis*, Plate 63c
Yellow-billed Cacique, *Amblycercus holosericeus*, Plate 63d
Bronzed Cowbird, *Molothrus aeneus*, Plate 64a
Great-tailed Grackle, *Quiscalus mexicanus*, Plate 64b

34. Tanagers

Tanagers comprise a large New World group of beautifully colored, small passerine birds, most of which are limited to tropical areas. They are among the tropics' most common and visible birds, primarily owing to their habit of associating in *mixed-species flocks* that gather in the open, often near human habitation, to feed in fruit trees, and they are a treat to watch. All told, there are some 230 species of tanagers (Family Emberizidae, Subfamily Thraupinae), the group including the *typical tanagers,* the *honeycreepers,* and the *euphonias.* Some of the tanagers migrate north or south to breed in temperate areas of North and South America (four breed in the USA, including the WESTERN TANAGER, among the most colorful of North American birds). Tanagers inhabit all forested and shrubby areas of the American tropics, over a wide range of elevations, and are particularly numerous in wet forests and forest edge areas. Not devotees of the dark forest interior, they prefer the lighter, upper levels of the forest canopy and more open areas; some prefer low, brushy habitat.

Tanagers vary from 9 to 28 cm (3.5 to 11 in) in length, with most concentrated near the smaller end of the range. They are compact birds with fairly short and thick bills and short to medium-long tails. Tanagers' outstanding physical attribute is their bright coloring – they are strikingly marked with patches of color that traverse the entire spectrum, rendering the group among the most fabulously attired of birds. It has been said of the typical tanagers (genus *Tangara*) that they must "exhaust the color patterns possible on sparrow-sized birds" (F.G. Stiles and A.F. Skutch 1989). Yellows, reds, blues and greens predominate, although a relatively few species buck the trend and appear in plain blacks, browns, or grays. The sexes usually look alike. Euphonias are small, stout tanagers, whose appearances, all species being slightly different, revolve around a common theme: blue-black above, with yellow foreheads, breasts, and bellies. Honeycreepers are also usually brilliantly colored, although the Costa Rican representatives of the group are mostly green.

Natural History
Ecology and Behavior
Most tanager species associate in mixed-species tanager flocks usually together with other types of birds; finding five or more tanager species in a single group is common. A mixed flock will settle in a tree full of ripe fruit and enjoy a meal. These flocks move through forests or more open areas, searching for fruit-laden trees. Although tanagers mostly eat fruit, some also take insects from foliage or even out of the air. And although most species are arboreal, a few are specialized ground foragers, taking seeds and bugs. Tanagers usually go after small fruits that can be swallowed whole, such as berries, plucking the fruit while perched. After plucking it, a tanager rotates the fruit a bit in its bill, then mashes it and swallows. (Ecologists divide frugivorous birds into *mashers*, such as tanagers, and *gulpers*, such as trogons and toucans, which swallow fruit whole and intact.) One explanation is that mashing permits the bird to enjoy the sweet juice prior to swallowing the rest of the fruit. This fits with the idea that mashers select fruit based partially on taste, whereas gulpers, which swallow intact fruit, do not (D.J. Levey *et al.* 1994).

Some tanagers, such as the *ant-tanagers*, are frequent members of mixed-species flocks (along with antbirds, woodcreepers and others) that spend their days following army ant swarms, feeding on insects that rush from cover at the approach of the devastating ants (see p. 157). Euphonias specialize on mistletoe berries, but eat other fruits and some insects as well. The honeycreepers are tanagers that are specialized for nectar feeding, their bills and tongues modified to punch holes in flower bottoms and suck out nectar; they also feed on some fruits and insects.

Some tanagers are altitudinal migrants, seasonally moving to higher or lower elevation habitats.

Breeding
Most tanagers appear to breed monogamously, although a number of bigamists have been noted (BLUE-GRAY and SCARLET-RUMPED TANAGERS, Plate 64, among them). Breeding is concentrated from February to June, during the transition from dry to wet season, when fruit and insects are most plentiful. In many species, male and female stay paired throughout the year. Males of many species give food to females in *nuptial feeding*, and during courtship displays make sure that potential mates see their brightly colored patches. Either the female alone or the pair builds a cup nest in a tree or shrub. Two eggs are incubated by the female only for 12 to 18 days and young are fed by both parents for 12 to 18 days prior to their fledging. A pair of tiny euphonias build a nest with a roof and a side entrance, often within a bromeliad plant.

Ecological Interactions
Tanagers, as *mashing* frugivores, sometimes drop the largest seeds from the fruits they consume before swallowing but, nonetheless, many seeds are ingested; consequently, these birds are active seed dispersers (see Close-Up, p. 179). Some ecologists believe tanagers to be among the most common dispersers of tropical trees and shrubs, that is, they are responsible for dropping the seeds that grow into the trees and shrubs that populate the areas they inhabit. Euphonias, for example, are crucial for the mistletoe life cycle because, after eating the berries, they deposit their seed-bearing droppings on tree branches, where the seeds germinate, the mistletoe plants starting out there as epiphytes.

Some of the tanager species form groups that replace each other ecologically with changing altitude. A good example is a set of three look-alike species, all green, yellow, and grayish, the ASHY-THROATED TANAGER, COMMON BUSH-TANAGER (Plate 66), and SOOTY-CAPPED BUSH-TANAGER (Plate 66). The first inhabits more lowland and foothill areas of the Atlantic slope of Costa Rica, the second occupies middle elevations (400 to 2200 m, 1300 to 7200 ft), the third only high mountain areas, from 2000 m (6500 ft) to above timberline.

Lore and Notes

The word *tanager* comes from Brazilian Tupi Indian word *tangara*, which is also used as the genus name for a group of tanagers.

Status

Only one of the Costa Rican tanagers is currently threatened or endangered although the populations of several others have been much reduced in the past few decades owing to forest cutting. The BLACK-CHEEKED ANT-TANAGER, its range limited to Costa Rica, is rare and endangered and it is thought that it soon might be found only in the Osa Peninsula's wooded Corcovado National Park. Another species, the BLUE-AND-GOLD TANAGER, can be considered near-threatened. Fortunately, despite being among tropical America's most beautiful birds, tanagers are not favorites of the international pet trade, probably because they have never been popularized as cage birds outside their native regions. However, several of the euphonias, such as the BLUE-HOODED EUPHONIA, are increasingly scarce and the reason may be that, although they are not hunted for the international trade, they *are* prized as cage birds within Central American countries. Several of South America's tanagers, especially in Brazil, are considered threatened or endangered, primarily owing to habitat loss.

Profiles

Blue-gray Tanager, *Thraupis episcopus*, Plate 64c
Scarlet-rumped Tanager, *Ramphocelus passerinii*, Plate 64d
Yellow-crowned Euphonia, *Euphonia luteicapilla*, Plate 65a
Olive-backed Euphonia, *Euphonia gouldi*, Plate 65b
Scrub Euphonia, *Euphonia affinis*, Plate 65c
Yellow-throated Euphonia, *Euphonia hirundinacea*, Plate 65d
Golden-browed Chlorophonia, *Chlorophonia callophrys*, Plate 66a
Common Bush-tanager, *Chlorospingus ophthalmicus*, Plate 66b
Sooty-capped Bush-tanager, *Chlorospingus pileatus*, Plate 66c
Dusky-faced Tanager, *Mitrospingus cassinii*, Plate 66d
Palm Tanager, *Thraupis palmarum*, Plate 67a
Shining Honeycreeper, *Cyanerpes lucidus*, Plate 67b
Red-legged Honeycreeper, *Cyanerpes cyaneus*, Plate 67c
Scarlet-thighed Dacnis, *Dacnis venusta,* Plate 67d
Silver-throated Tanager, *Tangara icterocephala*, Plate 68a
Green Honeycreeper, *Chlorophanes spiza*, Plate 68b
Speckled Tanager, *Tangara guttata*, Plate 68c
Bay-headed Tanager, *Tangara gyrola*, Plate 68d
Golden-hooded Tanager, *Tangara larvata*, Plate 68e

35. Sparrows and Grosbeaks

The New World *sparrows* and *grosbeaks* are large, diverse groups, totaling about 320 species, that include some of Central America's most common and visible passerine birds. The groups' classification is continually revised, but here we can consider them to be subfamilies within the larger Family Emberizidae: the sparrows, *seedeaters*, *towhees*, and *grassquits* in Subfamily Emberizinae, and the grosbeaks, *saltators*, and *buntings* in Subfamily Cardinalinae. These groups are almost *cosmopolitan* in distribution in the New World, meaning representatives occur just about everywhere, in all kinds of habitats and climates, from Alaska and northern Canada south to Tierra del Fuego. In fact, one species, the SNOW BUNTING, a small black and white bird, breeds farther north than any other land bird, in northern Alaska, Canada, and Greenland.

Sparrows are generally small birds, 9 to 22 cm (3.5 to 9 in) in length, with relatively short, thick, conical bills that are specialized to crush and open seeds. In some species, the upper and lower halves of the bill can be moved from side-to-side, the better to manipulate small seeds. Sparrows have relatively large feet that they use in scratching the ground to find seeds. Coloring varies greatly within the group but the plumage of most is dull brown or grayish, with many sporting streaked backs. The sexes generally look alike.

Natural History
Ecology and Behavior

Sparrows are mostly seed eaters, although many are considered almost omnivorous and even those that specialize on seeds for much of the year often feed insects to their young. Some species also eat fruit. Sparrows in Costa Rica mainly inhabit open areas such as grassland, parkland, brushy areas, and forest edge. They are birds of thickets, bushes, and grasses, foraging mostly on the ground or at low levels in bushes or trees. Because many species spend large amounts of time in thickets and brushy areas, they can be quite inconspicuous.

Most species are strongly territorial, a mated pair aggressively excluding other members of the species from sharply defined areas. In the typical sparrows, pairs often stay together all year; other species within the group often travel in small family groups. Sometimes, territories are defended all year round and almost all available habitat in a region is divided into territories. The result is that those individuals that do not own territories must live furtively on defended territories, always trying to avoid the dominant territory owner, retreating when chased, and waiting for the day when the owner is injured or dies and the territory can be taken over. Only when one of these *floaters* ascends in the hierarchy to territory ownership status can he begin to breed. In species that have this kind of territorial system, such as the common RUFOUS-COLLARED SPARROW (Plate 70), the floater individuals that live secretly on other individual's territories, waiting and watching, were termed by their discoverer an avian *underworld*, and the name has stuck.

Whereas in North America sparrows constitute perhaps the most important group of seed-eating birds, they are less dominant in the Neotropics. Other groups of birds, such as pigeons (see p. 126), occupy more of the seed-eating "niche" in Central American countries than do sparrows and, as a consequence, one encounters sparrows much more often in North than in Central America.

Breeding

Most sparrows are monogamous breeders. The female of the pair usually builds a cup-shaped or, more often in the tropics, a domed nest, from grasses, fine roots and perhaps mosses and lichens. Nests are concealed on the ground or low in a shrub or tree. The female alone incubates 2 to 3 eggs, for 12 to 14 days. Both male and female feed nestlings, which fledge after 10 to 15 days in the nest. Most breeding is accomplished from March through August. Some species, such as the RUFOUS-COLLARED SPARROW, breed almost continually through the year.

Ecological Interactions

HOUSE SPARROWS (Plate 70) are small gray, brown, and black birds that currently enjoy an almost worldwide distribution, living very successfully in close association with humans. Nests are often placed in buildings. Formally, however, this bird is not a New World sparrow at all, but a member of an Old World family, the Passeridae; until recently, it was restricted to the Eastern Hemisphere. How and why these sparrows arrived in the West, and the unintended consequences of their arrival, is a cautionary tale of human interference in the natural distribution of animals. European settlers brought House Sparrows and other garden birds, such as starlings, to North America and released them, so that the animals around their new homes in the New World would resemble the animals they remembered from their old homes, an ocean away. A small number of House Sparrows released on the East Coast of the USA in the 1800s spread to the north, west, and south, and, after rapidly colonizing all of North America, are still spreading. House Sparrows reached Costa Rica in 1974 and are now successfully ensconced there in most urban and suburban areas, where they compete for food with native sparrows, such as RUFOUS-COLLAREDS. Species such as the House Sparrow that, owing to people's machinations, are now distributed outside of their natural ranges are said to be *introduced*, as opposed to naturally occurring species, which are termed *indigenous* or *native*. A species that spreads far beyond its original distribution, whether aided by people or not, is called, in ecological terms, an *invader*.

Lore and Notes

In addition to their reputation for ecological success, the New World sparrows are known especially as a group that is the subject of frequent scientific research, and therefore as one that has contributed substantially to many areas of our knowledge about birds. For instance, studies of North America's SONG SPARROW and the Neotropic's RUFOUS-COLLARED SPARROW provided the basis for much of the information we have about avian territoriality and many other kinds of behavior. Also, the WHITE-CROWNED SPARROW has been the species of choice for many researchers for over 30 years for investigations of bird physiology and the relationships between ecology and physiology.

Status

None of Central America's sparrows or grosbeaks are currently considered threatened. Many are among the most abundant and frequently observed birds in the areas that they inhabit. In Costa Rica, the COCOS FINCH, restricted to Cocos Island, is considered vulnerable to threat. A few sparrows of Mexico and South America are threatened or endangered, as are a few sparrow subspecies in the USA.

Profiles

Buff-throated Saltator, *Saltator maximus*, Plate 69a
Black-faced Grosbeak, *Caryothraustes poliogaster*, Plate 69b
Orange-billed Sparrow, *Arremon aurantiirostris*, Plate 69c
Variable Seedeater, *Sporophila aurita*, Plate 69d
Striped-headed Sparrow, *Aimophila ruficauda*, Plate 70a
Yellow-faced Grassquit, *Tiaris olivacea*, Plate 70b
Rufous-collared Sparrow, *Zonotrichia capensis*, Plate 70c

House Sparrow, *Passer domesticus*, Plate 70d
Black-striped Sparrow, *Arremonops conirostris*, Plate 70e

Environmental Close-Up 3
Frugivory: Animals That Eat Fruit and the Trees That Want Them To

Frugivory From the Animal's Point of View

A key feature of tropical forests, and of the animal communities that inhabit them, is the large number of birds (cotingas, finches, manakins, parrots, orioles, tanagers, toucans, and trogons make up a partial list) that rely on fruit as a diet staple. Some mammals, particularly bats, also eat fruit, but I will concentrate in this discussion on the many Neotropical birds that are partly or wholly *frugivorous* (fruit-eating). Frugivory represents a trade, each participant – the fruit-bearing tree and the fruit-eating bird – offering the other something of great value (and therefore it is a kind of *mutualism* – see p. 35). The complex web of relationships between avian fruit-eaters and fruit-producing trees is particularly interesting because it nicely demonstrates ecological interactions between plant and animal, between food producer and food consumer, between predator and prey, and the mutual dependence sometimes engendered by such relationships.

Benefits of Frugivory for Birds

Most small and medium-sized tropical forest birds eat either fruits or insects, or they eat both. But it is the fruit-eating habit that accounts for much of the incredible ecological success of birds in the tropics. Many more bird species occupy the Earth's tropical areas than temperate zones and, ecologists believe, about 20% of the difference is directly attributable to the tropical birds' superior abilities to exploit fruit resources. In fact, probably 50% of tropical bird biomass (the summed weight of all tropical birds alive at one time) is supported by fruit-eating. One would think, therefore, that fruit must be tremendously profitable "prey" for birds, and in several ways it is:

1   Fruit is conspicuous. First consider insects as food. Palatable insects are often small and/or inconspicuous; they hide or blend in extremely well with their surroundings. Finding such insects is a chore that takes a lot of time. Ripe fruit, on the other hand, usually attracts attention to itself, being sweet-smelling, brightly colored, and displayed out in the open.
2   Fruit is easy to stalk, run down, catch, kill, and devour. Insects, as far as we can tell, are absolutely loath to be eaten – they run, hide, and resist to the end; some even spray noxious chemicals at their attackers. Fruit, however, never attempts escape and, in fact, when it is ripe and so most attractive to frugivores, it is most easily separated from the tree that bears it.
    The underlying reason for points (1) and (2), which becomes more clear when considering frugivory from the trees' point of view (see below), is that fruits are *made* to be consumed by animals. It is their *raison d'etre*. Owing to this, trees could hardly be expected to make their fruit difficult to locate or pluck. Thus we have a major ecological truth: insects benefit by not being eaten, but unless a fruit is eaten, the plant gains nothing from the effort to produce it.

3 Fruit is abundant. When a bird locates a tree with fruit, there is often a large amount available for consumption. Thus, meeting a day's nutritional requirements means finding one or, at most, a few, fruit-bearing trees.

4 Fruit in the tropics is usually available year-round.

There are wide-ranging consequences of points (3) and (4) for avian frugivores. That fruit is always available and abundant means that birds can safely specialize on it – evolve special ways to pluck, eat, and digest it – without encountering times of the year when no fruit is available, forcing the birds to search for food that they are ill-equipped to handle. Owing to its abundance, species that concentrate on fruit often are quite successful, meaning that within a given area the numbers of individuals of these species can be quite large. But the greatest influence of frugivory on the lives of birds is that, because fruit is abundant and easy to locate and eat, birds can fulfill nutritional needs in only a few hours, leaving many hours each day available to pursue other activities. In contrast, an avian *insectivore* or *piscivore* (specializing on insects or fish, respectively), to survive may have to hunt most of each day.

The spare time frugivory permits birds probably allows for the development of *polygamous* and *promiscuous* breeding in tropical birds (see Close-Up, p. 182). Take the manakins and cotingas that breed promiscuously. Males establish display sites on tree branches or on ground *courts*. Several of these display sites near each other constitute a *lek*. Females visit leks, attracted by the males' vocalizations and dancing display antics, compare the males displaying, and choose one or more to mate with. Afterwards, the females go off by themselves to nest and raise their young. At their leks, male manakins, for instance, spend up to 80% to 90% of daylight hours during the breeding season displaying and trying to attract females (the more they are able to convince to mate with them, the more offspring the males will have in the next generation). The free time frugivory affords permits both the prolonged display time in these breeding systems as well as the requisite ability of females to raise young themselves.

Also, when an animal's usual food is fairly scarce or difficult to locate or catch, to insure adequate supplies for themselves and their young, birds may need to defend individual territories and struggle to keep out other members of their species. Furthermore, male and female may need to continue their pairing past actual mating because one parent foraging alone cannot provide sufficient food for the young. But establishing a territory to defend the fruit it holds is unnecessary because there is usually fruit enough for all that want it. (In fact, usually birds cannot eat all the fruit that ripens on a tree.) It is far more efficient to forage in groups, to be *social* feeders, as are toucans and parrots, and so each day to have help in finding trees bearing ripe fruit (sometimes easier said than done because trees within a small area usually do not ripen simultaneously).

Problems of Frugivory

Have birds encountered difficulties in the process of specializing on fruit? Yes, there *are* some associated problems:

1 Fruits, although providing plentiful carbohydrates and fats, are relatively low in protein, so these birds, although easily meeting their daily calorie needs, sometimes have "protein deficits" that they must ease by feeding occasionally on insects or other animals (the occasional snail or frog, the odd lizard). Few bird species eat fruit exclusively. The ones that do, such as bellbirds (p. 160), need make special provision for their all-fruit diet. For instance, because

rapidly-growing young need good amounts of protein, bellbird nestlings, fed only fruit by their parents, grow relatively slowly, and so spend perhaps 50% more time in the nest than nonfrugivorous birds of the same size. Also, these birds tend to feed on unusual fruits that are high in proteins and fats, such as avocados.

2   Eating liquidy fruit pulp means that frugivores consume a lot of water, which is both bulky and heavy, and which must be transported for a time (which uses up energy) and disposed of regularly.

3   The birds' nutrition comes from the fleshy fruit pulp. The seeds that are eaten incidentally are usually indigestible and must be, like water, carried for a while and then disposed of – either by regurgitation or after being passed through the digestive tract.

4   When a species specializes on a particular type of fruit, it becomes vulnerable to any temporary or permanent decline in the fruit's availability. (While this is true, it appears that most avian frugivores avoid such vulnerability by not being overly specialized. In an observational study at one Costa Rican forest site – Monteverde – that followed the feeding habits of 70 fruit-eating species, researchers discovered that each bird species consumed, on average, 10 species of fruits.)

Frugivory From the Tree's Point of View

It is clear what birds get from frugivory, but what of the trees, which are picked clean of the fruit that they spend so much time and energy producing? The answer is that the trees, by having birds eat, transport, and then drop their seeds, achieve efficient reproduction – something well worth their investment in fruit. The trees make use of birds as winged, animate, seed *dispersal agents*.

Why don't trees just let their seeds drop to the ground? It turns out that seeds dropped near the parent tree usually do not survive. They die because they must compete with the much larger parent for sun and other nutrients. Seeds carried some distance from the parent tree have a better chance of germination and survival, and they will not compete with the parent tree (also, because in the tropics trees of the same species usually do not grow near each other, seeds dropped by birds are unlikely to be regularly competing with any trees of the same species). Thus, seed dispersal by birds enhances a parent tree's prospects for successful reproduction, and also allows the tree to colonize new sites with trees bearing copies of its genetic material. Also, insects that eat seeds find them more easily on the ground beneath the plant than if they are scattered more widely over the forest.

The tree's use of bird power for seed dispersal is exquisitely fine-tuned. As seeds are being readied, fruit is green, hard, and bitter-tasting – unappealing fare to birds (and to people!). When the seeds mature and are ready for dispersal and germination, the surrounding fruit brightens in color, becomes softer and easier to pluck from the tree, and in a *coup de grace*, trees inject sugars into fruits, making them sweet and very attractive.

Not all birds attracted to fruits are good seed dispersers. Some, notably the parrots, eat and digest seeds, acting as predators rather than dispersers.

Ecological Consequences of Frugivory For Birds, Trees, and Ecosystems

As tropical birds have benefited in several ways by specialization on fruit, so too have trees. In fact, ecologists now suspect that seed dispersal by birds and other vertebrate animals was and is responsible for the initial spread and current domination of the Earth by flowering plants. They estimate that upwards of 80% of trees and shrubs in tropical wet forests have their seeds dispersed by animals. These plants provide the nutrients to support large, healthy populations of frugivorous birds and bats. Moreover, the great species diversity of plants in the tropics may be largely linked to frugivorous animals continually eating fruits and spreading seeds into new areas. Such constant dispersal, which also allows continual, healthy genetic mixing, is beneficial for plant populations, always working to decrease the chances that individual species will go extinct. In fact, the more successful a tree species is at being "preyed upon" by birds, the more its seeds will be dropped over a wide area, and the more abundant it will become.

One potential problem for trees, though, is that if their fruit is eaten by only one or two bird species, that strict dependence for seed dispersal brings vulnerability. If the bird that disperses such a *specialist* tree for some reason declines in abundance and becomes extinct, so too, in short order, will the tree species. Examples of such occurrences are on record. For instance, when *Dodo* birds (see p. 128) were eliminated from the Indian Ocean's island of Mauritius, the tree species for which they were the sole dispersal agents were endangered. (Luckily, turkeys introduced to the island by people seem able to replace the Dodo there as a tree seed disperser.) Most tree species, however, enjoy the seed dispersal services of at least several bird species.

The trades that the birds and trees make, the conflicting strategies to survive and complete their life cycles, are fascinating. Think about it from one evolutionary perspective: the beneficial aspect of the interaction for the tree – having a bird transport its seeds – is the negative aspect for the animal, which has no desire to carry seeds from which it gets no benefit. The beneficial aspect for the bird – the fruit pulp that the plant manufactures to attract animals – is the negative part of the interaction for the plant, which loses the energy and nutrients required to make the fruit. Frugivory is one of the tropic's most important and compelling ecological interactions, and one that currently attracts strong interest from ecological researchers. Frugivory may even have been a causative factor in the early evolution of color vision, as the first fruit-eaters that could easily distinguish ripe and unripe fruit plainly would have had advantages over those that could not.

Environmental Close-Up 4
Avian Mating Systems and Birds That Cheat

Introduction: Fidelity and Infidelity

Many behavioral characteristics of animals are held up as outstanding examples of clean, natural, even ethical, living – a deer's grace and gentleness, a fox's cleverness, a mother cat's concern for her young, the beaver's work ethic – examples that people would do well to emulate. But there are some aspects of animals' behavior that we would probably do better to avoid imitating. The first that comes to mind, of course, is the somewhat nasty habit many have of killing and eating each other. Another is their highly questionable fidelity to their mates. Humans, you will be surprised to learn, even with their spotty record, may in this area be able to teach other animals a thing or two.

First, a word about *mating systems*, or breeding relationships between the sexes. Traditionally, various animal mating systems have been classified by the number of mates males and females have during each breeding period. *Monogamous* individuals have one mate and *polygamous* individuals have more than one mate (polygamy can be divided into two types: *polygyny*, in which one male mates with several females; and *polyandry*, in which one female mates with several males). Finally, some species employ *promiscuous* mating systems, in which individuals, it seems to us, mate indiscriminately, or nearly so. During the 1960s and 1970s, biologists who studied animal behavior began to realize that these divisions were not really so clear cut. Rather, there was more of a continuum of mating systems. A better way to view those relationships, it was thought, was as a battle between the sexes to monopolize breeding resources and mates. Monogamy could be viewed as the evolutionary result when neither sex could monopolize more than a single mate. Polygyny could be viewed as the result when males of a species, by establishing and defending territories with abundant food and nest resources, were able to lure, monopolize, and support several females.

Throughout this period of thinking about animal mating systems, one underlying assumption did not change, and that was that the males and females that lived together – nested together, in the case of birds – mated only with each other. The assumption made sense because animals, like people, always seemed to go through a selection process when searching for mates. Presumably, mates were chosen for traits that increased the likelihood that breeding efforts would be successful, the resulting kids happy, healthy, and possessed of good genes. Despite the name, even promiscuous breeders, it was thought, did not randomly choose partners for their brief mating relationships, but carefully chose mates based on some telltale physical or behavioral characteristics. Careful selection makes sense. After all, these are the individuals with whom the choosers are going to mix genes and have kids. Why then, the argument goes, after carefully selecting a mate, should an animal even consider cheating?

I will discuss only birds here because much of the research in this field has been with birds, but the ideas translate to other animal groups as well. Observers had long noticed occasional cases of birds being unfaithful to their mates. Often the behaviors were secretive, a male of a pair sneaking off to mate with another female while his current mate incubated a clutch of eggs, a female copulating with a neighboring male territory owner while her own mate was away, feeding off their territory. But the instances that were actually witnessed were few and usually ascribed to sick or "abnormal" behavior. Starting in the mid-1970s, some experiments were conducted with wild birds that suggested that *extra-pair copulations*, that is, matings between individuals that were not paired and did not nest together, might be a lot more common than initially thought. Biologists actually did *vasectomies* on small songbirds during the breeding season. They used for their experiments the Red-winged Blackbird, a strongly territorial, polygynous species that tends to nest in marshes. After their vasectomies, male Redwings could not have fertilized their females' eggs. Yet the experimenters discovered that about 70% of nests on the territories of vasectomized males had fertile eggs. The strong implication was that the female Redwings were mating not just with the male that owned the territory on which they built their nests – their supposed mates – but with other males, probably adjacent territory owners, as well.

One possible interpretation of the vasectomy experiments, however, was that female Redwings noticed something odd about their vasectomized mates, something in their behavior that people could not see, and, to assure that their eggs were fertilized, copulated with other males. In other words, the females in this situation may have pursued an unusual behavioral strategy of mating with neighbors, something they would not have done normally. Settlement of the controversy awaited the development of techniques in molecular biology during the 1980s, such as DNA fingerprinting, that permitted unequivocal assignments of paternity to be made. After taking blood samples from supposed parents and their kids, these tests determine for sure whether the parents who tend the nests in which the kids hatch are the actual genetic, or *biological*, parents of those kids. (If not, then they would be referred to as only the *social* parents.) At first with considerable surprise, and then with dawning realization of the truth, biologists found, in species after species, that extra-pair copulations (and, of course, *extra-pair fertilizations*; *EPCs* and *EPFs*, in biological shorthand), were frequent. Male and female birds were fooling around, and the behavior was very common, not rare.

How Much Do Birds Cheat?

By now, the genetic paternity of nestlings has been determined for wild populations of more than 60 bird species. For a few, no evidence of EPFs was found. But for about 50 species, between 1% and 75% of all offspring produced in a population were found to be the result of extra-pair matings. For a classically monogamous species, such as the Indigo Bunting, a small blue songbird in the sparrow group, biologists found in a North Carolina population that about 35% of young were sired by other than the supposed father. For Red-winged Blackbirds in a Washington State population, the proportion was similar. During 400 hours of monitoring over three breeding seasons, a researcher witnessed 375 Redwing copulations in the wild, of which 66 (18%) were EPCs. Fully 88% of the females watched during that period participated in at least one EPC; in other words, they were all doing it. In fact, the observer discovered that it was not only males looking to particpate in EPCs, but that females actually did the same – they solicited EPCs from neighboring males! Subsequent DNA fingerprinting of these birds revealed the consequences of the cheating: 34% of 403 nestlings born on the territories had been sired via EPFs, and 54% of tested nests held at least one nestling that had been sired by a male other than the supposed father. Sometimes a single nest held young that had been fathered by 2 or 3 different males. In almost all cases, it was males owning neighboring territories that proved to be the biological fathers of EPF nestlings.

Why Cheat? Birds Have Their Reasons ...

The high number of species in which extra-pair fertilizations occur, and the high proportion of individuals in any population that participate, tell us that we have discovered a common feature of bird breeding systems. (And of the breeding systems of other animals, as well. For instance, DNA fingerprints indicate that male and female Black Bears in Canada mate with multiple partners during each breeding effort.) The big question, of course, is why. Usually, when biologists ask why an animal engages in a particular behavior, what they are really asking is: What is the *adaptive significance* of the behavior – how does it lead to increased reproductive success, to better success at passing genes to future generations? For males, the reason for their participation in EPCs is clear. By mating with more females (in the Redwing's case, those in addition to the 1 to 10 females that already nest on their territories) and fertilizing their eggs, males should be able to increase their annual breeding success – the number of young that fledge each year for which they are the biological father. But why should females participate? The usual argument is that females carefully select the male they decide to mate with, perhaps using some combination of his personal traits and the qualities of the territory he owns. Following such a careful selection, why should she then copulate with other males? Could it be that by doing so she somehow increases her breeding success? The now-not-so-surprising answer is: yes, she does.

There are a number of possible ways that a female could have more or better offspring by mating with more than one male. Some males may be infertile or (in polygynous species) have low sperm counts after mating with all of the other females in their harems, so an individual female, by mating with her own male as well as with other males, may be ensuring that all of her eggs are fertilized (laying an unfertilized egg is a great waste of energy). A female that mates with several males may increase the genetic diversity or quality of her offspring, which could increase their chances of long-term survival. Finally, a female that mates with another male may obtain some immediate help from that male. The reason that he would help her is that, although he probably cannot know for sure, it is possible that he is the biological father of one or more of the young in her nest; it is to his benefit to be sure that those young survive and prosper. This last reason was tested with Red-winged Blackbirds. Sure enough, a male with whom a female had engaged in EPCs was more likely to permit the female to stay at seed-feeders on his territory than were other males with whom she had not mated, and the male was also more aggressive in helping defend her nest from a potential nest predator than were other males. So, did these females benefit reproductively? Females that had engaged in EPCs had a greater percentage of their eggs hatch than did females that did not cheat, and, in the end, fledged, on average, about a half chick more from their nests.

So female Redwings, and females of many other species as well, make many more choices about breeding partners than we initially believed. A female can choose a mate – the male on whose territory she will nest – by his personal characteristics and/or by the quality of his territory, but she is not limited to mating with only that choice. She can still exercise future choices of additional males with which to engage in EPCs. A main lesson here is that there can be quite a difference between an animal's social mating system – what we see going on, such as an apparently monogamous relationship – and its actual, biological, mating system. Thirty years ago it was generally believed that more than 80% of bird species were monogamous; but how many of those species are *biologically* monogamous? Probably few. As for comparisons with people, who, of course, often consider themselves to belong to a monogamous species, I leave it to the individual reader.

A final note: As of this writing, most of the species tested for EPCs have been birds from temperate latitudes. Tropical birds may behave differently. One idea is that, because of longer breeding seasons, female birds in the tropics will find it harder to find EPC mates because not all members of the species are breeding at exactly the same time. If true, then tropical birds may have higher fidelity to their mates than temperate birds, not because of a higher moral calibre, but simply owing to a lack of opportunity. For instance, a recent report on a DNA-based analysis of the mating system of DUSKY ANTBIRDS in Panama showed no evidence of EPFs; all youngsters in 9 families examined were genetically linked to both parents (R.C. Fleischer *et al.* 1997).

Chapter 8

Mammals

Introduction

Leafing through this book, the reader will have noticed the profiles of many more birds than mammals. This may at first seem discriminatory, especially when it is recalled that many people themselves are mammals and, owing to that direct kinship, are probably keenly interested and motivated to see and learn about mammals. Are not mammals as good as birds? Why not include more of them? There are several reasons for the discrepancy – good biological reasons. One is that, even though the tropics generally have more species of mammals than temperate or arctic regions, the total number of mammal species worldwide, and the number in any region, is less than the number of birds. In fact, there are in total only about 4000 mammal species, as compared to 9000 birds, and the relative difference is reflected in Costa Rica's fauna. But the more compelling reason not to include more mammals in a book on commonly sighted wildlife, is that, even in regions sporting high degrees of mammalian diversity, mammals are relatively rarely seen – especially by short-term visitors. Most mammals lack that basic protection from predators that birds possess, the power of flight. Consequently, mammals being considered delicious fare by any number of predatory beasts (eaten in good numbers by reptiles, birds, other mammals, and even the odd amphibian), most are active nocturnally, or, if day active, are highly secretive. Birds often show themselves with abandon, mammals do not. Exceptions are those mammals that are beyond the pale of predation – huge mammals and fierce ones. But there are no elephants or giraffes in Costa Rica, nor prides of lions. Another exception is monkeys. They are fairly large and primarily arboreal, which keeps them safe from a number of kinds of predators, and thus permits them to be noisy and conspicuous.

A final reason for not including more mammals in the book is that fully half of those occurring in Costa Rica are bats, for the most part nocturnal animals that, even if spotted, are very difficult for anyone other than experts to identify to species.

General Characteristics of Mammals

If birds are feathered vertebrates, mammals are hairy ones. The group first arose, so fossils tell us, approximately 245 million years ago, splitting off from the primitive reptiles during the late Triassic Period of the Mesozoic Era, before the birds did the same. Four main traits distinguish mammals and confer upon them great advantage over other types of animals that allowed them in the past to prosper and spread and continue to this day to benefit them: *hair* on their bodies which insulates them from cold and otherwise protects from environmental stresses; *milk production* for the young, freeing mothers from having to search for specific foods for their offspring; the bearing of *live young* instead of eggs, allowing breeding females to be mobile and hence, safer than if they had to sit on eggs for several weeks; and *advanced brains*, with obvious enhancing effects on many aspects of animal lives.

Classification of Mammals

Mammals are quite variable in size and form, many being highly adapted – changed through evolution – to specialized habitats and lifestyles, for example, bats specialized to fly, marine mammals specialized for their aquatic world. The smallest mammals are the *shrews*, tiny insect eaters that weigh as little as 2.5 g (a tenth of an ounce). The largest are the *whales*, weighing in at up to 160,000 kg (350,000 lb, half the weight of a loaded Boeing 747) – as far as anyone knows, the largest animals ever.

Mammals are divided into three major groups, primarily according to reproductive methods. The *monotremes* are an ancient group that actually lays eggs and still retains some other reptile-like characteristics. Only three species survive, the *platypus* and two species of *spiny anteaters*; they are fairly common inhabitants of Australia and New Guinea. The *marsupials* give birth to live young that are relatively undeveloped. When born, the young crawl along mom's fur into her *pouch*, where they find milk supplies and finish their development. There are about 240 marsupial species, including kangaroos, koalas, wombats, and opossums; they are limited in distribution to Australia and the Neotropics (the industrious but road-accident-prone VIRGINIA OPOSSUM also inhabits much of Mexico and the USA). The majority of mammal species are *eutherians*, or *true* mammals. These animals are distinguished from the other groups by having a *placenta*, which connects a mother to her developing babies, allowing for long internal development. This trait, which allows embryos to develop to a fairly mature form in safety, and for the female to be mobile until birth, has allowed the true mammals to be rather successful, becoming, in effect, the dominant vertebrates on land for millions of years. The true mammals include those with which most people are intimately familiar: rodents, rabbits, cats, dogs, bats, primates, elephants, horses, whales – everything from house mice to ecotravellers.

The 4000 species of living mammals are divided into about 20 orders and 115 families. Approximately 200 species occur in Costa Rica and, again, half of those are bats.

Features of Tropical Mammals

Costa Rica is distinguished as one of the few New World countries that has living today about the same species of mammals as inhabited the area when it was first colonized by Europeans. There are several Costa Rican mammals that may be *endemic* – found there and nowhere else: six species of rodents, one or two carnivores, and three shrews.

There are several important features of tropical mammals and their habitats that differentiate them from temperate zone mammals. First, tropical mammals face different environmental stresses than do temperate zone mammals, and respond to stresses in different ways. Many temperate zone mammals, of course, must endure cold winters, snow, and low winter food supplies. Many of them respond with *hibernation*, staying more or less dormant for several months until conditions improve. Tropical mammals do not encounter extreme cold or snow, but they face dry seasons, up to 5 months long, that sometimes severely reduce food supplies. But for some surprising reasons, they cannot alleviate this stress by hibernating, waiting for the rainy season to arrive and increase food supplies. When a mammal in Canada or Alaska hibernates, so too do most of its predators. This is not the case in the tropics. A mammal sleeping away the dry season in a burrow would be easy prey to snakes and other predators. Moreover, a big danger to sleeping mammals would be … army ants! These voracious insects are very common in the tropics and would quickly eat a sleeping mouse or squirrel. Also, external parasites, such as ticks and mites, which are inactive in extreme cold, would continue to be very active on sleeping tropical mammals, sucking blood and doing considerable damage. Last, the great energy reserves needed to be able to sleep for an extended period through warm weather may be more than any mammal can physically accumulate. Therefore, tropical mammals need to stay active throughout the year. One way they counter the dry season's reduction in their normal foods is to switch food types seasonally. For instance, some rodents that eat mostly insects during the rainy season switch to seeds during the dry; some bats that feed on insects switch to dry-season fruits (D.H. Janzen & D.E. Wilson 1983).

The abundance of tropical fruit brings up another interesting difference between temperate and tropical mammals: a surprising number of tropical mammals eat a lot of fruit, even among the carnivore group, which, as its name implies, should be eating meat. All the carnivores in Costa Rica, save the MOUNTAIN LION and NEOTROPICAL OTTER (Plate 78), are known to eat fruit – the dogs, cats, raccoons, weasels – and some seem to prefer it. Upon reflection, that these mammals consume fruit makes sense. Fruit is very abundant in the tropics, available all year, and, at least when it is ripe, easily digested by mammalian digestive systems. A consequence of such *frugivory* (fruit-eating) is that many mammals have become, together with frugivorous birds, major dispersal agents of fruit seeds, which they spit out or which travel unharmed through their digestive tracts. These mammals, therefore, spread fruit tree seeds as they travel, seeds that eventually germinate and become trees (see Close-Up, p. 179). Some biologists believe that, even though the carnivores plainly are specialized for hunting down, killing, and eating animal prey, it is possible that fruit was always a major part of their diet (D.H. Janzen & D.E. Wilson 1983).

Finally, there are some differences in the *kinds* of mammals inhabiting tropical and temperate regions. For instance, bears are nowhere to be found in Costa Rica (in fact, there is only a single Neotropical bear species, distributed sparsely from Panama to northern South America), nor are most social rodents like beavers and prairie dogs. Rabbits are few in number of species and usually in their abundances, also. On the other hand, some groups occur solely in the tropics or do fabulously there. There are about 50 species of New World monkeys, all of which occur in tropical areas (but only 4 occur in Costa Rica). Arboreal mammals such as monkeys and sloths are plentiful in tropical forests probably because there is a rich, resource-filled, dense canopy to occupy and feed in. Also, the closed canopy blocks light to the ground, which only allows an undergrowth that is sparse and poor in resources and consequently permits few opportunities for mammals to live and feed there. Bats thrive in the tropics, being very successful both in terms of number of species and in their abundances. Nine families of bats occur in Costa Rica, including more than 100 species; only 4 families and 40 species occur in the entire USA, an area more than 150 times larger than Costa Rica's. While all the North American bats are insect eaters, the Costa Rican bats are quite varied in lifestyle, among them being fruit-eaters, nectar-eaters, and even a few that consume animals or their blood (D.H. Janzen & D.E. Wilson 1983).

The social and breeding behaviors of various mammals are quite diverse. Some are predominantly solitary animals, males and females coming together occasionally only to mate. Others live in family groups. Some are rigorously territorial, others are not. Details on social and breeding behavior are provided within the individual family descriptions that follow.

Seeing Mammals in Costa Rica

No doubt about it, mammals are tough. One can go for two weeks and, if in the wrong places at the wrong times, see very few of them. A lot of luck is involved – a tapir, a small herd of peccaries, a porcupine just happens to cross the trail just a bit ahead of you. A three-toed sloth is by chance spotted in a tree. For instance, at Palo Verde National Park, I woke up early to birdwatch. Walking down a gravel road in the pre-dawn grayness, a small anteater, a NORTHERN TAMANDUA (Plate

75), strolled slowly out of the forest, almost bumped into my legs, detoured around me, and walked back into the forest on the other side of the road. I offer three pieces of mammal-spotting advice. First, if you have time and are a patient sort, stake out a likely looking spot near a stream or watering hole, be quiet, and wait to see what approaches. Second, try taking strolls very early in the morning; at this time, many nocturnal mammals are quickly scurrying to their day shelters. Third, although only for the stout-hearted, try searching with a flashlight at night around field stations or campgrounds. After scanning the ground (for safety's sake as well as for mammals), shine the light toward the middle regions of trees, and look for bright, shiny eyes reflecting the light. You will certainly stumble across

Table 6 Mammal Biodiversity Around Costa Rica: Where to See the Most Species (adapted from Janzen 1983).

O = opossum, S = shrew, B = bat, P = primate, A = anteater/sloth, R = rabbit, RO = rodent, C = carnivore, D = deer/peccary, T = tapir

| Site | Habitat type | Number of species of | | | | | | | | | |
		O	S	B	P	A	R	RO	C	D	T	Total
La Selva Biological Reserve	lowland wet	5	0	65	4	6	1	16	14	4	1	116
Osa Peninsula; Corcovado National Park	low & middle elevation wet	8	0	80	4	7	1	20	17	4	1	142
San Vito area; Wilson Botanical Garden	middle elevation wet	10	3	80	3	6	4	13	27	2	0	148**
Cerro de la Muerte*	highland wet	0	2	16	0	0	1	10	6	1	1	37
Monteverde Cloud Forest Reserve	middle & high elevation wet	6	2	32	3	4	1	16	14	3	1	82
Guanacaste area; Palo Verde National Park	lowland dry	4	0	39	3	3	1	11	16	2	0	79
San José area	middle elevation wet	5	2	57	2	6	1	16	12	0	0	101

Total number of mammal species known to occur in Costa Rica = 205.

* High in the Talamanca Mountains, along the Pan-American Highway (Route 2), between Cartago and San Isidro.

** Some species have not been seen but are suspected to occur in this area.

some kind of mammal or another; then it is simply a matter of whether you scare them more than they scare you.

Some mammals, of course, are reliably seen. Monkeys, for instance, are seen by visitors to many of Costa Rica's national parks, and tapirs and peccaries are frequently sighted at Corcovado National Park. Banish all thoughts right now of ever encountering *El Tigre*, the Jaguar, regularly found now only in localized regions of the country; few are actually encountered, although their tracks on the beach are a common sight at Corcovado.

Family Profiles

1. Opossums

Marsupials are an ancient group, preceding in evolution the development of the *true*, or *placental*, mammals, which eventually replaced the less-advanced marsupials over most parts of the terrestrial world. Marsupials alive today in the Australian and Neotropical regions therefore are remnants of an earlier time when the group's distribution spanned the Earth. Of the eight living families of marsupials, only three occur in the New World, and only one, the *opossums*, occurs in Costa Rica. That family, Didelphidae, is distributed widely over the northern Neotropics (with one member, the VIRGINIA OPOSSUM, reaching deeply northwards into the USA). Nine species represent the family in Costa Rica. They are a diverse group, occupying essentially all of the country's habitats except high mountain areas. Some, such as the COMMON OPOSSUM (Plate 71), are abundant and frequently sighted, while others are more obscure.

All opossums are basically alike in body plan, although species vary considerably in size. Their general appearance probably has not changed much during the past 40 to 65 million years. As one nature writer put it, the opossums scurrying around today are much the same as the ones dinosaurs encountered (J.C. Kricher 1989). Basically, these mammals look like rats, albeit in the case of some, such as the Common Opossum, like large rats. Their distinguishing features are a long, hairless tail, which is *prehensile* (that is, opossums can wrap it around a tree branch and hang from it), and large, hairless ears. Females in most of the opossums have pouches for their young on their abdomens, but a few groups of species do not. Opossum hindfeet have five digits each, one digit acting as an opposable thumb. The hindfeet of the WATER OPOSSUM (Plate 71) are webbed. The Common Opossum, Costa Rica's largest, grows to nearly a meter (3 ft) in length, if the long tail is included. A large adult of the species can weigh up to 5 kg (11 lb), but most weigh 1 to 2.5 kg (2 to 5 lb). Some of the species are much smaller, the MEXICAN MOUSE OPOSSUM, for instance, being only 25 to 30 cm (10 to 12 in) in length, tail included, and weighing only 100 g (4 oz). Opossums come in a narrow range of colors – shades of gray, brown, and black. Male and female opossums generally look alike, but males are usually larger than females of the same age.

Natural History
Ecology and Behavior
Most opossums are night-active *omnivores*, although some also can be seen during the day. Their reputation is that they will eat, or at least try to eat, almost any-

thing they stumble across or can catch; mostly they take fruit, eggs, and invertebrate and small vertebrate animals. The COMMON OPOSSUM forages mainly at night, often along ponds and streams, sometimes covering more than a kilometer per night within its home range, the area within which it lives and seeks food. Opossums that have been studied are not territorial – they do not defend part or all of their home ranges from others of their species. Some opossums forage mainly on the ground, but most are good climbers and are able to forage also in trees and shrubs; and some species are chiefly arboreal. After a night's foraging, an opossum spends the daylight hours in a cave, a rock crevice, or a cavity in a tree or log. Most opossums are unsociable animals, usually observed singly. The exception is during the breeding season, when males seek and court females, and two or more may be seen together.

Predators on opossums include owls, snakes, and carnivorous mammals. Some opossums apparently are somewhat immune to the venom of many poisonous snakes. The response of the Common Opossum to threat by a predator is to hiss, growl, snap its mouth, move its body from side to side, and finally, to lunge and bite. They often try to climb to escape. The VIRGINIA OPOSSUM is famous for faking death ("playing possum") when threatened, but that behavior is rare or absent in the Common Opossum and others.

Breeding

Female opossums give birth only 12 to 14 days after mating. The young that leave the reproductive tract are only about 1 cm (a half inch) long and weigh less than half a gram. These tiny opossums, barely embryos, climb unassisted along the mother's fur and into her pouch. There they grasp a nipple in their mouth. The nipple swells, essentially attaching the young; they remain there, attached, for about 2 months. Usually more young are born (up to 20) than make it to the pouch and attach correctly. In studies, 6 young, on average, are found in females' pouches (that have up to 13 nipples). Following the pouch phase, the female continues to nurse her young for another month or more, often in a nest she constructs of leaves and grass in a tree cavity or burrow. Female COMMON OPOSSUMS in Costa Rica have 2 litters per year, most often in February and July.

Ecological Interactions

The COMMON OPOSSUM has what can be considered a *commensal* relationship with people. Throughout Central America, populations of these mammals are concentrated around human settlements, particularly around garbage dumps, where they feed. They also partake of fruit crops and attack farmyard birds. Consequently, opossums are more likely to be seen near towns or villages than in uninhabited areas. Of course, these opossums pay a price for the easy food – their picture commonly is found in the dictionary under "roadkill."

Lore and Notes

COMMON OPOSSUMS are known as foul-smelling beasts. Their reputation probably stems from the fact that they apparently enjoy rolling about in fresh animal droppings. Also, when handled, they employ some unattractive defense mechanisms – tending to squirt urine and defecate.

Status

None of Costa Rica's opossum species are considered threatened or endangered, although one, the WATER OPOSSUM is uncommon in some areas. Opossum meat is not regarded as tasty, so these mammals are rarely hunted for food. In the past there was a trade in the fur of the CENTRAL AMERICAN WOOLLY OPOSSUM (Plate 71), but that is no longer the case. Opossums, chiefly COMMON and VIRGINIA OPOSSUMS, are killed intentionally near human settlements to protect fruit crops and poultry, and unintentionally but abundantly, by cars.

Profiles

Common Opossum, *Didelphis marsupialis*, Plate 71a
Central American Woolly Opossum, *Caluromys derbianus*, Plate 71b
Water Opossum, *Chironectes minimus*, Plate 71c
Gray Four-eyed Opossum, *Philander opossum*, Plate 71d

2. Bats

Of all the kinds of mammals, perhaps we can comprehend the lives, can mentally put ourselves into the skins, of nonhuman primates (monkeys and apes) best, and of *bats*, least. That is, monkeys, owing to their similarities to people, are somewhat known to us, familiar in a way, but bats are at the other extreme: foreign, exotic, mysterious. The reasons for their foreignness are several. Bats, like birds, engage in sustained, powered flight – the only mammals to do so ("rats with wings," in the memorable phrasing of a female acquaintance). Bats are active purely at night – every single species. Bats navigate the night atmosphere chiefly by "sonar," or *echolocation*: not by sight or smell but by broadcasting ultrasonic sounds – extremely high-pitched chirps and clicks – and then gaining information about their environment by "reading" the echos. Athough foreign to people's primate sensibilities, bats, precisely because their lives are so very different from our own, are increasingly of interest to us. In the past, of course, bats' exotic behavior, particularly their nocturnal habits, engendered in most societies not ecological curiosity but fear and superstition.

Bats are flying mammals that occupy the night. They are widely distributed, inhabiting most of the world's tropical and temperate regions, excepting some oceanic islands. With a total of about 980 species, bats are second in diversity among mammals only to rodents. Ecologically, they can be thought of as nighttime equivalents of birds, which dominate the daytime skies. Bats of the Neotropics, although often hard to see and, in most cases, difficult for anyone other than experts to identify, are tremendously important mammals, and that is why they are treated here. Their diversity and numbers tell the story: 39% of all Neotropical mammal species are bats, and there are usually as many species of bats in a Neotropical forest than of all other mammal species combined. Researchers estimate that most of the mammalian biomass (the total amount of living tissue, by weight) in any given Neotropical region resides in bats. Of the 200 or so species of mammals that occur in Costa Rica, fully half (105) are bats. Some of the more common and more interesting bats are profiled here.

Bats have true wings, consisting of thin, strong, highly elastic membranes that extend from the sides of the body and legs to cover and be supported by the elongated fingers of the arms. (The name of the order of bats, Chiroptera, refers to the wings: *chiro*, meaning hand, and *ptera*, wing.) Other distinctive anatomical features include bodies covered with silky, longish hair; toes with sharp, curved claws that allow the bats to hang upside down and are used by some to catch food; scent glands that produce strong, musky odors; and, in many, very odd-shaped folds of skin on their noses (noseleaves) and prominent ears that aid in echolocation. Like birds, bat's bodies have been modified through evolution to

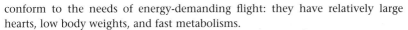

conform to the needs of energy-demanding flight: they have relatively large hearts, low body weights, and fast metabolisms.

Bats, although they come in a variety of sizes, are sufficiently standardized in form such that all species are easily recognized by everyone as bats. Females in most species are larger than males, although there are exceptions, such as the NECTAR BAT (Plate 73), in which males are larger. Because few people get near enough to resting or flying bats to examine them closely, I describe the forms of individual species only in the plate section. It will suffice to say that the bats under our consideration here range from tiny, 5-g (one-fifth of an ounce) bats with 5-cm (2 in) wingspans (the BLACK MYOTIS; Plate 73) to the New World's largest bat, which weighs up to 200 g (7 oz) and has a wingspan up to 80 cm (31 in; the FALSE VAMPIRE BAT; Plate 72).

Natural History
Ecology and Behavior
Neotropical bats are renowned for their insect-eating ways. Indeed, most species specialize on insects. They use their sonar not just to navigate the night but to detect insects, which they catch on the wing, pick off leaves, or scoop off the ground. Bats use several methods to catch flying insects. Small insects may be captured directly in the mouth; some bats use their wings as nets and spoons to trap insects and pull them to their mouth; and others scoop bugs into the fold of skin membrane that connects their tail and legs, then somersault in midair to move the catch to their mouth. Small bugs are eaten immediately on the wing, while larger ones, such as large beetles, are taken to a perch and dismembered. Not all species, however, are insectivores. Neotropical bats have also expanded ecologically into a variety of other *feeding niches*: some specialize in eating fruit, feeding on nectar and pollen at flowers, preying on vertebrates such as frogs or birds, eating fish, or even, in the case of the COMMON VAMPIRE BAT (Plate 72), sipping blood.

Bats spend the daylight hours in day roosts, usually tree cavities, shady sides of trees, caves, rock crevices, or, these days, in buildings or under bridges. Some bats make their own individual roosting sites in trees by biting leaves so that they fold over, making small *tents* that shelter them from predators as well as from the elements. More than one species of bat may inhabit the same roost, although some species will associate only with their own kind. For most species, the normal resting position in a roost is hanging by their feet, head downwards, which makes taking flight as easy as letting go and spreading their wings. Many bats leave roosts around dusk, then move to foraging sites at various distances from the roost. Night activity patterns vary, perhaps serving to reduce food competition among species. Some tend to fly and forage intensely in the early evening, become less active in the middle of the night, then resume intense foraging near dawn; others are relatively inactive early in the evening, but more active later on. Bats do not fly continuously after leaving their day roosts, but group together at a *night roost*, a tree for instance, where they rest and bring food. Fruit-eaters do not rest in the tree at which they have discovered ripe fruit, where predators might find them, but make several trips per night from the fruit tree to their night roost. Bats are highly social animals, roosting and often foraging in groups.

Most of the species decribed below are common representatives of groups of bats, each of which differs anatomically, ecologically, and behaviorally.

GREATER FISHING BAT (Plate 72). Relatively large bats, fishing bats roost in hollow trees and buildings near fresh or salt water. They have very large hind feet and claws that they use to pull fish, crustaceans, and insects from the water's surface. These bats fly low over still water, using their sonar to detect the ripples of a fish just beneath or breaking the water's surface. Grabbing the fish with their claws, they then move it to their mouth, land, hang upside down, and feast.

FALSE VAMPIRE BAT (Plate 72). The New World's largest bat, with wingspans to 80 cm (2.5 ft), False Vampire Bats feed on vertebrates such as birds, rodents, and other bats. (The name originates with the mistaken belief of early European explorers that the largest, meanest-looking bat in the region must be the bloodsucker of which they had heard so many tales.) Some of the animals they prey on weigh as much as they do, but they are fierce, with large canine teeth, shearing molars, and powerful jaw muscles. They roost in small groups, usually a pair of adults and their recent offspring. Apparently, False Vampires, although they forage alone, are good family bats: young pups at night are left in the day roost to be guarded by an adult or subadult family member; the returning foragers are greeted with mutual "kissing" when they return (one observer compared it to the mutual muzzle licking and nosing practiced by wolves when they greet one another). "Babysitter" bats may be fed by the returning foragers.

JAMAICAN FRUIT-EATING BAT (Plate 72). A medium-sized fruit-eater of wet and dry forests, these bats also take insects and pollen from flowers. They pluck fruit and carry it to a night roost 25 to 200 m (80 to 650 ft) away to eat it. Observers estimate that nightly each bat carries away from trees more than its own weight in fruit. Jamaican Fruit Bats roost in caves, hollow trees, or in foliage. Breeding is apparently polygynous (a single male mates with more than one female), because small roosts are always found to contain one male plus several females (up to 11) and their dependent young.

COMMON VAMPIRE BAT (Plate 72). Vampire bats are the only mammals that feed exclusively on blood; the only true mammal parasites. Day roosts are in hollow trees and caves. At night vampires fly out, using both vision (they have larger eyes and better vision than most bats) and sonar to find victims, usually large mammals. They not only fly well, they are also agile walkers, runners, and hoppers, of great assistance in perching on, feeding on, and avoiding swats by their prey. They use their sharp incisor teeth to bite the awake or sleeping animal, often on the neck, and remove a tiny piece of flesh. An anti-clotting agent in the bat's saliva keeps the small wound oozing blood. The vampire laps up the oozing blood – they do not suck it out. The feeding is reported to be painless (we won't ask how researchers know this, but, with a shudder, we can guess). Because blood is such a nutritious food, these bats need only about 15 ml (half a fluid ounce) a day. Vampires breed at any time of the year; young are fed blood from the mother's mouth for several months until they can get their own.

NECTAR BAT (Plate 73). These are small bats with a misleading name. Although they can hover for a few seconds at flowers to take pollen or nectar, most of their omnivorous diet consists of fruit and insects. They roost in large groups in both dry and wet forest habitats. Young use their teeth to cling to their mothers' fur after birth, being carried along during foraging trips; pups can fly on their own at about a month old.

SHORT-TAILED FRUIT BAT (Plate 73). These are small, very common bats that live in large groups, up to several hundred, usually in caves or tree cavities. They are primarily fruit-eaters, but also seasonally visit flowers for nectar. Usually they pick fruit from a tree, then return to a night roost to consume it. After giving birth, females carry their young for a week or two during their nightly foraging; older young are left in the day roost. Because of their abundance and frugivory, these bats are important dispersers of tree seeds in Neotropical forests.

SUCKER-FOOTED BAT (Plate 73). These tiny bats have circular adhesive cups on their thumbs and feet. They roost most commonly in small family groups (2 to 9) in rolled up banana or Heliconia leaves or fronds. The "sucker" cups adhere to the leaves. When in a few days the leaf matures and unfurls, the family must seek a new home. Interestingly, unlike most bats, the Sucker-foots in their roosts adhere head upwards. They are common in lowland rain forests and gardens and often can be spotted by peering up into banana or palm fronds.

BLACK MYOTIS (Plate 73). These are tiny, common bats that are distributed widely over the Neotropics. They roost in large groups in hollow trees and buildings; males usually roost separately from females and their young. At sunset they leave the roost in search of flying insects, and return just before dawn. Young are carried by the mother for a few days after birth, but are then left behind with other young in the roost when the female leaves to forage. Pups can fly at about 3 weeks of age, are weaned at 5 to 6 weeks, and are reproductively mature at only 4 months.

GREATER WHITE-LINED BAT (Plate 73). These tiny animals are one of the most frequently encountered bats of Costa Rica's lowland forests. By day they roost in groups of 5 to 50 in hollow trees or caves, rocks, or buildings; they are often seen under overhangs at ecotourist facilities. They leave roosts just before dark to commence their insect foraging, which they do under the forest canopy, usually within 300 m (1000 ft) of their roosts. Individual males defend territories in the day roosts, and they have harems of up to 9 females each. After birth, a mother carries her pup each night from the day roost and leaves it in a hiding place while she forages. Pups can fly at about 2 weeks old, but continue to nurse for several months.

Breeding

Bat mating systems are diverse, various species employing monogamy, polygyny, and/or promiscuity (see Close-Up, p. 182); the breeding behavior of many species has yet to be studied in detail. Some Costa Rican species breed at particular times of the year, but others have no regular breeding seasons. Most bats produce a single pup at a time.

Ecological Interactions

Bats are beneficial to forests and to people in a number of ways. Many Neotropical plants have bats, instead of bees or birds, as their main pollinators. These species generally have flowers that open at night and are white, making them easy for bats to find. They also give off a pungent aroma that bats can home in on. Nectar-feeding bats use long tongues to poke into flowers to feed on nectar – a sugary solution – and pollen. As a bat brushes against a flower, pollen adheres to its body, and is then carried to other plants, where it falls and leads to cross-pollination. Fruit-eating bats, owing to their high numbers, are important seed dispersers (see Close-Up, p. 179), helping to regenerate forests by transporting and dropping fruit seeds onto the forest floor. Also, particularly helpful to humans, bats each night consume enormous numbers of annoying insects.

Bats eat a variety of vertebrate animals; unfortunately for some of them they play right into the bat's hands … uh, feet. Some bats that specialize on eating frogs, it has been discovered, can home in on the calls that male frogs give to attract mates. These frogs are truly in a bind: if they call, they may attract a deadly predator; if they do not, they will lack for female company. However, some types of bat prey have developed anti-bat tactics. Several groups of moth species, for instance, can sense the ultrasonic chirps of some echolocating insectivorous bats; when they do, they react immediately by flying erratically or diving down into vegetation, decreasing the success of the foraging bats. Some moths even make their own clicking sounds, which apparently confuse the bats, causing them to break off approaches. The interaction of bats and their prey animals is an active field of animal behavior research because the predators and the prey have both developed varieties of tactics to try to outmaneuver or outwit the other.

Relatively little is known about which predators prey on bats. The list however, includes birds-of-prey (owls, hawks), snakes, other mammals such as opossums, cats, and (yes) people, and even other bats, such as the carnivorous FALSE VAMPIRE BAT. Squirrel Monkeys actually hunt tent-roosting bats that they find in tree leaves. Tiny bats, such as the 3 to 5 g (less than one-fifth of an ounce) BLACK MYOTIS, are even captured by large spiders and cockroaches. Bats, logically, are usually captured in or near their roosts, where predators can reliably find and corner them. One strong indication that predation is a real concern to bats is that many species reduce their flying in bright moonlight. Bats showing this "lunar phobia" include the JAMAICAN FRUIT-EATING BAT and SHORT-TAILED FRUIT BAT. On the other hand, others, like the very small GREATER WHITE-LINED BAT, do not decrease their activity levels under full moons.

Lore and Notes

Bats have frightened people for a long time. The result, of course, is that there is a large body of folklore that portrays bats as evil, associated with or incarnations of death, devils, witches, or vampires. Undeniably, it was bats' alien lives – their activity in the darkness, flying ability, and strange form – and people's ignorance of bats, that were the sources of these myriad superstitions. Many cultures, worldwide, have evil bat legends, from Japan and the Philippines, to Europe, the Middle East, and Central and South America. Even the Australian Aborigines were not immune. One of their legends concerning the origin of death features a large bat that guarded the entrance to a cave. The first man and woman on Earth were warned to stay away from the bat. The woman, curious, approached the bat, which grew frightened and flew off (notice how women are always the bad guys in these stories?). The cave housed Death, which, with its bat guard gone, escaped into the world, with chronic, fatal consequences for people.

Many ancient legends tell of how bats came to be creatures of the night. But the association of bats with vampires – blood-sucking monsters – may have originated in recent times with Bram Stoker, the English author who in 1897 published *Dracula* (the title character, a vampire, could metamorphose into a bat). Vampire bats are native only to the Neotropics. Stoker may have heard stories of their blood-lapping ways from travellers, and for his book, melded the behavior of these bats with legends of vampires from India and from Slavic Gypsy culture. Although not all New World cultures imparted evil reputations to bats, it is not surprising, given the presence of vampire bats, that some did. The Mayans, for instance, associated bats with darkness and death; there was a "bat world," a part of the underworld ruled by a bat god, through which dead people had to pass.

Speaking of Vampire Bats, these bats presumably are much more numerous today than in the distant past because they now have domesticated animals as prey. Before the introduction of domesticated animals to the Neotropics, Vampires would have had to seek blood meals exclusively from mammals such as deer and peccaries; now they have, over large parts of their range, herds of large domesticated animals to feed on. In fact, examinations of blood meals reveal that Vampire Bats in settled areas feed almost exclusively on ranch and farm animals – cattle, horses, poultry, etc. By the way, Vampire Bats rarely attack people, although it is not unheard of. In some regions, they may transmit rabies.

Status

Determining the statuses of bat populations is difficult because of their nocturnal behavior and habit of roosting in places that are hard to census. With some exceptions, all that is known for most Neotropical species is that they are common or not common, widely or narrowly distributed. Some species are known from only a few museum specimens, or from their discovery in a single cave, but that does not mean that there are not healthy but largely hidden wild populations. Because many forest bats roost in hollow trees, deforestation is obviously a primary threat. For example, the HONDURAN WHITE BAT, a tiny fruit-eater, is now apparently limited to the Caribbean lowlands of southern Central America, and is threatened by further habitat loss. All of the bats profiled here are common or, in the case of the FALSE VAMPIRE BAT, naturally fairly rare. Many bat populations in temperate regions in Europe and the USA are known to be declining and under continued threat by a number of agricultural, forestry, and architectural practices. Traditional roost sites have been lost on large scales by mining and quarrying, by the destruction of old buildings, and by changing architectural styles that eliminate many building overhangs, church belfries, etc. Many forestry practices advocate the removal of hollow, dead trees, which frequently provide bats with roosting space. Additionally, farm pesticides are ingested by insects, which are then eaten by bats, leading to death or reduced reproductive success.

Costa Rican conservationists realized more than 10 years ago that bats, although important members of local ecosystems, were still mostly feared and routinely destroyed by citizens. Deciding that the root causes were a lack of information about bats combined with belief in myths and misinformation, they conducted a successful 17-month long "Educational Campaign about the Importance of Bats in Tropical America." The project created and distributed educational materials about bats, conducted lectures throughout the country, and tried to generate positive publicity about bats in the news media.

Profiles

Greater Fishing Bat, *Noctilio leporinus*, Plate 72a
False Vampire Bat, *Vampyrum spectrum*, Plate 72b
Jamaican Fruit-eating Bat, *Artibeus jamaicensis*, Plate 72c
Common Vampire Bat, *Desmodus rotundus*, Plate 72d
Nectar Bat, *Glossophaga soricina*, Plate 73c
Short-tailed Fruit Bat, *Carollia perspicillata*, Plate 73a
Sucker-footed Bat, *Thyroptera tricolor*, Plate 73b
Black Myotis, *Myotis nigricans*, Plate 73d
Greater White-lined Bat, *Saccopteryx bilineata*, Plate 73e

3. Primates

People's reactions to *monkeys* (in Spanish, *monos*) are interesting. All people, it seems, find monkeys striking, even transfixing, when first encountered, but then responses diverge. Many people adore the little primates and can watch them for hours, whether it be in the wild or at zoos. But others, myself included, find them a bit, for want of a better word, unalluring; we are slightly uncomfortable around them. What is so intriguing is that it is probably the same characteristic of monkeys that both so attracts and repels people, and that is their quasi-humanness. Whether or not we acknowledge it consciously, it is doubtless this trait that is the source of all the attention and importance attached to monkeys and apes. They look like us, and, truth be told, they act like us, in a startlingly large number of ways. Aristotle, 2300 years ago, noted similarities between human and nonhuman primates, and Linnaeus, the Swedish originator of our current system for classifying plants and animals, working more than 100 years pre-Darwin, classed people together in the same group with monkeys. Therefore, even before Darwin's ideas provided a possible mechanism for people and monkeys to be distantly related, we strongly suspected there was a link; the resemblance was too close to be accidental. Given this bond between people and other primates, it is not surprising that visitors to parts of the world that support nonhuman primates are eager to see them and very curious about their lives. Fortunately, Costa Rica provides homes for several species of monkeys, some of them still sufficiently abundant in protected areas to be readily located and observed.

Primates are distinguished by several anatomical and ecological traits. They are primarily arboreal animals. Most are fairly large, very smart, and highly social – they live in permanent social groups. Most have five very flexible fingers and toes per limb. Primates' eyes are in the front of the skull, facing forward (eyes in the front instead of on the sides of the head are required for binocular vision and good depth perception, without which swinging about in trees would be an extremely hazardous and problematic affair), and primates have, for their sizes, relatively large brains. Female primates give birth usually to a single, very helpless infant.

Primates are distributed mainly throughout the globe's tropical areas and many subtropical ones, save for the Australian region. They are divided into four groups:

1 *Prosimians* include several families of primitive primates from the Old World. They look the least like people, are mainly small and nocturnal, and include lemurs, lorises, galago (bushbaby), and tarsiers.
2 *Old World Monkeys* (Family Cercopithecidae) include baboons, mandrills, and various monkeys such as rhesus and proboscis monkeys.
3 *New World Monkeys* (Family Cebidae) include many kinds of monkeys and the tiny marmosets.
4 The *Hominoidea* contains the gibbons, orangutans, chimpanzees, gorillas, and ecotravellers.

New World monkeys, in general, have short muzzles and flat, unfurred faces, short necks, long limbs, and long tails that are often used as fifth limbs for climbing about in trees. They are day-active animals that spend most of their time in trees, usually coming to the ground only to cross treeless space that they cannot traverse within the forest canopy. About 40 species of New World Monkeys are distributed from southern Mexico to northern Argentina; four or five occur in Costa Rica.

Squirrel monkeys, the name presumably referring to the agile way they run and jump through trees, occur from Central America to Amazonia. The RED-BACKED

SQUIRREL MONKEY (Plate 74), the species in Costa Rica, now occupies only small areas of the Pacific coasts of Panama and Costa Rica. They are small, slender animals, only weighing about 0.6 kg (1.3 lb). They have orange, gold, or olive-colored bodies and black heads with white eye mask, chin, and ears. Several species of *capuchin monkeys* range from southern Central America through Amazonia. Costa Rica's representative is the WHITE-FACED (or WHITE-THROATED) CAPUCHIN (Plate 74), a moderate-sized monkey, black with white or yellowish head, face, shoulders and upper chest. Adults weigh between 2.5 and 3.5 kg (5 to 7 lb); males are slightly larger than females. *Spider monkeys*, named for their long, slender limbs, range from southern Mexico to Brazil's lower Amazon region. CENTRAL AMERICAN SPIDER MONKEYS (Plate 74) are large and weigh up to 8 kg (17 lb). They have strong, prehensile tails and long, thin limbs. Coat color is variable – they are black, brown, or reddish, with lighter underparts and a whitish, unfurred facial mask and muzzle. *Howler monkeys*, named for the tremendous roaring calls they give at dawn and dusk, occur from Central America to northern South America. Costa Rica's MANTLED HOWLER MONKEYS (Plate 74), like spider monkeys, are large, weighing between 4 and 7 kg (9 to 16 lb). They are all black save for a noticeable fringe of brown or blonde hair on their sides (the "mantle"); males are larger than females. Howlers are among the New World's largest monkeys. A fifth species, the NIGHT MONKEY, may occur rarely in some Costa Rican locations.

Natural History
Ecology and Behavior
Squirrel Monkeys. Squirrel monkeys in Costa Rica are denizens of a few lowland wet forest areas of the Pacific coast, although, in other parts of their range, in South America, they are more common and occupy a variety of habitat types. They are highly arboreal, spending 90% or more of daylight hours moving through the forest canopy, looking for insects to eat, and also small fruits and some leaves. They are highly skilled gymnasts, running and jumping along branches and from tree to tree. Groups (*troops*) in Costa Rica are usually small, with less than 10 individuals, but in South America, where these monkeys are more common, troops of 20 to 50 or more are typical. A troop usually consists of several adult males and many females and their dependent young, although during nonbreeding portions of the year the sexes may separate into one-sex groups. Squirrel monkeys apparently do not defend exclusive territories: observers have noticed that the home ranges of troops frequently overlap. During a one-month period, a troop may range back and forth over an area (home range) of about 2 sq km (0.75 sq mile). These monkeys are commonly spotted in trees near water – along lakeshores, rivers, and swamps.

White-faced Capuchins. These monkeys are abundant residents of the wet lowland forests on Costa Rica's Caribbean slope and of dryer deciduous forests on the Pacific slope. They are highly arboreal, but also versatile – they forage over all levels of the forest, from canopy to lower tree trunks, and also occasionally come to the ground to feed. Their diet is broad, consisting mainly of ripe fruit and insects, but also bird eggs, young birds, baby squirrels, and small lizards. (Although they rarely attack larger animals, one male capuchin was observed to attack a 1.7-m (6-ft) long Green Iguana (Plate 18) and break off and eat the end of its tail.) In one study, a troop was found to consume 20% animal prey (mostly insects), 65% fruit, and 15% green plant material; but insects make up 50% or more of the diet during some periods of the year. Capuchins are very active monkeys, spending 80% or more of daylight hours moving through the forest, foraging in any number of ways, such as looking through leaves and leaf litter, pulling bark off trees, and rolling over sticks and logs. A troop, 2 to 20 strong (often 6 to 10), consisting usually of a single adult male plus females and their young, travels an average of about 2 km (1.2 miles) per day, while remaining within a fairly small home range of a few square kilometers (about a square mile). Troops maintain exclusive territories, aggressively defending their turf whenever they meet other troops at territorial boundaries.

Spider Monkeys. Spider monkeys are found in Costa Rican rainforests and deciduous forests at a wide range of elevations. They are extremely arboreal, rarely descending to the ground. They stay mostly within a forest's upper canopy, moving quickly through trees using their fully prehensile tail as a fifth limb to climb, swing, and hang. Spider monkeys eat ripe fruit, young leaves, and flowers. Troops in Panama were observed to feed on 80% fruit and 20% leaves and other plant materials. During the day, troops, varying in size from 2 to 25 or more (groups of 100 or more have been reported), range over wide swaths of forest, but stay within a home range of 2.5 to 4.0 sq km (1 or 2 sq miles). Troops usually consist of an adult male and several females and their dependent offspring. Spider monkeys are commonly observed in small groups, often two animals, but frequently they are members of a larger troop; the troop breaks up daily into small foraging parties, then coalesces each evening at a mutual sleeping tree.

Howler Monkeys. Howlers inhabit a variety of forest habitat types, but apparently prefer lowland wet evergreen forests. Like the other Costa Rican monkeys, they are highly arboreal and rarely come to the ground; typically they spend most of their time in the upper reaches of the forest. In contrast to the other monkey species, howlers are relatively slow-moving and more deliberate in their canopy travels. They eat fruit and a lot of leafy material; in fact, in one Costa Rican study, leaves comprised 64% of their diet, fruit and flowers, 31%. Owing to their specialization on a super-abundant food resource – leaves – their home ranges need not be, and are not, very large. Most troops have between about 10 and 20 individuals, usually several adult males plus females and associated young. Howlers are slow-moving and often quiet, frequently inconspicuous and on trails people may pass directly below howlers without noticing them. They are most assuredly not inconspicuous, however, when the males let loose with their incredible roaring vocalizations (females also roar occasionally). Their very loud, piercing choruses of roars, at dawn, during late afternoon, and, frequently, during heavy rain, are a characteristic and wonderful part of the rainforest environment. (The initial response of a newcomer to the Neotropics, upon being awakened in the morning by howling howlers, is sure to be "Now what the heck is *that?*"). These vocalizations are probably used by the howlers to communicate with other troops, to advertise their locations and to defend them; although troops of these monkeys do not maintain exclusive territories, they do appear to defend current feeding sites. The males' howling can be heard easily at 3 km (1.8 miles) away in a forest or 5 km (3 miles) away across water.

Breeding

Female monkeys in Costa Rica usually produce a single young that is born furred and with its eyes open. RED-BACKED SQUIRREL MONKEYS, which live up to 21 years in captivity, begin reproducing at 3 (females) to 5 (males) years old. The young cling to their mother after birth and are not truly independent of her until about a year old. Pregnancy is between 160 and 172 days. Mating is during the dry season, with births occurring during the wet season. Female WHITE-FACED CAPUCHINS reach sexual maturity at 3 to 4 years of age, then give birth at 1-to-2 year intervals. Most births occur during the dry season. Young cling to the mother's fur immediately following birth, and are carried by the mothers for 5 to 6 months, until they can travel on their own. Pregnancy is about 180 days. Capuchins live up to 46 years in captivity. CENTRAL AMERICAN SPIDER MONKEYS appear to have no regular breeding seasons. Females reach sexual maturity at about 4 years old (males at about 5), then give birth every 2 to 4 years after pregnancies of about 230 days. Young, which weigh about 500 g (a pound) at birth, are carried by the mother for up to 10 months and are nursed for up to a year. Upon reaching sexual maturity, young females leave their troops to find mates in other troops; males remain with their birth troop. Spider monkeys have lived for 33 years in captivity. Female MANTLED HOWLERS reach sexual maturity at 3 to 4 years of age. They give birth following pregnancies of about 180 days. At 3 months, youngsters begin making brief trips away from their mothers, but until a year old, they continue to spend most of their time on their mother's back; they are nursed until they are 10 to 12 months old. Howlers have survived in the wild for up to 20 years.

Ecological Interactions

A variety of predatory animals prey on Costa Rica's monkeys, including Boa Constrictors (Plate 16), birds-of-prey such as eagles, arboreal cats such as Jaguarundi and Margay (Plate 77), and people. Other causes of death are disease (for instance, many monkey populations in the Caribbean lowlands of Panama and Costa Rica crashed during the early 1950s because of an outbreak of yellow fever) and parasite infestations, such as that by *botflies*. Botflies lay their eggs on mosquitos, monkeys being exposed when infected mosquitos land on them to feed. Botfly larvae burrow into a monkey's skin, move into the bloodstream, and often find their way to the neck region. Many howlers, for instance, are observed to have severe botfly infestations of their necks, seen as swollen lumps and the holes created when adult botflies emerge from the monkey's body. In one Panamanian study, members of a howler population were found each to have an average of 2 to 5 botfly parasites; several monkeys in the study died, apparently of high levels of botfly infestation.

Monkeys are especially crucial elements of rainforest ecosystems because they are seed dispersers for many hundreds of plant species, particularly of the larger canopy trees. Mammals transport seeds that stick to their fur from the producing tree to the places where the seeds eventually fall off. Mammals that are *frugivores* (fruit-eaters) also carry fruit away from a tree, then eat the soft parts and drop the seeds, which may later germinate; or they eat the fruit whole and transport the seeds in their digestive tracts. The seeds eventually fall, unharmed, to the ground and germinate (see Close-Up, p. 179). Monkeys, it turns out, are major seed dispersers. For example, in Panama, where they were studied, a troop of WHITE-FACED CAPUCHINS was estimated to disperse each day more than 300,000 tiny seeds of a single tree species; up to two-thirds of the seeds that passed through the monkeys' digestive systems later germinated (a proportion that was actually higher than seeds that made it to the ground without passing through an animal gut). Monkeys also assist plants in another way: Capuchins eat so many insects that they remove from trees and other plants that they must have a significant effect in reducing insect damage to trees. Because some monkeys eat leaves, they also harm trees, but reports are very rare of primates stripping all the leaves from trees, killing them. Also, monkeys at times are seed predators. They extract seeds from fruit and chew them, destroying them, and also eat young fruits and nuts that contain seeds too undeveloped to ever germinate.

Capuchin troops are quite noisy as they forage, moving quickly about in trees and also vocalizing. A variety of other mammals take advantage of capuchin foraging, apparently attracted by the noise; squirrel monkeys have been observed following capuchins, picking up bugs that the capuchins scare up as they move, and various ground-dwellers such as agouti (Plate 76) and peccaries (Plate 80) congregate under foraging troops, feeding on dropped fruit.

Lore and Notes

The current range of the RED-BACKED SQUIRREL MONKEY, restricted to fragmented regions on the Pacific coasts of Panama and Costa Rica, is at least 500 km (300 miles) distant from the nearest South American squirrel monkey populations. The discontinuous nature of the distributions is puzzling, and it has led biogeographers to suggest that squirrel monkeys may have arrived in Central America only with the help of people; that is, they may have been introduced there by travellers from South to Central America in Pre-Columbian times.

Owing to their active lifestyles, intelligence, and mischievousness, capuchins are sought after as pets and as "organ-grinder" monkeys; consequently, they are probably the most numerous captive monkeys in North America and Europe. Trade in capuchins for pets, however, is now illegal.

A cautionary note: wildlife guides are sometimes able to find quiet howler monkeys by locating their droppings beneath trees. But ecotravellers be warned – these monkeys have reputations for sending their droppings downwards, directly toward the heads of people standing below them.

Status

All New World monkeys are listed in CITES Appendix I or II as endangered species (I) or species that, although they may not be currently threatened, need to be highly regulated in trade or they could soon become threatened (II). Main menaces to monkeys are deforestation – elimination of their natural habitats – and poaching for trade and meat. The larger monkeys especially, spiders and howlers, are often hunted for their meat, and therefore are usually rare near human settlements. (Those who eat monkeys claim that spider monkey is best.) CENTRAL AMERICAN SPIDER and MANTLED HOWLER MONKEYS are endangered, CITES Appendix I and USA ESA listed; however, even given their fragmented populations, both are still fairly abundant in protected areas of Costa Rica. The RED-BACKED SQUIRREL MONKEY, also CITES Appendix I and USA ESA listed, is highly endangered in Costa Rica. Only a few fragmented, Pacific coastal, populations survive, at Manuel Antonio National Park and in and around Corcovado National Park. In 1985, the entire Costa Rican population was estimated at less than 3000. Only Costa Rica's WHITE-FACED CAPUCHIN is not officially considered to be threatened. Large expanses of protected forest are required for continued survival of Costa Rica's "monos."

Profiles

Red-backed Squirrel Monkey, *Saimiri oerstedii*, Plate 74a
White-faced Capuchin, *Cebus capucinus*, Plate 74b
Mantled Howler Monkey, *Alouatta palliata*, Plate 74c
Central American Spider Monkey, *Ateles geoffroyi*, Plate 74d

4. Anteaters, Armadillos, and Sloths

Anteaters, *armadillos*, and *sloths* are three types of very different and different-looking mammals that, somewhat surprisingly, are closely related. The group they belong to is the Order Edentata, meaning, literally, *without teeth*. Since all but the anteaters have some teeth, the name is a misnomer. The *edentates* are New World mammals specialized to eat ants and termites, or to eat leaves high in the forest canopy. Although the edentates might look and behave differently, they are grouped together because they share certain skeletal features and aspects of their circulatory and reproductive systems that indicate close relationships. Because anteaters and sloths are so different and found only in the tropical and semi-tropical forests of Central and South America, they are perhaps the quintessential mammals of the region, the way that toucans and parrots are the quintessential Neotropical birds. Although if given a choice of mammals, most visitors to Costa Rica might prefer to see a Jaguar, it is far more likely that the characteristic Neotropical mammal that they spot will be one of the far more common sloths or anteaters.

Anteaters. The anteater family, Myrmecophagidae, has 4 species, all restricted to Neotropical forests. Three of the species occur in Costa Rica: the very rare, 2-m-long (6.5 ft) GIANT ANTEATER, the smaller NORTHERN TAMANDUA (Plate 75), and the very small SILKY ANTEATER (Plate 75). Because the last species is a nocturnal tree-dweller, only the Northern Tamandua is likely to be seen. Fairly common inhabitants of rainforests, they have long cone-shaped snouts, large hooked claws on each front foot, noticeable ears, and a conspicuously dense coat of yellowish or brownish hair, with black on the belly and sides (a black *vest*, biologists say). Tamanduas weigh between 3 and 6 kg (6 to 13 lb). The anteater shape is unmistakeable, and once you've studied a picture, you'll know one when you see one.

Armadillos. Armadillos are strange ground-dwelling mammals that, probably owing to the armor plating on their backs, are ecologically quite successful. The family, Dasypodidae, contains about 20 species that are distributed from the southern tip of South America to the central USA. Only two species occur in Costa Rica, NAKED-TAILED and NINE-BANDED ARMADILLOS (Plate 75). Because the former is wholly nocturnal, only the Nine-banded, the species that extends to the USA, is likely to be encountered in Costa Rica. These armadillos, which weigh from 3 to 4 kg (6 to 9 lb), are grayish or yellowish with many crosswise plates of hard, horn-like material on their backs (bony plates underlie the outer horny covering). The plating produces a look that makes them unmistakeable.

Sloths. What can one say? There is nothing else like a sloth. They vaguely resemble monkeys, but their slow-motion lifestyle is the very antithesis of the primates' hyperkinetic life. There are two families of sloths, the two-toed and three-toed varieties, distinguished by the number of claws per foot. All told, there are 5 sloth species, two of which occur in Costa Rica – HOFFMAN'S TWO-TOED and

BROWN-THROATED THREE-TOED SLOTHS (Plate 75). Only the more common three-toed is likely to be spotted by most visitors, as the two-toed is mostly active only at night. Three-toed Sloths (Family Bradypodidae, meaning *slow-footed*), which weigh, on average, about 4 kg (9 lb), are pale yellowish or brown with a round, white face with dark side stripes. Their hair is long and stiff, producing a shaggy look. Long limbs end in feet with three curved claws that they use as hooks to hang from tree branches.

Natural History
Ecology and Behavior

Anteaters. Anteaters are mammals highly specialized to feed on ants and termites; some also dabble in bees. From an anteater's point of view, the main thing about these social insects is that they live in large colonies, so that finding one often means finding thousands. The anteaters' strong, sharp, front claws are put to use digging into ant colonies in or on the ground, and into termite nests in trees (the very abundant, dark, globular, often basket-ball sized *termitaries* attached to the trunks and branches of tropical trees); their long, thin snouts are used to get down into the excavation, and their extremely long tongues, coated with a special sticky saliva, are used to extract the little bugs. Anteaters have prehensile tails for hanging about and moving in trees, allowing them to get to hard-to-reach termite nests. Particular about their food, anteaters don't generally go after army ants or large, stinging ants that might do them harm. Tamanduas rest in hollow trees or other holes during midday, but are otherwise active, including nocturnally. They forage both on the ground and in trees, usually solitarily. Each individual's home range, the area in which it lives and seeks food, averages about 70 hectares (170 acres). Anteaters are fairly slow-moving animals and their metabolic rates low because, although ants and termites are plentiful and easy to find, they don't provide a high nutrition, high energy diet.

Sloths. Three-toed Sloths are active both during the day and at night, spending almost all their time in trees, feeding on leaves. "Active" is probably the wrong word to describe their behavior. Sloths, particularly the three-toed ones, move incredibly slowly – so much so that in the not-too-distant past it was thought that a sloth spent its entire life moving about slowly in a single tree. Detailed observations have shown that sloths do indeed switch trees, but, on average, only once every two days. When switching, they do not cross open ground, but move between the trees' overlapping branches. This is smart, both because slowly descending to the ground and then climbing another tree would be a waste of time and energy and because a slow-moving sloth on the ground would be easy, defenseless prey for a variety of predators – snakes, large cats, and eagles. (One person clocked a female sloth on the ground as moving only 4.5 m, or 14 ft, in a minute – and that was in rapid response to the call of her offspring!) Apparently, sloths normally come down from their elevated perches only about once per week, to urinate and defecate at the base of a tree. Why they do so, instead of letting go from the heights, remains a mystery. During the 30 minutes or so it takes the sloth to dig a small hole, void itself, and cover the droppings, the animal is dangerously vulnerable to predators. Consuming only leaves provides a nutritionally poor diet and, as a result, sloths have very low metabolic rates and relatively low body temperatures; in fact, at night, sloths save energy by having their body temperatures decline to almost match that of the environment. Sloths are solitary and apparently territorial – only one per tree is permitted (or a female together with her young). Look for sloths in large, leafy trees (particularly Cecropias), especially at night – often they can be spotted hanging upside down, their hook-like claws grasping the branches.

Armadillos. Some armadillos feed mainly on ants and termites, but the NINE-BANDED ARMADILLO is more omnivorous, eating many kinds of insects, small vertebrates, and also some plant parts. These armadillos, as is characteristic of their kind, have long claws for digging for food and for digging burrows. Usually they spend the day foraging alone, but several family members may share the same sleeping burrow. They are generally slow-moving creatures that, if not for their armor plating, would be easy prey for predators. When attacked, they curl up into a ball so that their armor faces the attacker, their soft abdomen protected at the center of the ball. Few natural predators can harm them. However, like opossums, they are frequently hit on roads by automobiles.

Breeding

Female anteaters bear one offspring at a time, and lavish attention on it. At first the newborn is placed in a secure location, such as in a tree cavity, and the mother returns to it at intervals to nurse. Later, when it is old enough, the youngster rides on the mother's back. After several months, when the young is about half the mother's size, the two part ways. Breeding may be at any time of year. Sloths also produce one young at a time. Following 6 months of pregnancy, the offspring is born. It is then carried about and fed by the mother for about 4 months, at which point it is put down and must forage for itself. Until it is a year old or so, the juvenile forages within its mother's home range; then it moves out on its own. Sloths not only move slowly, they grow slowly. Apparently they do not reach sexual maturity until they are 3 years old, and they may live for 20 to 30 years. Female armadillos, after 70-day pregnancies, produce several young at a time, usually 4. For some unknown reason, each litter of armadillo young arises from a single fertilized egg so that if a female has 4 young, they are always identical quadruplets.

Ecological Interactions

The theory of the *ecological niche* suggests that two or more species that are virtually identical in their lifestyles and resource use cannot coexist within the same habitat or, at least, not for long. Competition among the species for resources will eventually drive the poorer competitors to extinction. If true, how do several species of anteater all occur in the same tropical forest? After all, they all eat ants and termites. Ecologists believe that the SILKY and GIANT ANTEATERS, and the NORTHERN TAMANDUA, coexist in some of the same places because they are different sizes and, although they eat the same food, their activity patterns differ sufficiently so as to reduce competition. For instance, Silky Anteaters are strictly nocturnal, but Giant Anteaters and Tamandua are also active during the day. The Silky is arboreal, the Giant is ground-dwelling, and Tamandua are both.

Some of the hair on sloths often has a blue-green tinge to it. Intriguingly, this coloring turns out to be caused by algae – miniscule plants – that live out their lives on the hairs. Not only do sloths support plants on their bodies, they support insects as well. It seems that a number of different beetle and moth species spend at least parts of their life cycles living on sloths. One moth species, a "sloth moth," lives as an adult moth on a sloth, reproducing by laying its eggs in sloth droppings.

Lore and Notes

GIANT ANTEATERS are also known as Ant Bears, for obvious reasons.

Status

Overall, the edentate mammals are not doing badly, but all suffer population declines from habitat destruction. One problem in trying to determine the status of their populations is that many are nocturnal and some of the armadillos spend most of their time in burrows. The result is that nobody really knows the real health of some populations. The GIANT ANTEATER (CITES Appendix II listed) has been rare in Central America for over 100 years, and may be extinct now in most of the region. It is fairly common only on the savannas of Venezuela and Colombia. If it survives in Costa Rica, it is only in the remotest forests. NORTHERN TAMANDUA are found throughout Costa Rica but, outside of protected areas, they are sometimes killed as pests by locals. The SILKY ANTEATER is thought to be fairly common, but because its populations naturally are sparse and also because it is so difficult to spot, good information is lacking. Costa Rica's two sloth species apparently are fairly common, although, again, there is no good information on their populations (the two-toed is CITES Appendix III listed for Costa Rica). Some biologists suspect that three-toed sloths are one of the most abundant larger mammals of Neotropical forests. One sloth, Brazil's MANED THREE-TOED SLOTH, is endangered (USA ESA listed). Armadillos are common in Costa Rica and other parts of their ranges, but because they are hunted for meat, their populations are often sparse around heavily settled areas. NINE-BANDED ARMADILLOS may be one of the most abundant mammals of Central American forests. NAKED-TAILED ARMADILLOS (CITES Appendix III listed for Costa Rica) also may be common but, owing to their nocturnal lifestyles, no one knows for sure. In South America, the GIANT ARMADILLO, which weighs up to 30 kg (65 lb) and is killed for meat, is now endangered (CITES Appendix I and USA ESA listed) from overhunting.

Profiles

Hoffman's Two-toed Sloth, *Choloepus hoffmanni*, Plate 75a
Brown-throated Three-toed Sloth, *Bradypus variegatus*, Plate 75b
Nine-banded Armadillo, *Dasypus novemcinctus*, Plate 75c
Silky Anteater, *Cyclopes didactylus*, Plate 75d
Northern Tamandua, *Tamandua mexicana*, Plate 75e

5. Rodents

Ecotravellers discover among *rodents* an ecological paradox: although by far the most diverse and successful of the mammals, rodents are, with a few obvious exceptions in any region, relatively inconspicuous and rarely encountered. The number of living rodent species globally approaches 1750, fully 43% of the approximately 4050 known mammalian species. Probably in every region of the world save Antarctica, rodents – including the mice, rats, squirrels, chipmunks, marmots, gophers, beaver, and porcupines – are the most abundant land mammals. More individual rodents are estimated to be alive at any one time than individuals of all other types of mammals combined. Rodents' near-invisibility to people, particularly in the Neotropics, derives from the facts that most rodents are very small, most are secretive or nocturnal, and many live out their lives in subterranean burrows. That most rodents are rarely encountered, of course, many people do not consider much of a hardship.

Rodent ecological success is likely related to their efficient, specialized teeth and associated jaw muscles, and to their broad, nearly omnivorous diets. Rodents are characterized by having four large incisor teeth, one pair front-and-center in the upper jaw, one pair in the lower (other teeth, separated from the incisors, are located farther back in the mouth). With these strong, sharp, chisel-like front teeth, rodents "make their living" gnawing (*rodent* is from the Latin *rodere*, to gnaw), cutting, and slicing vegetation, fruit, and nuts, killing and eating small animals, digging burrows, and even, in the case of beaver, imitating lumberjacks.

Rodents are distributed throughout the world except for Antarctica and some Arctic islands. The Neotropics contain some of the largest and most interesting of the world's rodents. About 50 species occur in Costa Rica. Only a few of these are commonly spotted by visitors and so warrant coverage here – a few squirrels, a porcupine, and two larger rodent representatives, the PACA and CENTRAL AMERICAN AGOUTI (Plate 76). Squirrels are members of the Family Sciuridae, a world-wide group of more than 350 species that occurs on all continents except Australia and Antarctica. The family includes ground, tree, and flying squirrels. Only 5 species occur in Costa Rica. Family Erethizontidae contains the 15 species of New World porcupines, which are distributed throughout the Americas except for the southern third of South America. A single species is native to Costa Rica. Last, two families that are restricted to tropical America contain a few large, common rodents: Family Agoutidae contains the Paca, and Family Dasyproctidae includes the Agouti.

Most of the world's rodents are small mouse-like or rat-like mammals that weigh less than a kilogram (2.2 lb); they range, however, from tiny pygmy mice that weigh only a few grams to South America's pig-like CAPYBARA, behemoths at up to 50 kg (110 lb). Costa Rica's two most visible tree squirrels, RED-TAILED and VARIEGATED SQUIRRELS (Plate 76), are moderate-sized squirrels with short ears, relatively long legs, and long, bushy tails. Red-tailed Squirrels are reddish or brown, whereas Variegated Squirrels, as the name suggests, are highly variable in color, both individually and geographically. Many are reddish or brown with a darker back, and a mixed black and white tail that produces a grizzled gray appearance. Porcupines generally are fairly large, heavyset rodents, but the Costa Rican species, the MEXICAN HAIRY PORCUPINE (Plate 76), is a relatively small, thin member of the group, weighing between 1.5 and 2.5 kg (3.3 to 5.5 lb). Their bodies are covered with long, dark hair that covers most of their spines. They have short limbs, longish prehensile tails, small eyes, mostly hidden ears, and a hairless snout. CENTRAL AMERICAN AGOUTI and PACA are large, almost pig-like rodents, usually brownish, with long legs, short hair, and squirrel-like heads. Paca weigh up to 10 kg (22 lb), twice the weight of an Agouti. Males are slightly larger than females.

Natural History
Ecology and Behavior
RED-TAILED and VARIEGATED SQUIRRELS are day-active tree squirrels, generally seen in trees and, occasionally, foraging on the ground. Red-tails typically occupy wet forested areas, from low to mid-range elevations. Variegated Squirrels occupy forest edge and more open areas, and drier areas, in Costa Rican lowlands. These squirrels eat a wide variety of foods: fruit (especially berries), nuts, some insects, leaves, flowers, even bark and fungi. Red-tailed Squirrels during a Panamanian study were noted feeding at 21 different plant species. Both squirrels cache food

for later meals by burying it in the ground or placing it in tree cavities. Female Red-tails are territorial, defending exclusive living and feeding areas from other females. Males are not territorial; their home ranges, the areas over which they range daily in search of food, overlap those of other males and those of females. Variegated Squirrels appear to be territorial. Home ranges in these tree squirrels range from about 0.5 to 4 hectares (1 to 10 acres), depending on habitat quality, that is, on the amount of food available per unit area. MEXICAN HAIRY PORCUPINES are solitary, nocturnal animals, almost always found in trees. They move slowly along branches, using their *prehensile* tail as a fifth limb, to feed on leaves, green tree shoots, and fruit. During the day they sleep in tree cavities or on branches hidden amid dense vegetation. They are found mostly in higher-elevation forests.

PACA are usually active only at night, foraging for fruit, nuts, seeds, and vegetation. Along with CENTRAL AMERICAN AGOUTI, they can sit up on their hind legs and eat, holding their food with their front paws, much like a squirrel or rat. They sleep away daylight hours in burrows. Several observers have noted that Paca, if startled or threatened, will freeze, and, if chased, will dive into nearby water, around which they are usually found. The smaller Agouti are naturally day-active, but have become increasingly nocturnal in their habits in areas where they are intensively hunted. Agouti mainly eat seeds and fruit, but also flowers, vegetation, and insects. Both Paca and Agouti appear to live in monogamous pairs on territories, although male and female tend to forage alone. When threatened or startled, Agouti usually run, giving warning calls or barks as they go, presumably to warn nearby relatives of danger. Agouti and Paca, large and tasty, are preyed on by a variety of mammals and reptiles, including large snakes and such carnivores as Jaguarundi (Plate 77).

Breeding

Relatively little is known of the breeding behavior of most Neotropical tree squirrels and of many other rodents. Tree squirrel nests consist of a bed of leaves placed in a tree cavity or a ball of leaves on a branch or in a tangle of vegetation. One to 3 young are born per litter, usually 2. Female Red-tails have 2 or 3 litters per year. Actual mating in this species takes place during *sex chases*, during which 4 or more males chase a female for several hours, the female apparently choosing which male or males she mates with. Pregnancy is about 45 days; young nurse for 8 to 10 weeks. Breeding tends to be during the dry season, from late December through March. MEXICAN HAIRY PORCUPINES have 1 to 3 young per litter. Pregnancy periods are relatively long, and, as a result, the young are *precocial* – born eyes open and in an advanced state. They are therefore mobile and quickly able to follow the mother. CENTRAL AMERICAN AGOUTI and PACA also have precocial young, usually in litters of 1 or 2. A day after their birth, a mother Agouti leads her young to a burrow where they hide, and to which she returns each day to feed them. Pregnancies for Agouti and Paca last 115 to 120 days.

Ecological Interactions

Rodents are important ecologically primarily because of their great abundance. They are so common that they make up a large proportion of the diets of many carnivores. For instance, in a recent study of Jaguar, it was discovered that rodents were the third most frequent prey of the large cats, after sloths and iguanas. In turn, rodents, owing to their ubiquitousness and numbers, are themselves important predators on seeds and fruit. That is, they eat seeds and seed-containing fruit, digesting or damaging the seeds, rendering them useless to the plants that produced them for reproduction. Of course, not every seed is damaged (some fall to the ground as rodents eat, others pass unscathed through their digestive tracts), and so rodents, at least occasionally, also act as seed dispersers (see Close-Up, p. 179). Burrowing is another aspect of rodent behavior that has significant ecological implications because of the sheer numbers of individuals that participate. When so many animals move soil around (rats and mice, especially), the effect is that over several years the entire topsoil of an area is turned, keeping soil loose and aerated, and therefore more suitable for plant growth.

Lore and Notes

Through the animals' constant gnawing, rodents' chisel-like incisors wear down rapidly. Fortunately for the rodents, their incisors, owing to some ingenious anatomy and physiology, continue to grow throughout their lives, unlike those of most other mammals.

Contrary to folk wisdom, porcupines cannot "throw" their quills, or spines, at people or predators. Rather, the spines detach quite easily when touched, such that a predator snatching a porcupine in its mouth will be impaled with spines and hence, rendered very unhappy. The spines have barbed ends, like fishhooks, which anchor them securely into the offending predator.

PACA meat is considered to be among the most superior of wild meats, because it is tasty, tender, and lacks much of an odor; as such, when it can be purchased in Costa Rica, it is very expensive. Both Agouti and Paca are favorite game animals throughout their ranges.

Status

Both RED-TAILED and VARIEGATED SQUIRRELS are common, widespread species, not presently threatened. The Variegated, in particular, adapts well to human disturbance of forested areas and thrives near human settlements – for example, on farms and plantations. These squirrels are hunted for meat in parts of their ranges. DEPPE'S SQUIRREL, a small, brown tree squirrel, is now threatened in Costa Rica owing to deforestation (CITES Appendix III listed). The precise status of MEXICAN HAIRY PORCUPINE populations is unknown, but they are thought to be secure. The same is true for many other species of New World porcupines – little is known about them, but most appear not to be presently threatened. These nocturnal rodents are hunted for meat in some areas. One species, southeastern Brazil's BRISTLE-SPINED PORCUPINE, is now highly endangered (USA ESA listed). PACA are hunted for meat throughout their broad geographic range, but, although scarce in heavily hunted areas, they are secretive enough and broadly enough distributed over Central and South America to still maintain many healthy populations. There are still dense populations of CENTRAL AMERICAN AGOUTI in relatively undisturbed regions of Costa Rica.

Profiles

Red-tailed Squirrel, *Sciurus granatensis*, Plate 76a
Variegated Squirrel, *Sciurus variegatoides*, Plate 76b
Central American Dwarf Squirrel, *Microsciuris alfari,* Plate 76c
Mexican Hairy Porcupine, *Coendou mexicanus*, Plate 76d
Paca, *Agouti paca*, Plate 76e
Central American Agouti, *Dasyprocta punctata*, Plate 76f

6. Carnivores

Carnivores are the ferocious mammals – the cat that sleeps on your pillow, the dog that takes table scraps from your hand – that are specialized to kill and eat other vertebrate animals. Four families within the Order Carnivora have Costa Rican representatives: *felids* (cats), *canids* (dogs), *procyonids* (raccoons), and *mustelids* (weasel-like things). They have in common that they are primarily ground-dwelling animals and have teeth customized to grasp, rip, and tear flesh – witness their large, cone-shaped canines. Most are meat-eaters, but many are at least somewhat *omnivorous,* taking fruits and other plant materials. Only two wild members of the dog family, Canidae, occur in Costa Rica, the COYOTE and GRAY FOX (Plate 77); because they are common mammals that range into North America, they are pictured but not detailed here. In total there are about 37 species of cat, Family Felidae, with representatives inhabiting all continents but Australia and Antarctica. Because all 6 species that occur in Central America are fairly rare, most to the point of being endangered, and because of their mainly nocturnal habits, it is rare to see even a single wild cat on any brief Costa Rican trip. More than likely, all that will be observed of cats are traces; some tracks in the mud near a stream or scratch marks on a tree trunk or log.

All of the cats are easily recognized as such. They come in two varieties – spotted and not spotted. The 4 spotted species generally are yellowish, tan, or cinnamon on top and white below, with black spots and stripes on their heads, bodies, and legs. The smallest is the ONCILLA, or LITTLE SPOTTED CAT, the size of a small house cat. Next in size is the MARGAY (Plate 77), which is the size of a large house cat, weighing 3 to 5 kg (6 to 11 lb). OCELOTS (Plate 77) are the size of medium-sized dogs and weigh 7 to 14 kg (15 to 30 lb). Last, the JAGUAR (Plate 77) is the largest New World cat and the region's largest carnivore, sometimes nearly 2 m long (6.5 ft), and weighing between 60 and 120 kg (130 to 260 lb). The two unspotted cats are the mid-sized JAGUARUNDI (Plate 77), which is blackish, brown, gray, or reddish, and the PUMA, or MOUNTAIN LION, which is tan or grayish and almost as large as the Jaguar. Female cats often are smaller than males, up to a third smaller in the Jaguar.

The Mustelid family is comprised of about 70 species of small and medium-sized, slender-bodied carnivores that are distributed globally except for Australia and Antarctica. Included in the family are the weasels, skunks, mink, otters, and badgers, animals that occupy diverse habitats, including, in the case of otters, the water. Mustelids generally have long, thin bodies, short legs, long tails, and soft, dense fur. Seven species occur in Costa Rica, but only 3 are commonly sighted. The TAYRA (TIE-rah, Plate 78) is a medium-sized, mink-like animal, being long and slender and mostly black or brown; they weigh up to 5 kg (11 lb). STRIPED HOG-NOSED SKUNKS (Plate 78) weigh about 4 kg (9 lb) and are black with white stripes. NEOTROPICAL OTTERS (Plate 78) are short-legged and brownish and usually weigh about 11 kg (25 lb). Males are larger than females in many mustelid species.

The Raccoons, or Family Procyonidae, are a New World group of about 15 species (for several reasons, the Asian pandas were thought until recently to be procyonids). This is a very successful group of small and medium-sized mammals that occupy a range of habitats, usually where there are trees. Six species occur in Costa Rica, but 3 are rarely seen. The more visible ones are the NORTHERN RACCOON, the WHITE-NOSED COATI (kah-WAH-tee), and the KINKAJOU (Plate

79). In general, procyonids have long, pointed muzzles, short legs, and long tails that more often than not are noticeably ringed. Northern Raccoons (3 to 6 kg, 6 to 13 lb) are brownish or grayish with black tipped outer hairs that produce a salt-and-pepper look. They have strongly banded tails and a distinguishing black face mask that surrounds their eyes. Coatis (4 to 5 kg, 9 to 11 lb), brown or reddish with dark face masks, are more slender than raccoons and have very long, banded tails that, like a cat, they hold erect as they walk. Kinkajous (2 to 3 kg, 5 to 7 lb) have extremely long tails and, in contrast to raccoons and coatis, are uniformly brownish. Their heads are rounder and their snouts shorter and broader than other procyonids. As with the felids and mustelids, male procyonids are often a bit larger than females.

Natural History
Ecology and Behavior

Felids. The cats are finely adapted to be predators on vertebrate animals. Hunting methods are extremely similar among the various species. Cats do not run to chase prey for long distances. Rather, they slowly stalk their prey or wait in ambush, then capture the prey after pouncing on it or after a very brief, fast chase. Biologists are often impressed by the consistency in the manner that cats kill their prey. Almost always it is with a sharp bite to the neck or head, breaking the neck or crushing the skull. Retractile claws, in addition to their use in grabbing and holding prey, give cats good abilities to climb trees, and some of them are partially arboreal animals, foraging and even sleeping in trees. Aside from some highly social large cats of Africa, most cats are solitary animals, foraging alone, individuals coming together only to mate. Some species are territorial but in others individuals overlap in the areas in which they hunt. Cats, with their big eyes to gather light, are often nocturnal, especially those of rainforests, but some are also active by day. When inactive, they shelter in rock crevices or burrows dug by other animals. Cats are the most carnivorous of the carnivores; their diets are more centered on meat than any of the other families. Little is known of the natural history of forest-dwelling ONCILLAS; they eat birds and small rodents. MARGAYS are mostly-arboreal forest cats; they forage in trees for rodents and birds. OCELOTS eat rodents, snakes, lizards, and birds. They are probably more common than Oncillas and Margays and, although quite secretive, they are the most frequently seen of the spotted cats. Active mainly at night, they often spend daylight hours asleep in trees. *El Tigre*, the JAGUAR, can be active day or night. These cats inhabit low and middle elevation forests, hunting for large prey such as peccary and deer, but also monkeys, sloths, rodents, birds, lizards, even caiman. JAGUARUNDI are both day and night active, and are seen fairly frequently in forests. They eat small rodents, rabbits, and birds. PUMA occupy various habitat types and prey on deer and other large mammals. They are rare in Central America, the total population of the region probably no more than a few hundred.

Mustelids. Most of the mustelids are strongly carnivorous, although some, such as the ones detailed below, eat a number of other foods. These are powerful animals, sometimes capable of killing prey as large as, or even larger than themselves. Like the cats, they kill with swift crushing bites to the head or neck. TAYRAS are tree climbers, active both day and night. Singly or sometimes in pairs or family groups, they search the ground and in trees for a variety of foods – fruit, bird eggs or nestlings, lizards, rodents, rabbits, and insects. Although they are very wary animals, still, they are among the most frequently sighted of the mustelids.

STRIPED HOG-NOSED SKUNKS are nocturnal. They forage solitarily, rooting about a good deal in the leaf litter and soil, looking for insects, snails, and small vertebrates such as rodents and lizards; occasionally they take fruit. Skunks, what with their spray defenses (see below), usually move quite leisurely, apparently knowing that they are well protected from most predators. NEOTROPICAL OTTERS forage alone or in pairs. They are active both during the day and at night, hunting in streams, rivers, and ponds for fish and crustaceans such as crayfish. Although otters always remain in or near the water, they spend their inactive time in burrows on land. Adapted for moving swiftly and smoothly through water, they move on land awkwardly, with a duck-like waddle.

Procyonids. The distinctive ecological and behavioral traits of the procyonids are that:

1   although classified as carnivores, they are omnivorous;
2   they are mostly nocturnal in their activities (except for the coati);
3   as a group, they have a great propensity to climb trees.

NORTHERN RACCOONS forage either singly or in small groups composed of a mother and her young. They eat fruit and all sorts of small animals, both vertebrates and invertebrates, not to mention garbage around human settlements. Exhibiting a high degree of manual dexterity and sensitivity of their "fingers," raccoons actually search for food in ponds and streams by lowering only their front paws into the water and feeling for frogs, crabs, crayfish, etc. When not active, raccoons seek shelter in burrows or in tree or rock crevices. Coatis are known for their daylight activity and for the fact that, unlike others of the family, they are quite social. They usually group together in small bands, most commonly several adult females and their young. Males tend to be solitary animals, joining a female band only for several weeks during the breeding season. Coatis are as comfortable foraging in trees as they are on the ground; they search for fruit, lizards, mice, insects and, in the great raccoon tradition, they are also denizens of trash heaps. KINKAJOUS spend most of their time in trees, foraging for fruits and arboreal vertebrates. Alone among the procyonids, their tail is fully prehensile, permitting them to grasp branches with it and hang upside down. Kinkajous are nocturnal, and relatively little is known of their behavior in the wild. With a flashlight, they can often be spotted moving about tree branches at night, making squeaking sounds; several are often found feeding together in a single tree. Adult procyonids probably have a relatively low rate of predation, but their enemies would include boas, raptors, cats, and Tayras.

Breeding

Felids. Male and female cats of the Neotropics come together only to mate; the female bears and raises her young alone. She gives birth in a den that is a burrow, rock cave, or tree cavity. The young are sheltered in the den while the female forages; she returns periodically to nurse and bring the kittens prey to eat. Most of the cats have 1 or 2 young at a time, although PUMA and JAGUAR may have up to 4. Pregnancy is about 75 days in the smaller cats, about 100 in the large ones. Juvenile Jaguars remain with their mother for up to 18 months, learning to be efficient hunters, before they go off on their own.

Mustelids. Female mustelids give birth in dens under rocks or in crevices, or in burrows under trees. Pregnancy for TAYRA, skunks, and otters usually lasts about

60 to 70 days. Tayra produce an average of 2 young per litter, skunk, 2 to 5, and otter, 2 or 3. As is true for many of the carnivores, mustelid young are born blind and helpless.

Procyonids. In all the Costa Rican procyonids, females raise young without help from males. Young are born in nests made in trees (NORTHERN RACCOONS in North America also give birth in rock crevices and in tree cavities). Duration of pregnancy varies from about 65 days in raccoons, to 75 days in the WHITE-NOSED COATI, to about 115 days in KINKAJOUS. Raccoons have 3 to 7 young per litter, coatis, 1 to 5 young, and Kinkajous, always only one.

Ecological Interactions

The 6 species of Costa Rican cats are quite alike in form and behavior. Therefore, according to ecological theory, they should compete strongly for the same resources, competition that if unchecked, should drive some of the species to extinction. But are all the cats really so similar? One major difference is size. ONCILLA are very small, MARGAY a bit bigger, and JAGUARUNDI larger than that. OCELOT are next in size. The two large cats, PUMA and JAGUAR, are somewhat similar in size, but Puma live in more diverse habitats than do Jaguar. Prey the animals take also varies. The smallest cats take small rodents and birds, the medium-sized cats take larger rodents and birds, and the large cats take larger prey such as large mammals. Biologists believe that these kinds of differences among similar species permit sufficient "ecological separation" to allow somewhat peaceful coexistence.

Lore and Notes

JAGUAR rarely attack people, who normally are given a wide berth; these cats tend to run away quickly when spotted. Recently there have been widely circulated reports of PUMA attacking people in the USA, but this seems more due to people moving to live in prime Puma habitat, which is increasingly limited, than to a desire on the cat's part for human prey. Cats in Costa Rica are sometimes seen walking at night along forest trails or roads. General advice if you happen to stumble across a large cat: do not run because that often stimulates a cat to chase. Face the cat, make yourself large by raising your arms, and make as much loud noise as you can.

Mustelids have a strong, characteristic odor, *musk*, that is produced by secretions from scent glands around their backsides. The secretions are used to communicate with other members of the species and to mark habitats, presumably also for signalling. In skunks, these glands produce particularly strong, foul-smelling fluids that with startling good aim can be violently squirted in a jet at potential predators. The fluids are not toxic, cannot cause blindness as is sometimes commonly believed, but they can cause temporary, severe irritation of eyes and nose. Predators that approach a skunk once rarely repeat the exercise.

One facet of mustelid natural history that is particularly helpful to people, though not universally appreciated, is that these carnivores eat a staggering number of rodents. For instance, it has been calculated that weasels each year in New York State eat some 60 million mice and millions of rats. In fact, in the past, TAYRA were kept as pets in parts of South America to protect homes and belongings from rodents.

One aspect of the natural history of NORTHERN RACCOONS with which many people are familiar is their habit of washing their food before eating it. In fact, their species' name, *lotor*, is Latin for *the washer*. Unfortunately, this piece of folk wisdom is untrue. In captivity, many raccoons dip their food in their water dishes, but this is now believed to be simply a substitute for the way raccoons in the wild reach for prey in the water. Raccoons in the wild eat what they find, no dipping required.

Sometimes the name *coatimundi* is used for a coati, but the longer term is often incorrect. "Coati" is an Indian name for the species. "Coati-mundi" apparently was used by Indians to refer to solitary coati (usually males, because females travel in groups). Thus, coatimundi is not really a synonym for coati.

Status

All of the Neotropical cats are now threatened or actually endangered. Their forest habitats are increasingly cleared for agricultural purposes; they were, and still are to a limited extent, hunted for their skins, and large cats are killed as potential predators on livestock and pets. The 4 species profiled here and the PUMA are all CITES Appendix I and USA ESA listed, although the JAGUARUNDI and Puma are listed for only parts of their ranges. Jaguar have been eliminated from most of Costa Rica and are present only in small numbers in protected areas, including Tortuguero, Santa Rosa, and Corcovado National Parks.

Many mustelids in the past were trapped intensively for their fur, which is often soft, dense, and glossy, just the ticket, in fact, to create coats of otter or weasel, mink or marten, sable or fisher. NEOTROPICAL OTTERS, although still widespread in the Americas, are sufficiently rare to be considered endangered (CITES Appendix I and USA ESA listed). Skunks are common, their populations healthy, and TAYRA are common animals that usually do well even where people disturb their natural habitats. Another Costa Rican mustelid, the GRISON (Plate 78), a grayish and black weasel-like animal, is fairly rare and is regulated by Costa Rican authorities as possibly threatened (CITES Appendix III listed).

None of the Costa Rican procyonids are currently threatened. Raccoons, coatis, and KINKAJOUS are all fairly common. Relatively little is known about another species, the CRAB-EATING RACCOON (Plate 79), so information on its population sizes is scarce. Two other species, the OLINGO (Plate 79) and the CACOMISTLE, possibly will be threatened in the future, and are listed by Costa Rican authorities as species to watch. One type of Olingo, possibly a separate species that occurs solely in Costa Rica, may be endangered.

Profiles

Coyote, *Canis latrans*, Plate 77a
Gray Fox, *Urocyon cinereoargenteus*, Plate 77b
Ocelot, *Leopardus pardalis*, Plate 77c
Margay, *Leopardus wiedii*, Plate 77d
Jaguar, *Panthera onca*, Plate 77e
Jaguarundi, *Herpailurus yaguarondi*, Plate 77f
Tayra, *Eira barbara*, Plate 78a
Striped Hog-nosed Skunk, *Conepatus semistriatus*, Plate 78b
Hooded Skunk, *Mephitis macroura*, Plate 78c
Neotropical Otter, *Lutra longicaudis*, Plate 78d
Grison, *Galictis vittata*, Plate 78e
Long-tailed Weasel, *Mustela frenata*, Plate 78f
Northern Raccoon, *Procyon lotor*, Plate 79a
Crab-eating Raccoon, *Procyon cancrivorus*, Plate 79b

White-nosed Coati, *Nasua narica*, Plate 79c
Kinkajou, *Potos flavus*, Plate 79d
Olingo, *Bassaricyon gabbii*, Plate 79e

7. Peccaries and Deer

Peccaries and *deer* are the two Neotropical representatives of the Artiodactyla, the globally distributed order of hoofed mammals (ungulates) that have an even number of toes on each foot. (Order Perissodactyla, p. 219, are ungulates with odd numbers of toes.) Other *artiodactyls* are pigs, hippos, giraffes, antelope, bison, buffalo, cattle, gazelles, goats, and sheep. In general, the group is specialized to feed on leaves, grass, and fallen fruit. The truth be told, peccaries look like mid-sized pigs; and deer are self-explanatory. Three peccary species comprise the Family Tayassuidae. They are confined in their distributions to the Neotropics, although one species pushes northwards into the southwestern USA; two species, the COLLARED and WHITE-LIPPED PECCARIES (Plate 80), occur in Costa Rica. Collared Peccaries are more abundant than the White-lipped, occur in more habitats, and are seen more frequently. Collareds are found in rainforests, deciduous forests, and areas of scattered trees and shrubs, including agricultural areas (where they raid crops). White-lippeds are denizens only of rainforests. The two deer species that occur in Costa Rica, WHITE-TAILED and RED BROCKET DEER (Plate 80) are members of Family Cervidae, which is 36 species strong and distributed almost worldwide.

Peccaries are small to medium-sized hog-like animals covered with coarse longish hair, with slender legs, large heads, small ears, and short tails. They have enlarged, sharp and pointed, tusk-like canine teeth. The Collared Peccary is the smaller of the two species, adults typically weighing between 17 and 30 kg (35 to 65 lb). They come in black or gray as adults, with a band of lighter-colored hair at the neck that furnishes their name; youngsters are reddish-brown or buff-colored. The White-lipped Peccary, so named for the white patch of hair on its chin, weighs from 25 to 40 kg (55 to 85 lb). Deer are large mammals, reddish, brown, or gray. They have long, thin legs, short tails, and big ears. Males have antlers that they shed each year and regrow. White-tailed Deer have white markings around their eyes, on their muzzles, and, appropriately, on their tails. Central American White-tailed Deer (30 to 50 kg, 65 to 110 lb) are, in general, slightly larger than Red Brocket Deer (24 to 48 kg, 50 to 100 lb), but usually smaller, by a third to a half, than members of their species in the USA and Canada. Very young deer are usually spotted with white.

Natural History
Ecology and Behavior
Peccaries are day-active, highly social animals, rarely encountered singly. COLLARED PECCARIES travel in small groups of 3 to 25 or so, most frequently 6 to 9; WHITE-LIPPED herds generally are larger, often 50 to 100 or more (smaller herds occur where they are heavily hunted). Peccaries travel single file along narrow forest paths, spreading out when good foraging sites are found. These animals are omnivores, but mainly they dig into the ground with their snouts, *rooting* for vegetation. They feed on roots, underground stems, and bulbs, but also leaves, fruit (especially the White-lipped), insects, and even small vertebrates that they stumble across. Because White-lipped Peccaries are larger than Collareds and travel in larger groups, they need to wander long distances each day to locate enough food.

Like pigs, peccaries like to wallow in mud and shallow water, and there is usually a wallowing spot within their home range, the area within which a group lives and forages. During dry seasons, peccaries may gather in large numbers near lakes or streams. Because peccaries are hunted by people, they are usually quiet, wary, and therefore, sometimes hard to notice or approach. Peccaries are preyed upon by large snakes such as boas, and probably by Puma and Jaguar (Plate 77).

Deer are *browsers* and *grazers*, that is, they eat leaves and twigs from trees and shrubs that they can reach from the ground (browsing), and grass (grazing). The RED BROCKET DEER, in particular, also eats fruit and flowers, chiefly those that have already fallen to the ground. WHITE-TAILED DEER inhabit open places and forest edge areas, rarely dense forest, whereas the Red Brocket Deer is a forest species that wanders through trailless terrain. The large, branched antlers of male White-tails make moving through dense forest a dubious business; male Red Brockets, on the other hand, have short, spike-like, rearwards-curving antlers – plainly better for maneuvering in their dense jungle habitats. Both White-tails and Red Brockets are active during daylight hours and also often at night; Red Brocket Deer are most commonly seen during early mornings and at dusk. White-tails travel either solitarily or in small groups, whereas Red Brockets are almost always solitary. Deer are *cud-chewers*. After foraging and filling a special chamber of their stomach, they find a sheltered area, rest, regurgitate the meal into their mouths and chew it well so that it can be digested. Predators on deer include the big cats – Puma and Jaguar; eagles may take young fawns.

Breeding
Female peccaries have either 1 or 2 young at a time, born 4 to 5 months after mating. The young are precocial, meaning that they can walk and follow their mother within a few days of birth. Newborns have been noticed in Costa Rica during May. Deer, likewise, give birth to 1 or 2 young that, within a week or two, can follow the mother. Until that time, they stay in a sheltered spot while their mother forages, returning at intervals to nurse them.

Lore and Notes
Both species of peccary enjoy reputations for aggressiveness toward humans, but experts agree that the reputation is exaggerated. There are stories of herds panicking at the approach of people, stampeding, even chasing people. These are large enough beasts, with sufficiently large and sharp canine teeth, to do damage. If you spot peccaries, err on the side of caution; watch them from afar and leave them alone. Be quiet and they might take no notice of you; their vision apparently is poor. If charged, a rapid retreat into a tree could be a wise move.

When a WHITE-TAILED DEER spots a predator or person that has not yet spotted it, the deer slinks away with its head and tail down, the white patch under the tail concealed. But when the deer is alarmed – it spots a predator stalking it or hears a sudden noise – it bounds off with its tail raised, its white rump and white tail bottom exposed, almost like a white flag. Animal behaviorists believe that the white is a signal to the deer's party, relatives likely to be among them, that a potential predator has been spotted and that they should flee.

The COLLARED PECCARY ranges northwards into the USA's Arizona, New Mexico, and Texas, where it is known locally simply as the PECCARY, or JAVELINA.

Status

Peccaries were hunted for food and hides long before the arrival of Europeans to the New World, and such hunting continues. COLLARED PECCARIES, listed in CITES Appendix II, are still locally common in protected, wilderness, and more rural areas. WHITE-LIPPED PECCARIES, also CITES Appendix II listed, are less common, and less is known about their populations; they may soon be threatened. Deer are likewise hunted for meat, skins, and sport. Deer range widely in Costa Rica but, due to hunting pressures, they are numerous only in the protected environs of national parks and wildlife preserves. RED BROCKET DEER employ excellent anti-hunting tactics, being solitary animals that keep to dense forests.

Profiles

Collared Peccary, *Tayassu tajacu*, Plate 80b
White-lipped Peccary, *Tayassu pecari*, Plate 80c
White-tailed Deer, *Odocoileus virginianus*, Plate 80d
Red Brocket Deer, *Mazama americana*, Plate 80e

8. Tapir

Tapirs (TAE-peers) are relatively small, funny-looking relatives of the horse and rhinoceros and the only members of that group to occur naturally in the New World. (Horses were brought from Asia by people.) Tapirs, horses, and rhinos belong to an order of mammals called the Perissodactyla, which refers to the fact that all of its members have an odd number of toes on each foot. Only four species of tapirs comprise the Family Tapiridae, three residing in the Neotropics and one in Asia. BAIRD'S TAPIR (Plate 80) is the only one to occur in Costa Rica, and it is now fairly rare; owing to its scarcity, spotting it is often a priority for visitors eager to see mammalian wildlife. This tapir used to be common in many of Costa Rica's habitats, including grassy swamps, rainforests, forested hillsides, and flooded grasslands. Now it is found in only small numbers, and then only where it is protected from hunting, mainly in national parks.

Baird's Tapir is the largest of the Neotropical tapirs, and a substantial animal, stocky and up to 2 m (6 ft) long, with short legs and a long snout somewhat reminiscent of a horse's. Weighing between 150 and 300 kg (330 to 660 lb), they have the distinction of being Central America's largest native terrestrial mammal. Tapirs have short, sparse hair – from a distance they appear almost hairless – and short tails. The long snout, or *proboscis*, consists of an enlarged, elongated upper lip. Tapirs are blackish to dark- or reddish-brown in color. Youngsters have a characteristic lighter brown coloring with white or yellowish spots and stripes.

Natural History
Ecology and Behavior

Tapirs are mainly nocturnal, but are also seen foraging during daylight hours. They are herbivores, feasting on leaves, twigs, grass, fruit, and perhaps some seeds. As *browsers*, they walk along, stopping occasionally to munch on low plants. Apparently tapirs are very particular about the types of plants they consume, relying at least partially on a highly developed sense of smell to choose the right stuff; their vision is quite poor. The distinctive tapir snout is used both to shovel food into the mouth and to reach food that the tongue and teeth cannot. Tapirs are not very social; they are usually encountered in ones or twos, for instance, a female and her young. These mammals have a strong affinity for water and are excellent swimmers; if they are disturbed, they often seek refuge in the water. Usually there is a bathing and wallowing site within their home range, the area within which they live and forage; sometimes tapirs sleep in the water.

Breeding
Relatively little is known about breeding in wild tapirs. A single offspring is born to a female BAIRD'S TAPIR 13 months after mating. At first, the youngster stays in a secluded spot while its mother forages elsewhere and periodically returns to nurse. After 10 days or so, the youngster can follow the mother, and stays with her for up to a year. When it is about two-thirds the mother's size, it goes its separate way. Mothers are reputed to attack people that threaten their dependent young.

Ecological Interactions
At least two researchers have noted that tapirs, which can become infested with blood-sucking, disease-carrying ticks, have let other mammals – a coati in one case, a tame peccary in the other – approach them and pick and eat the ticks on their bodies. If this occurs regularly, it is a *mutualistic* association: tapirs obviously benefit because they are freed temporarily from the harmful ticks, and the tick-eaters receive the nutritional value of the bloodsuckers (yech!).

Lore and Notes
During a recent visit to Corcovado National Park's Sirena station, an adult BAIRD'S TAPIR emerged each evening from the forest to feast on fruit fallen beneath a particular fig tree. The individual appeared not to take the slightest notice of the curious humans that approached it to within a meter or two. Several ecotourists were overheard to comment on the tapir's evident inelegance; such behavior, it should be noted, is considered bad form within range of the animal's hearing.

Status
Because they are hunted for meat, and also due to deforestation, BAIRD'S TAPIR is now rare and considered an endangered species, listed by both CITES Appendix I and USA ESA. Tapirs are rarely seen because of their low population sizes, because they are active mostly at night, and because, owing to hunting, they are very shy and cautious animals. They are usually seen by short-term visitors to Costa Rica only in Corcovado National Park and perhaps in Santa Rosa National Park.

Profile
Baird's Tapir, *Tapirus bairdii*, Plate 80a

Environmental Close-Up 5
Why Are There So Many Species in the Tropics?

The feature of the tropics – particularly of tropical forests – that most strikes ecologists is the high degree of *species diversity*. Simply put, far more species occur in the tropics than in any other region of the world. In fact, recent estimates are that tropical rainforests, which cover only about 7% of the Earth, contain at least half (and maybe much more) of all species of organisms. Some estimates are that 80% or more of the world's terrestrial species reside in the tropics. For almost any kind of living thing – various types of plants, insects, reptiles, birds, etc. – diversity, or *species richness*, is greater in the tropics than in temperate or arctic regions. For instance, examine the information in the table below, which compares species richness for various animal groups in tropical Costa Rica with that in several larger, temperate zone areas. Although Costa Rica is the smallest in land size among the four locations, it has far more indigenous animals of all kinds than the other places (except for salamanders, which are a predominantly temperate-zone group).

Because climate-related species richness patterns are so general, ecologists believe that there must be a powerful single reason or a variety of reasons to explain them. Indeed, some ecologists think that identifying the factors underlying these patterns is one of the most important pursuits of their field – a "Holy Grail" of ecology, it has been called. Several ideas are beginning to emerge in the research and writings of various biologists.

An early idea concerned the relative environmental stability between tropical and temperate regions. Ecologists reasoned that if a given environment, such as the tropics, were to be very stable climatically for a long time, many millennia, then more species could accumulate there over time by the development of new species (evolution) and the arrival of others (immigrants that evolved in other regions and then expanded their range into the tropics). A stable, relatively non-harsh climate (such as found today in many parts of the tropics) would also encourage low extinction rates; put another way, species that live in stable tropical climates should tend to be very successful for a long time. According to this idea, the fact that fewer species occupy temperate regions today is consistent with the recent history of temperate regions, which were covered with glaciers during the last ice age (ending only 10,000 years ago), and which even now experience harsher, more seasonal climates than do tropical areas. Increasingly, however, ecologists doubt this hypothesis, the main reason being that, it turns out, tropical regions have *not* been as stable climatically as originally thought. New techniques of historical climate analysis (for instance, analysis of pollen samples taken from deep in the earth) suggest that when temperate regions were covered with ice during the last glaciation, many regions that today are tropical rainforest were actually covered with other habitat types such as dry forest or savanna,

Table 7 The Number of Species of Various Types of Animals that Occur in Several Geographic Areas (modified from N.G. Hairston 1994).

	North Carolina, USA	Great Britain	New Zealand	Costa Rica
Climate	Temperate	Temperate	Temperate	Tropical
Land area (km^2)	84,625	143,201	160,000	51,000
No. of species of:				
Salamanders	49	3	0	35
Frogs & Toads	29	4	3	120
Lizards	10	3	6	68
Snakes	37	3	0	127
Mammals	31	46	2	205
Breeding birds (approx.)	167	240	300	600

More likely, some combination of environmental factors, both physical and biological, create the lush species richness of the tropics. Plants grow better in warm, continuously wet environments, conditions that pretty much define the tropics. Plants, of course, live on a combination of sun, water, and atmospheric carbon dioxide gas, capturing the sun's energy to manufacture from these components their own energy-containing nutrient (a simple sugar called *glucose*, the end product of photosynthesis). The photosynthetic process of plants is ecologically termed *primary production* because it is the initial creation of energy-containing matter upon which the rest of ecosystems depend for sustenance. Better growing conditions in the tropics means that there will be more plants there than in other regions. Many animals – *herbivores* – eat plants; more plants means that more herbivores can be supported. Other animals, *carnivores*, eat the herbivores, and so plants indirectly support them, too. Logically, then, in tropical regions, with their greater overall primary production, more energy is produced and so more kinds of animals can be supported (not to mention greater numbers of individuals). Animals, aside from depending on plants for food, also live in, on, or around plants. More plants in the tropics therefore provide more living space, more physical *niches*, for animals to occupy, and so support more animal species in this way also. Furthermore, when animals do not need to devote much of their energy toward surviving extreme temperatures or aridness, as do those that live in temperate and arctic regions, they can channel that extra energy into reproduction. Animals in the warm, wet tropics, therefore, can reproduce prolifically, which, although certainly not on the minds of the breeding individuals, is a good way to enhance species survival and success.

The relationships between the physical environment and primary production of plants is not the only hypothesis that might correctly explain geographic patterns of species richness, but it is one gaining increasing acceptance. It is an idea that is especially helpful for the budding ecologists and conservationists among ecotravellers to consider and understand because it nicely ties together several main aspects of the field of ecology, and neatly illustrates the encompassing interdependence of plants, animals, and the physical environment. Plants depend on the physical environment for their growth and success; animals depend on plants for theirs; and plants, in turn, as described elsewhere in the book (p. 179), often depend on animals for pollination to complete their reproductive cycles. With these interactions in mind, a traveller can enter the tropical forest and perhaps better enjoy the splendors of the species richness all around.

References

Blaustein A.R., D.B. Wake and W.P. Sousa (1994) Amphibian declines: judging stability, persistence, and susceptibility of populations to local and global extinctions. *Conservation Biology* **8**: 60–71.

Boag D. (1982) *The Kingfisher*. Blandford Press, Poole, UK.

Bowes A.L. (1964) *Birds of the Mayas*. West-of-the-Wind Publications, Big Moose, New York, USA.

Emmons L.H. (1997). *Neotropical Rainforest Mammals: A Field Guide*, 2nd ed. University of Chicago Press, Chicago, USA.

Fleischer R.C., C.L. Tarr, E.S. Morton, A. Sangmeister and K.C. Derrickson (1997) Mating system of the dusky antbird, a tropical passerine, as assessed by DNA fingerprinting. *Condor* **99**: 512–514.

Fuertes L.A (1914) Impressions of the voices of tropical birds. *Bird Lore* **16**: 342–349.

Greene H.W. and R.L. Seib (1983) *Micrurus nigrocinctus* (Coral Snake). In: *Costa Rican Natural History*, D.H. Janzen (Ed) (pp. 406–408). University of Chicago Press, Chicago USA.

Hairston N.G. (1994) *Vertebrate Zoology: An Experimental Field Approach*. Cambridge University Press, Cambridge, UK.

Janzen D.H. (1983) *Costa Rican Natural History*. University of Chicago Press, Chicago, USA. (an edited work with many contributors)

Janzen D.H. and D.E. Wilson (1983) Mammals. In: *Costa Rican Natural History*, D.H. Janzen (Ed) (pp. 426–442). University of Chicago Press, Chicago, USA.

Kricher J.C. (1989) *A Neotropical Companion: An Introduction to the Animals, Plants and Ecosystems of the New World Tropics*. Princeton University Press, Princeton, New Jersey, USA.

Levey D.J., T.C. Moremond and J.S. Denslow (1994) Frugivory: An overview. In: *La Selva: Ecology and Natural History of a Neotropical Rain Forest*, L.A. McDade, K.S. Bawa, H.A. Hespenheide and G.S. Hartshorn (Eds) (pp. 282–298). University of Chicago Press, Chicago, USA.

Perrins C.M. (1985) Trogons. In: *The Encyclopedia of Birds*, C.M. Perrins and A.L.A. Middleton (Eds) (pp. 264–265). Facts on File Publications, New York, USA.

Peterson C.R., A.R. Gibson and M.E. Dorcas (1993) Snake thermal ecology. In: *Snakes: Ecology and Behavior*, R.A. Seigel and J.T. Collins (Eds) (pp. 241–314). McGraw-Hill, New York, USA.

Primack R.B. (1993) *Essentials of Conservation Biology*. Sinauer Associates, Sunderland, Massachusetts, USA.

Skutch A.F. (1958) Life history of the White-whiskere Soft-wing *Malacoptila panamensis*. *Ibis* **100**: 209–231.

ch A.F. (1963) Life history of the Rufous-tailed Jacamar *Galbula ruficauda*. *Ibis* **105**: 354–368.

Skutch A.F. (1971) Life history of the Broad-billed Motmot, with notes on the Rufous Motmot. *Wilson Bulletin* **83**: 74–94.

Stiles F.G. and D.H. Janzen (1983) *Cathartes aura* (Turkey Vulture). In: *Costa Rican Natural History*, D.H. Janzen (Ed) (pp. 560–562). University of Chicago Press, Chicago, USA.

Stiles F.G. and A.F. Skutch (1989) *A Field Guide to the Birds of Costa Rica*. Cornell University Press, Ithaca, New York, USA.

Strauch J.G. (1983) *Calidris alba* (Sanderling). In: *Costa Rican Natural History*, D.H. Janzen (Ed) (pp. 556–557). University of Chicago Press, Chicago, USA.

Zug G. (1983) *Bufo marinus* (Marine Toad). In: *Costa Rican Natural History*, D.H. Janzen (Ed) (pp. 386–387). University of Chicago Press, Chicago, USA.

Habitat Photos

1 Rainforest trail at the Organization for Tropical Study's La Selva Biological Reserve. Notice the buttressed tree trunks and large-leaved understory plants. Lowland wet forest habitat; northern Caribbean lowlands.

2 Hiking the wonderful trails at La Selva Biological Reserve. Lowland wet forest habitat; northern Caribbean lowlands.

3 Along the road to the Organization for Tropical Study's Palo Verde Biological Research Station, Palo Verde National Park during the dry season. Lowland dry forest habitat, northern Pacific lowlands.

4 Coastal canal and seasonally flooded rainforest, Tortuguero National Park. Lowland wet forest habitat, northern Caribbean lowlands.

5 Santa Rosa National Park during the dry season. Lowland dry forest habitat, northern Pacific lowlands.

6 Arenal Volcano as seen from the northwest; in the Tilarán Range, it tops off at 1633 m (5350 ft).

7 Rainforest waterfalls at Rara Avis, a private nature reserve and ecotourism resort near Braulio Carrillo National Park. Middle elevation forest habitat; northern Caribbean slope.

8 Puerto Viejo River at La Selva Biological Reserve; freshwater habitat.

9 Along the Sirena River, Corcovado National Park. Lowland wet forest and freshwater habitats; southern Pacific lowlands.

10 View of the Tempisque River floodplain and marshes, taken from cliffs above Palo Verde Biological Research Station, Palo Verde National Park. Freshwater habitat; northern Pacific lowlands.

11 Dark sand tropical beach at Manuel Antonio National Park. Marine habitat; southern Pacific lowlands.

12 Papaya grove near the small settlement of Muelle. Agricultural habitat; northern Caribbean lowlands.

13a,b Foggy day at the Organization for Tropical Study's Las Cruces Biological Station/Wilson Botanical Garden. Middle elevation wet forest; southern Pacific slope.

14 Middle elevation rainforest near San Vito; southern Pacific slope.

15 Striking green rainforest canopy at about 1400 m (4600 ft) near Cacao Volcano, Guanacaste Range, northwestern Costa Rica. Highland cloud forest habitat.

16 Dark interior of the cloud forest at Monteverde Cloud Forest Reserve. Highland forest habitat; northern Pacific slope.

17 Passion flower (*Passiflora vitifolia*) vine in

18 Treeferns in lower elevation rainforest (at 300 m, 1000 ft), Braulio Carrillo National Park. Northern Caribbean lowlands.

19 High elevation rainforest in the mountains of the Central Range, Braulio Carrillo National Park.

Identification Plates

Plates 1–80

Abbreviations on the Identification Plates are as follows:

M;   male
F;   female
IM; immature

The species pictured on any one plate are usually the correct size relative to each other, but sometimes this was impossible to accomplish.

Plate 1a

Purple Caecilian
Gymnopis multiplicata
Dos Cabezas = two heads
Soldas = welded

ID: Wormlike, limbless, long (to 40 cm, 16 in) and wide (to 2.5 cm, 1 in); head a bit flattened; small eyes covered by skin; body encircled by ringed creases. Purplish in color, except for a few small white patches, one on the head.

HABITAT: Low and middle elevation wet forests and warm, moist places in other habitats; found on or under the ground.

PARKS: CABR, CHNP, CONP, LSBR, MANP, MVCR, PVNP, TONP

Plate 1b

Mountain Salamander
(also called Monteverde Salamander, La Palma Salamander)
Bolitoglossa subpalmata
Escorpión = scorpion
Salamandras = salamander

ID: A small black or brown salamander with spots or blotches of tan, brown, or orange; black eyes; coloring varies extensively at higher elevations; to 6 cm (2.5 in).

HABITAT: Middle and high elevation wet forests; found in wet areas, on ground or vegetation, often in bromeliad epiphytes; also under rocks and logs.

PARKS: BCNP, IVNP, LANP, MVCR, PONP, WIBG

Plate 1c

Ring-tailed Salamander
(also called Climbing Salamander, Robust Mushroom-tongue Salamander)
Bolitoglossa robusta
Escorpión = scorpion
Salamandras = salamander

ID: A mid-sized salamander usually black with whitish speckles, although some are reddish on top; yellow or orange ring around upper part of tail; black eyes; to 13 cm (5 in).

HABITAT: Middle and high elevation wet forests; found in wet areas, often on vegetation.

PARKS: BCNP, IVNP, LANP, MVCR, PONP, RVNP

Plate 1d

Marine Toad (also called Cane Toad)
Bufo marinus
Sapo Grande = giant toad
Sapo Común = common toad

ID: A large, warted, ugly toad; large, triangular glands on each side of the head behind brown eyes; females are mottled, combinations of dusky brown, tan, and chocolate; males generally are uniformly brown; to 20 cm (8 in).

HABITAT: Low, middle, and some higher elevation forests; found in open and semi-open areas, often in and around buildings.

PARKS: ARVL, BCNP, CABR, CHNP, CNWR, CONP, LANP, LSBR, MANP, MVCR, PVNP, RVNP, SRNP, TONP, WIBG

Plate I 237

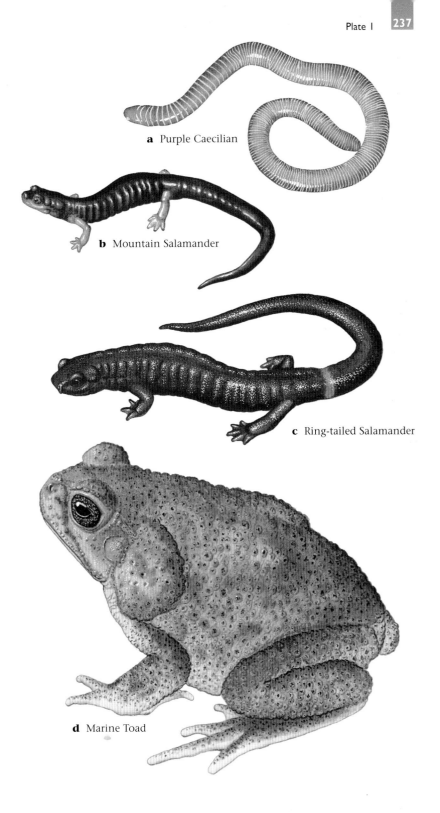

a Purple Caecilian

b Mountain Salamander

c Ring-tailed Salamander

d Marine Toad

Plate 2 (*See also*: Toads, p. 54)

Plate 2a

Green Climbing Toad
(also called Evergreen Toad)
Bufo coniferus
Sapo Cornudo = horned toad

ID: Mid-sized frog highly variable in color; greenish, yellow-greenish, or brown, often with black and white splotches; parallel rows of spine-tipped warts run down their sides; glands on head behind eyes are small and often triangular; brown and green eyes; to 9 cm (3.5 in).

HABITAT: Middle elevation wet forests; found on the ground or in small pools or ponds.

PARKS: BCNP, CONP, LSBR, MVCR, WIBG

Plate 2b

Litter Toad
(also called Truando Toad)
Bufo haematiticus
Sapito de Hojarasca = little leaf litter toad

ID: Brown or beige toad with black spots; the back is usually lighter-colored and the contrasting sides darker brown or black; head glands behind brown or black eyes are oval in shape; to 8 cm (3 in).

HABITAT: Low and middle elevation wet forests; found on the ground and in small pools.

PARKS: ARVL, BCNP, CABR, CHNP, CNWR, CONP, LANP, LSBR, MANP, MVCR, TONP, WIBG

Plate 2c

Golden Toad
(also called Orange Toad, Monteverde Toad, Alajuela Toad)
Bufo periglenes
Sapo Dorado de Monteverde = monteverde golden toad
Sapito Dorado = little golden toad

ID: A small, colorful toad; males (on top in illustration) yellow or orange, females black with red spots ringed with yellow; to 6 cm (2.5 in).

HABITAT: Middle elevation wet forests; found on the ground or in small pools.

PARKS: MVCR

Note: This species is endangered or already extinct, CITES Appendix I and USA ESA listed.

Plate 2d

Harlequin Frog
(also called Veragosa Stubfoot Toad)
Atelopus varius
Sapo Arlequín = harlequin toad

ID: A small, rainbow-colored frog; usually black with spots or markings of yellow, orange, green, and/or blue; to 5 cm (2 in).

HABITAT: Low, middle, and high elevation wet forests; found on the ground and along streams.

PARKS: CABR, IVNP, LANP, MANP, MVCR, PONP, RVNP, WIBG

Note: This species regulated in Costa Rica for conservation purposes, CITES Appendix III listed; the subspecies that occurs in Panama is endangered.

Plate 2 239

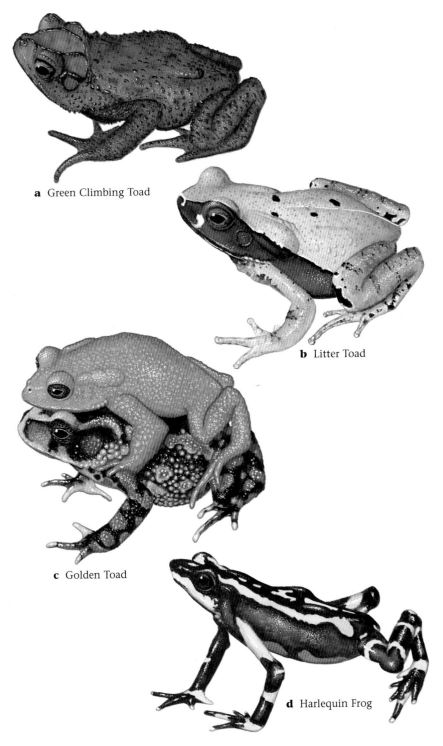

a Green Climbing Toad

b Litter Toad

c Golden Toad

d Harlequin Frog

Plate 3a

Mexican Burrowing Toad
Rhinophrynus dorsalis
Alma de Vaca = soul of the cow
Sapo Borracho = drunk toad

ID: Medium-sized, odd-looking frog described as resembling a blob of jelly; smooth, moist skin of the back is gray, reddish brown, dark brown, or purplish black, with red, orange, or yellow lines and spots (often there is a single line down the center of the back); small eyes; fat legs; inflates like blowfish when scared; to 9 cm (3.5 in).

HABITAT: Dry forests and wet pastures, fields, ditches of northern Pacific lowlands; found on the ground.

PARKS: PVNP, SRNP

Plate 3b

Common Dink Frog
(also called Tink Frog, Caretta Robber Frog)
Eleutherodactylus diastema
Martillito = little hammer

ID: Small brown or grayish frog; often has dark bars or spots on back and legs, although coloring is highly variable; eyes brown/silver; its name refers to loud, metallic calls given by males at night; 2.5 cm (1 in).

HABITAT: Low and middle elevation wet forests; often found in shrubs or trees, especially on bromeliad epiphytes.

PARKS: ARVL, BCNP, CHNP, CNWR, CONP, LSBR, MANP, MVCR, RVNP, TONP

Plate 3c

Common Rain Frog
(also called Fitzinger's Robber Frog)
Eleutherodactylus fitzingeri
Ranita piedra = little rock frog

ID: A small light or dark brown frog with a yellow stripe down back and yellowish spots in thigh area; eyes brownish; 5 cm (2 in).

HABITAT: Low and middle elevation wet forests; terrestrial, but also climbs vegetation.

PARKS: BCNP, CABR, CHNP, CNWR, CONP, LANP, LSBR, MANP, MVCR, PVNP, RVNP, SRNP, TONP, WIBG

Plate 3d

Bransford's Litter Frog
(also called Bransford's Robber Frog)
Eleutherodactylus bransfordii

ID: Small brownish frog with warty skin, usually with spots; some with light stripe down back; individuals even within the same small area are highly variable in skin color, markings, and skin texture; in many regions, these are the most abundant frogs found on the ground; 3 cm (1 in).

HABITAT: Low and middle elevation wet forests; found on the ground or hidden below the leaf litter.

PARKS: ARVL, BCNP, CHNP, CNWR, CONP, LANP, LSBR, MANP, MVCR, PVNP, RVNP, SRNP, TONP

Plate 3   **241**

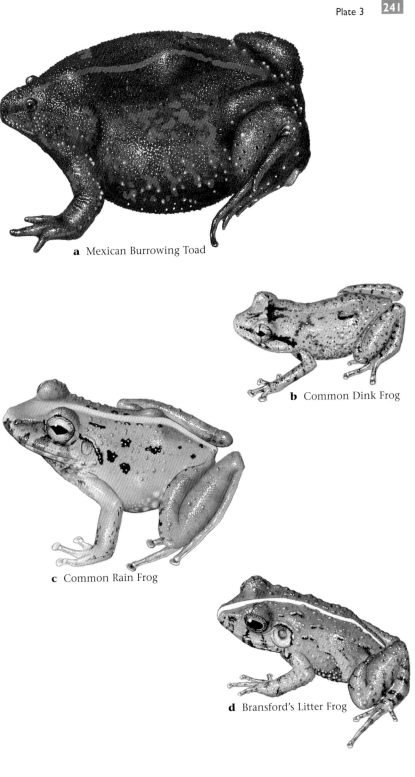

a Mexican Burrowing Toad

b Common Dink Frog

c Common Rain Frog

d Bransford's Litter Frog

Plate 4a

Smoky Jungle Frog
(also called Smoky Frog, South
American Bullfrog)
Leptodactylus pentadactylus
Rana Ternero = calf frog
Rana Toro = bull frog
ID: A large frog, brown, gray, or purplish gray,
often with dark spots; lips with light and dark bars;
skin secretions can be irritating to people; to 16
cm (6 in).

HABITAT: Dry and wet low and middle elevation
forests; found in burrows or in rock crevices,
often near rivers or streams.

PARKS: ARVL, BCNP, CHNP, CNWR, CONP, LANP,
LSBR, MANP, MVCR, PVNP, RVNP, SRNP, TONP,
WIBG

Plate 4b

Mudpuddle Frog
(also called Tungara Frog, Foam Toad)
Physalaemus pustulosus
Sapito Tungara = little tungara toad
ID: Small brownish frog with rough (pustular) skin;
resembles a toad, but lacks a toad's big glands on
the head behind the eyes; to 3.5 cm (1.5 in).

HABITAT: Forests, pastures, and gardens of
Pacific lowlands and middle elevations; found on
the ground or under leaf litter.

PARKS: CABR, CONP, MANP, PVNP, SRNP, WIBG

Plate 4c

Red-eyed Leaf Frog
(also called Gaudy Leaf Frog, Red-eyed
Treefrog)
Agalychnis callidryas
Rana Calzonuda = stupid frog or
underwear frog
Rana Verde de Arbol = green treefrog
ID: Largish treefrog, with large toes with
considerable webbing; colors vary, but often has
a pale or dark green back, sometimes with white
or yellow spots; top of the thigh is green; blue-
purple patches on rear of limbs; vertical bars on
sides; often, hands and feet are orange; eyes are
ruby red; to 5 to 7 cm (2 to 3 in).

HABITAT: Lowland wet forests, Caribbean and
Pacific slopes; found in trees, small pools,
swamps.

PARKS: BCNP, CABR, CHNP, CNWR, CONP, LSBR,
MANP, MVCR, TONP, WIBG

Plate 4d

Misfit Leaf Frog
Agalychnis saltator
Rana de Arbol = treefrog
ID: Mid-sized treefrog with pale bright green back
(becoming red-brown at night), often with white
spots outlined in black; sides and top of thigh blue
to purple; large toes with considerable webbing;
dark red eyes; 4 to 6 cm (1.5 to 2.5 in).

HABITAT: Lowland wet forests, northern
Caribbean slope; found on vegetation and in
ponds and small pools.

PARKS: BCNP, LSBR, TONP

Plate 4   243

a Smoky Jungle Frog

b Mudpuddle Frog

c Red-eyed Leaf Frog

d Misfit Leaf Frog

Plate 5a

Meadow Treefrog
(also called Gunther's Costa Rican Treefrog)
Hyla pseudopuma
Rana de Arbol = treefrog

ID: Usually tan or brown but males during breeding periods are bright yellow; yellow or yellow-green on limbs; a dark line starts behind each eye and continues along the sides; to 5 cm (2 in).

HABITAT: Middle and high elevation wet forests; mostly arboreal and often found around bromeliad epiphytes, but also occurs in small pools.

PARKS: BCNP, IVNP, LANP, MVCR, RVNP, WIBG

Plate 5b

Variegated Treefrog
(also called Hourglass Treefrog)
Hyla ebraccata
Rana de Arbol = treefrog

ID: Tiny frog with a short, blunt snout, yellowish tan or yellow back with or without large dark brown splotches (sometimes hourglass-shaped); yellowish thighs; often, dark bands on legs; in some, dark stripes start at the snout and run along both sides; webbed fingers and toes; to 3.5 cm (1.5 in).

HABITAT: Low and some middle elevation wet forests and seasonally dry forests, Pacific and Caribbean slopes; usually found on understory shrubs or in or near ponds.

PARKS: BCNP, CABR, CHNP, CNWR, CONP, LSBR, MANP, TONP, WIBG

Plate 5c

Boulenger's Snouted Treefrog
Scinax boulengeri
Ranita de Boulenger = Boulenger's little frog

ID: Small treefrog, rather flattened so it can squeeze into small tree crevices; dark brown head and back; dark brown barred with green and black; rough, warted skin; long snout; hands not webbed; to 5 cm (2 in).

HABITAT: Low and some middle elevation forests, Pacific and Caribbean slopes; found on small trees, bromeliad epiphytes, understory shrubs, or near ponds.

PARKS: BCNP, CABR, CHNP, CNWR, CONP, LSBR, MANP, PVNP, SRNP, TONP, WIBG

Plate 5d

Gladiator Frog
(also called Rosenberg's Treefrog)
Hyla rosenbergi
Rana de Arbol = treefrog

ID: Largish frog, yellowish tan or brown above, blotched, with a thin, dark line in the middle of the back running from tip of snout to rump; black or dark markings on sides and limbs; females often have the black line but no other black markings; webbed fingers and toes; to 8 cm (3 in).

HABITAT: Low and some middle elevations, southern Pacific slope; found in or near small pools.

PARKS: CONP

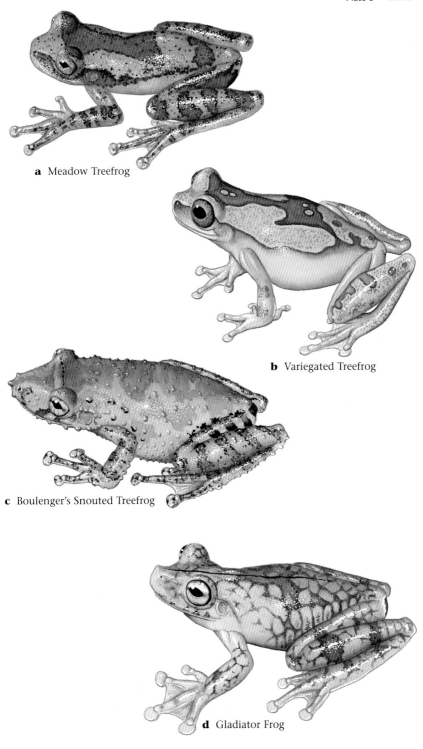

a Meadow Treefrog

b Variegated Treefrog

c Boulenger's Snouted Treefrog

d Gladiator Frog

Plate 6 (*See also*: Treefrogs, p. 59; True Frogs, p. 61)

Plate 6a

Masked Treefrog
(also called Granada Cross-banded Treefrog)
Smilisca phaeota
Rana Mascarada = masked frog

ID: A larger treefrog, pale green or tan with darker green or brown markings; dark marks around eyes; upper lip often silvery white; usually a light stripe on the outer part of front legs; light barring on rear legs; eyes brown and black; to about 7 cm (3 in).

HABITAT: Low and middle elevation wet forests, Pacific and Caribbean slopes; found on vegetation and in small pools.

PARKS: BCNP, CNWR, CONP, LANP, LSBR, MVCR, TONP, WIBG

Plate 6b

Drab Treefrog
(also called Costa Rican Smilisca, Veragua Cross-banded Treefrog)
Smilisca sordida
Rana de Arbol = treefrog

ID: Light brown, red-brown, or grayish mid-sized treefrog; back has darker gray, brown, or green markings; sides are brown with lighter-colored spots; limbs marked with brown or olive bands; eyes brown or silver mixed with black; to 6.5 cm (2.5 in).

HABITAT: Low and middle elevation wet forests, Pacific and Caribbean slopes; occurs on vegetation, especially bromeliad epiphytes, and in small pools.

PARKS: BCNP, CHNP, CONP, LANP, LSBR, MVCR, PVNP, TONP, WIBG

Plate 6c

Mexican Treefrog
Smilisca baudinii
Rana de Arbol = treefrog

ID: Largish treefrog with short, bluntly rounded snout; pale green or brown above with darker blotches; limbs marked with dark bands; dark eye bar; often, vertical dark bars on upper lip; to 6 cm (2.5 in).

HABITAT: Low and middle elevation wet forests and drier areas, Caribbean and northern Pacific slopes; found in trees and low vegetation.

PARKS: AVNP, BCNP, CHNP, CNWR, LSBR, PVNP, SRNP, TONP

Plate 6d

Vaillant's Frog
(also called Web-footed Frog)
Rana vaillanti
Rana = frog

ID: A large frog with greenish head and shoulders; body and limbs shading to brown, bronze, or grayish with black flecks; sides sometimes gray or gray-brown with black spots; dark bars on rear legs; toes fully webbed; to 11 cm (4.5 in).

HABITAT: Lowland forests of Pacific and Caribbean slopes; found in quiet water of rivers, streams, ponds, near shore.

PARKS: BCNP, CABR, CHNP, CNWR, CONP, LSBR, PVNP, SRNP, TONP

Plate 6   247

a Masked Treefrog

b Drab Treefrog

c Mexican Treefrog

d Vaillant's Frog

Plate 7a

Brilliant Forest Frog
(also called Warszewitsch's Frog)
Rana warszewitschii
Rana = frog

ID: A mid-sized slender frog, brownish with green spots or splotches, or uniformly green; sometimes with dark face mask; legs brownish and darkly barred; dark brown rear thighs with yellow spots or markings; eyes brown and gold; to 8 cm (3 in).

HABITAT: Low, middle, and higher elevation wet forests, Caribbean and Pacific slopes; found in and along rivers and streams, ponds, small pools.

PARKS: BCNP, CHNP, CONP, LANP, LSBR, MVCR, TONP, WIBG

Plate 7b

Leopard Frog
"Rana pipiens"
Rana = frog

ID: Several closely related frog species in the genus *Rana* look somewhat alike and are often confused, even by experts; the scientific consensus now is that the Leopard Frog in Costa Rica actually consists of two or even three different species: *Rana forreri* (Forrer's Grass Frog) in the Pacific lowlands; *Rana taylori* (Peralta Frog) in the Caribbean lowlands and Meseta Central; and perhaps a third species in the Talamanca Mountain highlands. Leopard frogs are usually brown and green/olive mixed, with dark circles and ovals on their backs; legs and arms with dark bands; to about 10 cm (4 in).

HABITAT: Low, middle, and high elevation wet forests, Caribbean and Pacific slopes; found in and along rivers and streams, ponds, small pools.

PARKS: CABR, CHNP, IVNP, LANP, MANP, MVCR, PVNP, TONP, WIBG

Plate 7c

Fleischmann's Glass Frog
Hyalinobatrachium fleischmanni
Rana de Vidrio = glass frog

ID: Tiny translucent frog with a rounded snout; lime green with yellow spots and yellow hands; organs/bones visible through abdominal skin; 2.5 cm (1 in).

HABITAT: Middle and higher elevation wet forests, Caribbean and southern Pacific slopes; found along rivers and streams, in vegetation.

PARKS: BCNP, CONP, IVNP, LANP, MVCR, PONP, RVNP, WIBG

Plate 7d

Emerald Glass Frog
(also called Nicaragua Giant Glass Frog)
Centrolene prosoblepon
Rana de Vidrio = glass frog

ID: Tiny translucent frog, dark green often with black spots; pale green hands; organs/bones visible through abdominal skin; to 3.5 cm (1.4 in).

HABITAT: Low, middle, and higher elevation wet forests, Caribbean and southern Pacific slopes; found along rivers and streams, in vegetation.

PARKS: BCNP, CONP, IVNP, LANP, LSBR, MVCR, PONP, RVNP, TONP, WIBG

Plate 7   249

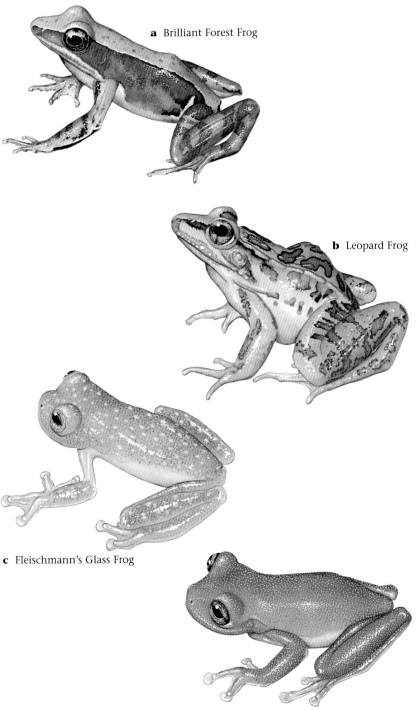

a Brilliant Forest Frog

b Leopard Frog

c Fleischmann's Glass Frog

d Emerald Glass Frog

Plate 8a

Green Poison-arrow Frog
(also called Green and Black Poison-
arrow Frog)
Dendrobates auratus
Rana Venenosa = poisonous frog
ID: Largish poison-arrow frog; bright blue, green,
or turquoise, or dark green with brownish or black
splotches; 2.5 to 4 cm (1 to 1.5 in).

HABITAT: Low and some middle elevation wet
forests, Caribbean and southern Pacific slopes;
found on forest floor or low vegetation.

PARKS: BCNP, CABR, CHNP, CNWR, CONP, TONP

Plate 8b

Granular Poison-arrow Frog
Dendrobates granuliferus
Rana Venenosa = poisonous frog
ID: Tiny bright red or yellow-olive frog with black-
spotted or bluish green and black-spotted rear
legs; back is very rough, or granular; to 2.3 cm (1
in).

BITAT: Lowland wet forests, southern Pacific
slope; found on ground or low vegetation.

PARKS: CONP, MANP

Plate 8c

Strawberry Poison-dart Frog
(also called Red and Blue or Flaming
Poison-dart Frog)
Dendrobates pumilio
Ranita Roja = little red frog
Rana Con Blue Jeans = blue jeans frog
ID: Small, bright red frog, often with varying
amounts of black flecks; red, blue, green, or black
limbs; smooth back; to 2.5 cm (1 in).

HABITAT: Low and some middle elevation wet
forests, Caribbean slope; found on ground or low
vegetation.

PARKS: BCNP, CHNP, CNWR, LSBR, TONP,

Plate 8d

Lovely Poison-dart Frog
Phyllobates lugubris
Rana Venenosa = poisonous frog
ID: A small, black frog with narrow, paired, gold,
pale-yellow, or yellow-green stripes running from
snout to rump; to 2.4 cm (1 in).

HABITAT: Low elevation wet forests, Caribbean
slope; found on forest floor or low vegetation.

PARKS: BCNP, CHNP, LSBR, TONP

Plate 8e

Orange and Black Poison-dart Frog
(also called Golfodulcean Poison-dart
Frog)
Phyllobates vittatus
Rana Venenosa = poisonous frog
ID: A small black frog with wide, paired orange
stripes on its back and turquoise-mottling on its
limbs; 2 to 3 cm (1 in).

HABITAT: Low elevation wet forests, southern
Pacific slope; found on forest floor or low
vegetation.

PARKS: CONP

Plate 8   251

a Green Poison-arrow Frog

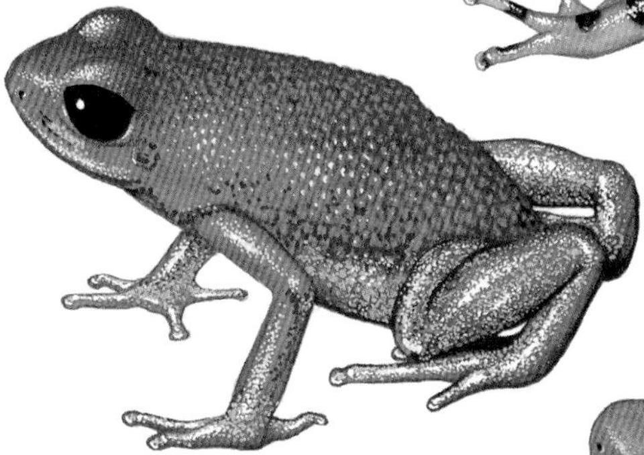

b Granular Poison-arrow Frog

c Strawberry Poison-dart Frog

d Lovely Poison-dart Frog

e Orange and Black Poison-dart Frog

Plate 9a

Spectacled Caiman
(or, simply, Caiman)
Caiman crocodilus
Lagarto = alligator
Cuajipalo or Guajipal

ID: A large, brown or olive-brown, crocodile-like reptile, often with noticeable dark bars marking back and tail; to about 2.5 m (8 ft) in total length, although most are 2 m (6 ft) or less. Distinguished from American Crocodile by (1) having a broad, rounded snout, and (2) lacking the crocodile's 2 teeth, one on each side of the lower jaw, that project outside the mouth. *Spectacled* refers to the bony ridges around the front of its eyes.

HABITAT: Caribbean and Pacific lowlands, freshwater or brackish water; in or near creeks, streams, ponds, beaches, swamps.

PARKS: BCNP, CABR, CHNP, CNWR, CONP, LSBR, MANP, PVNP, SRNP, TONP

Note: This species regulated for conservation purposes, CITES Appendix II listed.

Plate 9b

American Crocodile
Crocodylus acutus
Lagarto Negro = black alligator
Lagarto Amarillo = yellow alligator
Cocodrilo

ID: A large, brown, olive, or grayish crocodile, to as long as 7 m (21 ft), but most are much smaller; individuals longer than 4 m (13 ft) are rare. Dark bands on back and tail may be visible in younger individuals. Distinguished from Caiman by (1) longer, more slender, more pointed snout, and (2) having one large tooth on each side of lower jaw that projects sharply upwards, fitting into a notch on upper jaw, that can be seen when jaws are closed.

HABITAT: Pacific and Caribbean coastal lowlands, in brackish or freshwater; in or near swamps, mangrove swamps, rivers.

PARKS: CABR, CHNP, CONP, LSBR, PVNP, SRNP, TONP

Note: This species listed as endangered, CITES Appendix I and USA ESA.

Plate 9c

Brown Land Turtle
(also called Brown Wood Turtle)
Rhinoclemmys annulata
Tortuga Parda Terrestre = brown land turtle
Jicote

ID: A mid-sized land turtle with a high, fairly flat-topped back that is black, brown with orange blotches, or tan with yellow blotches; underneath black or dark brown, often with yellow markings; yellow or red stripes on head; yellow chin with dark spots; yellow scales with dark markings on front legs; toes not webbed; to 20 cm (8 in).

HABITAT: Low and middle elevation wet forests, Caribbean slope; primarily terrestrial, but also occasionally found in small pools and ponds.

PARKS: BCNP, CHNP, CNWR, LSBR, TONP

Plate 9d

Black River Turtle
(also called Black Wood Turtle)
Rhinoclemmys funerea
Tortuga Negra del Río = black river turtle
Jicote

ID: A large aquatic turtle with a brown or black high domed back; underneath black with yellow markings (seams); black head with yellow/orange stripes; jaw and chin yellow/orange with black spots; skin of neck and legs black with yellow/orange markings; webbed toes; to 32 cm (12 in).

HABITAT: Wet forests, mainly Caribbean slope; found in or around marshes, swamps, ponds, streams, rivers.

PARKS: BCNP, CHNP, CNWR, LANP, LSBR, TONP, WIBG

Plate 9   253

a Spectacled Caiman

b American Crocodile

c Brown Land Turtle

d Black River Turtle

Plate 10a
Red Turtle
(also called Painted Wood Turtle)
Rhinoclemmys pulcherrima
Tortuga Roja = red turtle

ID: A brightly colored land turtle with a high domed back; back is brown around the edges but the larger side and top plates are usually decorated with patterns of red-orange, yellow, and black; underneath yellow with a wide, central dark bar; head green or brown with reddish stripes; jaw and chin yellow/orange, often with dark markings; front legs with red or yellow scales with black markings; toes slightly webbed; to 23 cm (9 in).

HABITAT: Low elevation Pacific coastal areas; more common in cleared areas near streams, than in forests; found often after rains on roads or in pastures, but also in streams, pools, ponds.

PARKS: CABR, PVNP, SRNP

Plate 10b
Snapping Turtle
Chelydra serpentina
Tortuga Lagarto = alligator turtle

ID: A large, mean aquatic turtle; brown, tan, olive, or black back often caked with mud or aquatic vegetation; usually 3 ridges of sharp bumps along back; underneath yellow to tan; very large head with scales on its side and back; tail as long as shell; to 45 cm (18 in), although most are smaller.

HABITAT: Fresh and brackish water at low and middle elevations; found in marshes, ponds, lakes, streams, rivers with abundant aquatic vegetation.

PARKS: CABR, CHNP, CNWR, CONP, MANP, PVNP, SRNP, TONP

Plate 10c
White-lipped Mud Turtle
Kinosternon leucostomum
Tortuga caja = box turtle

ID: A mid-sized dark brown or black turtle; head brown with whitish jaws, sometimes with dark markings; a yellowish stripe on each side of the head from eye to neck; underneath yellow with darker markings (seams); to 18 cm (7 in).

HABITAT: Low and some middle elevation freshwater habitats, Pacific and Caribbean slopes; prefers quiet water with abundant vegetation in marshes, swamps, streams, rivers, ponds; also terrestrial.

PARKS: CABR, CHNP, CNWR, CONP, MANP, TONP, WIBG

Plate 10d
Central American Mud Turtle
(also called Narrow-bridged Mud Turtle)
Kinosternon angustipons
Tortuga caja = box turtle

ID: A smallish, aquatic brown turtle; head dark brown on top, lighter-colored on sides; limbs gray or brownish; underneath yellow; to 12 cm (5 in).

HABITAT: Warm, shallow freshwater areas with slow currents over the Caribbean lowlands; found in swamps, marshes, creeks, ponds.

PARKS: CHNP, CNWR, LSBR, TONP

Plate 10 255

a Red Turtle

b Snapping Turtle

c White-lipped Mud Turtle

d Central American Mud Turtle

Plate 11a
Green Sea Turtle
Chelonia mydas
Tortuga Verde = green turtle
Tortuga Blanca = white turtle
ID: A medium to large sea turtle with black, gray, greenish, or brown heart-shaped back, often with bold spots or streaks; yellowish white underneath; males' front legs each have one large, curved claw; name refers to greenish body fat; to 1.5 m (5 ft).

HABITAT: Caribbean and Pacific coasts; feeds in shallow ocean water, lays eggs on beaches.

PARKS: CHNP, CONP, MANP, SRNP, TONP

Note: This species listed as endangered, CITES Appendix I and USA ESA.

Plate 11b
Hawksbill Sea Turtle
Eretmochelys imbricata
Tortuga Carey = tortoise shell turtle
ID: A small to mid-sized sea turtle; shield-shaped back mainly dark greenish brown; yellow underneath; head scales brown or black; jaws yellowish with dark markings; chin and throat yellow; 2 claws on each front leg; narrow head and tapering hooked "beak" give the species its name; to 90 cm (35 in).

HABITAT: Feeds in clear, shallow ocean water near rocks and reefs, and also in shallow bays, estuaries, and lagoons; lays eggs on beaches.

PARKS: CHNP, CONP, MANP, SRNP, TONP

Note: This species listed as endangered, CITES Appendix I and USA ESA.

Plate 11c
Leatherback Sea Turtle
Dermochelys coriacea
Tortuga Baula
ID: Largest of the world's sea turtles, to lengths of 1.7 m (5 ft) or more and weights of 550+ kg (1200+ lb). Back is black or brown, smooth, covered with a continuous layer of black, often white-spattered, leathery skin (instead of the hardened plates of other sea turtles); 7 ridges along back running front to rear; no claws on limbs; no scales on skin except in youngsters; front limbs up to 1 m (3 ft) long.

HABITAT: An open-ocean turtle, but occasionally feeds in shallow water of bays and estuaries; lays eggs on beaches.

PARKS: CHNP, CONP, MANP, SRNP, TONP

Note: This species listed as endangered, CITES Appendix I and USA ESA.

Plate 11d
Olive Ridley Sea Turtle
(also called Pacific Sea Turtle)
Lepidochelys olivacea
Tortuga Lora = parrot turtle
Carpintera = carpenter
ID: A small sea turtle; wide, olive-colored, heart-shaped back a bit flattened, with a ridge down the middle; males have long, thick tails that extend beyond the top shell, and a curved claw on each front limb; skin is olive above, lighter-colored below; to 70 cm (28 in).

HABITAT: Open ocean and coastal areas, in bays, lagoons, near reefs; lays eggs on beaches.

PARKS: CONP, MANP, SRNP

Note: This species listed as endangered, CITES Appendix I and USA ESA.

Plate 11 257

a Green Sea Turtle

b Hawksbill Sea Turtle

c Leatherback Sea Turtle

d Olive Ridley Sea Turtle

Plate 12a

Mussurana
Clelia clelia
Zopilote = vulture
Víbora de Sangre = blood viper (young
snakes only)
ID: A large, uniformly-colored black, brown, or
grayish snake, to 2.5 m (8 ft); youngsters are bright
red or pink with black and yellow heads.

HABITAT: Caribbean and Pacific slopes, in all but
the driest lowlands; found on the ground, usually
in open areas such as open forests and pastures.

PARKS: BCNP, CABR, CHNP, CNWR, CONP, LSBR,
MANP, MVCR, PVNP, TONP, WIBG

Note: This species regulated for conservation
purposes, CITES Appendix II listed.

Plate 12b

Indigo Snake
Drymarchon corais
Zopilote = vulture
ID: A large, long snake, beige, brown, or olive-
colored; often has noticeable black lines radiating
under eye and a short black bar just behind and to
the side of the head; black eyes; to 4 m (13 ft).

HABITAT: Low and middle elevations, Caribbean
and Pacific slopes; found on the ground or in the
water in swamps, marshes, along riverbeds; also
climbs low plants.

PARKS: BCNP, CABR, CNWR, CONP, LSBR, MANP,
MVCR, PVNP, SRNP, TONP, WIBG

Plate 12c

Blunt-headed Tree Snake
(also called Chunk-headed Snake,
Blunt-headed Vine Snake)
Imantodes cenchoa
Bejuquilla = little vine snake
Ojo de Gato = cat-eye snake
ID: Small, very slim snake with a thin neck but
noticeably wide, squarish head; very large,
bulging eyes; body compressed side-to-side;
either dark-colored with a few blackish brown
splotches, or pale orange or tan with many
blotches; to 1 m (3.3 ft).

HABITAT: Low and middle elevation forests,
Caribbean and Pacific slopes; arboreal, usually
found in small, outer branches of shrubs and
trees; especially in and around bromeliad
epiphytes.

PARKS: BCNP, CABR, CHNP, CNWR, CONP, LSBR,
MANP, MVCR, PVNP, SRNP, TONP, WIBG

Plate 12d

Brown Vine Snake
Oxybelis aeneus
Bejuquilla = little vine snake
ID: A very slender snake with a slim, elongated
head; brown, pale gray, or yellowish gray,
sometimes spotted with tiny black and white dots;
sides of head and under head yellowish or whitish
(sometimes with red stripes); eyes yellow or
beige; to 2 m (6.5 ft). (There is also a Green Vine
Snake, a separate species, common in Caribbean
lowland areas such as TONP).

HABITAT: Low and middle elevations, drier areas
of Caribbean and Pacific slopes; arboreal.

PARKS: BCNP, CABR, CNWR, CONP, LSBR, MANP,
MVCR, PVNP, SRNP, WIBG

Plate 12 259

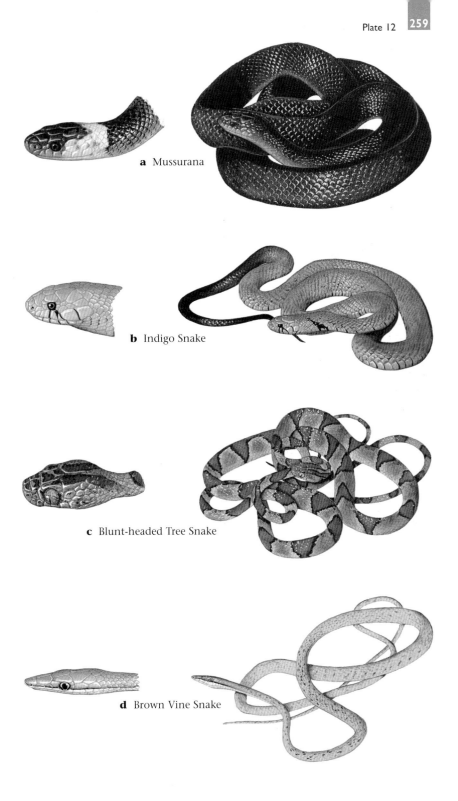

a Mussurana

b Indigo Snake

c Blunt-headed Tree Snake

d Brown Vine Snake

Plate 13a

Roadguard
Conophis lineatus
Guarda Camino = roadguard

ID: A mid-sized snake, dark gray/brown or olive with light and dark lengthwise stripes; cone-shaped head; to 1.3 m (4 ft).

HABITAT: Low elevations of dry northern Pacific slope, but also found in some southern Pacific areas; prefers open areas in forests, pastures, roadsides.

PARKS: CABR, CONP, MANP, PVNP, SRNP

Plate 13b

Speckled Racer
Drymobius margaritiferus
Ranera = frog-eater

ID: A black or green snake spotted all over with yellow, orange, or bluish dots; head black, often with yellow marking; eyes black; to 1.2 m (4 ft).

HABITAT: Low and middle elevation forests, Caribbean and Pacific slopes; terrestrial, often found in thickets and near water.

PARKS: BCNP, CHNP, LSBR, MVCR, PVNP, SRNP, TONP, WIBG

Plate 13c

Mica
(also called Tropical Chicken Snake, Tropical Rat Snake)
Spilotes pullatus
Zopilote = vulture

ID: A mid-sized snake, variable in color, but often shiny black with yellow markings and bands; chin whitish and black; yellow under head and extending rearwards, changing to a black belly; large brown/black eyes; to 2.2 m (7.2 ft).

HABITAT: Low and middle elevations, Caribbean and Pacific slopes; wet forest, brushy woodland, open areas around farms, settlements; arboreal and terrestrial; usually found near water.

PARKS: BCNP, CABR, CHNP, CNWR, CONP, LSBR, MANP, MVCR, PVNP, TONP

Plate 13d

Green Parrot Snake
(also called Green Tree Snake)
Leptophis ahaetulla
Culebra Lora = parrot snake

ID: A slender snake, bright green on top; belly ranges from lighter green to whitish; chin often light blue; black eyestripe in many Costa Rican individuals; large yellow and black eyes; to 2 m (6.5 ft).

HABITAT: Low and middle elevation wet forests, Caribbean and Pacific slopes; found on ground and in small trees and shrubs, usually near water.

PARKS: BCNP, CHNP, CNWR, CONP, LSBR, MVCR, TONP, WIBG

Plate 13 261

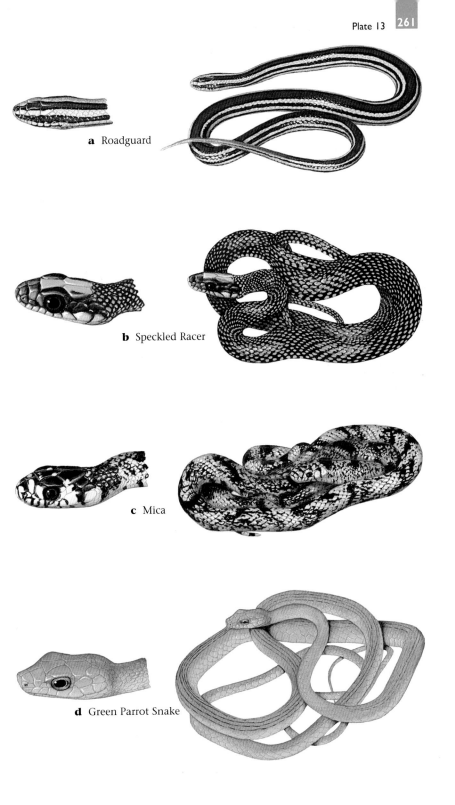

a Roadguard

b Speckled Racer

c Mica

d Green Parrot Snake

Plate 14 (*See also*: Colubrid Snakes, p. 79)

Plate 14a

Bird-eating Snake
(also called Puffing Snake)
Pseustes poecilonotus
Sabanera = savannah snake
ID: Black, dark brown, or green body with yellow/orange bars or blotches; yellow lips, throat and belly; to 2.5 m (8 ft).

HABITAT: Low, middle, and higher elevation wet forests, Caribbean and Pacific slopes; usually more open areas; found in trees and shrubs.

PARKS: ARVL, BCNP, CABR, CHNP, CNWR, CONP, IVNP, LANP, LSBR, MANP, MVCR, PONP, RVNP, TONP, WIBG

Plate 14b

Tropical Kingsnake
(also called Milk Snake)
Lampropeltis triangulum
Coral Falsa = false coral snake
ID: A medium-sized snake; body is repeated pattern of red, whitish, and black rings, with reds the widest and whites the narrowest; in some individuals, white rings are replaced by orange; the ringed pattern fades in larger, longer individuals, which turn mostly all-black; a coral snake mimic (see p. 85); to 1.8 m (6 ft).

HABITAT: Low, middle, and higher elevation wet forests; moutainsides, hillsides, agricultural areas; found on the ground, often concealed in leaf litter.

PARKS: ARVL, BCNP, CNWR, CONP, IVNP, LANP, LSBR, MANP, MVCR, PONP, PVNP, RVNP, TONP, WIBG

Plate 14c

Skink-eater
(also called Neck-band Snake)
Scaphiodontophis annulatus
Coral Falsa = false coral snake
ID: A small, thickish snake with two forms: in one, rings of dull red, yellow, and black run down the entire body; in the other, the rings cover only the first third of the body, with the remainder being solid light brown or olive; a coral snake mimic (see p. 85); to 1 m (3.3 ft).

HABITAT: Low and middle elevation wet forests, Caribbean and Pacific slopes; terrestrial, found on or under leaf litter, often in rocky areas or near streams or swamps.

PARKS: BCNP, CABR, CHNP, CNWR, CONP, LSBR, MANP, MVCR, TONP, WIBG

Plate 14d

Harlequin Snake
(also called Black-banded Snake)
Scolecophis atrocinctus
Coral Falsa = false coral snake
ID: A small snake with black and light rings that alternate along the length of its body; light rings are orange on top, pale on sides; light blue belly; black eyes; a coral snake mimic (see p. 85); to 60 cm (2 ft).

HABITAT: Low and middle elevation wet forests, northern Pacific slope; found on the ground and in low vegetation.

PARKS: MVCR, PVNP

Plate 14 **263**

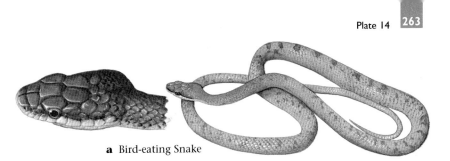

a Bird-eating Snake

b Tropical Kingsnake

c Skink-eater

b Harlequin Snake

Plate 15a

Fer-de-lance
Bothrops asper
Terciopelo = velvet
Toboba Rabo Amarillo = yellowtail
viper (young males only)
Toboba Tiznada = sooty viper (on
Pacific coast)

ID: A large, fairly slender snake with a triangular head; brown, olive, gray, or black back covered with a series of beige and brown or black triangles on each side (when viewed from above the series of triangles resemble hourglass figures or X's); dark stripe on each side of head behind eye; yellowish under head; tan or brown eyes; to 2.5 m (8 ft).

HABITAT: Low and middle elevation wet forests and open areas; Caribbean slope and parts of Pacific slope; found in some drier forests near watercourses; partly arboreal as juveniles, terrestrial as adults.

PARKS: BCNP, CABR, CHNP, CNWR, CONP, LSBR, MANP, MVCR, TONP, WIBG

Plate 15b

Eyelash Viper
(also called Palm Viper or Eyelash
Palm Pit-viper)
Bothriechis schlegelii
Toboba de Pestaña = eyelash viper
Oropel = tinsel viper (yellow form)
Bocaracá

ID: A slender, triangle-headed snake; individuals of different colors may occur in the same area: (1) green, olive, or grayish with brown, tan, or rust-colored markings on head and body (not shown), (2) reddish yellow or (3) bright golden yellow, sometimes with black back spots; small dark stripe often behind eye; 2 or 3 horny, spine-like, scales jut out over each eye (the "eyelashes"); yellow or beige eyes; to 75 cm (30 in).

HABITAT: Low and middle elevation wet forests of Caribbean and Pacific slopes; arboreal; often hangs from vegetation with prehensile tail.

PARKS: BCNP, CABR, CHNP, CNWR, CONP, LSBR, MANP, MVCR, TONP, WIBG

Plate 15c

Jumping Viper
(also called Jumping Pit-viper)
Atropoides nummifer
Mano de Piedra = rock-hand
Timbo
Patoca

ID: A thickset, stocky pit-viper with a triangular brown head with dark eye-stripes and a tan or grayish-brown body with dark brown or black blotches; the name refers to its vaunted ability to launch itself and strike at long distance, but actually only over about half its body length; to 80 cm (32 in).

HABITAT: Low and middle elevation wet forests, Caribbean and Pacific slopes; usually found on the ground, but also low in trees.

PARKS: BCNP, CABR, CHNP, CNWR, CONP, MANP, WIBG

Plate 15d

Tropical Rattlesnake
Crotalus durissus
Cascabel = rattlesnake

ID: A stout rattlesnake with a triangular brown head and a brown body with a pattern of darker triangles or diamonds; 2 stripes run from the top of the head along the neck; a noticeable ridge runs along the middle of the back; to 1.5 m (5 ft).

HABITAT: Low elevation dry forest, northern Pacific slope; found in open areas, forest clearings, dry grasslands, on the ground or in rock crevices.

PARKS: PVNP, SRNP

Plate 15   265

a Fer-de-lance

b Eyelash Viper

c Jumping Viper

d Tropical Rattlesnake

Plate 16 (*See also*: Dangerous Snakes, p. 83)

Plate 16a
Bushmaster
Lachesis muta
Cascabel muda = mute rattlesnake
Matabuey = ox killer
Platonegro = blackplate
Mapaná

ID: The largest New World venomous snake; broad, rounded triangle head, brown or blackish with dark eyestripes; body yellowish, red-brown, gray-brown, or tan with a pattern of brown or black blotches in diamond shapes; conspicuous ridge running along the middle of the back; often longer than 2 m (6.5 ft) and sometimes to 3.5 m (11.5 ft).

HABITAT: Low and middle elevation wet forests over parts of the Caribbean and southern Pacific slopes; terrestrial, often found near large buttressed trees or fallen logs.

PARKS: BCNP, CHNP, CNWR, CONP, LSBR, TONP, WIBG

Plate 16b
Rainforest Hognosed Pit-viper
Porthidium nasutum
Tamagá

ID: A fairly stocky pit-viper; tip of snout of rounded triangle head is strongly upturned, providing the basis for the name; tan, brown, or reddish-, grayish, or yellowish brown, often with triangular or rectangular light or dark blotches; dark brown eyes; to 60 cm (24 in).

HABITAT: Low and middle elevation wet forests, Caribbean and southern Pacific slopes; prefers open areas, clearings; often found near logs, stumps, litter piles.

PARKS: BCNP, CHNP, CNWR, CONP, LSBR, TONP, WIBG

Plate 16c
Boa Constrictor
Boa constrictor
Bécquer
Boa

ID: A large, shiny, handsome snake with a long triangular head, often with a single stripe along its top, and dark eyestripes; brown or grayish body with dark blotches; the tail, often with browns, reds, and yellows, is usually brighter and more colorful than the body; to 2.5 m (8 ft).

HABITAT: Low and middle elevation wet and dry forests, Caribbean and Pacific slopes; often found in open areas on the ground or in vegetation, trees, especially near human settlements.

PARKS: BCNP, CABR, CHNP, CNWR, CONP, LANP, LSBR, MANP, MVCR, PVNP, RVNP, SRNP, TONP, WIBG

Note: This species regulated for conservation purposes, CITES Appendix II listed.

Plate 16d
Central American Coral Snake
Micrurus nigrocinctus
Coral = coral snake
Coralillo = little coral snake

ID: A small, colorful snake with a small head and short tail; head is generally black and yellow, with the snout being all black; the body has alternating rings of red, black, and yellow, or only red and black; yellow rings, when present, are very narrow; to 1 m (3.3 ft).

HABITAT: Low and middle elevation wet and dry forests, Caribbean and Pacific slopes; found on the ground in forests, but also basking in open areas, and in rocky hillsides.

PARKS: BCNP, CABR, CHNP, CNWR, CONP, LANP, LSBR, MANP, MVCR, PVNP, SRNP, TONP, WIBG

Plate 16 **267**

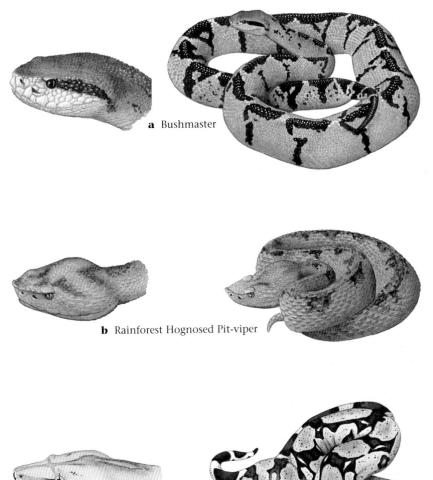

a Bushmaster

b Rainforest Hognosed Pit-viper

c Boa Constrictor

d Central American
Coral Snake

Plate 17a

Pelagic Sea Snake
(also called Yellow-bellied Sea Snake)
Pelamis platurus
Culebra del Mar = sea snake
Serpiente Pelágica = pelagic snake

ID: Typically yellow with a wide, dark stripe along its back, but some individuals are nearly all yellow and others, nearly all black; thin, smallish head; oar-shaped tail; rarely longer than 80 cm (32 in).

HABITAT: Marine, Pacific Ocean; usually lives fairly far from shore, but often found stranded or dead on beaches.

PARKS: CONP, MANP, SRNP

Plate 17b

Leaf Litter Gecko
(also called Costa Rican Scaly-eyed Gecko)
Lepidoblepharis xanthostigma
Gallego de Hojarasca = leaf litter gecko

ID: A small gecko with narrow, pointed-oval head; heavy, cylindrical tail; velvety skin with granular scales on back; dark brown or brownish lavender back marbled with lighter areas; head and tail less dark; sometimes a pair of white lines running down sides of back; chin and throat yellowish with brown dots; to 4 cm (1.5 in), plus tail.

HABITAT: Low and middle elevation wet forests, Caribbean and Pacific slopes; found in the leaf litter, often hidden under leaves, and especially in cacao groves and other tree plantations.

PARKS: ARVL, BCNP, CABR, CHNP, CNWR, CONP, LANP, LSBR, MANP, RVNP, TONP, WIBG

Plate 17c

Central American Smooth Gecko
(also called Turnip-tail Gecko)
Thecadactylus rapicauda
Escorpión Tobobo = viper scorpion

ID: A large gecko with triangular head, distinct from neck; brownish lavender, tan, or gray with darker blotches or bands; dark eyestripe running to shoulder; various kinds of scales on body; partly webbed hands and feet; newly-grown tails (see p. 93) often greatly enlarged (the "turnip") and lighter in color than body; to 11 cm (4.5 in), plus tail.

HABITAT: Low elevation wet forests, Caribbean and southern Pacific slopes; found often in houses and buildings, and on rocks near human settlements.

PARKS: CABR, CHNP, CNWR, CONP, LSBR, MANP, TONP

Plate 17d

Yellowbelly Gecko
Phyllodactylus tuberculosus

ID: Mid-sized gecko with oval snout; head widens behind eyes; distinct neck; light brown, tan, or grayish with spots; darker markings often on head, sides, legs; often, dark bars on tail; smaller and larger bumps ("tubercles") along back, the larger ones arranged in distinct rows; to 6.5 cm (2.5 in), plus tail.

HABITAT: Low elevation dry forests, northern Pacific slope; found on rocks near human settlements and in buildings.

PARKS: PVNP, SRNP

Plate 17   269

a Pelagic Sea Snake

b Leaf Litter Gecko

c Central American Smooth Gecko

d Yellowbelly Gecko

Plate 18a

Green Iguana
(also called Common Iguana)
Iguana iguana
Garrobo

ID: Very large lizard with a tall crest consists of long, sickle-shaped scales) running from neck to tail ; short head with prominent eye and large circular scale (larger than eye) at angle of the jaw; large dewlap (skin sac) hangs from throat; usually greenish or brownish with wavy black bands on body and tail; to 2 m (6.5 ft), including very long tail.

HABITAT: Low elevation wet forests and forest edge areas, Caribbean and Pacific slopes; along streams and rivers in drier areas; found on the ground and in trees, sometimes on sunny, leafy branches as high as 20 m (65 ft).

PARKS: BCNP, CABR, CHNP, CNWR, CONP, LSBR, MANP, PVNP, SRNP, TONP

Note: This species regulated for conservation purposes, CITES Appendix II listed.

Plate 18b

Basilisk
(also called Jesus Christ Lizard)
Basiliscus basiliscus
Chisbala = flying bullet
Lagartija Jesucristo = Jesus Christ lizard
Garrobo

ID: Medium to large brown or olive lizard with dark cross bands along body, often a light stripe along lips and sides, and large, continuous crests along the head, back, and tail (less prominent in females and young); small ones are good at running quickly across the surface of water (see p. 90), providing the irreverent name; to 1 m (3.3 ft) long, including tail.

HABITAT: Lowlands of Pacific slope; found along streams and bodies of water; terrestrial but also climbs trees, low vegetation. (Another basilisk species occurs along the Caribbean slope and is commonly seen at sites such as TONP.)

PARKS: CABR, CONP, MANP, MVCR, PVNP, SRNP, WIBG

Plate 18c

Ctenosaur
(also called Black Iguana)
Ctenosuara similis
Iguana Negra = black iguana
Garrobo

ID: Large lizard with a tan, olive, or olive-brown body with (usually 4) dark cross-wise bands; banded limbs; pale-brown, weakly-banded tail with circular rows of scales; back often with red/orange spots; old males have short crest (1 cm, a half inch, high) of vertical scales; brown eyes; to 1.2 m (4 ft), including tail.

HABITAT: Low elevation wet and dry areas on Pacific slope, particularly along Pacific beaches; found on the ground and in trees.

PARKS: CABR, CONP, MANP, MVCR, PVNP, SRNP

Plate 18 271

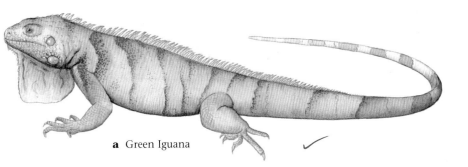

a Green Iguana

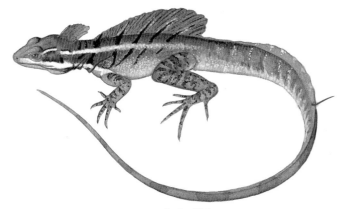

b Basilisk

c Ctenosaur

Plate 19a

Big-headed Anole
(also called Pug-nosed Anole)
Anolis capito
Lagartija = lizard
Galleguillo

ID: Mid-sized greenish-yellow, greenish-brown, brown, or tan lizard with spots, streaks, bars, and/or mottling; distinct neck; some females with wide light or light and dark stripes down back; male throat sac greenish yellow; to about 10 cm (4 in), plus very long tail.

HABITAT: Low and middle elevation wet forests; found on trees and ground; day-active.

PARKS: BCNP, CHNP, CNWR, CONP, LANP, LSBR, MANP, MVCR, TONP, WIBG

Plate 19b

Ground Anole
(also called Humble Anole)
Anolis humilis
Galleguillo de Hojarasca = leaf litter lizard

ID: A small, stout-bodied lizard, dark brown or brownish olive with a wide light or bronze stripe running down its back with, usually, V-shaped markings; males with red-orange and yellow throat fan; brown eyes; to 4 cm (1.5 in), plus tail.

HABITAT: Low and middle elevation wet forests, Caribbean and southern Pacific slopes; found in the leaf litter, especially near buttresses of large trees in forests and tree plantations.

PARKS: BCNP, CABR, CHNP, CNWR, LSBR, MVCR, TONP, WIBG

Plate 19c

Slender Anole
(also called Border Anole)
Anolis limifrons
Galleguillo

ID: A small, extremely slender lizard, with long, thin limbs; pale olive or olive-brown, often with a reddish tinge; white lips continuous with a white, diffuse stripe along body; males have a whitish and yellowish throat fan; to 5 cm (2 in), plus tail.

HABITAT: Low and middle elevation wet forests, Caribbean and Pacific slopes; found on ground and vegetation especially in forest edge areas and disturbed areas such as gardens, groves, and plantations.

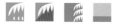

PARKS: BCNP, CHNP, CNWR, CONP, LSBR, MVCR, TONP

Plate 19d

Green Spiny Lizard
Sceloporus malachiticus
Lagartija Espinosa = thorny lizard

ID: A mid-sized lizard with body covered with coarse, spine-tipped scales; green, olive, or brown (but can darken to black); tail sometimes bluish; black mark on side of neck; throat and belly with blue blotches; to 9 cm (3.5 in), plus tail.

HABITAT: Middle and higher elevation wet forest areas, Pacific and northern Caribbean slopes; found on the ground but also climbs; prefers sunny, open areas, forest edge, clearings, gardens, rock walls, buildings.

PARKS: ARVL, BCNP, IVNP, LANP, MVCR, PONP, WIBG

Plate 19 273

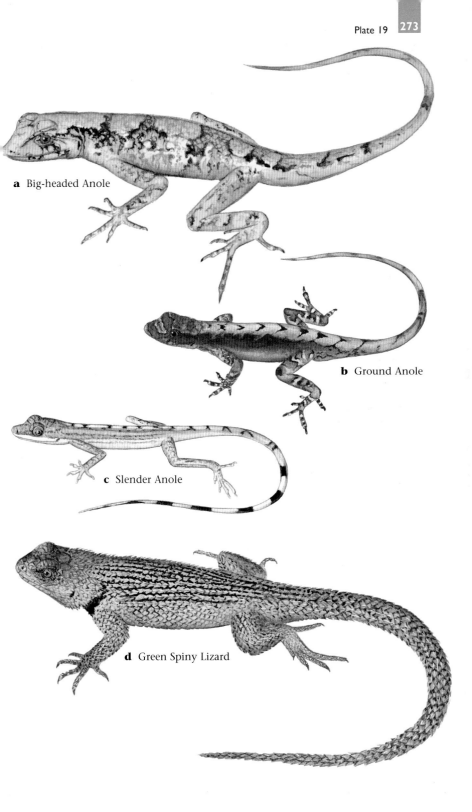

a Big-headed Anole

b Ground Anole

c Slender Anole

d Green Spiny Lizard

Plate 20a

Litter Skink
(also called Brown Forest Skink)
Sphenomorphus cherriei
Lucia de Hojarasca = leaf litter skink

ID: Small lizard with longish head, body, and tail; small legs; shiny bronze/brown back with dark spots; sides darker; black eyestripes extend along neck to body; yellowish area under eye extends to side of body; to 6.5 cm (2.5 in), plus tail.

HABITAT: Low and middle elevation wet forests and forest edges, Caribbean and Pacific slopes; usually found on the ground, in leaf litter; prefers open areas, tree groves.

PARKS: BCNP, CHNP, CNWR, CONP, LSBR, MVCR, PVNP, TONP, WIBG

Plate 20b

Central American Whiptail
(also called Central American Ameiva)
Ameiva festiva
Chisbala

ID: A mid-sized lizard, olive or brown with a conspicuous yellow, whitish, or bluish stripe down center of back; yellow, white or bluish dashes or dots along the sides; youngsters with bluish tail; to 12 cm (5 in), plus tail.

HABITAT: Low elevation wet forests, Caribbean and southern Pacific slopes; found on the ground or in low vegetation.

PARKS: BCNP, CHNP, CNWR, CONP, LSBR, MVCR, TONP, WIBG

Plate 20c

Barred Whiptail
(also called Rainbow Ameiva)
Ameiva undulata
Chisbala

ID: Mid-sized brown or greenish brown lizard, sometimes with whitish stripes; sides brown, or dark brown, sometimes with vertical green-blue bars; to 10 cm (4 in), plus tail.

HABITAT: Low elevation dry areas, northern Pacific slope; found on the ground in the leaf litter in forest and forest edge habitats; also in thickets, tree groves, and agricultural areas.

PARKS: CABR, MVCR, PVNP, SRNP

Plate 20d

Deppe's Whiptail
(also called Seven-lined Racerunner, Blackbelly Racerunner)
Cnemidophorus deppei
Chisbala

ID: A small, slender lizard with narrow, pointed head and long toes; blackish or dark brown body, sometimes with pale green areas; 7 or 8 narrow cream-colored stripes down the back; to 8 cm (3 in), plus long tail.

HABITAT: Northern Pacific coastal sites; found in open areas, sandy spots with little vegetation, beach dunes.

PARKS: CABR, PVNP, SRNP

Plate 20   275

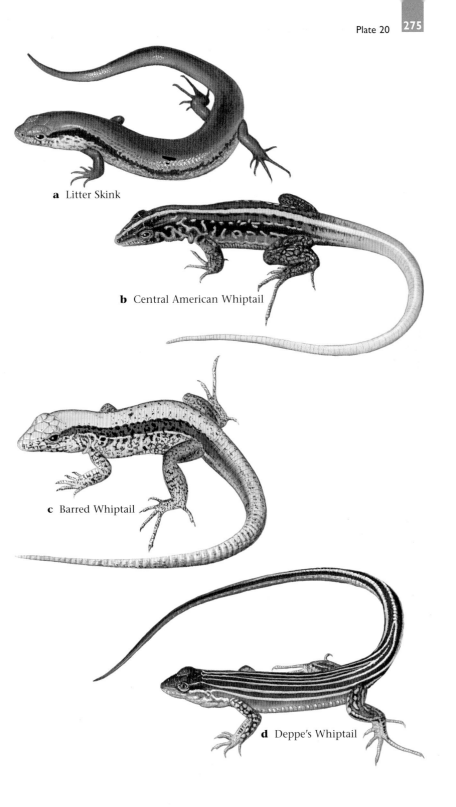

a Litter Skink

b Central American Whiptail

c Barred Whiptail

d Deppe's Whiptail

Plate 21a

Brown Booby
Sula leucogaster
Monjita = little nun
Alcatraz = gannet
Piquero moreno

ID: A mid-sized seabird with brown back, brown neck, white belly, and yellowish, cone-shaped, sharply pointed bill; pointed wings; to 66 cm (26 in); wingspan to 1.4 m (4.8 ft). Pacific coast males have grayish neck and bill.

HABITAT: Marine habitat, Caribbean and Pacific coasts; found along shores and around islands.

PARKS: CHNP, CONP, MANP, SRNP, TONP

Plate 21b

Magnificent Frigatebird
Fregata magnificens
Zopilote de Mar = sea vulture
Tijereta de Mar = sea scissors
Rabihorcado Magno = magnificent pitch-fork tail
Fragata

ID: Large, black seabird with long, narrow, pointed wings, long, forked tail, and long gray bill with down-curved tip; male with reddish throat patch; female with white belly; immature bird has white head and belly; to 90 cm (3 ft); wingspan to 2 m (6 ft).

HABITAT: Marine habitat, Caribbean and Pacific coasts; found along shores and around islands; often seen soaring high over coastal areas.

PARKS: CHNP, CONP, MANP, PVNP, SRNP, TONP

Plate 21c

Laughing Gull
Larus atricilla
Gaviota Reidora = laughing gull

ID: Smallish seabird, white with grayish back and tops of wings; white ring around eye; bill reddish-gray; adults during breeding have black heads and reddish bills; 40 cm (16 in); wingspan 1 m (3.3 ft).

HABITAT: Marine habitat, Caribbean and Pacific coasts; found along shores, beaches, islands; also seen inland near mudflats, river outlets, lake edges.

PARKS: CHNP, CONP, MANP, PVNP, SRNP, TONP

Plate 21d

Brown Pelican
Pelecanus occidentalis
Pelicano Moreno, Pelicano Pardo = brown pelican
Alcatraz = gannet

ID: Large, brownish seabird with blackish (during breeding) or white (nonbreeding) neck and very long bill with large throat pouch; head yellowish and bill reddish during breeding; immature bird is overall brown with lighter belly; 1 m (3.3 ft); wingspan to 2.1 m (7 ft).

HABITAT: Marine habitat, Caribbean and Pacific coasts; found along shores, beaches, islands.

PARKS: CHNP, CONP, MANP, PVNP, SRNP, TONP

Note: This species considered endangered over parts of its range, USA ESA listed.

Plate 21e

Olivaceous Cormorant
(also called Neotropic Cormorant)
Phalacrocorax brasilianus
Cormorán Neotropical = neotropical cormorant
Pato Chancho = pig duck

ID: A blackish or brownish mid-sized waterbird with brownish yellow facial skin and gray or black bill with down-curved tip, and long tail; 64 cm (2 ft); wingspan to 1 m (3.3 ft).

HABITAT: Found in and around lakes, rivers, lagoons in lowland areas and near shore in the Caribbean and Pacific; often seen in rivers and lakes diving for fish.

PARKS: BCNP, CABR, CHNP, CNWR, CONP, MANP, PVNP, SRNP, TONP, WIBG

Plate 21 277

a Brown Booby

b Magnificent
Frigatebird

e Olivaceous Cormorant

c Laughing Gull

d Brown Pelican

Plate 22a
Anhinga
Anhinga anhinga
Pato Aguja = needle duck
ID: Large, black waterbird with long, sharply pointed bill; silvery-white streaks on wings; black (males) or buffy-brown (females) neck and head; to 90 cm (3 ft); wingspan to 1.1 m (3.8 ft).

HABITAT: Found in and around lakes, rivers, lagoons, and marshes in Caribbean and Pacific lowland areas; often seen swimming with only head and neck above water, or perched with wings spread to dry.

PARKS: CABR, CHNP, CNWR, CONP, PVNP, TONP

Plate 22b
Jabiru Stork
Jabiru mycteria
Galán Sin Ventura = unlucky fellow
Jabirú
ID: A very large, white, wading bird with black head and huge, black bill; reddish area at bottom of neck; to 1.4 m (4.5 ft) tall; wingspan to 2.3 m (7.5 ft).

HABITAT: Aquatic habitats in only a few lowland areas; found around streams, rivers, ponds, lakes, but most often in marshes.

PARKS: CNWR, PVNP

Plate 22c
Wood Stork
Mycteria americana
Cigueñón = big wood stork
ID: Large, white wading bird with black head, neck, and bill; black shows under wings in flight; to 1 m (3.3 ft) tall; wingspan to 1.5 m (5 ft).

HABITAT: Aquatic habitats in some lowland areas; found around streams, rivers, ponds, lakes, but most often in marshes, including saltwater marshes.

PARKS: CNWR, PVNP, SRNP

Plate 22d
Roseate Spoonbill
Ajaia ajaja
Espátula Rosada = pink spatula
Garza Rosada = pink heron
ID: A large pink or light red wading bird with white neck and large, easily noticeable, spoon-shaped bill; immature bird is whitish to slightly pink; to 80 cm (2.7 ft); wingspan to 1.3 m (4.2 ft).

HABITAT: Lowland aquatic sites, mostly on Pacific slope; found around ponds, lakes, marshes, including saltwater marshes.

PARKS: CNWR, CONP, PVNP, SRNP

Plate 22e
White Ibis
Eudocimus albus
Ibis Blanco = white ibis
ID: Large white wading bird with thin, downward-curved, red bill and red legs; black wing tips noticeable in flight; immature bird is brownish; to 62 cm (2 ft); wingspan to 97 cm (38 in).

HABITAT: Lowland aquatic habitats of Caribbean and Pacific slopes; found along shorelines, beaches, mangroves, streams and rivers, ponds, lakes, and marshes.

PARKS: CONP, PVNP, SRNP

Plate 22 **279**

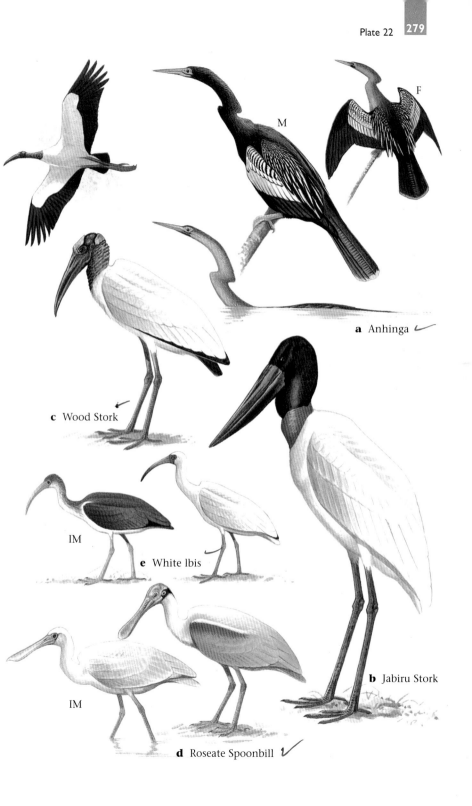

a Anhinga

c Wood Stork

e White Ibis

d Roseate Spoonbill

b Jabiru Stork

M

F

IM

IM

Plate 23 (*See also*: Herons and Egrets, p. 108)

Plate 23a

Boat-billed Heron
Cochlearius cochlearius
Pico-cuchara = spoon-bill
Chocuaco

ID: Medium-sized grayish heron with large head and very large, broad bill; top of head and inconspicuous crest black; belly rusty brown; immature bird has less black and more brown; to 50 cm (20 in).

HABITAT: Aquatic habitats over Caribbean and Pacific lowlands; found in or near marshes, swamps, rivers, mangroves, often perched in trees.

PARKS: CABR, CHNP, CNWR, CONP, LSBR, MANP, PVNP, SRNP, TONP

Plate 23b

Little Blue Heron
Egretta caerulea
Garceta Azul = little blue heron

ID: Medium-sized blue-gray heron with purplish or brownish red head and neck and grayish bill; legs vary in color but often grayish or black; immatures are white with dark tipped grayish bill, lighter-colored legs; to 66 cm (26 in); wingspan to 1 m (3.3 ft).

HABITAT: Aquatic habitats over Caribbean and Pacific lowlands; found in coastal areas and in or near ponds, rivers, marshes, mangroves.

PARKS: CABR, CHNP, CNWR, CONP, LSBR, MANP, PVNP, SRNP, TONP

Plate 23c

Tricolored Heron
Egretta tricolor
Garceta Tricolor = tricolored heron

ID: Medium-sized gray or bluish gray heron with brownish purple neck and chest; white throat and belly; yellowish bill with darker tip; yellowish legs; 66 cm (26 in); wingspan to 91 cm (36 in).

HABITAT: Aquatic habitats over Caribbean and Pacific lowlands; found in coastal areas and in or near ponds, rivers, marshes, mangroves.

PARKS: CABR, CHNP, CNWR, CONP, LSBR, MANP, PVNP, SRNP, TONP

Plate 23d

Snowy Egret
Egretta thula
Garceta Nivosa = snowy egret
Garza Blanca = white egret

ID: Medium-sized all-white heron with black bill and legs; immature bird is similar but back of legs yellowish green and with some gray on bill; to 64 cm (25 in); wingspan to 1 m (3.3 ft).

HABITAT: Aquatic habitats over Caribbean and Pacific lowlands; found in coastal areas and in or near ponds, rivers, marshes.

PARKS: CABR, CHNP, CNWR, CONP, LSBR, MANP, PVNP, SRNP, TONP

Plate 23   281

a Boat-billed Heron

b Little Blue Heron

IM

c Tricolored Heron

d Snowy Egret

IM

Plate 24a

Cattle Egret
Bubulcus ibis
Garza del Ganado = cattle egret
Garcilla Bueyera = ox egret

ID: A smaller, white heron with thickish neck, yellow bill, and dark legs; yellowish buff color on head, chest, and back during breeding; bill and legs reddish during breeding; immature bird is white with yellowish bill; 50 cm (20 in); wingpsan to 91 cm (36 in).

HABITAT: Agricultural areas at low and mid-elevations, Caribbean and Pacific slopes; found foraging in fields or following tractors; also marshes.

PARKS: ARVL, BCNP, CABR, CHNP, CNWR, CONP, LANP, LSBR, MANP, MVCR, PVNP, RVNP, SRNP, TONP, WIBG

Plate 24b

Great Egret
Casmerodius albus
Garceta Grande = big egret

ID: Large all-white heron with yellow bill and dark legs; 1 m (3.3 ft); wingspan to 1.3 m (4.3 ft).

HABITAT: Aquatic habitats over Caribbean and Pacific lowlands and some mid-elevations; found along coasts and inland around marshes, lakes, ponds, rivers.

PARKS: CABR, CHNP, CNWR, CONP, LSBR, MANP, PVNP, SRNP, TONP

Plate 24c

Bare-throated Tiger Heron
Tigrisoma mexicanum
Garza-tigre Cuellinuda = bare-throated tiger heron

ID: Large brownish heron with fine black stripes on neck, back and sides; head black and gray; throat yellow; immature bird is more of a chestnut-brown, has brown and black mottled wings, and lacks gray and black on its head; to 80 cm (2.7 ft).

HABITAT: Aquatic habitats over Caribbean and Pacific lowlands; found along coasts and inland around marshes, lakes, ponds, rivers.

PARKS: CABR, CHNP, CNWR, CONP, LSBR, MANP, PVNP, SRNP, TONP

Plate 24d

Green Heron
Butorides striatus
Garcilla Verde = little green heron

ID: Small heron with grayish green back, maroon or reddish brown neck, and black on top of head; yellowish or orange legs; immature bird is darker and heavily streaked; to 45 cm (18 in); wingspan to 60 cm (24 in).

HABITAT: Aquatic habitats at low- and mid-elevations on Caribbean and Pacific slopes; found along coasts in mangroves and inland around marshes, lakes, ponds, rivers.

PARKS: BCNP, CABR, CHNP, CNWR, CONP, LANP, LSBR, MANP, MVCR, PVNP, SRNP, TONP, WIBG

Plate 24 283

b Great Egret

a Cattle Egret

IM

d Green Heron

IM

c Bare-throated Tiger Heron

Plate 25a

Gray-necked Wood-rail
Aramides cajanea
Rascón Cuelligrís = gray-necked water rail
Pone-pone

ID: Mid-sized marsh bird with long, reddish legs, gray head and neck, yellowish bill, olive/brownish back, reddish brown chest; to 40 cm (16 in).

HABITAT: Low and middle elevation forests of Caribbean and Pacific slopes; found in wet forest areas and around streams, rivers, marshes, mangroves.

PARKS: ARVL, BCNP, CABR, CHNP, CNWR, CONP, LANP, LSBR, MANP, MVCR, PVNP, RVNP, SRNP, TONP, WIBG

Plate 25b

Purple Gallinule
Porphryula martinica
Gallina de Agua = water hen
Gallareta Morada = purple hen

ID: Striking mid-sized wading bird with bluish violet head, neck, and chest; green wings; red and yellow bill; light blue forehead; yellow legs; immature bird is light brown with greenish wings; to 40 cm (16 in).

HABITAT: Aquatic habitats at low and middle elevations, Caribbean and Pacific slopes; found in marshes and along lake and pond shores.

PARKS: ARVL, BCNP, CABR, CHNP, CNWR, CONP, LANP, LSBR, MANP, MVCR, PVNP, RVNP, SRNP, TONP, WIBG

Plate 25c

Northern Jacana
Jacana spinosa
Jacana Centroamericana = Central American jacana
Gallina de Agua = water hen

ID: Smallish wading bird with black head, neck, and chest; bright brown wings, back, and belly; yellow bill and forehead; greenish legs and very long toes; yellow under wings seen in flight; immature bird is brown with white chest/belly and black on top of head and eyestripe; to 25 cm (10 in).

HABITAT: Low and middle elevations, Caribbean and Pacific slopes; found in ponds, marshes, wet fields.

PARKS: BCNP, CABR, CHNP, CNWR, CONP, LANP, LSBR, MANP, MVCR, PVNP, SRNP, TONP, WIBG

Plate 25d

Sunbittern
Eurypyga helias
Garza del Sol = sun egret
Pájaro Sol = sunbird

ID: Chicken-sized bird with long, thin bill, slender neck, black head with white stripes; body intricately patterned in brown, black, white, and yellow; 48 cm (19 in).

HABITAT: Low and middle elevations, Caribbean and southern Pacific slopes; found in larger streams and rivers, forest streams and swamps.

PARKS: BCNP, CABR, CNWR, CONP, LANP, LSBR, MVCR, TONP, WIBG

Plate 25 285

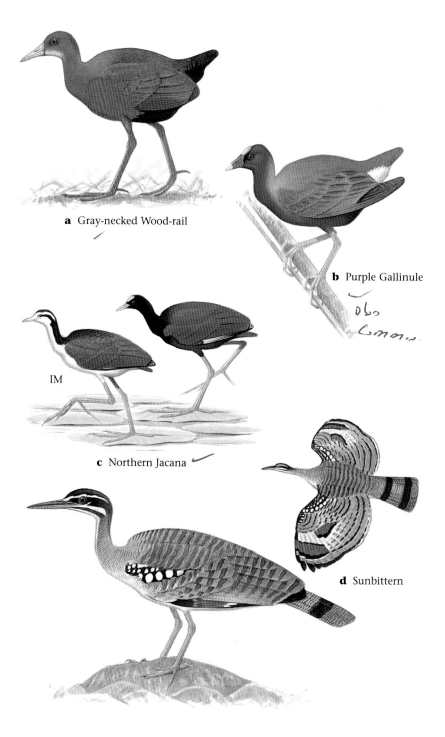

a Gray-necked Wood-rail

b Purple Gallinule

IM

c Northern Jacana

d Sunbittern

Plate 26a

Sungrebe
Heliornis fulica
Perrito de Agua = little water dog
Pato Cantil

ID: Smallish duck-like bird, brownish olive and white, with black and white stripes on head and neck; longish tail; straight, nonduckish bill; to 30 cm (1 ft).

HABITAT: Caribbean lowlands and some sites along southern Pacific slope; found in and along wooded streams and rivers, often in brushy areas.

PARKS: BCNP, CHNP, CNWR, CONP, LANP, LSBR, TONP

Plate 26b

Black-bellied Whistling Duck
Dendrocygna autumnalis
Pijije Común
Piche

ID: Slender, medium-sized duck, rust-colored with black belly; bill and feet red; immature bird is dull brown with grayish belly and dark bill; to 55 cm (22 in).

HABITAT: Aquatic habitats over Caribbean and Pacific lowlands; found in ponds, lakes, marshes, wet grassy areas.

PARKS: BCNP, CABR, CNWR, CONP, LANP, LSBR, PVNP, RVNP, SRNP, TONP

Plate 26c

Muscovy Duck
Cairina moschata
Pato Real = royal duck
Pato Alzado = imperial duck

ID: Large, chunky duck, mostly black with greenish gloss, and white wing patches; male has feathered crest on head and red "warts" on face; female lacks red warts, is a bit smaller and has a smaller crest; immature bird is brownish; to 85 cm (34 in).

HABITAT: Lowlands over Caribbean and Pacific slopes; found in wooded streams, rivers, and swamps; also in mangroves.

PARKS: BCNP, CABR, CHNP, CNWR, CONP, LANP, LSBR, PVNP, SRNP, TONP

Plate 26d

Double-striped Thick-knee
Burhinus bistriatus
Alcaraván Americano = American curlew

ID: Large brownish shorebird with noticeably large head with big yellow eyes; black stripe and white stripe above eye; brownish streaked chest; white belly; long yellow legs; shortish bill; 50 cm (20 in).

HABITAT: Low elevations over northern Pacific slope; found in pastures, fields, grasslands, cleared areas; night active.

PARKS: PVNP, SRNP

Plate 26 287

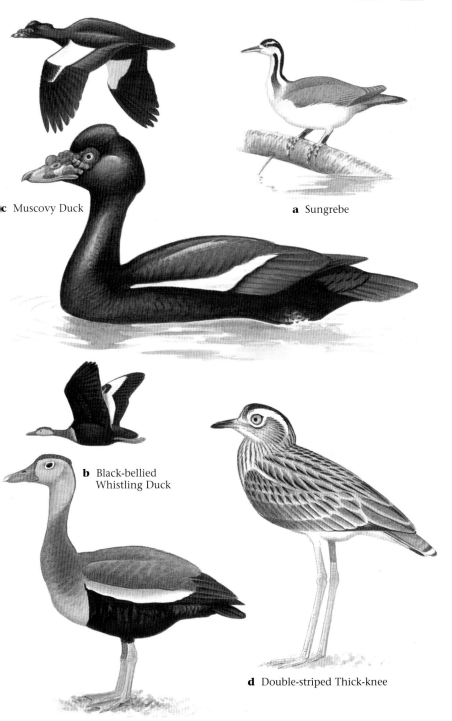

c Muscovy Duck

a Sungrebe

b Black-bellied
Whistling Duck

d Double-striped Thick-knee

Plate 27a

Spotted Sandpiper
Actitis macularia
Andarríos Maculado = spotted river walker

ID: Small brownish shorebird; white chest and belly, spotted with black during breeding season; whitish eyestripe, straight brownish bill; yellowish legs; to 20 cm (8 in).

HABITAT: Aquatic habitats at low-, mid-, and some higher-elevation sites throughout Caribbean and Pacific slopes; found along ocean shores and around lakes, ponds, rivers; also mangroves, marshes.

PARKS: ARVL, BCNP, CABR, CHNP, CNWR, CONP, LANP, LSBR, MANP, MVCR, PVNP, RVNP, SRNP, TONP, WIBG

Note: This species is a nonbreeding seasonal migrant.

Plate 27b

Sanderling
Calidris alba
Playerito Arenero = little beach sand-eater

ID: Small light gray shorebird with darker shoulder area and white head, chest and belly; straight black bill and black legs; to 20 cm (8 in).

HABITAT: Sandy shorelines, mudflats, along Caribbean and Pacific coasts.

PARKS: CHNP, CONP, MANP, PVNP, SRNP, TONP

Note: This species is a nonbreeding seasonal migrant.

Plate 27c

Western Sandpiper
Calidris mauri
Correlimos Occidental = western dune runner

ID: Small gray or gray-brown shorebird with white chest and belly; black legs and long, black bill with drooping tip; more brown on head and wings during breeding season; 16 cm (6.5 in).

HABITAT: Low- and mid-elevation aquatic habitats over Caribbean and Pacific slopes; found along coastlines on beaches and mudflats, and around lakes and ponds.

PARKS: CHNP, CNWR, CONP, MANP, PVNP, SRNP, TONP

Note: This species is a nonbreeding seasonal migrant.

Plate 27d

Black-bellied Plover
Pluvialis squatarola
Chorlito Gris = gray plover

ID: Medium-sized brown, grayish, and white shorebird; grayish brown chest mixed with white; white belly; black bars on tail; short black bill; gray legs; black throat and chest during breeding season; 30 cm (12 in).

HABITAT: Coastal areas, usually along the Pacific; found on beaches, mudflats, mangroves; occasionally along rivers near coast.

PARKS: CABR, CONP, MANP, PVNP, SRNP

Note: This species is a nonbreeding seasonal migrant.

Plate 27e

Whimbrel
Numenius phaeopus
Zarapito Trinador = warbling curlew

ID: Large gray-brown shorebird with black striped head and long, black bill that turns downward; to 45 cm (18 in).

HABITAT: Coastal areas, more so along the Pacific; found along sandy and rocky beaches, on mudflats; occasionally along rivers near coast.

PARKS: CABR, CHNP, CONP, MANP, SRNP, TONP

Plate 27 289

a Spotted Sandpiper

b Sanderling

c Western Sandpiper

d Black-bellied Plover

e Whimbrel

Plate 28a
Gray-headed Chachalaca
Ortalis cinereiceps
Chachalaca Cabecigrís = gray-headed chachalaca

ID: Largish olive-colored bird with lighter belly, small gray head, and reddish throat; dark tail with lighter tip; reddish brown wing tips seen in flight; gray bill; to 53 cm (21 in).

HABITAT: Low and middle elevations over Caribbean and southern Pacific slopes; found in trees in woodland areas, thickets, around clearings, and along watercourses; walks along tree branches.

PARKS: BCNP, CABR, CHNP, CNWR, CONP, LANP, LSBR, MANP, TONP

Plate 28b
Plain Chachalaca
Ortalis vetula
Chachalaca Olivacea = olivaceous chachalaca

ID: Similar to Gray-headed Chachalaca (see above), but belly is darker, yellowish orange, and lacks reddish brown wing tips; black bill; to 53 cm (21 in).

HABITAT: Dry forests of northern Pacific lowlands and dry and wet forests at various elevations on Nicoya Peninsula; found in trees in forest interior, at forest edge, and in savannah areas.

PARKS: PVNP, SRNP

Note: This species is vulnerable in some regions, CITES Appendix III listed for Guatemala and Honduras.

Plate 28c
Crested Guan
Penelope purpurascens
Pava Crestada = crested guan

ID: Large, turkey-like, brown bird with crest on head and red throat sac; white spots/streaks on chest; reddish legs; to 90 cm (3 ft).

HABITAT: Low- and mid-elevation forests over Caribbean and Pacific slopes; found in canopy or on ground.

PARKS: ARVL, BCNP, CABR, CHNP, CNWR, CONP, LANP, LSBR, MANP, MVCR, PVNP, RVNP, SRNP, TONP, WIBG

Plate 28d
Black Guan
Chamaepetes unicolor
Pava Negra = black guan
Granadera = grenadier

ID: Large blackish bird with blue face and red legs; to 60 cm (2 ft).

HABITAT: Higher elevation forests, Caribbean and Pacific slopes; found in trees walking along branches or on ground.

PARKS: ARVL, BCNP, IVNP, LANP, MVCR, PONP, RVNP

Plate 28e
Great Curassow
Crax rubra
Pavón = peacock
Granadera = grenadier
Pajuila

ID: Very large chicken-like bird with conspicuous, curly, head crest and long tail; male is black with white belly and has yellow "knob" on bill; female is mostly brownish or red-brown with white and black barred head; to 91 cm (3 ft).

HABITAT: Low- and mid-elevation forests, Caribbean and Pacific slopes; found walking on ground in forest interior and at forest edges.

PARKS: BCNP, CABR, CNWR, CONP, LANP, LSBR, PVNP, RVNP, SRNP, WIBG

Note: This species is vulnerable in some regions, CITES Appendix III listed for Costa Rica, Guatemala, and Honduras.

Plate 28 291

a Gray-headed Chachalaca

b Plain Chachalaca

c Crested Guan

d Black Guan

F

M

e Great Curassow

Plate 29a

Spotted-bellied Bobwhite
Colinus leucopogon
Codorniz Vientrimanchada = spotted-bellied quail

ID: Small ground bird, brownish with round white spots on breast (more pronounced in females); white stripe above eye, dark stripe through eye; black bill; gray legs; to 23 cm (9 in).

HABITAT: Low and middle elevations of northern Pacific slope and Central Valley; found in fields, pastures, scrubby woodlands, grassland.

PARKS: MVCR, PVNP, RVNP, SRNP

Plate 29b

Great Tinamou
Tinamus major
Tinamú Grande = great tinamou
Gallina de Monte = mountain hen
Gongolona

ID: Large, thick-set bird, olive-brownish with darker bars; gray legs; very small tail; slender bill; to 45 cm (18 in).

HABITAT: Low and middle elevation wet forests, Caribbean and southern Pacific slopes; found usually on the ground, but rests in trees.

PARKS: BCNP, CABR, CHNP, CNWR, CONP, LANP, LSBR, MANP, TONP, WIBG

Plate 29c

Thicket Tinamou
Crypturellus cinnamomeus
Tinamú Canelo = cinnamon tinamou
Gongolona

ID: Mid-sized, thick-set bird, brownish with conspicuous dark bars; chest and belly cinnamon; red legs; very small tail; slender bill; to 28 cm (11 in).

HABITAT: Low and middle elevation drier forests of northern Pacific slope; found on the ground.

PARKS: PVNP, RVNP, SRNP

Plate 29d

Slaty-breasted Tinamou
Crypturellus boucardi
Tinamú Pizarroso = slaty-breasted tinamou

ID: Mid-sized, thick-set bird with dark gray head and chest, brownish back and wings; white throat; red legs; very small tail; slender bill; female with light brown/buffy wing bars; to 28 cm (11 in).

HABITAT: Low elevation wet forests of northern Caribbean slope; found on the ground.

PARKS: BCNP, CNWR, LSBR, TONP

Plate 29   293

a Spotted-bellied Bobwhite

b Great Tinamou

c Thicket Tinamou

M

F

d Slaty-breasted Tinamou

Plate 30a

Turkey Vulture
Cathartes aura
Zopilote Cabecirrojo = red-headed
vulture
Zopilote = vulture
ID: Large black bird with featherless red head and neck, whitish bill, and yellowish, flesh, or light red legs; resident birds (non-migratory) with white band on back of neck; underside of wing in flight is black in front, grayish behind; wings held in shallow V during soaring flight; to 80 cm (32 in); wingspan to 1.7 m (5.8 ft).

HABITAT: Found countrywide, usually below 2100 m (7000 ft); usually seen in the air, circling above open areas and many other kinds of habitats.

PARKS: ARVL, BCNP, CABR, CHNP, CNWR, CONP, LANP, LSBR, MANP, MVCR, PONP, PVNP, RVNP, SRNP, TONP, WIBG

Plate 30b

Black Vulture
Coragyps atratus
Zopilote Negro = black vulture
Zopilote = vulture
ID: Large black bird with featherless black head and neck; whitish legs; underside of wing in flight shows a whitish area near wing tip; wings held flat out during soaring flight; to 66 cm (26 in); wingspan to 1.4 m (4.8 ft).

HABITAT: Found countrywide, usually below 2000 m (6500 ft); usually spotted in the air, circling above villages, towns, garbage dumps, other open areas.

PARKS: ARVL, BCNP, CABR, CHNP, CNWR, CONP, LANP, LSBR, MANP, MVCR, PONP, PVNP, RVNP, SRNP, TONP, WIBG

Plate 30c

King Vulture
Sarcoramphus papa
Zopilote Rey = king vulture
ID: Large white bird with featherless, multi-colored head, black wings, gray neck, orange bill; underside of wing in flight is white in front, black behind; to 81 cm (32 in); wingspan to 2 m (6.5 ft).

HABITAT: Found countrywide, usually below 1400 m (4500 ft); usually seen in the air, circling above forested or partly wooded areas.

PARKS: BCNP, CABR, CHNP, CNWR, CONP, LANP, LSBR, MANP, MVCR, PVNP, SRNP, TONP, WIBG

Plate 30 295

a Turkey Vulture

b Black Vulture

c King Vulture

Plate 31 (*See also*: Raptors, p. 122)

Plate 31a

Crested Caracara
Polyborus plancus
Caracara Cargahuesos = bone-carrier
caracara

ID: A large black bird with barred neck, black, white, and reddish head, white throat, light-colored, hooked bill, and yellow legs; to 60 cm (2 ft); wingspan to 1.3 m (4.3 ft).

HABITAT: Open habitats over lowland areas of the Pacific slope – grasslands, pastures, forest edge areas; more common in northern than southern areas.

PARKS: CABR, CONP, MANP, PVNP, SRNP

Plate 31b

Yellow-headed Caracara
Milvago chimachima
Caracara Cabecigualdo = yellow-headed caracara

ID: A mid-sized bird with blackish brown back and wings, light tawny head, chest and belly; black line through eye; tail light with dark bars; hooked bill and legs are dark or pale bluish or greenish; to 43 cm (17 in); wingspan to 74 cm (29 in).

HABITAT: Open habitats over lowland areas of the southern Pacific slope – grasslands, pastures, forest edge areas.

PARKS: CABR, CONP, MANP

Plate 31c

Laughing Falcon
Herpetotheres cachinnans
Guaco
Halcón Guaco

ID: Largish brown bird with tawny or buffy head, chest, and belly; black mask around eyes; tail black with light bars; dark, hooked bill; to 55 cm (22 in).

HABITAT: Open and semi-open areas over lowlands of Caribbean and Pacific slopes; found in forest edge areas, grasslands, agricultural areas.

PARKS: ARVL, BCNP, CABR, CHNP, CNWR, CONP, LANP, LSBR, MANP, MVCR, PVNP, RVNP, SRNP, TONP, WIBG

Plate 31d

Collared Forest Falcon
Micrastur semitorquatus
Halcón de Monte Collarejo = collared forest falcon

ID: Largish bird with dark, hooked bill, long, yellowish legs, and dark tail with light bars. Two forms: light form has black back and wings, white or tawny chest and belly, white face; dark form is mostly black, with chest and belly barred with white or light brown; to 51 cm (20 in).

HABITAT: Low and middle elevation wooded areas, Caribbean and Pacific slopes; found in forest interiors and edges.

PARKS: ARVL, BCNP, CABR, CNWR, CONP, LANP, LSBR, MANP, MVCR, PVNP, RVNP, SRNP, WIBG

Plate 31 297

a Crested Caracara

b Yellow-headed Caracara

c Laughing Falcon

d Collared Forest Falcon

BARRED FIRST

Plate 32a

American Swallow-tailed Kite
Elanoides forficatus
Halcón tijerilla = little scissors falcon
Elanio Tijereta

ID: Largish white and black bird with black, deeply forked tail; underside of wing in flight is white in front, black behind; to 60 cm (2 ft); wingspan to 1.2 m (4 ft).

HABITAT: Low and middle elevations over Caribbean and southern Pacific slopes; often seen soaring over forested areas.

PARKS: ARVL, BCNP, CABR, CNWR, CONP, LANP, LSBR, MANP, MVCR, RVNP, TONP, WIBG

Plate 32b

Gray-headed Kite
Leptodon cayanensis
Gavilán Cabecigris = gray-headed kite

ID: Largish white and black bird with gray head; black above, white below; underside of wing in flight is black in front, black with gray bars behind; tail with light and dark bars; dark, hooked bill; grayish legs; to 53 cm (21 in).

HABITAT: Low elevation wooded areas, Caribbean and Pacific slopes; found in forest edge areas and along wooded waterways.

PARKS: BCNP, CABR, CNWR, CONP, LSBR, MANP, PVNP, SRNP, TONP

Plate 32c

Common Black Hawk
Buteogallus anthracinus
Gavilán Cangrejero = crab-eater hawk

ID: Large, mostly black bird with dark, hooked bill, yellow legs; shortish black tail with wide white bar; 56 cm (22 in); wingspan to 1.3 m (4.2 ft).

HABITAT: Lowlands (primarily coastal areas) of Caribbean and Pacific slopes; found in trees near water: ocean shores, rivers, streams, marshes.

PARKS: CABR, CHNP, CONP, LSBR, MANP, PVNP, SRNP, TONP

Plate 32d

White Hawk
Leucopternis albicollis
Gavilán Blanco = white hawk

ID: Large white bird with black on wings and black bar on tail; yellow legs; underside of wing in flight is white with black edge; to 58 cm (23 in).

HABITAT: Low and middle elevations, Caribbean and southern Pacific slopes; found in forested and forest edge areas.

PARKS: BCNP, CABR, CHNP, CNWR, CONP, LSBR, MANP, MVCR, TONP, WIBG

Plate 32 **299**

b Gray-headed Kite

a American Swallow-tailed Kite

c Common Black Hawk

d White Hawk

Plate 33a

Roadside Hawk
Buteo magnirostris
Gavilán Chapulinero = grasshopper-eater hawk

ID: Mid-sized brownish gray hawk with grayish head and chest; gray and brown barred belly; tail with light and dark bars; yellow legs; to 40 cm (16 in).

HABITAT: Low and middle elevations, Caribbean and Pacific slopes; found in open wooded areas, grasslands, forest edges, agricultural areas, roadsides.

PARKS: BCNP, CABR, CHNP, CNWR, CONP, LSBR, MANP, PVNP, SRNP, TONP

Plate 33b

Osprey
Pandion haliatus
Aguila Pescadora = fishing eagle
Gavilán Pescador = fishing hawk

ID: Large brownish bird with white head; dark stripe through eye; gray legs; wing in flight has backward "bend;" underside of wing white with darker stripes and markings; to 60 cm (2 ft); wingspan to 1.8 m (6 ft).

HABITAT: Lowlands (primarily coastal areas) of Caribbean and Pacific slopes; seen flying or perched in trees near water – ocean shores, mangroves, ponds, lakes.

PARKS: BCNP, CABR, CHNP, CNWR, CONP, LSBR, MANP, PVNP, SRNP, TONP

Note: This species is a nonbreeding seasonal migrant.

Plate 33c

Broad-winged Hawk
Buteo platypterus
Gavilán Aludo = broad-winged hawk
Gavilán Pollero = chicken-eater hawk

ID: Mid-sized brown hawk with reddish brown and white striped chest and belly; black tail with white bars; underside of wings in flight mostly white; yellow legs; 41 cm (16 in); wingspan to 86 cm (34 in).

HABITAT: Low-, mid-, and higher-elevations, Caribbean and Pacific slopes; seen soaring or perched in more open areas such as forest edge, grasslands.

PARKS: ARVL, BCNP, CABR, CHNP, CNWR, CONP, LANP, LSBR, MANP, MVCR, PVNP, RVNP, SRNP, TONP, WIBG

Note: This species is a nonbreeding seasonal migrant.

Plate 33d

Swainson's Hawk
Buteo swainsoni
Gavilán de Swainson = Swainson's hawk
Gavilán = hawk

ID: Large brown hawk, 2 forms. Light form with white throat, chest with large brown band, light belly, white and grayish or brownish under wings. Dark form with dark brown throat, chest, belly; underside of wing in flight dark brown in front, grayish behind; to 53 cm (21 in); wingspan to 1.3 m (4.3 ft).

HABITAT: Usually seen soaring over northern Caribbean, southern Pacific slopes, but may be spotted countrywide.

PARKS: ARVL, BCNP, CABR, CHNP, CNWR, CONP, LANP, LSBR, MANP, MVCR, PONP, PVNP, RVNP, SRNP, TONP, WIBG

Note: This species is a nonbreeding seasonal migrant.

Plate 33   301

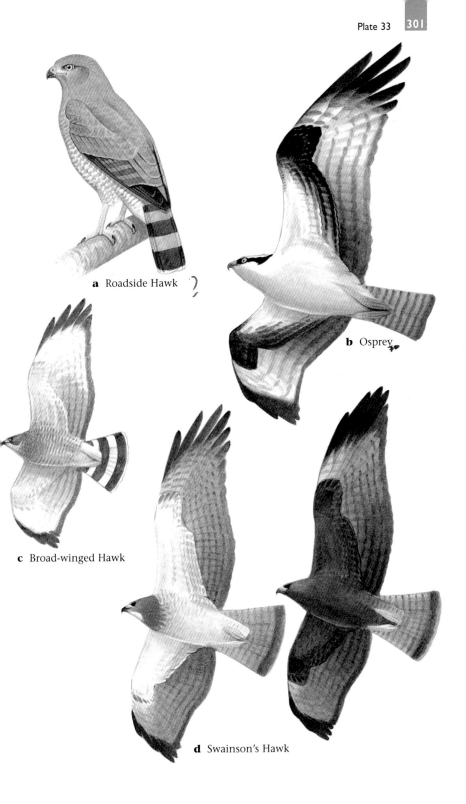

a Roadside Hawk

b Osprey

c Broad-winged Hawk

d Swainson's Hawk

Plate 34a

Band-tailed Pigeon
Columba fasciata
Paloma Collareja = necklace pigeon
ID: Large grayish or brownish pigeon with yellow bill and legs; purplish gray head; iridescent greenish patch with white bar at back of neck; to 35 cm (14 in).

HABITAT: High elevation forested areas, Caribbean and Pacific slopes; found high in trees in forests, forest edge areas, tree plantations.

PARKS: ARVL, BCNP, IVNP, LANP, MVCR, PONP, RVNP, WIBG

Plate 34b

Red-billed Pigeon
Columba flavirostris
Paloma Piquirroja = red-billed pigeon
ID: Large, dark reddish purplish pigeon with brown back; belly and tail gray; bill whitish and red; reddish legs; 33 cm (13 in).

HABITAT: Low and middle elevations, particularly northern Pacific slope; less common on Caribbean slope; found in open wooded areas, forest edge, clearings, grassland, agricultural areas.

PARKS: BCNP, CABR, CNWR, CONP, LSBR, MANP, MVCR, PVNP, RVNP, SRNP, TONP

Plate 34c

Short-billed Pigeon
Columba nigrirostris
Paloma Piquicorta = short-billed pigeon
Dos Tontos Son = two fools they are
ID: Mid-sized purplish brown or ruddy brown pigeon with short, black bill; reddish legs; 27 cm (11 in).

HABITAT: Low and middle elevation wet forest, Caribbean and southern Pacific slopes; found in trees or on ground in more open areas such as forest edges and clearings.

PARKS: BCNP, CABR, CHNP, CNWR, CONP, LANP, LSBR, MANP, MVCR, RVNP, TONP, WIBG

Plate 34d

Blue Ground-dove
Claravis pretiosa
Tortolita Azulada = bluish turtle dove
Tortolita = turtle dove
ID: Smallish dove with yellowish bill; male bluish gray with lighter face, chest, and belly; dark spots and bars on wings; sides of tail black; female brownish with reddish brown bars on wings; to 20 cm (8 in).

HABITAT: Low and middle elevation wet forests, countrywide; found usually on the ground in open areas, pastures, fields, open woodlands, and at forest edges.

PARKS: ARVL, BCNP, CABR, CHNP, CNWR, CONP, LSBR, MANP, PVNP, TONP, WIBG

Plate 34e

Ruddy Ground-dove
Columbina talpacoti
Tortolita Rojiza = reddish turtle dove
Tortolita = turtle dove
ID: Smallish dove with yellow or brown bill; male reddish brown with gray head; black spots on wings; female duller, less reddish; 16.5 cm (6.5 in).

HABITAT: Low and middle elevations, Caribbean and southern Pacific slopes (also parts of Nicoya Peninsula); found usually on ground in open areas: pastures, fields, woodland clearings.

PARKS: BCNP, CABR, CHNP, CNWR, CONP, LSBR, MANP, PVNP, TONP, WIBG

Plate 34 303

a Band-tailed Pigeon

b Red-billed Pigeon

c Short-billed Pigeon

M

F

d Blue Ground-dove ✓

e Ruddy Ground-dove

Plate 35a

Common Ground-dove
Columbina passerina
Tortolita Común = common turtle dove
Tortolita = turtle dove
ID: Small dove with reddish or yellowish bill with dark tip; male gray with black "scaling" on neck and chest, black spots on wings, pinkish tinge on underparts; reddish brown wing patches seen in flight; female brownish with less scaling; black spots on wings; 15 cm (6 in).

HABITAT: Dry lowland forests of northern Pacific slope, and Central Valley; found usually on the ground in open areas: pastures, agricultural areas, roadsides, woodland clearings.

PARKS: CABR, PVNP, SRNP

Plate 35b

Inca Dove
Columbina inca
Tortolita Colilarga = long-tailed turtle dove
Tortolita = turtle dove
ID: Small pale gray dove with black linings on feathers that yields a "scaled" appearance; longish tail with white edges; reddish brown wing patches seen in flight; to 20 cm (8 in).

HABITAT: Low and middle elevations, northern Pacific slope; found usually on the ground in open areas such as pastures, fields, lawns, woodland clearings, forest edges.

PARKS: CABR, MANP, MVCR, PVNP, SRNP

Plate 35c

White-tipped Dove
Leptotila verreauxi
Paloma Coliblanca = white-tailed dove
ID: Mid-sized dove with gray or grayish brown head; brown back and wings; lighter-colored face; pinkish or violet tinge to head and chest; tail dark with white edging at end; blue skin around eye; black bill; male has iridescent sheen on neck; to 28 cm (11 in).

HABITAT: Low and middle elevation wet and dry forests over Pacific slope; found usually on ground in open areas such as agricultural areas, gardens, open woodlands, forest edges.

PARKS: CABR, CONP, MANP, MVCR, PVNP, SRNP, WIBG

Plate 35d

White-winged Dove
Zenaida asiatica
Paloma Aliblanca = white-winged dove
ID: Mid-sized brownish dove with black spot on side of face below blue-ringed eye; grayish belly; white bar on wing, seen mostly in flight; sides of tail tipped with white; male has iridescent sheen on neck; to 28 cm (11 in).

HABITAT: Lowland dry forest, northern Pacific slope; found on ground in more open areas, such as pastures, open woodlands, forest edges.

PARKS: ARVL, CABR, PVNP, SRNP

Plate 35e

Ruddy Quail-dove
Geotrygon montana
Paloma-Perdiz Rojiza = ruddy quail dove
ID: Fairly small reddish brown dove with red bill; purplish red legs; males with facial stripe, lighter-colored face and throat, and iridescent purple sheen on back; female darker olive-brown with lighter underparts; to 24 cm (9.5 in).

HABITAT: Wet forests at low and middle elevations, Caribbean and Pacific slopes; found usually on ground along moist forest trails, shady plantations, gardens.

PARKS: BCNP, CNWR, CONP, LSBR, MANP, MVCR, PVNP, WIBG

Chested gray

Plate 35   305

Common Ground-dove

b Inca Dove

c White-tipped Dove

d White-winged Dove

F

e Ruddy Quail-dove

M

Plate 36a

Scarlet Macaw
Ara macao
Guacamaya Roja
Lapa Roja

ID: Very large, long-tailed red parrot with big patches of yellow on wings and blue on wings and tail; to 86 cm (34 in).

HABITAT: Lowland forests of Pacific slope and some parts of northern Caribbean slope; usually found high in tree canopy in wooded and forest edge areas, often near water.

PARKS: CABR, CONP, PVNP, SRNP

Note: This species is endangered, CITES Appendix I listed.

Plate 36b

Mealy Parrot
Amazona farinosa
Loro Verde = green parrot
Loro = parrot

ID: A large green parrot with blue tinge on top of head; touches of red and blue on wings, seen mostly in flight; end of tail lighter green or yellowish; whitish eye-ring; to 38 cm (15 in).

HABITAT: Lowland wet forest, Caribbean and southern Pacific slopes; found in tree canopy in wooded areas, forest edges, tree plantations.

PARKS: BCNP, CABR, CHNP, CNWR, CONP, LSBR, MANP, TONP, WIBG

Plate 36c

Red-lored Parrot
Amazona autumnalis
Loro Frentirrojo = red-lored parrot
Loro = parrot

ID: Mid-sized green parrot with red forehead and blue tinge on head feathers; often some yellow on face; red and blue patches on wings, seen mostly in flight; to 34 cm (13 in).

HABITAT: Low and middle elevation wet forests, Caribbean and southern Pacific slopes; found in tree canopy in wooded areas, forest edges, tree plantations.

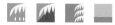

PARKS: BCNP, CABR, CHNP, CNWR, CONP, LSBR, MANP, MVCR, RVNP, TONP, WIBG

Plate 36d

Yellow-naped Parrot
Amazona auropalliata
Lora de Nuca Amarilla = yellow-naped parrot
Loro = parrot

ID: A mid-sized green parrot with yellow patch on back of neck; red and blue patches on wings, seen mostly in flight; end of tail light green; to 34 cm (13 in).

HABITAT: Dry forests of northern Pacific slope; found in tree canopy in wooded areas, forest edges, and in agricultural areas.

PARKS: CABR, PVNP, SRNP

Plate 36 307

b Mealy Parrot

Fly Shand.

a Scarlet Macaw

c Red-lored Parrot

d Yellow-naped Parrot

Plate 37a

White-fronted Parrot
Amazona albifrons
Loro Frentiblanco = white-fronted parrot
Loro = parrot

ID: Mid-sized green parrot with red on face, including around eyes; white forehead; blue at top of head; red and blue patches on wings, seen mostly in flight; to 28 cm (11 in).

HABITAT: Dry forests of northern Pacific slope; found in tree canopy in wooded areas, forest edges, and in agricultural areas.

PARKS: MVCR, PVNP, RVNP, SRNP

Plate 37b

White-crowned Parrot
Pionus senilis
Loro Coroniblanco = white-crowned parrot
Loro = parrot

ID: A smallish, dark green parrot with white fore-head and white throat; blue or greenish blue head and upper breast; brownish or bronze shoulder patches; blue under wings and red under tail, seen in flight; to 25 cm (10 in).

HABITAT: Lowland wet forests, Caribbean and southern Pacific slopes; found in tree canopy in wooded areas, forest edges, and in agricultural areas.

PARKS: BCNP, CABR, CHNP, CNWR, CONP, LSBR, MANP, RVNP, TONP, WIBG

Plate 37c

Brown-hooded Parrot
Pionopsitta haematotis
Loro Cabecipardo = brown-headed parrot
Loro = parrot

ID: A small green parrot with brownish head, neck, and chest; dark face; red spot on side of head; red and blue patches on wings, seen in flight; to 22 cm (8.5 in).

HABITAT: Lowland wet forests, Caribbean and southern Pacific slopes; found in tree canopy in wooded areas, forest edges, and in agricultural areas.

PARKS: BCNP, CABR, CHNP, CNWR, CONP, LSBR, MANP, MVCR, RVNP, TONP, WIBG

Plate 37d

Orange-fronted Parakeet
Aratinga canicularis
Perico Frentinaranja = orange-fronted parakeet
Perico = parakeet

ID: Smallish green parrot with orange forehead and blue on top of head; olive or brownish breast; yellow eye-ring; blue on wings, seen mostly in flight; long green tail often with bluish tip; to 22 cm (9 in).

HABITAT: Low elevation wet and dry forests, northern Pacific slope; found in tree canopy in wooded and forest edge areas.

PARKS: MVCR, PVNP, RVNP, SRNP

Plate 37e

Orange-chinned Parakeet
Brotogeris jugularis
Periquito Barbinaranja = orange-chinned parakeet
Perico = parakeet

ID: Small green parrot with orange chin and brownish shoulders; extensive yellow patches under wings, seen in flight; to 18 cm (7 in).

HABITAT: Low and middle elevation wet and dry forests, Caribbean and Pacific slopes; found in tree canopy in more open wooded areas, forest edges, plantations.

PARKS: BCNP, CABR, CHNP, CNWR, CONP, LSBR, MANP, MVCR, PVNP, RVNP, SRNP, TONP, WIBG

Plate 37 309

a White-fronted Parrot

b White-crowned Parrot

c Brown-hooded Parrot

d Orange-fronted Parakeet

e Orange-chinned Parakeet

Plate 38a

Striped Cuckoo
Tapera naevia
Cuclillo Listado = striped cuckoo
ID: Mid-sized brown bird with short bushy crest; whitish stripe above eye; black-striped brown back; whitish to light brownish chest; smallish down-curved bill; to 30 cm (12 in).

HABITAT: Lower elevation wet forests, Caribbean and southern Pacific slopes; found in trees and on the ground in more open sites – forest edges, pastures, plantations, scrub areas.

PARKS: CABR, CNWR, CONP, LSBR, MANP, WIBG

Plate 38b

Squirrel Cuckoo
Piaya cayana
Cuco Ardilla = squirrel cuckoo
Pájaro Ardilla = squirrel bird
ID: Large reddish brown bird with grayish belly; long tail with, on its underside, alternating bars of black and white; to 48 cm (19 in).

HABITAT: Low, middle, and some higher elevation wooded areas, Caribbean and Pacific slopes; found in trees in more open, wooded habitats, such as forest edges and tree plantations.

PARKS: ARVL, BCNP, CABR, CHNP, CNWR, CONP, IVNP, LSBR, MANP, MVCR, PONP, PVNP, RVNP, SRNP, TONP, WIBG

Plate 38c

Smooth-billed Ani
Crotophaga ani
Garrapatero Piquiliso = smooth-billed tick-eater
Tijo
ID: A mid-sized dull black bird with relatively huge, humped bill and long tail; iridescent sheen on head, neck, breast; to 35 cm (14 in).

HABITAT: Low and middle elevations, southern Pacific slope; found in small flocks in more open habitats such as scrub areas, fields, pastures, and other agricultural sites.

PARKS: CONP, MANP, WIBG

Plate 38d

Groove-billed Ani
Crotophaga sulcirostris
Garrapatero Piquiestriado = groove-billed tick-eater
Tijo
ID: A mid-sized all black bird with relatively huge, humped bill having conspicuous ridges; iridescent sheen on head, breast; long tail; to 30 cm (12 in).

HABITAT: Low and middle elevations, Caribbean and northern Pacific slopes; found in small flocks in more open habitats such as scrub and open wooded areas, fields, pastures, and other agricultural sites.

PARKS: ARVL, BCNP, CABR, CHNP, CNWR, LANP, LSBR, MANP, MVCR, PONP, PVNP, RVNP, SRNP

Plate 38   311

a Striped Cuckoo

b Squirrel Cuckoo

c Smooth-billed Ani

d Groove-billed Ani

Plate 39a

Spectacled Owl
Pulsatrix perspicillata
Buho de Anteojos = spectacled owl
Morococo

ID: Large owl with dark brown head, back, and chest; whitish, buffy, or light brown belly; white "spectacles" around eyes; white on throat; to 46 cm (18 in).

HABITAT: Low and middle elevation wet and dry forest, Caribbean and Pacific slopes; found in forest interior and in more open areas around forest edge, tree plantations, etc.

PARKS: ARVL, BCNP, CABR, CNWR, CONP, LANP, LSBR, MANP, MVCR, PVNP, RVNP, SRNP, TONP

Plate 39b

Pacific Screech-owl
Otus cooperi
Lechucita Sabanera = little savannah owl

ID: A mid-sized brown owl with dark streaks on chest; longish ear tufts, or "horns;" to 23 cm (9 in).

HABITAT: Low and some middle elevations, northern Pacific slope; found in wooded areas, as well as in semi-open sites such as forest edges, trees along waterways and near buildings and roads.

PARKS: PVNP, RVNP, SRNP

Plate 39c

Ferruginous Pygmy-owl
Glaucidium brasilianum
Mochuelo Común

ID: A small grayish brown or reddish brown owl with white streaks on chest, belly; fine white streaks on head; brown or black tail with paler bars; black spot on side of neck; to 16 cm (6.5 in).

HABITAT: Low and some middle elevations, northern Pacific slope; found in wooded areas, as well as in semi-open sites such as forest edges, grassland and agricultural areas with trees; day-active.

PARKS: PVNP, SRNP

Plate 39d

Pauraque
Nyctidromus albicollis
Tapacaminos Común = common road-blocker
Cuyeo

ID: Mid-sized brown bird with fine brown mottling and black spots or streaks; whitish band on throat; light brown chest/belly with fine black bars; longish tail with white stripes in male, white tips in female; white or light-colored band on wings, seen in flight; to 28 cm (11 in).

HABITAT: Low, middle, and some higher elevation sites, Caribbean and Pacific slopes; found resting on the ground during the day in shady spots in grasslands, pastures, open woodlands, forest edges; active at night.

PARKS: ARVL, BCNP, CABR, CHNP, CNWR, CONP, LANP, LSBR, MANP, MVCR, PVNP, RVNP, SRNP, TONP, WIBG

Plate 39e

Lesser Nighthawk
Chordeiles acutipennis
Añapero Menor

ID: Mid-sized gray-brown bird with light and dark brown and black markings; whitish band on throat; light brown chest/belly with fine black bars; white or light-colored band on wings, seen in flight; male has white band on tail; to 23 cm (9 in).

HABITAT: Lowlands of Pacific slope and along Caribbean coast; found on the ground or on low tree branches in more open areas, often near water – grasslands, pastures, beaches; active at night.

PARKS: CABR, CHNP, CONP, MANP, PVNP, SRNP, TONP

Plate 39   313

b Pacific Screech-owl

a Spectacled Owl

c Ferruginous Pygmy-owl

e Lesser Nighthawk

d Pauraque

Plate 40a

White-collared Swift
Streptoprocne zonaris
Vencejo Collarejo = collared swift
Vencejo = swift

ID: A mid-sized black bird (for a swift, fairly large) with white ring encircling neck; squarish or slightly notched tail; long, slender, swept-back wings; to 21 cm (8.5 in). Top and bottom views shown.

HABITAT: Low, middle, and higher elevations, Caribbean and Pacific slopes; seen flying above all types of habitats; flies continuously.

PARKS: ARVL, BCNP, CABR, CHNP, CNWR, CONP, IVNP, LANP, LSBR, MANP, MVCR, PONP, PVNP, RVNP, SRNP, TONP, WIBG

Plate 40b

Gray-rumped Swift
Chaetura cinereiventris
Vencejo Lomigrís = gray-rumped swift
Vencejo = swift

ID: A small glossy black bird with gray rump and throat; short, squarish tail; long, slender, swept-back wings; 10 cm (4 in). Top and bottom views shown.

HABITAT: Lower elevations, Caribbean slope; seen flying above all types of habitats; flies continuously.

PARKS: BCNP, CHNP, CNWR, LSBR, TONP

Plate 40c

Barn Swallow
Hirundo rustica
Golondrina Tijereta = scissors swallow
Golondrina = swallow

ID: Small, slender, dark blue bird with narrow, swept-back wings and deeply forked tail; reddish-brown forehead, throat, and chest; light brown or tawny belly; thin dark band across chest; to 17 cm (6.5 in).

HABITAT: Low and middle elevations, Caribbean and Pacific slopes, particularly along coasts; often seen flying low over open areas – fields, pastures, lawns, waterways.

PARKS: BCNP, CABR, CHNP, CNWR, CONP, LSBR, MANP, MVCR, PVNP, SRNP, TONP, WIBG

Note: This species is a nonbreeding seasonal migrant.

Plate 40d

Southern Rough-winged Swallow
Stelgidopteryx ruficollis
Golondrina Alirrasposa Sureña = southern rough-winged swallow
Golondrina = swallow

ID: Small gray-brown bird with swept-back, dark wings and shortish, notched tail; tawny or cinnamon throat and upperchest; whitish rump and belly; to 13 cm (5 in).

HABITAT: Low and middle elevations, Caribbean and southern Pacific slopes; seen in the air over more open habitats – grasslands, scrub areas, pastures, roads, streams.

PARKS: BCNP, CABR, CHNP, CNWR, CONP, LSBR, MANP, MVCR, PVNP, RVNP, SRNP, TONP, WIBG

Plate 40   315

b Gray-rumped Swift

a White-collared Swift

c Barn Swallow

d Southern
Rough-winged
Swallow

Plate 41a

Blue and White Swallow
Notiochelidon cyanoleuca
Golondrina Azul y Blanco = blue and white swallow
Golondrina = swallow

ID: Small glossy blue bird with short, notched tail; dark wings and tail; white chest and belly; to 11 cm (4.5 in).

HABITAT: Middle and high elevation sites, Caribbean and Pacific slopes; found flying over open habitats – pastures, scrub areas, grasslands, buildings.

PARKS: ARVL, BCNP, IVNP, LANP, MVCR, PONP, RVNP, WIBG

Plate 41b

Mangrove Swallow
Tachycineta albilinea
Golondrina Lomiblanca = white-back swallow

ID: Small glossy dark green bird with dark wings and short, dark, notched tail; narrow white line over eye; white chest, belly, and rump; to 12 cm (4.5 in).

HABITAT: Low and some middle elevations, Caribbean and Pacific slopes; seen flying over water and wet sites – rivers, large streams, ponds, lakes, lagoons, marshes, wet pastures.

PARKS: ARVL, BCNP, CABR, CHNP, CNWR, CONP, LSBR, MANP, PVNP, SRNP, TONP

Plate 41c

Green Hermit
Phaethornis guy
Ermitaño Verde = green hermit
Ermitaño = hermit

ID: Fairly large dark green or bluish green hummingbird with very long, down-curved bill; black stripe through eye; light brown or buff-colored throat; white-tipped tail; female with light facial stripes, grayish chest/belly, and long tail; to 16 cm (6.5 in).

HABITAT: Higher elevation wet forests, Caribbean and Pacific slopes; found around flowers in forest interior and in more open areas – forest edges, tree plantations.

PARKS: ARVL, BCNP, LANP, LSBR, MVCR, PONP, RVNP, WIBG

Plate 41d

Long-tailed Hermit
Phaethornis superciliosus
Ermitaño Colilargo = long-tailed hermit
Ermitaño = hermit

ID: Fairly large brownish or greenish brown hummingbird with long, white-tipped tail and very long, down-curved bill; black and light eye-stripes; light brown to gray-brown chest/belly; to 16 cm (6.5 in).

HABITAT: Low elevation wet forests, Caribbean and Pacific slopes; found around flowers in the forest interior and at forest edges, particularly near waterways.

PARKS: BCNP, CABR, CHNP, CNWR, CONP, LSBR, MANP, MVCR, RVNP, TONP

Plate 41e

Little Hermit
Phaethornis longuemareus
Ermitaño Enano = dwarf hermit
Ermitaño = hermit

ID: Small brownish or greenish brown hummingbird with down-curved bill; black and light facial stripes; cinnamon chest/belly; tail brownish with light tip; 9 cm (3.5 in).

HABITAT: Low and middle elevation forests, Caribbean and Pacific slopes; found near flowers in the forest interior and forest edge areas, particularly near watercourses; also in gardens.

PARKS: BCNP, CABR, CHNP, CNWR, CONP, LSBR, MANP, MVCR, PVNP, RVNP, SRNP, TONP, WIBG

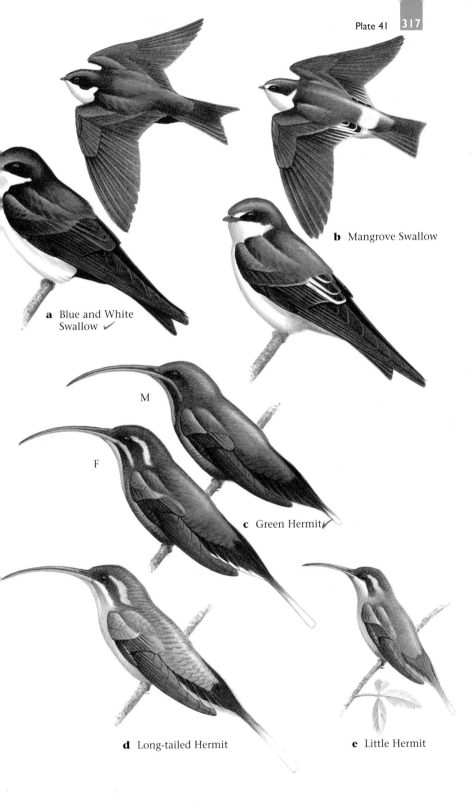

Plate 41 317

b Mangrove Swallow

a Blue and White Swallow

M

F

c Green Hermit

d Long-tailed Hermit

e Little Hermit

Plate 42a
Crowned Woodnymph
Thalurania colombica
Ninfa Violeta y Verde = violet and green nymph

ID: Small hummingbird with fairly straight bill, slightly down-curved at tip; male with glossy green throat, chest and rump, purple head and belly, dark wings, and dark, forked tail; female greenish with light gray throat and chest; to 10 cm (4 in).

HABITAT: Low elevation wet forests, Caribbean and southern Pacific slopes; found near flowers in forest interior and at forest edges, tree plantations, gardens with trees.

PARKS: BCNP, CABR, CHNP, CNWR, CONP, LSBR, MANP, MVCR, RVNP, TONP, WIBG

Plate 42b
Steely-vented Hummingbird
Amazilia saucerrottei
Colibrí Coliazul = blue-tailed hummingbird

ID: Small green hummingbird with straight bill; brownish rump; blue/black, notched tail; 9 cm (3.5 in).

HABITAT: Wooded regions of northern Pacific slope; found near flowers in forest interior and also at forest edge, tree plantations, gardens.

PARKS: MVCR, PVNP, RVNP, SRNP

Plate 42c
Cinnamon Hummingbird
Amazilia rutila
Colibrí Canela = cinnamon hummingbird

ID: Mid-sized green hummingbird with cinnamon chest/belly, straight bill, and reddish brown tail; to 10 cm (4 in).

HABITAT: Low and some middle elevations, northern Pacific slope; found near flowers in forest interior and more open sites – forest edges, brushy areas.

PARKS: PVNP, RVNP, SRNP

Plate 42d
Rufous-tailed Hummingbird
Amazilia tzacatl
Colibrí Rabirrufa = rufous-tailed hummingbird

ID: Mid-sized green hummingbird with grayish belly and reddish brown, squarish or slightly notched tail; straight red and black bill; to 10 cm (4 in).

HABITAT: Low and middle elevations, Caribbean and Pacific slopes; found near flowers in forest interior and more open sites – forest edge, scrub areas, plantations, other agricultural areas.

PARKS: ARVL, BCNP, CABR, CHNP, CNWR, CONP, LANP, LSBR, MANP, MVCR, PVNP, RVNP, SRNP, TONP, WIBG

Plate 42e
Striped-tailed Hummingbird
Eupherusa eximia
Colibrí Colirrayado = striped-tailed hummingbird

ID: Smallish green hummingbird with straight bill; reddish brown on wings; dark tail with white lines; whitish belly; female with grayish-white throat/chest/belly and green spots on sides; 9 cm (3.5 in).

HABITAT: Middle and some higher elevation wet forests, Caribbean and Pacific slopes; found around flowers in forest interior but also semi-open sites such as forest edges, scrub areas, and tree plantations.

PARKS: ARVL, BCNP, LANP, MVCR, RVNP, WIBG

Plate 42

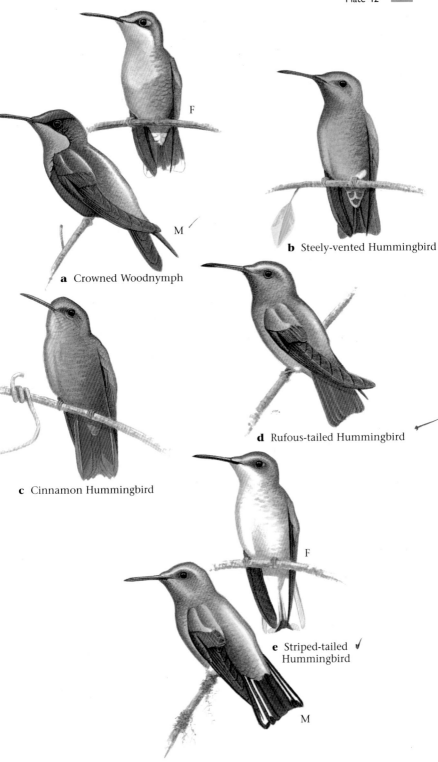

a Crowned Woodnymph

F

M

b Steely-vented Hummingbird

c Cinnamon Hummingbird

d Rufous-tailed Hummingbird

e Striped-tailed ✓
Hummingbird

F

M

Plate 43a

Purple-throated Mountain-gem
Lampornis calolaema
Colibrí Montañés Gorgimorado = purple-throated mountain-gem

ID: Mid-sized greenish hummingbird with straight bill and white line behind eye; male with purple throat, green chest, gray belly, dark tail; female with cinnamon throat/chest, white-tipped dark tail; to 10 cm (4 in).

HABITAT: High and some middle elevation wet forests, mostly over northern half of the country; found around flowers in forest interior but also semi-open sites such as forest edges and tree plantations.

PARKS: ARVL, BCNP, IVNP, MVCR, PONP, RVNP, WIBG

Plate 43b

Violet Sabrewing
Campylopterus hemileucurus
Ala de Sable Violáceo = violet sabrewing

ID: A large hummingbird with down-curved bill and white patches at end of tail; male with blue violet head/chest/belly, dark green back, dark wings; female with blue violet throat, gray chest/belly; to 15 cm (6 in).

HABITAT: Middle and high elevation forests, Caribbean and Pacific slopes; found near flowers in forest interior and more open sites at forest edges, tree plantations.

PARKS: ARVL, BCNP, IVNP, LANP, MVCR, PONP, RVNP, WIBG

Plate 43c

Green Violet-ear
Colibri thalassinus
Colibrí Verde Orejivioláceo = green violet-ear

ID: Mid-sized green hummingbird with slightly down-curved bill; violet patch behind eye; bluish patch on chest; dark bar across tail; to 10 cm (4 in).

HABITAT: High elevation forests, Caribbean and Pacific slopes, southern two-thirds of the country; prefers more open sites such as forest edges, scrub areas, tree plantations.

PARKS: ARVL, BCNP, IVNP, LANP, MVCR, PONP, WIBG

Plate 43d

Green-crowned Brilliant
Heliodoxa jacula
Brillante Frentiverde = green-crowned brilliant

ID: Large green hummingbird with straight bill; male with white mark behind eye, violet patch on throat, and dark, forked tail; female with white markings behind and below eye; white chest/belly with green spots; dark forked tail with white tip; to 13 cm (5 in).

HABITAT: High elevation wet forests, Caribbean slope and parts of Pacific slope; found around flowers in forest interior and forest edge areas.

PARKS: ARVL, BCNP, IVNP, LANP, MVCR, PONP, WIBG

Plate 43e

Magenta-throated Hummingbird
Calliphlox bryantae
Estrellita Gorgimorada = purple-throated little star

ID: Small greenish hummingbird with two whitish patches on rump, straight bill; male with purple throat, white mark behind eye, white band across chest, reddish brown belly, forked tail; female with light brown throat, whitish chest band, some reddish brown on chest/belly, tail reddish brown with black bar; to 9 cm (3.5 in).

HABITAT: High elevation forests, mostly over Pacific slope; found near flowers in semi-open sites such as forest edges, clearings, tree plantations.

PARKS: LANP, MVCR, WIBG

Plate 43 321

a Purple-throated
Mountain-gem

M

F

c Green Violet-ear

M

F

b Violet Sabrewing

F

M

d Green-crowned
Brilliant

M

F

e Magenta-throated
Hummingbird

Plate 44a

Resplendent Quetzal
Pharomachrus mocinno
Fenix del Bosque = forest phoenix
Quetzal

ID: Male is unmistakeable: a large bright green bird with red belly, green crest on head, white underneath tail, yellow bill, and a few extremely long tail feathers (streamers); female, lacking streamers, is duller green with brown-gray chest, red belly, white and black barred tail, and two-toned bill: dark above, yellow below; to 37 cm (14.5 in), plus very long tail streamers in males.

HABITAT: High elevation wet forests, Caribbean and Pacific slopes; found in tree canopy in forest interior and forest edge areas.

PARKS: BCNP, IVNP, LANP, MVCR, PONP

Note: This species is endangered, CITES Appendix I and USA ESA listed.

Plate 44b

Slaty-tailed Trogon
Trogon massena
Trogón Coliplomizo = slaty-tailed trogon
Trogón

ID: Male is largish green bird with red belly, red/orange eye-ring and bill, and gray-black under tail; female is mostly gray with red belly and two-toned bill: black above, reddish below; to 30 cm (12 in).

HABITAT: Low and some middle elevation wet forests, Caribbean and southern Pacific slopes; found in tree canopy in forest interior and semi-open sites such as forest edges, tree plantations.

PARKS: BCNP, CABR, CHNP, CNWR, CONP, LSBR, RVNP, TONP, WIBG

Plate 44c

Violaceous Trogon
Trogon violaceus
Trogón Violaceo = violaceous trogon
Trogón

ID: Mid-sized bird with yellow belly, dark bill, black and white barred tail; male with black and dark blue/violet head and chest, greenish back, yellow eye-ring; female with gray head, back, and chest, white eye-ring; to 24 cm (9.5 in).

HABITAT: Low elevation wet and dry forests, Caribbean and Pacific slopes; found in tree canopy in forest interior and in more open areas such as around clearings, forest edges, streams and rivers, and in tree plantations.

PARKS: BCNP, CABR, CHNP, CNWR, CONP, LSBR, MANP, PVNP, SRNP, TONP

Plate 44d

Black-throated Trogon
Trogon rufus
Trogón Cabeciverde = green-headed trogon
Trogón

ID: Mid-sized bird with yellow belly and bill, pale bluish eye-ring, and black and white barred tail; male with green head, chest, and back, and black throat; female with brownish head, chest, and back; to 23 cm (9 in).

HABITAT: Low and some middle elevation wet forests, Caribbean and southern Pacific slopes; found in forest interior and more open areas such as forest edge, near rivers and streams, and around tree plantations.

PARKS: BCNP, CABR, CHNP, CONP, LSBR, MVCR, RVNP, TONP, WIBG

Plate 44e

Black-headed Trogon
Trogon melanocephalus
Trogón Cabecinegro = black-headed trogon
Trogón

ID: Mid-sized bird with yellow belly, black/gray head and chest, pale bluish eye-ring, dark bill, and, seen from below, large white patches on black tail; male with greenish back and blue rump; female with grayish back; to 27 cm (10.5 in).

HABITAT: Low and some middle elevation sites, northern Pacific slope (sometimes also in northern Caribbean region); found in tree canopy in forest edge areas.

PARKS: CABR, PVNP, RVNP, SRNP

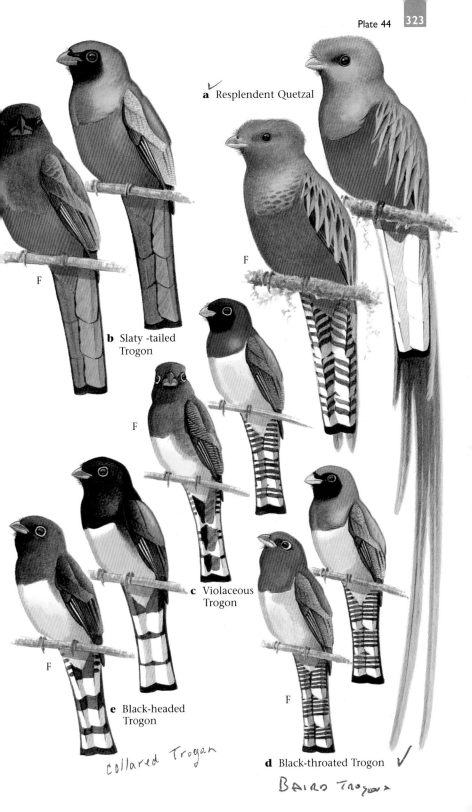

Plate 44 **323**

a Resplendent Quetzal

F

b Slaty-tailed Trogon

F

F

c Violaceous Trogon

F

e Black-headed Trogon

Collared Trogan

d Black-throated Trogon

BAIRD Trogons

Plate 45 (*See also*: Jacamars and Puffbirds, p. 145)

Plate 45a

Rufous-tailed Jacamar
Galbula ruficauda
Jacamar Rabirrufo = rufous-tailed jacamar
Jacamar

ID: Slender, bright green bird with long tail and long, straight, stiletto bill; reddish brown belly and underside of tail; wide green bar across chest; male with white throat, female with light brown/tan throat; to 23 cm (9 in).

HABITAT: Low and some middle elevation sites, Caribbean and southern Pacific slopes; found in more open wooded areas such as forest edges, along rivers and streams, in tree plantations.

PARKS: BCNP, CABR, CHNP, CNWR, CONP, LSBR, MANP, MVCR, TONP, WIBG

Plate 45b

White-necked Puffbird
Bucco macrorhynchos
Buco Collarejo = necklace buco

ID: Mid-sized, heavy-looking, black and white bird with biggish head and thick, black bill; white forehead, throat, and belly; black bar across chest; black on top of head; black wings and tail; to 25 cm (10 in).

HABITAT: Low elevation forests, Caribbean and Pacific slopes; found in tree canopy in more open sites such as forest edges, clearings, along waterways.

PARKS: BCNP, CABR, CHNP, CNWR, CONP, LSBR, MANP, PVNP, SRNP, TONP

Plate 45c

White-fronted Nunbird
Monasa morphoeus
Monja Frentiblanca = white-fronted nunbird
Monja Cariblanca = white-faced nunbird

ID: Largish gray bird with black head; long red-orange bill down-curved at tip; white feathers above and below bill; to 29 cm (11.5 in).

HABITAT: Low elevation wet forests, Caribbean slope; found usually in small flocks in tree canopy in more open sites such as forest edges, tree plantations.

PARKS: BCNP, CHNP, LSBR, TONP

Plate 45d

White-whiskered Puffbird
Malacoptila panamensis
Buco Barbón = bearded buco

ID: Smallish, puffy-looking cinnamon-brown bird with streaked chest/belly; whitish feathers above and below bill; fine light brown spots/streaks on head; largish bill, dark above, lighter below; female similar to male, but darker, grayish brown; to 19 cm (7.5 in).

HABITAT: Low and some middle elevation wet forests, Caribbean and Pacific slopes; found in forest interior and along forest edges, tree plantations.

PARKS: BCNP, CABR, CHNP, CONP, LSBR, MANP, TONP, WIBG

Plate 45   325

b White-necked Puffbird

a Rufous-tailed Jacamar

F   M

d White-whiskered Puffbird

F   M

c White-fronted Nunbird

Plate 46 (*See also*: Kingfishers, p. 147)

Plate 46a

Ringed Kingfisher
Ceryle torquata
Martín Pescador Collarejo = necklace martin fisher
Martín Pescador = martin fisher

ID: Large blue-gray bird with ragged head crest, brownish belly, white neck-band and throat, and large, heavy bill; female with bluish bar across chest; to 40 cm (16 in).

HABITAT: Low elevation aquatic sites, Caribbean and Pacific slopes; found along streams, rivers, lakes, ponds, lagoons, estuaries, mangroves.

PARKS: BCNP, CABR, CHNP, CNWR, CONP, LSBR, MANP, PVNP, RVNP, SRNP, TONP

Plate 46b

Belted Kingfisher
Ceryle alcyon
Martín Pescador Norteño = northern martin fisher
Martín Pescador = martin fisher

ID: Largish blue-gray bird with ragged head crest, white belly, white neck-band and throat, bluish bar across chest, and large, heavy bill; female has reddish brown bar across belly; to 33 cm (13 in).

HABITAT: Low elevation aquatic sites, Caribbean and Pacific slopes; found along seashore, streams, rivers, lakes, ponds, lagoons.

PARKS: CABR, CHNP, CNWR, CONP, LSBR, MANP, PVNP, SRNP, TONP

Note: This species is a nonbreeding seasonal migrant.

Plate 46c

Amazon Kingfisher
Chloroceryle amazona
Martín Pescador Amazónico = Amazon martin fisher
Martín Pescador = martin fisher

ID: Mid-sized green and white bird with long, heavy bill; conspicuous green head crest; white belly, white neck-band and throat; male has wide reddish brown bar across chest; to 28 cm (11 in).

HABITAT: Low elevation aquatic sites, Caribbean and Pacific slopes; found along rivers, larger streams, lakes.

PARKS: BCNP, CABR, CHNP, CNWR, CONP, LSBR, MANP, PVNP, TONP

Plate 46d

Green Kingfisher
Chloroceryle americana
Martín Pescador Verde = green martin fisher
Martín Pescador = martin fisher

ID: Smallish green and white bird with long, heavy bill; white belly, white neck-band and throat; male with wide reddish brown bar across chest; female with greenish bands across chest; smaller than Amazon Kingfisher, with less conspicuous head crest; to 19 cm (7.5 in).

HABITAT: Low and middle elevation aquatic sites, Caribbean and Pacific slopes; found along shoreline, rivers, larger streams, lakes, ponds, lagoons.

PARKS: ARVL, BCNP, CABR, CHNP, CNWR, CONP, LANP, LSBR, MANP, MVCR, PVNP, RVNP, SRNP, TONP, WIBG

Plate 46e

American Pygmy Kingfisher
Chloroceryle aene
Martín Pescador Enano = dwarf martin fisher
Martín Pescador = martin fisher

ID: Small green and reddish brown bird with long, heavy bill; reddish brown neck-band, throat, and chest; lower belly white; female with dark greenish bar across chest; to 13 cm (5 in).

HABITAT: Low elevation aquatic sites, Caribbean and Pacific slopes; found along small forest streams, ponds, pools, swamps.

PARKS: CABR, CHNP, CNWR, CONP, LSBR, PVNP, SRNP, TONP

Plate 46

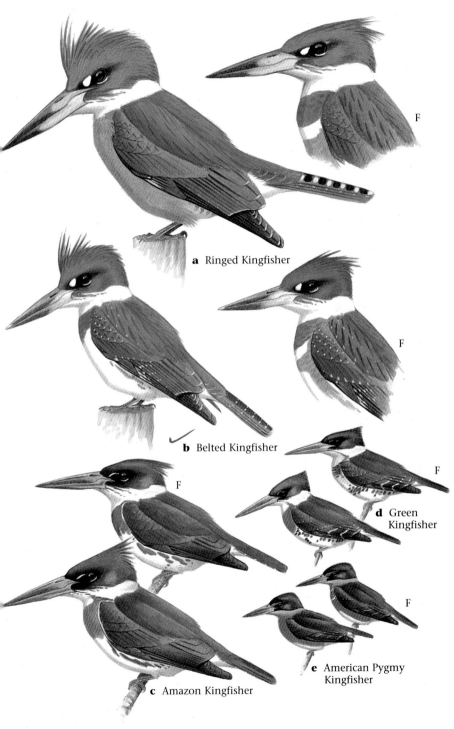

a Ringed Kingfisher

F

b Belted Kingfisher

F

d Green Kingfisher

F

c Amazon Kingfisher

F

e American Pygmy Kingfisher

F

Plate 47 (*See also*: Motmots, p. 148)

Plate 47a

Rufous Motmot
Baryphthengus martii
Momoto Canelo = cinnamon motmot
Pájaro Bobo = dumb bird

ID: Large green and reddish brown bird with long tail; longish down-curved bill; black mask around eyes; small dark spot on chest; bluish green on wings and lower belly; tail usually with "tennis racket" ends; to 46 cm (18 in).

HABITAT: Low elevation wet forests, Caribbean slope; found in tree canopy, generally in more open sites, such as near clearings or at forest edge.

PARKS: BCNP, CNWR, LSBR, TONP

Plate 47b

Blue-crowned Motmot
Momotus momota
Momoto Común = common motmot

ID: Large green bird with long tail; black facial mask with blue edging; longish down-curved bill; blue on head; bluish green throat; greenish to greenish brown chest and belly; small dark spot on chest; tail usually with "tennis racket" ends; to 39 cm (15.5 in).

HABITAT: Low and middle elevation forests, Pacific slope; found in forest interior and in more open areas such as forest edges, tree plantations, and, in drier regions, along watercourses.

PARKS: CABR, CONP, MANP, MVCR, PVNP, RVNP, SRNP, WIBG

Plate 47c

Broad-billed Motmot
Electron platyrhynchum
Momoto Piquiancho = broad-billed motmot

ID: Mid-sized green and reddish brown bird with long tail; longish down-curved bill; black mask around eyes; conspicuous dark spot on chest; bluish green chin/upper throat; reddish brown head, chest; green or bluish green belly; tail usually with "tennis racket" ends; to 32 cm (12.5 in).

HABITAT: Low and some middle elevation wet forests, Caribbean slope; found in tree canopy usually in more open sites such as forest edges.

PARKS: BCNP, CHNP, LANP, LSBR, TONP

Plate 47d

Turquoise-browed Motmot
Eumomota superciliosa
Momoto Cejiceleste = turquoise-browed motmot
Pájaro Bobo = dumb bird

ID: Mid-sized green and brownish green bird with long tail and longish down-curved bill; small black mask around eyes and black throat; turquoise or pale blue bar above eye; tail usually with "tennis racket" ends; to 33 cm (13 in).

HABITAT: Low and some middle elevation forests, northern Pacific slope; found in forest interiors and in more open areas such as forest edges and sites with scattered trees.

PARKS: PVNP, RVNP, SRNP

Plate 47 **329**

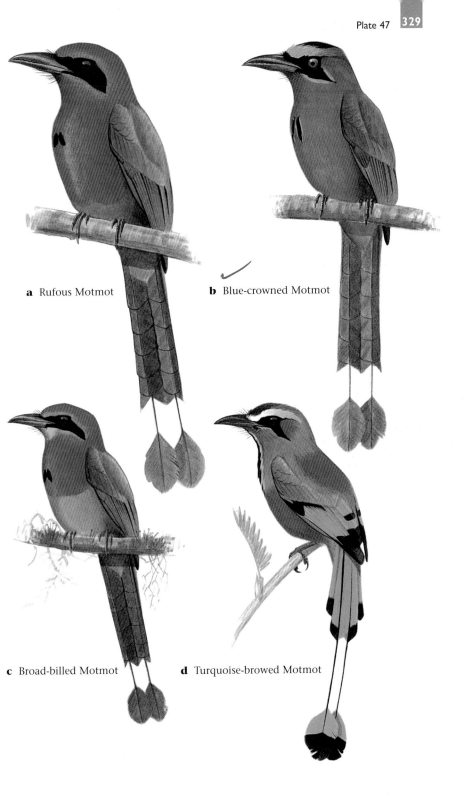

a Rufous Motmot

b Blue-crowned Motmot

c Broad-billed Motmot

d Turquoise-browed Motmot

Plate 48a

Olivaceous Piculet
Picumnus olivaceus
Carpenterito Oliváceo = little
olivaceous woodpecker
Pájaro Carpintero = carpenter bird
ID: Very small woodpecker with brownish green
or olive back; lighter, yellow-olive chest, belly;
dark tail with light stripes; male with orange
streaks/spots on forehead, white spots/streaks
around head; female lacks orange spots; 9 cm
(3.5 in).

HABITAT: Low and some middle elevation wet
forests, southern Pacific slope (and some parts of
northern Caribbean slope); prefers open
woodlands, forest edges, tree plantations,
gardens.

PARKS: CABR, CNWR, CONP, MANP, WIBG

Plate 48b

Hoffman's Woodpecker
Melanerpes hoffmannii
Carpintero de Hoffman = Hoffman's
woodpecker
Pájaro Carpintero = carpenter bird
ID: Smallish black and white barred bird with light
brown or brown-gray chest, yellowish belly,
yellow at back of neck; longish, straight bill; male
only has red on top of head; to 19 cm (7.5 in).

HABITAT: Low and middle elevations, northern
Pacific slope (and small parts of Caribbean slope);
prefers open, wooded sites such as forest edges,
tree plantations, gardens with trees.

PARKS: CABR, CNWR, MVCR, PVNP, RVNP, SRNP

Plate 48c

Red-crowned Woodpecker
Melanerpes rubricapillus
Carpintero Nuquirrojo = red-naped
carpenter
Pájaro Carpintero = carpenter bird
ID: Smallish black and white barred bird with light
brown, grayish, or olive chest and reddish belly;
male red at back of neck and top of head; female
red at back of neck and white on top of head;
longish, straight bill; to 18 cm (7 in).

HABITAT: Low and middle elevations, southern
Pacific slope; prefers open, wooded sites such as
forest edges, clearings, tree plantations.

PARKS: CABR, CONP, MANP, WIBG

Plate 48d

Black-cheeked Woodpecker
Melanerpes pucherani
Carpintero Carinegro = black-faced
woodpecker
Pájaro Carpintero = carpenter bird
ID: Smallish black and white barred bird with light
grayish or olive chest; reddish belly; yellow
forehead; black eye mask; white spot behind eye;
male red at back of neck and top of head; female
red at back of neck and black on top of head;
longish, straight bill; to 19 cm (7.5 in).

HABITAT: Low and some middle elevation wet
forests, Caribbean slope; found in tree canopy in
open, wooded sites such as forest edges,
clearings, tree plantations.

PARKS: BCNP, CHNP, CNWR, LSBR, TONP

Plate 48   331

a Olivaceous
Piculet

b Hoffman's
Woodpecker

F

M

d Black-cheeked
Woodpecker

F

M

ACORN

c Red-crowned
Woodpecker

Plate 49a

Lineated Woodpecker
Dryocopus lineatus
Carpintero Lineado = lineated woodpecker
Pájaro Carpintero = carpenter bird
ID: Large black bird with red crest on head; whitish stripe runs from edge of bill down along neck; 2 whitish stripes on back; light-colored, barred lower chest/belly; male has small red stripe on side of throat; female has black forehead; to 34 cm (13.5 in).

HABITAT: Low and some middle elevation forests, Caribbean and Pacific slopes; found in tree canopy in open, wooded sites such as forest edges and clearings.

PARKS: BCNP, CABR, CHNP, CNWR, CONP, LSBR, MANP, MVCR, PVNP, SRNP, TONP, WIBG

Plate 49b

Pale-billed Woodpecker
Campephilus guatemalensis
Carpintera Picoplata = silver-billed carpenter
Pájaro Carpintero = carpenter bird
ID: Large black bird with red head and crest; 2 whitish stripes on back form V; light-colored, barred lower chest/belly; female has black at front of crest; to 37 cm (14.5 in).

HABITAT: Low and some middle elevation forests, Caribbean and Pacific slopes; found in tree canopy in open, wooded sites such as forest edges and clearings, tree plantations, along rivers and streams.

PARKS: BCNP, CABR, CHNP, CNWR, CONP, LSBR, MANP, MVCR, PVNP, RVNP, SRNP, TONP, WIBG

Plate 49c

Collared Aracari
Pteroglossus torquatus
Tucancillo Collarejo = little necklace toucan
Pití
Cusingo
ID: Large, colorful bird with huge bill, light above, dark below; black head and chest; dark green back; yellow belly with dark cross-wise band and central black spot; red skin around eye; to 41 cm (16 in).

HABITAT: Low and some middle elevation forests, Caribbean and northern Pacific slopes; found in tree canopy in more open habitats such as forest edges, tree plantations, and, in drier forests, along rivers and streams.

PARKS: BCNP, CHNP, CNWR, LSBR, PVNP, RVNP, SRNP, TONP

Plate 49d

Fiery-billed Aracari
Pteroglossus frantzii
Tucancillo Piquianaranjado = little orange-billed toucan
ID: Large, colorful bird with huge, fiery red/orange and black bill; black head and chest; dark green back; small brown patch between black neck and green back; yellow belly with red cross-wise band and central black spot; to 43 cm (17 in).

HABITAT: Low and some middle elevation forests, southern Pacific slope; found in tree canopy in more open habitats such as forest edges, tree plantations.

PARKS: CABR, CONP, MANP, WIBG

Plate 49 333

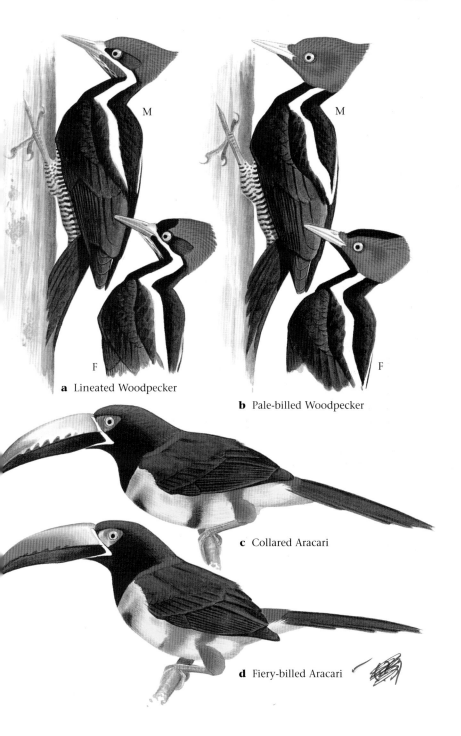

a Lineated Woodpecker

b Pale-billed Woodpecker

c Collared Aracari

d Fiery-billed Aracari

Plate 50a

Keel-billed Toucan
Ramphastos sulfuratus
Tucán Pico Iris = rainbow-billed toucan
Curré Negro

ID: A large, mostly black bird with yellow face and chest, yellowish green skin around eye, and that amazing, rainbow-colored (green-orange-blue) toucan's bill; to 47 cm (18.5 in).

HABITAT: Low and some middle elevation forests, Caribbean and parts of northern Pacific slopes; found in tree canopy in more open habitats such as forest edges, tree plantations, and, in drier forests, along rivers and streams.

PARKS: BCNP, CHNP, CNWR, LSBR, MVCR, RVNP, SRNP, TONP

Plate 50b

Chestnut-mandibled Toucan
Ramphastos swainsonii
Tucán de Swainson = swainson's toucan
Dios-te-dé = God gives you

ID: Large, mostly black bird with yellow face and chest; yellowish green skin around eye; large bill, yellow above, dark maroon or reddish brown below; to 56 cm (22 in).

HABITAT: Low and some middle elevation wet forests, Caribbean and southern Pacific slopes; found in tree canopy in more open habitats such as forest edges, tree plantations.

PARKS: BCNP, CABR, CNWR, CONP, LSBR, MANP, TONP, WIBG

Plate 50c

Emerald Toucanet
Aulacorhynchus prasinus
Tucancillo Verde = little green toucan

ID: Mid-sized green bird with blue throat; tail green above, brown below; large bill yellow above, black below; to 30 cm (12 in).

HABITAT: Middle and higher elevation wet forests, Caribbean and Pacific slopes; found in tree canopy in forest interior, edge areas, clearings, tree plantations.

PARKS: ARVL, BCNP, IVNP, LANP, MVCR, PONP, RVNP, WIBG

Plate 50 335

b Chestnut-mandibled
Toucan

a Keel-billed Toucan

c Emerald Toucanet

Plate 51a

Wedge-billed Woodcreeper
Glyphorhynchus spirurus
Trepadorcito Pico de Cuña = wedge-billed woodcreeper
Trepapalos = tree climbers

ID: Small brown bird with shortish, wedge-shaped black bill; light stripe through eye; other light streaks and spots on head; tan/buffy throat; light spots and streaks on brown chest; 15 cm (6 in).

HABITAT: Low, middle, and some higher elevation wet forests, Caribbean and southern Pacific slopes (and some parts of northern Pacific slope); found climbing up tree trunks in forest interior and in more open sites such as forest edges, tree plantations.

PARKS: BCNP, CABR, CHNP, CNWR, CONP, LSBR, MANP, MVCR, RVNP, TONP, WIBG

Plate 51b

Olivaceous Woodcreeper
Sittasomus griseicapillus
Trepadorcito Aceitunado = olivaceous woodcreeper
Trepapalos = tree climbers

ID: Small reddish brown bird with gray head and chest; dark, slender, straight bill; 15 cm (6 in).

HABITAT: Low elevation dry forest, northern Pacific slope, and middle and higher elevation wet forests, Caribbean and southern Pacific slopes; found climbing up tree trunks in forest interior and in more open sites such as forest edges, tree plantations; in drier areas, found along rivers and streams.

PARKS: BCNP, LANP, MVCR, PVNP, RVNP, SRNP, WIBG

Plate 51c

Streaked-headed Woodcreeper
Lepidocolaptes souleyetii
Trepador Cabecirrayado = streaked-headed Woodcreeper
Trepapalos = tree climbers

ID: Smallish brown bird with head, neck, chest, and belly heavily streaked with black, brown, and buff; tannish/buffy throat; long, narrow, down-curved bill; to 19 cm (7.5 in).

HABITAT: Low and some middle elevation forests, Caribbean and Pacific slopes; found climbing up tree trunks and along branches in open forested areas such as forest edges, clearings, gardens, tree plantations.

PARKS: ARVL, BCNP, CABR, CHNP, CNWR, CONP, LANP, LSBR, MANP, MVCR, PVNP, RVNP, SRNP, TONP, WIBG

Plate 51d

Barred Woodcreeper
Dendrocolaptes certhia
Trepador Barreteado = barred woodcreeper
Trepapalos = tree climbers

ID: Mid-sized brown bird with black barring pattern on head, back, chest, and belly; fairly heavy, dark bill; to 28 cm (11 in).

HABITAT: Low and some middle elevation forests, Caribbean and Pacific slopes; found in forest interior and in more open sites such as forest edges, tree plantations and, in drier areas, in trees along waterways.

PARKS: BCNP, CABR, CHNP, CNWR, CONP, LSBR, MANP, MVCR, PVNP, RVNP, SRNP, TONP, WIBG

Plate 51 337

b Oilvaceous
Woodcreeper

a Wedge-billed
Woodcreeper

c Streaked-headed
Woodcreeper

d Barred
Woodcreeper

Plate 52 (*See also:* Antbirds, p. 156)

Plate 52a

Barred Antshrike
Thamnophilus doliatus
Batará Barreteado

ID: Male is a small white-and-black barred bird with a mostly black head crest; female is reddish brown with black streaks on face, buffy throat, and light brown chest/belly; 15 cm (6 in).

HABITAT: Low and some middle elevation forests, Caribbean and Pacific slopes; found usually on the ground in open areas such as thickets but also in the forest interior and, in drier regions, near waterways.

PARKS: BCNP, CABR, CHNP, CNWR, LSBR, MANP, PVNP, RVNP, SRNP, TONP

Plate 52b

Bicolored Antbird
Gymnopithys leucaspis
Hormiguero Bicolor = bicolored anteater

ID: Smallish brown bird with white throat and chest; pale blue skin around eye; black in front of and behind eye; short tail; 14 cm (5.5 in).

HABITAT: Low and middle elevation wet forest, Caribbean and southern Pacific slopes; found in forest interior or edge, on or near the ground, usually feeding by following army ants.

PARKS: BCNP, CABR, CONP, LSBR, MANP, TONP, WIBG

Plate 52c

Black-faced Antthrush
Formicarius analis
Gallito Hormiguero Carinegro = little rooster black-faced anteater

ID: Mid-sized dark or olive brown bird with black cheeks and throat; grayish chest and belly; small amount of pale bluish skin around eye; long legs, short tail; to 18 cm (7 in).

HABITAT: Low and middle elevation wet forest, Caribbean and southern Pacific slopes; found in forest interior or edge, on or near the ground.

PARKS: BCNP, CABR, CHNP, CNWR, CONP, LSBR, MANP, MVCR, TONP, WIBG

Plate 52d

Dotted-winged Antwren
Microrhopias quixensis
Hormiguerito Alipunteado = little dotted-winged anteater

ID: Small black bird with white spots and bar on wing, white tail tips; male is almost all black; female more grayish with reddish brown throat/chest/belly; 11 cm (4.5 in).

HABITAT: Low and some middle elevation wet forest, Caribbean and southern Pacific slopes; found foraging on or near the ground in forest interior and more open sites such as forest edges, tree plantations, thickets.

PARKS: BCNP, CABR, CHNP, CNWR, CONP, LSBR, MANP, TONP, WIBG

Plate 52 **339**

a Barred Antshrike

F

M

b Bicolored Antbird

d Dotted-winged Antwren

F

M

c Black-faced Antthrush

Plate 53a

White-collared Manakin
Manacus candei
Saltarín Cuelliblanco = white-collared dancer

ID: Female is a small olive-green bird with yellowish belly, orange legs, and small, black bill; male with black on wings and top of head; black band across back; white throat, chest, and upper back; olive-green rump; yellow belly; orange legs; small, black bill; to 11 cm (4.25 in).

HABITAT: Low elevation wet forest, Caribbean slope; found in trees and in low thicket sites in more open wooded habitats – forest edges, tree plantations, along watercourses.

PARKS: BCNP, CHNP, CNWR, LSBR, TONP

Plate 53b

Long-tailed Manakin
Chiroxiphia linearis
Saltarín Colilargo = long-tailed dancer
Saltarín Toledo = toledo dancer

ID: Female is small, olive-green bird with lighter belly, orange legs, small, black bill; male is black with blue back, red crest on head, and two very long, black tail feathers; to 12 cm (5 in), plus long tail feathers.

HABITAT: Low and middle elevation dry and wet forests, northern Pacific slope; found in trees in forest interior and more open areas such as forest edges, particularly along swamps and watercourses.

PARKS: MVCR, PVNP, RVNP, SRNP

Plate 53c

Red-capped Manakin
Pipra mentalis
Saltarín Cabecirrojo = red-capped dancer

ID: Female is small olive-green bird with lighter belly, brownish legs and small brownish bill; male is black with red head and yellow thighs; 10 cm (4 in).

HABITAT: Low elevation wet forests, Caribbean and southern Pacific slopes; found low in trees in forest interior and around more open sites such as forest edges, clearings.

PARKS: BCNP, CABR, CHNP, CNWR, CONP, LSBR, MANP, TONP

Plate 53d

White-ruffed Manakin
Corapipo leucorrhoa
Saltarín Gorgiblanco = white-ruffed dancer

ID: Female is small olive-green bird with grayish throat, dark legs, and small, dark bill; male is bluish black with white throat, dark legs; to 10 cm (4 in).

HABITAT: Low and middle elevation wet forest, Caribbean and southern Pacific slopes; found low in trees in forest interior and around more open sites such as forest edges, clearings, tree plantations.

PARKS: BCNP, CNWR, CONP, LSBR, WIBG

Plate 53 **341**

M

b Long-tailed Manakin

M

F

F   **a** White-collared
Manakin

M

M

F

d White-ruffed
Manakin

F

c Red-capped Manakin

Plate 54a

Rufous Piha
Lipaugus unirufus
Piha Rojiza = rufous piha
ID: Mid-sized reddish brown bird with lighter throat and belly; dark, fairly thick bill; grayish legs; to 24 cm (9.5 in).

HABITAT: Low and some middle elevation wet forests, Caribbean and southern Pacific slopes; found in tree canopy and lower, usually in more open sites such as forest edges and clearings.

PARKS: BCNP, CABR, CHNP, CNWR, CONP, LSBR, MANP, TONP, WIBG

Plate 54b

Three-wattled Bellbird
Procnias tricarunculata
Pájaro Campana = bellbird
Campanero Tricarunculado
ID: Female is mid-sized olive-green bird with yellow-streaked chest and belly; male is brown with white head and three worm-like, hanging wattles; to 20 cm (12 in).

HABITAT: Higher elevation wet forests, Caribbean and Pacific slopes (occasionally down to low elevation regions); prefers tree canopy in forest interior and also more open sites such as forest edges, tree plantations.

PARKS: ARVL, BCNP, CABR, CONP, IVNP, LANP, LSBR, MANP, MVCR, PONP, PVNP, RVNP, WIBG

Plate 54c

Purple-throated Fruitcrow
Querula purpurata
Quérula Gorgimorada = purple-throated quérula
ID: Mid-sized black bird with grayish bill; male with dark purple throat; to 28 cm (11 in).

HABITAT: Low elevation wet forests, Caribbean slope; found in tree canopy often in more open, wooded areas – forest edges, tree plantations, etc.

PARKS: BCNP, CHNP, CNWR, LSBR, TONP

Plate 54d

Snowy Cotinga
Carpodectes nitidus
Cotinga Nivosa = snowy cotinga
ID: Mid-sized white or light gray bird with dark bill; male is pale gray above, white below; female is grayish with light gray or whitish chest/belly; to 22 cm (9 in). (The Yellow-billed Cotinga, which resembles the Snowy Cotinga but has a yellow bill, occurs only over the southern Pacific slope.)

HABITAT: Low elevation wet forests, Caribbean slope; found in tree canopy, particularly in more open wooded areas – forest edges, tree plantations, along waterways.

PARKS: BCNP, CHNP, CNWR, LSBR, TONP

Plate 54   343

a Rufous Piha

b Three-wattled Bellbird

M

F

d Snowy Cotinga

F

M

M

F

c Purple-throated
Fruitcrow

Plate 55 (*See also*: Tityra, A cotinga, p. 160; Flycatchers, p. 162)

Plate 55a

Masked Tityra
Tityra semifasciata
Tityra Carirroja = red-faced tityra
Calandria

ID: Mid-sized gray bird with black-tipped red bill, red skin around eye, and broad black bar on wing and tail; male with black on chin, forehead, and behind eye; white chest/belly; female is gray-brown with whitish throat and gray chest/belly; to 20 cm (8 in).

HABITAT: Low and middle elevation forests, Caribbean and Pacific slopes; found in tree canopy, usually in more open sites such as forest edges, clearings, tree plantations, along waterways.

PARKS: BCNP, CABR, CHNP, CNWR, CONP, LANP, LSBR, MANP, MVCR, PVNP, RVNP, SRNP, TONP, WIBG

Plate 55b

Tropical Kingbird
Tyrannus melancholicus
Pecho Amarillo = yellow chest
Tirano Tropical = tropical tyrant

ID: Mid-sized olive-colored bird with gray head; whitish throat; dark wings and dark, notched tail; dark bar through eye; yellow belly; reddish patch on top of head usually concealed; to 22 cm (8.5 in).

HABITAT: Low, middle, and some higher elevation sites, Caribbean and Pacific slopes; found in trees in open wooded areas, such as forest edges and tree plantations, and also in more open areas such as grasslands, pastures and other agricultural sites, and near human settlements.

PARKS: ARVL, BCNP, CABR, CHNP, CNWR, CONP, LANP, LSBR, MANP, MVCR, PVNP, RVNP, SRNP, TONP, WIBG

Plate 55c

Great Kiskadee
Pitangus sulphuratus
Bienteveo Grande = big good-to-see
Pecho Amarillo = yellow chest

ID: Mid-sized olive brown bird with reddish brown wings and bright yellow chest/belly; black and white head; yellow patch on top of head usually concealed; white throat; to 23 cm (9 in).

HABITAT: Low and middle elevations, Caribbean and Pacific slopes; found in trees in more open sites such as grasslands, pastures, forest edges, gardens, and along waterways.

PARKS: ARVL, BCNP, CABR, CHNP, CNWR, CONP, LANP, LSBR, MANP, MVCR, PVNP, RVNP, SRNP, TONP, WIBG

Plate 55d

Boat-billed Flycatcher
Megarhynchus pitangua
Mosquerón Picudo = big-billed fly-eater
Pecho Amarillo = yellow chest

ID: Mid-sized olive bird with bright yellow chest/belly; black and white head; yellow or orange patch on top of head usually concealed; white throat; distinguished from Great Kiskadee by wing color and larger bill; to 23 cm (9 in).

HABITAT: Low, middle, and some higher elevation sites, Caribbean and Pacific slopes; found in tree canopy in wooded area and more open sites such as forest edges, tree plantations, gardens, and along waterways.

PARKS: ARVL, BCNP, CABR, CHNP, CNWR, CONP, LANP, LSBR, MANP, MVCR, PVNP, RVNP, SRNP, TONP, WIBG

Plate 55 345

F

M

a Masked Tityra

b Tropical Kingbird

c Great Kiskadee

d Boat-billed Flycatcher

Plate 56a
Social Flycatcher
Myiozetetes similis
Mosquero Cejiblanco = white-browed
fly-eater
Pecho Amarillo = yellow chest

ID: Rather small olive or olive greenish bird with dark gray and white head; dark eye mask; reddish patch on top of head usually concealed; white throat; bright yellow chest/belly; very small black bill; to 17 cm (6.5 in).

HABITAT: Low, middle, and some higher elevation sites, Caribbean and Pacific slopes; found in trees in more open areas such as grasslands, pastures and agricultural sites, forest edges, along rivers and lakes, and in gardens.

PARKS: ARVL, BCNP, CABR, CHNP, CNWR, CONP, LANP, LSBR, MANP, MVCR, PVNP, RVNP, SRNP, TONP, WIBG

Plate 56b
Gray-capped Flycatcher
Myiozetetes granadensis
Mosquero Cabecigrís = gray-capped
fly-eater
Pecho Amarillo = yellow chest

ID: Closely resembles Social Flycatcher but has lighter gray head, whitish forehead, and less distinct white bar above eye; 16 cm (6.5 in).

HABITAT: Low, middle and some higher elevations, Caribbean and southern Pacific slopes; found in trees in semi-open sites such as forest edges, along waterways, tree plantations, gardens, farming areas.

PARKS: ARVL, BCNP, CABR, CHNP, CNWR, CONP, LANP, LSBR, MANP, MVCR, RVNP, TONP, WIBG

Plate 56c
Brown-crested Flycatcher
Myiarchus tyrannulus
Copetón Crestipardo = brown-crested
big tuft

ID: Mid-sized grayish olive or grayish brown bird with bushy head crest, gray throat and chest, yellowish belly; to 20 cm (8 in).

HABITAT: Low and middle elevations, northern Pacific slope; found in more open habitats such as forest edges, along waterways, marshes, mangrove swamps, open plantations, and gardens.

PARKS: MVCR, PVNP, RVNP, SRNP

Plate 56d
Dusky-capped Flycatcher
Myiarchus tuberculifer
Copetón Crestioscuro = dusky-capped
big tuft

ID: Smallish olive bird with very dark/blackish head, gray throat/chest, yellow belly; wings and tail brownish or grayish brown; 16 cm (6.5 in).

HABITAT: Low, middle, and some higher elevation forests, Caribbean and Pacific slopes; prefers more open parts of forests – forest edge areas, clearings, tree plantations, along waterways.

PARKS: ARVL, BCNP, CABR, CHNP, CNWR, CONP, LANP, LSBR, MANP, MVCR, PVNP, RVNP, SRNP, TONP, WIBG

Plate 56 347

a Social Flycatcher

b Gray-capped Flycatcher

c Brown-crested Flycatcher

d Dusky-capped
Flycatcher

Plate 57a

Ochre-bellied Flycatcher
Mionectes oleagineus
Mosquerito Aceitunado = little
olivaceous fly-eater
Mosquerito Ojenido
ID: Small olive-greenish bird with slightly darker
wings and tail and orangy-yellow belly; 13 cm
(5 in).

HABITAT: Low and middle elevation wet forests,
Caribbean and southern Pacific slopes; found in
forest interior and in semi-open sites such as
forest edges, clearings, tree plantations.

PARKS: BCNP, CABR, CHNP, CNWR, CONP, LSBR,
MANP, MVCR, PVNP, RVNP, TONP, WIBG

Plate 57b

Common Tody Flycatcher
Todirostrum cinereum
Espatulilla Común = little common
spatula
ID: Very small flycatcher with black head,
greenish gray back, black and yellow wings, black
tail with white tip, yellow chest/belly, pale yellow
eyes; 9.5 cm (3.75 in).

HABITAT: Low and middle elevations, Caribbean
and Pacific slopes; found in tree canopy in forest
edge areas, tree plantations, shady gardens.

PARKS: ARVL, BCNP, CABR, CHNP, CNWR, CONP,
LANP, LSBR, MANP, MVCR, PVNP, RVNP, SRNP,
TONP, WIBG

Plate 57c

Scissor-tailed Flycatcher
Tyrannus forficatus
Tijereta Rosada = pink scissors
ID: A mid-sized silver-gray bird with very long,
black, forked tail, black wings, reddish patch on
side under wing, whitish chest/belly; to 20 cm
(8 in), plus tail adds up to another 15 cm (6 in).

HABITAT: Lower elevations, northern Pacific
slope; found around very open sites such as
fields, pastures, grasslands, marshes, human
settlements.

PARKS: CABR, MANP, PVNP, SRNP

Note: This species is a nonbreeding seasonal
migrant.

Plate 57d

Long-tailed Tyrant
Colonia colonus
Mosquero Coludo = long-tailed
fly-eater
ID: Small black bird with whitish forehead and
gray head-cap, neck, and back; very long black
tail; to 15 cm (6 in), plus tail adds up to another
10 cm (4 in).

HABITAT: Low elevation wet forests, Caribbean
slope; found in tree canopy in semi-open sites
such as forest edges, clearings, tree plantations,
along waterways.

PARKS: BCNP, CHNP, CNWR, LSBR, TONP

Plate 57 349

a Ochre-bellied Flycatcher

c Scissor-tailed Flycatcher

d Long-tailed Tyrant

b Common Tody
Flycatcher

Plate 58a

Rufous-naped Wren
Campylorhynchus rufinucha
Soterrey Nuquirrufo = rufous-naped wren

ID: Small brown-and-black-barred bird (fairly large, however, for a wren) with black head top, black eyestripe, white chest/belly, thin black bill, gray legs; to 18 cm (7 in).

HABITAT: Low elevation dry forests, northern Pacific slope; found in more open sites, such as forest edges, trees and brushy areas along waterways, parklands, trees near human settlements.

PARKS: CABR, PVNP, RVNP, SRNP

Plate 58b

Banded-backed Wren
Campylorhynchus zonatus
Soterrey Matraquero

ID: Small black-and-whitish-barred bird (fairly large, however, for a wren) with white throat/chest with dark spots; light brown belly and legs; thin bill grayish above, light brown below; to 17 cm (6.5 in).

HABITAT: Low and middle elevations wet forests, Caribbean slope; prefers more open sites such as forest edges, clearings, tree plantations, along waterways, vegetation around human settlements.

PARKS: BCNP, CHNP, CNWR, LANP, LSBR, TONP

Plate 58c

Gray-breasted Wood-wren
Henicorhina leucophrys
Soterrey de Selva Pechigrís = gray-breasted jungle-wren

ID: Small brown bird with streaked black, dark brown, and white head, gray throat/chest, tawny or brown belly, black-barred wings, and short, black-barred tail; 11 cm (4.5 in).

HABITAT: Middle and high elevation wet forests, Caribbean and Pacific slopes; found low in trees and brush in forest interior and in more open sites such as forest edges, thickets.

PARKS: ARVL, BCNP, IVNP, LANP, MVCR, PONP, RVNP, WIBG

Plate 58d

White-breasted Wood-wren
Henicorhina leucosticta
Soterrey de Selva Pechiblanco = white-breasted jungle-wren

ID: Small brown bird with streaked black, dark brown, and white head, white throat/chest, tawny/light brown belly, black-barred wings, and short, black-barred tail; 10 cm (4 in).

HABITAT: Low and middle elevation wet forests, Caribbean and southern Pacific slopes; found low in trees in forest interior and more open areas such as forest edges, tree plantations.

PARKS: ARVL, BCNP, CABR, CNWR, LSBR, MVCR, RVNP, TONP, WIBG

Plate 58e

House Wren
Troglodytes aedon
Soterrey Cucarachero = cockroach-eating wren

ID: Small brown bird with black-barred wings and tail; lighter brown chest/belly; pale stripe above eye; 11 cm (4.5 in).

HABITAT: Low, middle, and high elevations, Caribbean and Pacific slopes; found mostly around houses and other structures, and open habitats such as pastures and low scrub.

PARKS: ARVL, BCNP, CABR, CHNP, CNWR, CONP, LSBR, MANP, MVCR, PVNP, RVNP, SRNP, TONP, WIBG

Plate 58 351

a Rufous-naped Wren

b Banded-backed Wren

c Gray-breasted Wood-wren

d White-breasted Wood-wren

e House Wren

Plate 59 (*See also:* Thrushes, p. 166)

Plate 59a

Sooty Robin
Turdus nigrescens
Mirlo Negruzco = blackish blackbird
ID: Mid-sized dark bird with orange bill, legs, eye-ring; whitish eye; male is blackish, female is brownish; 25 cm (10 in).

HABITAT: High elevations, southern Caribbean and southern Pacific slopes; found in very open habitats such as pastures and other agricultural areas, low scrub, and páramo (treeless sub-alpine habitat with shrubs and grasses).

PARKS: BCNP, IVNP, LANP, PONP

Plate 59b

Clay-colored Robin
Turdus grayi
Mirlo Pardo = brown blackbird
ID: Mid-sized brown or olive-brown bird with lighter brown chest/belly, dark-streaked throat, yellowish bill, brownish legs; to 24 cm (9.5 in).

HABITAT: Low, middle, and higher elevations, Caribbean and Pacific slopes; inhabits very open areas such as pastures, agricultural sites, human settlements, tree plantations, gardens, lawns.

PARKS: ARVL, BCNP, CABR, CHNP, CNWR, CONP, LANP, LSBR, MANP, MVCR, PVNP, RVNP, SRNP, TONP, WIBG

Plate 59c

Black-faced Solitaire
Myadestes melanops
Solitario Carinegro = black-faced solitaire
ID: Smallish gray bird with black face, gray-black wings and tail; orange bill and legs; to 18 cm (7 in).

HABITAT: Middle and high elevation wet forests, Caribbean and Pacific slopes; found in tree canopy or low shrubby areas, often in forest edge and other semi-open sites.

PARKS: ARVL, BCNP, LANP, MVCR, PONP, RVNP, WIBG

Plate 59 353

a Sooty Robin

b Clay-colored Robin

c Black-faced Solitaire

Plate 60a

White-throated Magpie-jay
Calocitta formosa
Urraca Copetona = big tufted magpie
Piapia Azul

ID: Large bird, blue above, white below; conspicuous crest on head; long blue tail; large black bill; 46 cm (18 in).

HABITAT: Low and middle elevations, northern Pacific slope; found in tree canopy in more open, wooded sites such as forest edges, trees along waterways, and especially around human settlements.

PARKS: CABR, MVCR, PVNP, RVNP, SRNP

Plate 60b

Brown Jay
Cyanocorax morio
Urraca Parda = brown magpie
Piapia

ID: Large dark brown bird with whitish lower chest and belly; tail partially white-tipped; largish black bill; to 40 cm (16 in).

HABITAT: Low, middle, and higher elevation deforested regions, Caribbean and parts of Pacific slopes; found in tree canopy in open, wooded sites such as forest edges, tree plantations, near human settlements.

PARKS: ARVL, BCNP, CABR, CHNP, CNWR, IVNP, LSBR, MANP, MVCR, PONP, RVNP, TONP

Plate 60c

Azure-hooded Jay
Cyanolyca cucullata
Urraca de Toca Celeste = azure-hooded magpie

ID: Mid-sized dark blue bird with black head, light blue top of head, dark red eyes; 28 cm (11 in).

HABITAT: Middle and higher elevation wet forests, Caribbean and Pacific slopes; found low in tree canopy in forest interior and forest edge areas.

PARKS: ARVL, BCNP, LANP, MVCR

Plate 60d

Long-tailed Silky-flycatcher
Ptilogonys caudatus
Capulinero Colilargo

ID: Mid-sized bluish gray bird with yellowish head with crest, light gray forehead; black, white, and yellow underneath tail; female olive instead of bluish gray, with lighter or whitish belly; small, dark bill; to 24 cm (9.5 in).

HABITAT: High elevation forests, southern Caribbean and southern Pacific slopes; found in tree canopy in semi-open sites such as forest edges, clearings, cut areas, tree plantations.

PARKS: BCNP, IVNP, LANP, PONP

Plate 60   355

b Brown Jay

a White-throated
Magpie-jay

c Azure-hooded Jay

d Long-tailed
Silky-flycatcher

Plate 61a

Buff-rumped Warbler
Phaeothlypis fulvicauda
Reinita = little queen
Reinita Guardaribera = riverside-guarding little queen

ID: Small brown or dark olive bird with buffy rump and upper part of tail; light stripe above eye; lighter chest/belly with darker spotting; to 14 cm (5.5 in).

HABITAT: Low and middle elevations, Caribbean and southern Pacific slopes; found on ground along streams and rivers.

PARKS: BCNP, CABR, CHNP, CNWR, CONP, LSBR, MANP, MVCR, TONP, WIBG

Plate 61b

Three-striped Warbler
Basileuterus tristriatus
Reinita = little queen
Reinita Cabecilistada = striped-head little queen

ID: Small olive-green bird with black stripes on tan/buff-colored head; yellowish chest/belly; brownish legs; 13 cm (5 in).

HABITAT: Middle elevation wet forests, Caribbean and southern Pacific slopes; found low in understory of forest interior and at forest edges.

PARKS: ARVL, BCNP, LANP, MVCR, WIBG

Plate 61c

Chestnut-sided Warbler
Dendroica pensylvanica
Reinita = little queen
Reinita de Costillas Castañas = chestnut-ribbed little queen

ID: Small olive-green bird with black tail, black wings with 2 yellowish bars, light gray chest/belly; male with brown streak on each side, female often with inconspicuous streak; 11 cm (4.5 in).

HABITAT: Low, middle, and some high elevation forests, Caribbean and Pacific slopes; found in tree canopy and shrubs in more open wooded sites such as forest edges, tree plantations, gardens.

PARKS: ARVL, BCNP, CABR, CHNP, CNWR, CONP, LANP, LSBR, MANP, MVCR, PVNP, RVNP, SRNP, TONP, WIBG

Note: This species is a nonbreeding seasonal migrant.

Plate 61d

Tennessee Warbler
Vermivora peregrina
Reinita = little queen
Reinita Verdilla = green little queen

ID: Small olive-green bird with grayish head, light-colored eyebrow, dark stripe through eye; whitish chest/belly; sharply pointed bill; 11 cm (4.5 in).

HABITAT: Low, middle, and some high elevation forests, Caribbean and Pacific slopes; found in tree canopy in more open sites such as forest edges, shady gardens, tree plantations, and, in drier regions, along waterways.

PARKS: ARVL, BCNP, CABR, CHNP, CNWR, CONP, LANP, LSBR, MANP, MVCR, PVNP, RVNP, SRNP, TONP, WIBG

Note: This species is a nonbreeding seasonal migrant.

Plate 61e

Slate-throated Redstart
Myioborus miniatus
Candelita Pechinegra = little black-chested candle

ID: Small dark gray or blackish bird with reddish brown patch on top of head; yellow chest/belly; black tail edged with white; to 13 cm (5 in).

HABITAT: Middle and higher elevation forests, Caribbean and Pacific slopes; found low in tree canopy in forest interior and more open sites such as forest edges, clearings, tree plantations, gardens.

PARKS: BCNP, LANP, MVCR, RVNP, WIBG

Plate 61 357

a Buff-rumped Warbler

b Three-striped Warbler

F

c Chestnut-sided Warbler

M

e Slate-throated Redstart

d Tennessee Warbler

Plate 62a

Bananaquit
Coereba flaveola
Reinita Mielera = honey-eater little queen

ID: Very small grayish olive bird with white eyestripe, gray throat, yellow chest/belly, and short, pointed, down-curved, black bill; 9 cm (3.5 in).

HABITAT: Low and middle elevation wet forests, Caribbean and southern Pacific slopes; found in tree canopy in more open wooded sites such as forest edges, gardens, plantations.

PARKS: ARVL, BCNP, CABR, CHNP, CNWR, CONP, LSBR, MANP, MVCR, RVNP, TONP, WIBG

Plate 62b

Tropical Gnatcatcher
Polioptila plumbea
Perlita Tropical = little tropical pearl

ID: Small gray bird with black wings; black tail edged with white; whitish chest/belly; straight black bill; male has black on top of head and black eyestripe; female has gray on top of head and gray eyestripe; 10 cm (4 in).

HABITAT: Low and middle elevations, Caribbean and Pacific slopes; found in tree canopy and shrubs in more open, wooded sites: forest edges, clearings, gardens, tree plantations, and, in drier regions, along waterways.

PARKS: ARVL, BCNP, CABR, CHNP, CNWR, CONP, LSBR, MANP, PVNP, SRNP, TONP, WIBG

Plate 62c

Streak-backed Oriole
Icterus pustulatus
Bolsero Dorsilistado = streak-backed oriole

ID: Mid-sized orange bird with black eye area, throat, and chest; black tail; black wings with white markings; black streaks on back; pointed, blackish bill; to 20 cm (8 in).

HABITAT: Low elevation drier forests, northern Pacific slope; found in tree canopy in more open, wooded sites such as forest edges and scrub or grassland areas with scattered trees.

PARKS: PVNP, SRNP

Plate 62d

Baltimore Oriole
Icterus galbula
Bolsero Norteño = northern oriole

ID: Male is smallish orange bird with black head and wings, black tail edged with orange; female is orangish olive with blackish wings and pale orange chest/belly; 18 cm (7 in).

HABITAT: Low, middle, and some higher elevations, Caribbean and Pacific slopes; found in tree canopy and shrubs in semi-open sites such as forest edges, tree plantations, gardens, arboretums.

PARKS: ARVL, BCNP, CABR, CHNP, CNWR, CONP, LSBR, MANP, MVCR, PVNP, RVNP, SRNP, TONP, WIBG

Note: This species is a nonbreeding seasonal migrant.

Plate 62   **359**

F

M

a Bananaquit

b Tropical Gnatcatcher

c Streak-backed Oriole

F

M

d Baltimore Oriole

Plate 63a

Montezuma's Oropendola
Psarocolius montezuma
Oropéndola de Montezuma =
Montezuma's oropendola
Oropéndola

ID: Large brown bird with black head, chest; yellow-edged tail; large black bill with orange tip; blue patch under eye; to 50 cm (20 in); male larger than female.

HABITAT: Low and some middle elevations, Caribbean slope; found in tree canopy in forest interior and in more open areas such as forest edges, clearings, tree plantations.

PARKS: BCNP, CHNP, CNWR, LSBR, RVNP, TONP

Plate 63b

Chestnut-headed Oropendola
Psarocolius wagleri
Oropéndola Cabecicastaña = chestnut-headed oropendola
Oropéndola

ID: Large dark brown bird with black back and wings; yellow-edged tail; large whitish bill; to 35 cm (14 in); male larger than female.

HABITAT: Low and middle elevations, Caribbean and parts of southern Pacific slopes; found in tree canopy in forest interior and in semi-open sites such as forest edges, clearings, tree plantations.

PARKS: ARVL, BCNP, CABR, CHNP, CNWR, CONP, LANP, LSBR, MANP, MVCR, TONP, WIBG

Plate 63c

Scarlet-rumped Cacique
Cacicus uropygialis
Cacique Lomiescarlata = scarlet-rumped cacique
Cacique

ID: Mid-sized black bird with red lower back (rump), pointed whitish bill, and light blue eyes; to 24 cm (9.5 in).

HABITAT: Low and some middle elevation wet forests, Caribbean and southern Pacific slopes; found high in tree canopy in forest interior and more open sites such as forest edges, clearings, tree plantations, shady gardens.

PARKS: BCNP, CABR, CHNP, CONP, LSBR, MANP, RVNP, TONP

Plate 63d

Yellow-billed Cacique
Amblycercus holosericeus
Cacique Picoplata = silver-billed cacique
Cacique

ID: Mid-sized all black bird with pointed yellow bill and yellow eyes; to 24 cm (9.5 in).

HABITAT: Low, middle, and higher elevations, Caribbean and southern Pacific slopes; found low in thickets with scattered trees and in open wooded areas such as forest edges and trees near water.

PARKS: ARVL, BCNP, CABR, CHNP, CNWR, CONP, LANP, LSBR, MANP, TONP, WIBG

Plate 63

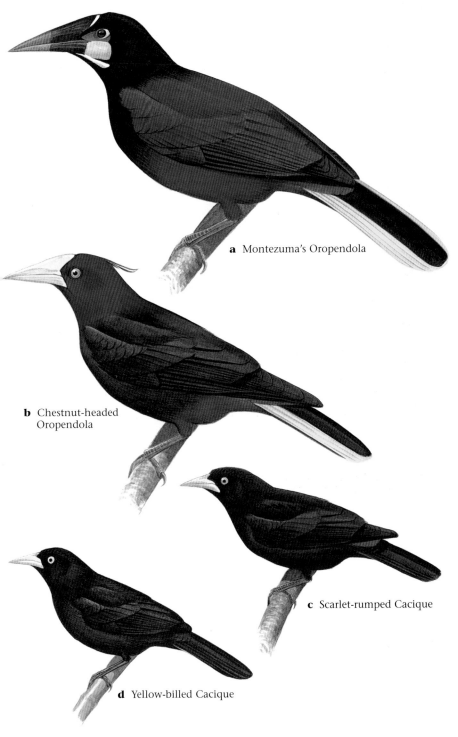

a Montezuma's Oropendola

b Chestnut-headed
Oropendola

c Scarlet-rumped Cacique

d Yellow-billed Cacique

Plate 64a
Bronzed Cowbird
Molothrus aeneus
Vaquero Ojirrojo = red-eyed cowboy
ID: Mid-sized blackish bird with greenish, bluish, or bronze gloss, black bill, red eyes; female is duller, browner; male especially has conspicuous area of raised feathers on back of neck; 20 cm (8 in).

HABITAT: Low and middle elevations, Caribbean and Pacific slopes; found in very open, deforested sites such as agricultural areas, pastures, along roads, in town parks, near human settlements.

PARKS: ARVL, CABR, CHNP, CNWR, CONP, LSBR, MANP, MVCR, PVNP, RVNP, SRNP, TONP, WIBG

Plate 64b
Great-tailed Grackle
Quiscalus mexicanus
Clarinero = clarion-player
Zanate Grande
ID: Male is largish black bird with purple gloss, especially on head and back, long black tail that folds to V-shape, large black bill, yellowish eye; female is brownish with darker wings and lighter eyestripe, yellowish eye, black bill; male to 43 cm (17 in); female to 33 cm (13 in).

HABITAT: Low and middle elevations, Caribbean and Pacific slopes; found in open habitats such as grasslands, pastures, roadsides and, in drier areas, along lakes and waterways.

PARKS: ARVL, BCNP, CABR, CHNP, CNWR, CONP, MANP, MVCR, PVNP, SRNP, TONP

Plate 64c
Blue-gray Tanager
Thraupis episcopus
Tangara Azuleja = blue-gray tanager
ID: Small pale blue-gray bird, darker on back, with bright blue wings and tail; small dark bill; female duller, darker overall; 15 cm (6 in).

HABITAT: Low, middle and higher elevation open areas, Caribbean and Pacific slopes; found in trees and shrubs near human settlements, town parks, forest edges.

PARKS: ARVL, BCNP, CABR, CHNP, CNWR, CONP, LANP, LSBR, MANP, MVCR, PVNP, RVNP, SRNP, TONP, WIBG

Plate 64d
Scarlet-rumped Tanager
Ramphocelus passerinii
Tangara Lomiescarlata = scarlet-rumped tanager
Sargento = sergeant
ID: Male is small black bird with red rump and light gray or pale blue bill with dark tip; female is yellowish olive or brownish olive with grayish head and throat, and orangish yellow rump, chest, and belly; females on Pacific slope similar but with chest and rump more orange; to 16 cm (6.5 in).

HABITAT: Low and middle elevations, Caribbean and southern Pacific slopes; found in trees, thickets, shrubs in more open habitats such as forest edges, pastures, and gardens.

PARKS: ARVL, BCNP, CABR, CNWR, CONP, LSBR, MANP, RVNP, TONP, WIBG

Plate 64   363

a Bronzed Cowbird

b Great-tailed Grackle

F

M

c Blue-gray Tanager

d Scarlet-rumped Tanager

F

M

Plate 65a

Yellow-crowned Euphonia
Euphonia luteicapilla
Eufonia Coroniamarilla = yellow-crowned euphonia
Monjita = little nun
Agüio

ID: Male is very small bluish black bird with black throat, yellow on top of head, and yellow chest/belly; female is olive-greenish with lighter green-to-yellowish chest/belly; 9.5 cm (3.75 in).

HABITAT: Low and middle elevations, Caribbean and southern Pacific slopes; found in semi-open sites such as forest edges, open woodlands, tree plantations.

PARKS: BCNP, CABR, CHNP, CNWR, CONP, LSBR, MANP, MVCR, RVNP, TONP, WIBG

Plate 65b

Olive-backed Euphonia
Euphonia gouldi
Eufonia Olivácea = olive euphonia
Monjito = little monk

ID: Very small greenish olive bird; male with brownish belly and yellow forehead; female with yellowish olive belly and reddish brown forehead; 9.5 cm (3.75 in).

HABITAT: Low and some middle elevations, Caribbean slope; found in tree canopy in forest interior and more open sites such as forest edges, tree plantations, and along rivers and streams.

PARKS: BCNP, CHNP, CNWR, LSBR, RVNP, TONP

Plate 65c

Scrub Euphonia
Euphonia affinis
Eufonia Gargantinegra = black-throated euphonia
Monjita = little nun
Agüio

ID: Male is very small bluish black bird with black throat, yellow forehead, and yellow chest/belly; female is olive-greenish with lighter green-to-yellowish chest/belly, grayish on top of head; 9.5 cm (3.75 in).

HABITAT: Low and middle elevations, northern Pacific slope; found in tree canopy in semi-open wooded sites such as forest edges and trees along waterways, and in open habitats with scattered trees.

PARKS: MVCR, PVNP, RVNP, SRNP

Plate 65d

Yellow-throated Euphonia
Euphonia hirundinacea
Eufonia Gorgiamarilla = yellow-throated euphonia

ID: Male is very small bluish black bird with yellow forehead and yellow throat, chest, and belly; female is greenish olive with yellowish throat, greenish yellow chest, whitish belly; 10 cm (4 in).

HABITAT: Low and middle elevations, northern Pacific slope; found in tree canopy in drier areas in trees along waterways, and in wetter areas, in semi-open sites such as forest edges, clearings, tree plantations.

PARKS: CNWR, MVCR, PVNP, RVNP, SRNP

Plate 65 365

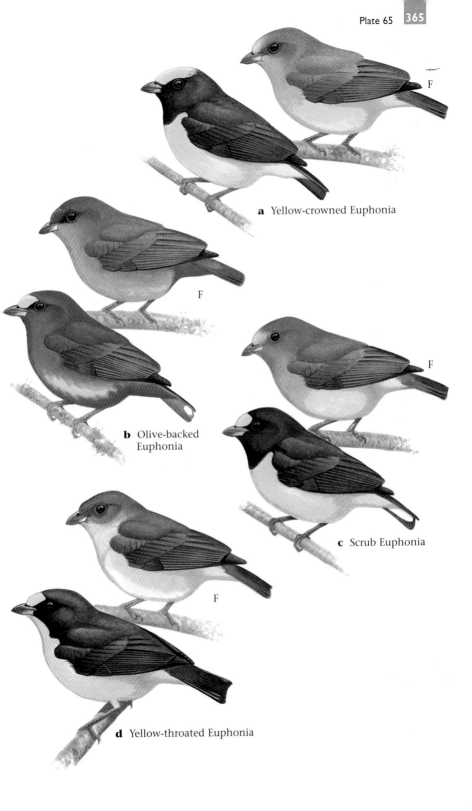

a Yellow-crowned Euphonia

F

b Olive-backed Euphonia

F

c Scrub Euphonia

F

d Yellow-throated Euphonia

Plate 66a

Golden-browed Chlorophonia
Chlorophonia callophrys
Clorofonia Cejidorada = golden-browed chlorophonia
Rualdo

ID: Male is small bright green bird with yellow forehead and yellow over the eye; blue on top of head; yellow chest/belly; female is a bit duller than male and lacks yellow over eye; 13 cm (5 in).

HABITAT: High elevation forests, Caribbean and Pacific slopes; found in tree canopy in semi-open sites such as forest edges, tree plantations, shady gardens.

PARKS: ARVL, BCNP, IVNP, LANP, MVCR, PONP, RVNP, WIBG

Plate 66b

Common Bush-tanager
Chlorospingus ophthalmicus
Tangara de Monte Ojerruda

ID: Small greenish olive bird with brown head, gray throat, yellowish olive chest, whitish belly; small white patch behind eye; to 14 cm (5.5 in).

HABITAT: Higher elevations, Caribbean and Pacific slopes; found in tree canopy in forest interior and in more open, wooded sites such as forest edges, tree plantations, clearings.

PARKS: ARVL, BCNP, LANP, MVCR, RVNP, WIBG

Plate 66c

Sooty-capped Bush-tanager
Chlorospingus pileatus
Tangara de Monte Cejiblanca = white-eyebrowed bush-tanager

ID: Small greenish olive bird with black head, gray throat, yellowish olive chest, whitish/pale gray belly; white stripe above and behind eye; to 13 cm (5.25 in).

HABITAT: High elevations, mostly over southern half of the country; found in tree canopy and shrubs in forest interior and more open sites such as forest edges, clearings, and brushy areas above treeline.

PARKS: BCNP, IVNP, LANP, MVCR, PONP

Plate 66d

Dusky-faced Tanager
Mitrospingus cassinii
Tangara Carinegruzca = dusky-faced tanager

ID: Mid-sized blackish olive bird; black head with greenish olive top; greenish olive chest/belly; pale eyes; 18 cm (7 in).

HABITAT: Low elevations, Caribbean slope; found in trees, shrubs, and thickets in more open sites such as forest edges, tree plantations, vegetation along waterways.

PARKS: BCNP, CNWR, LSBR, TONP

Plate 66   367

F

M

a Golden-browed Chlorophonia

b Common
Bush-tanager

c Sooty-capped
Bush-tanager

d Dusky-faced Tanager

Plate 67a

Palm Tanager
Thraupis palmarum
Tangara Palmera = palm tanager
ID: Smallish grayish olive bird with black wings, gray legs; 15 cm (6 in).

HABITAT: Low and middle elevations, Caribbean and southern Pacific slopes (occasionally northern Pacific also); found in open sites such as forest edges, tree plantations, gardens, pastures with trees, trees along waterways.

PARKS: BCNP, CABR, CHNP, CNWR, CONP, LSBR, MANP, MVCR, SRNP, TONP, WIBG

Plate 67b

Shining Honeycreeper
Cyanerpes lucidus
Mielero Luciente = shining honey-eater
ID: Male is small blue bird with black wings, tail, throat, and eyestripe; yellow legs; longish, thin, down-curved bill; female is green with streaked face, blue and white streaked chest, light yellowish belly and yellow legs; 10 cm (4 in).

HABITAT: Low and middle elevations, Caribbean and southern Pacific slopes; found in tree canopy in semi-open habitats such as forest edges, tree plantations, shady gardens.

PARKS: ARVL, BCNP, CABR, CHNP, CNWR, CONP, LSBR, MANP, RVNP, TONP, WIBG

Plate 67c

Red-legged Honeycreeper
Cyanerpes cyaneus
Mielero Patirrojo = red-legged honey-eater
ID: Male is small blue bird with black back, wings, tail, and eyestripe; turquoise top of head; red legs; longish, thin, down-curved bill; female is green with light eyestripe; yellowish green chest/belly with dull streaks; 12 cm (4.75 in).

HABITAT: Low and middle elevation drier forests, northern Caribbean and Pacific slopes; found in tree canopy usually in more open sites such as forest edges, tree plantations, gardens, and trees along waterways.

PARKS: ARVL, CABR, CNWR, CONP, MANP, PVNP, RVNP, SRNP, WIBG

Plate 67d

Scarlet-thighed Dacnis
Dacnis venusta
Mielero Celeste y Negro = sky-blue and black honey-eater
ID: Male is small blackish bird with blue-turquoise head, back, and rump; red thighs; small, pointed bill; female is dull bluish green with grayish throat/chest, yellowish belly, blackish wings and tail, red thighs; 12 cm (4.75 in).

HABITAT: Middle elevations, Caribbean and southern Pacific slopes, found in tree canopy in semi-open sites such as forest edges, tree plantations, gardens.

PARKS: ARVL, BCNP, CABR, CONP, LSBR, MANP, MVCR, WIBG

Plate 67   369

a Palm Tanager

F

b Shining
Honeycreeper

F

c Red-legged
Honeycreeper

F

d Scarlet-thighed Dacnis

Plate 68a

Silver-throated Tanager
Tangara icterocephala
Tangara Dorada = golden tanager
ID: Small yellow bird with blackish wings, black streaks on back, whitish throat, gray legs; female a bit duller than male; to 13 cm (5.25 in).

HABITAT: Low (occasionally), middle, and some higher elevation wet forests, Caribbean and Pacific slopes; found in tree canopy usually in more open settings such as forest edges, clearings, tree plantations.

PARKS: ARVL, BCNP, CABR, CONP, LANP, LSBR, MANP, MVCR, RVNP, WIBG

Plate 68b

Green Honeycreeper
Chlorophanes spiza
Mielero Verde = green honey-eater
ID: Male is small green bird with black head, black and yellowish down-curved bill, red eyes; female is paler green with even lighter chest/belly; 13 cm (5.25 in).

HABITAT: Low and middle elevation wet forests, Caribbean and Pacific slopes; found in tree canopy in forest interior and in more open places such as trees and shrubs at forest edges, clearings, shady gardens.

PARKS: BCNP, CABR, CHNP, CNWR, CONP, LSBR, MANP, RVNP, TONP, WIBG

Plate 68c

Speckled Tanager
Tangara guttata
Tangara Moteada = speckled tanager
ID: Small greenish bird heavily spotted with black on head, back, and chest; wings and tail black with green edging; yellow face; whitish belly; to 13 cm (5.25 in).

HABITAT: Low and middle elevation wet forests, Caribbean and southern Pacific slopes; found in tree canopy and shrubs usually in more open wooded sites such as forest edges, clearings, shady gardens.

PARKS: ARVL, BCNP, CABR, MANP, WIBG

Plate 68d

Bay-headed Tanager
Tangara gyrola
Tangara Cabecicastaña = chestnut-headed tanager
ID: Small green bird with brown head, bright blue chest, belly, and rump; 13 cm (5 in).

HABITAT: Low and middle elevation wet forests, Caribbean and southern Pacific slopes; prefers tree canopy in more open wooded sites such as forest edges, clearings, tree plantations.

PARKS: ARVL, BCNP, CABR, CONP, MANP, MVCR, WIBG

Plate 68e

Golden-hooded Tanager
Tangara larvata
Tangara Capuchidorada = golden-hooded tanager
Pájaro Arcoiris = rainbow bird
Pájaro Siete Colores = seven colors bird
ID: Small black bird with yellowish head; black on chin and around eye; bluish face, shoulders, rump; white belly; female's head greenish yellow often with dark spots; 13 cm (5 in).

HABITAT: Low and middle elevation wet forests, Caribbean and southern Pacific slopes; found in tree canopy in forest interior and semi-open sites such as forest edges, clearings, shady gardens.

PARKS: ARVL, BCNP, CABR, CHNP, CNWR, CONP, LSBR, MANP, TONP, WIBG

Plate 68 **371**

a Silver-throated Tanager

Brilliant Turquoise

M

F

b Green Honeycreeper

c Speckled Tanager

d Bay-headed Tanager

F

M

e Golden-hooded Tanager

Plate 69a

Buff-throated Saltator
Saltator maximus
Saltator Gorgianteado = buff-throated saltator

ID: Mid-sized olive-green bird with tan/buffy throat with black border; white chin; grayish face; white eyestripe; heavy blackish bill; 20 cm (8 in).

HABITAT: Low and middle elevations, Caribbean and southern Pacific slopes; inhabits semi-open sites such as forest edges, shady gardens and tree plantations, and very open areas such as low thickets and pastures.

PARKS: ARVL, BCNP, CABR, CHNP, CNWR, CONP, LSBR, MANP, MVCR, RVNP, TONP, WIBG

Plate 69b

Black-faced Grosbeak
Caryothraustes poliogaster
Picogrueso Carinegro = black-faced grosbeak

ID: Small olive-green bird with yellowish head and chest; black face; grayish belly; short, thick, black bill; to 18 cm (7 in).

HABITAT: Low and some middle elevation wet forests, Caribbean slope; found in tree canopy in forest interior and more open sites such as forest edges, clearings, tree plantations.

PARKS: BCNP, CHNP LSBR, MVCR, RVNP, TONP

Plate 69c

Orange-billed Sparrow
Arremon aurantiirostris
Pinzón Piquinaranja = orange-billed finch

ID: Small olive-green bird with black, white, and gray striped head, white throat, black chest, whitish belly; grayish sides; small orange bill; 15 cm (6 in).

HABITAT: Low and some middle elevation wet forests, Caribbean and southern Pacific slopes; found on ground and low in brush in forest interior and more open sites such as forest edges.

PARKS: BCNP, CABR, CHNP, CNWR, CONP, LSBR, MANP, RVNP, TONP, WIBG

Plate 69d

Variable Seedeater
Sporophila aurita
Espiguero Variable = variable grain-eater
Pius

ID: On Caribbean slope, male is small black bird with white patch on wings and small black bill; female is brownish olive with lighter chest/belly; on Pacific slope, black male has white rump, belly, and collar; female is dull brown or olive with lighter chest/belly; to 11 cm (4.25 in).

HABITAT: Low and middle elevations, Caribbean and southern Pacific slopes; found on or near ground in more open habitats, including forest edges, grasslands, pastures, gardens, roadsides.

PARKS: BCNP, CABR, CHNP, CNWR, CONP, LSBR, MANP, MVCR, PVNP, RVNP, TONP, WIBG

Plate 69   373

a Buff-throated Saltator

c Orange-billed Sparrow

b Black-faced Grosbeak

F

d Variable Seedeater

(M-Caribbean)   (M-Pacific)

Plate 70a

Striped-headed Sparrow
Aimophila ruficauda
Sabanero Cabecilistado = striped-headed savannah sparrow

ID: Smallish brown bird with black and white striped head; blackish streaks on back; whitish or grayish chest/belly; bill black above, tan below; 18 cm (7 in).

HABITAT: Low elevations, northern Pacific slope; found in semi-open and very open areas such as forest edges, low brushy scrub, grasslands, pastures.

PARKS: PVNP, RVNP, SRNP

Plate 70b

Yellow-faced Grassquit
Tiaris olivacea
Semillerito Cariamarillo = little yellow-faced seedeater

ID: Male is small greenish bird with yellow throat and eyestripe; black forehead, under eye, and chest; olive-grayish belly; female is olive-colored, duller all over, with hint of yellowish eyestripe and throat; 10 cm (4 in).

HABITAT: Low, middle, and some higher elevations, Caribbean and southern Pacific slopes; found in very open sites such as grasslands, pastures, lawns, fields, roadsides.

PARKS: ARVL, BCNP, CABR, CHNP, CNWR, LANP, LSBR, MANP, MVCR, WIBG

Plate 70c

Rufous-collared Sparrow
Zonotrichia capensis
Comemaiz = corn-eater
Chingolo

ID: Small brown bird with gray and black head with small crest; reddish brown on neck; black streaks on back; white throat; whitish belly; to 14 cm (5.5 in).

HABITAT: Middle and high elevation open areas, Caribbean and Pacific slopes; found in pastures, agricultural fields, grasslands, and around human settlements.

PARKS: BCNP, IVNP, LANP, MVCR, PONP, WIBG

Plate 70d

House Sparrow
Passer domesticus
Gorrión Común = common sparrow

ID: Male is a small brown bird with gray on top of head, whitish side of head, black throat/chest, black streaks on back, gray belly; female is duller brown above, grayish below, with light brown or buffy eyestripe; 14 cm (5.5 in).

HABITAT: Found around most villages, towns, and cities.

PARKS: Found around human settlements.

Plate 70e

Black-striped Sparrow
Arremonops conirostris
Pinzón Cabecilistado = striped-headed finch
Huevo Blanco = white egg

ID: Small greenish olive bird with gray and black striped head; yellowish olive wing patch seen in flight; white throat; whitish and grayish chest/belly; to 17 cm (6.5 in).

HABITAT: Low and middle elevations, Caribbean and southern Pacific slopes; found in open habitats such as fields, pastures, thickets, shady gardens, tree plantations.

PARKS: ARVL, BCNP, CABR, CHNP, CNWR, CONP, LSBR, MANP, MVCR, RVNP, TONP, WIBG

Plate 70 **375**

a Striped-headed Sparrow

M

F **b** Yellow-faced Grassquit

c Rufous-collared Sparrow

M **d** House Sparrow

F

e Black-striped Sparrow

Plate 71a

Common Opossum
(also called Southern Opossum)
Didelphis marsupialis
Zorro Pelón = bald fox
Zarigüeya = opossum
Raposa

ID: A large opossum with yellowish face; blackish or gray back; black ears; cheek area yellowish; to 42 cm (16 in), plus long, almost hairless, tail. (Virginia Opossum, *Didelphis virginiana*, is common over northwest Pacific slope; it closely resembles Common Opossum but has white cheeks.)

HABITAT: Countrywide below about 1500 m (5000 ft); nocturnal; found in trees and on the ground.

PARKS: BCNP, CABR, CHNP, CNWR, CONP, LANP, LSBR, MANP, MVCR, PVNP, SRNP, TONP, WIBG

Plate 71b

Central American Woolly Opossum
Caluromys derbianus
Zorro de Balsa = woolly fox

ID: A smaller, very furry opossum, reddish brown with a grayish face, dark stripe from nose to forehead, and gray patch on its back; light-colored front feet; last half of tail is hairless; to 30 cm (12 in), plus long tail.

HABITAT: Low and middle elevation wet and dry forests, Caribbean and Pacific slopes; nocturnal; arboreal.

PARKS: ARVL, BCNP, CABR, CHNP, CNWR, CONP, LANP, LSBR, MANP, MVCR, PVNP, RNVP, SRNP, TONP, WIBG

Plate 71c

Water Opossum
Chironectes minimus
Zorro de Agua = water fox

ID: A smaller opossum with webbed toes on rear feet; gray back with broad black/brown bands and a black stripe down its center; head blackish; cheeks and throat whitish; to 30 cm (12 in), plus tail.

HABITAT: Countrywide in both wet and dry forests, and cleared areas; swims; found in water or on ground along watercourses.

PARKS: ARVL, BCNP, CABR, CHNP, CNWR, CONP, LANP, LSBR, MANP, MVCR, PVNP, RNVP, SRNP, TONP, WIBG

Plate 71d

Gray Four-eyed Opossum
Philander opossum
Zorro de Cuatro Ojos = four-eyed fox

ID: An opossum with gray back and lighter-colored throat, chest, and belly; black face mask; black on top of head; a white mark above each eye; to 33 cm (13 in), plus hairless tail.

HABITAT: Low and middle elevation forests and agricultural areas, countrywide; prefers dense vegetation near water; nocturnal; found in trees but also on the ground.

PARKS: ARVL, BCNP, CABR, CHNP, CNWR, CONP, LANP, LSBR, MANP, MVCR, PVNP, RNVP, SRNP, TONP, WIBG

Plate 71 377

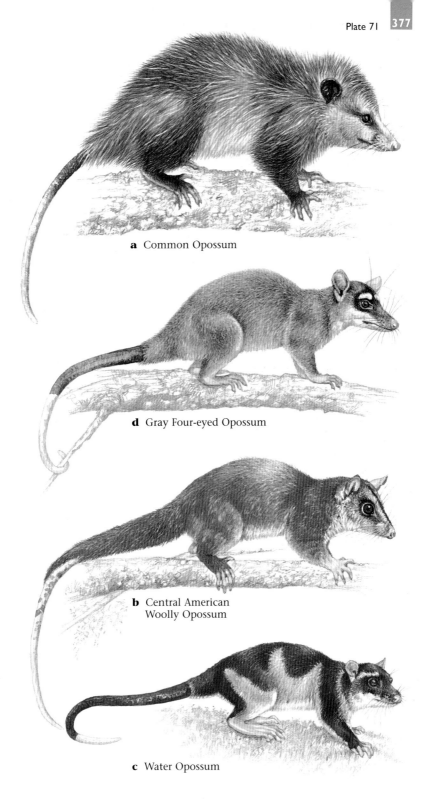

a Common Opossum

d Gray Four-eyed Opossum

b Central American
Woolly Opossum

c Water Opossum

Plate 72a

Greater Fishing Bat
(also called Greater Bulldog Bat)
Noctilio leporinus
Murciélago Pescador = fishing bat

ID: A large brown or reddish bat; usually one light stripe on its back; forward-pointing ears; lips split in the middle, with drooping folds of skin, like a bulldog; no noseleaf; head and body length to 9.7 cm (4 in), plus tail; wingspan to 60 cm (2 ft).

HABITAT: Lowlands of Caribbean and Pacific slopes, near water; roosts in hollow trees, caves; forages over water for small fish.

PARKS: CABR, CHNP, CNWR, CONP, LSBR, MANP, PVNP, SRNP, TONP, WIBG

Plate 72b

False Vampire Bat
Vampyrum spectrum
Vampiro Falso = false vampire bat

ID: A large bat (largest in the New World) with brown or rust-colored head and back; one light stripe along back; long, rounded ears; long, dog-like snout with prominent noseleaf; no tail; head and body length to 15 cm (6 in); wingspan to 80+ cm (2.5 ft).

HABITAT: Low and middle elevation forests, Caribbean and Pacific slopes; roosts in hollow trees; forages in more open areas both within and outside of forests.

PARKS: BCNP, CABR, CHNP, CNWR, CONP, LANP, LSBR, MANP, MVCR, PVNP, SRNP, TONP

Plate 72c

Jamaican Fruit-eating Bat
Artibeus jamaicensis
Murciélago Frutero Jamaicano = Jamaican fruit bat
Murciélago Come Frutas = fruit-eating bat

ID: A large, stout-bodied bat, black, brown, or grayish; large head usually with light stripes on face; short, broad snout with spear-shaped noseleaf; V-shaped row of small bumps on chin; head and body length to 10 cm (4 in); wingspan to 40 cm (16 in).

HABITAT: Low and middle elevation wet and dry forests, Caribbean and Pacific slopes; roosts in caves, hollow trees, under palm leaves; feeds on fruit.

PARKS: ARVL, BCNP, CABR, CHNP, CNWR, CONP, LANP, LSBR, MANP, MVCR, PVNP, RNVP, SRNP, TONP, WIBG

Plate 72d

Common Vampire Bat
Desmodus rotundus
Vampiro = vampire

ID: A mid-sized, dark brown bat with shiny fur; tips of hair on back often silvery white; short snout with U-shaped, fleshy, skin folds; large, sharp middle incisor and canine teeth; triangular, pointed ears; no tail; head and body length to 9.0 cm (3.5 in).

HABITAT: Low and middle elevation wet and dry forests, clearings, farm areas, Caribbean and Pacific slopes; roosts in trees, caves; nocturnal; often flies along riverbeds.

PARKS: ARVL, BCNP, CABR, CHNP, CNWR, CONP, LANP, LSBR, MANP, MVCR, PVNP, RNVP, SRNP, TONP, WIBG

Plate 72 379

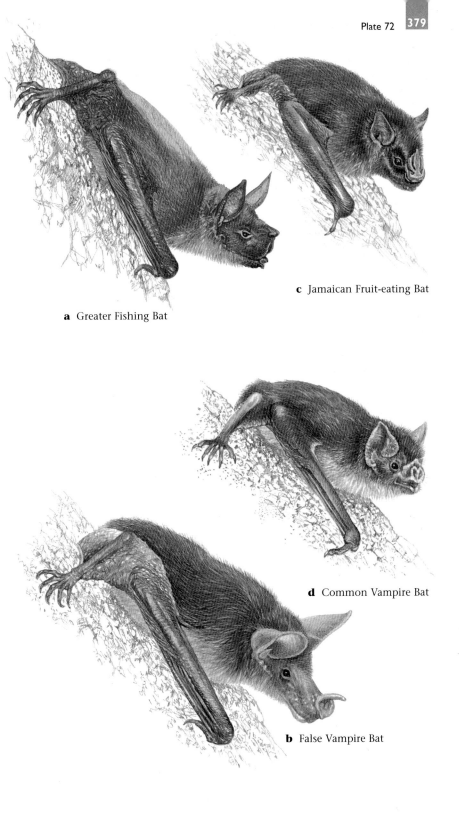

a Greater Fishing Bat

c Jamaican Fruit-eating Bat

d Common Vampire Bat

b False Vampire Bat

Plate 73a

Short-tailed Fruit Bat
(also called Seba's Short-tailed Bat)
Carollia perspicillata
Murciélago Candelero = candlestick bat

ID: A small brown or gray bat with short, narrow snout with relatively large, spear-shaped noseleaf; small warts on chin; triangular, pointed ears; head and body length to 6.5 cm (2.5 in).

HABITAT: Low and middle elevation forests, gardens, agricultural areas, Caribbean and Pacific slopes; roosts in trees, caves, riverbanks, buildings; prefers moist areas; feeds at fruit sources, flowers (especially at the *Piper* plant's candle-like flowering structures).

PARKS: BCNP, CABR, CHNP, CNWR, CONP, LANP, LSBR, MANP, PVNP, SRNP, TONP, WIBG

Plate 73b

Nectar Bat
(also called Common Long-tongued Bat)
Glossophaga soricina
Murciélago Lengualarga = long-tongued bat

ID: A small brown or gray bat with a long snout; small, spear-shaped noseleaf; short, blunt ears; lower lip with a V-shaped notch lined with small bumps; head and body length to 6.5 cm (2.5 in), plus short tail; wingspan to 28 cm (11 in).

HABITAT: Low and middle elevation wet and dry forests and open areas, Caribbean and Pacific slopes; roosts in caves, trees, bridges, buildings; forages within forest but also in open areas, dry stream beds, farms; hovers at flowers to feed on nectar.

PARKS: BCNP, CABR, CHNP, CNWR, CONP, LANP, LSBR, MANP, MVCR, PVNP, SRNP, TONP, WIBG

Plate 73c

Sucker-footed Bat
(also called Spix's Disk-winged Bat)
Thyroptera tricolor
Murciélago de Ventosas = sucker-footed bat

ID: A tiny brown bat with white or yellowish belly; short, narrow snout without a noseleaf; triangular, pointed ears; fleshy sucker disks near ankles and

thumbs for attaching to leaves; head and body length to 4.5 cm (2 in), plus tail.

HABITAT: Low elevation wet forests, gardens, farm areas, Caribbean and Pacific slopes; nocturnal; roosts in rolled up *Heliconia* and banana leaves.

PARKS: BCNP, CABR, CHNP, CNWR, CONP, LSBR, MANP, MVCR, RNVP, TONP, WIBG

Plate 73d

Black Myotis
(also called Little Brown Bat)
Myotis nigricans
Murciélago Pardo = brown bat

ID: A tiny dark brown or black bat with small pointed snout without noseleaf; triangular, pointed ears; head and body length to 5 cm (2 in), plus tail.

HABITAT: Low, middle, and higher elevation forests, gardens, agricultural areas; nocturnal; flies in more open areas, along trails, streams, etc.; roosts in trees, rock crevices, buildings.

PARKS: ARVL, BCNP, CABR, CHNP, CNWR, CONP, IVNP, LANP, LSBR, MANP, MVCR, PONP, PVNP, RNVP, SRNP, TONP, WIBG

Plate 73e

Greater White-lined Bat
(also called White-lined Sac-winged Bat)
Saccopteryx bilineata
Murciélago de Saco = sac bat

ID: Small, dark, brown to black bat with two white lines running along its back; grayish belly; head and body length to 5.5 cm (2 in), plus short tail.

HABITAT: Lowlands over Caribbean and Pacific slopes; roosts in hollow trees, caves, but also in/on buildings, under roofs; forages at dusk, often near water.

PARKS: BCNP, CABR, CHNP, CNWR, CONP, LSBR, MANP, PVNP, SRNP, TONP

Plate 73 381

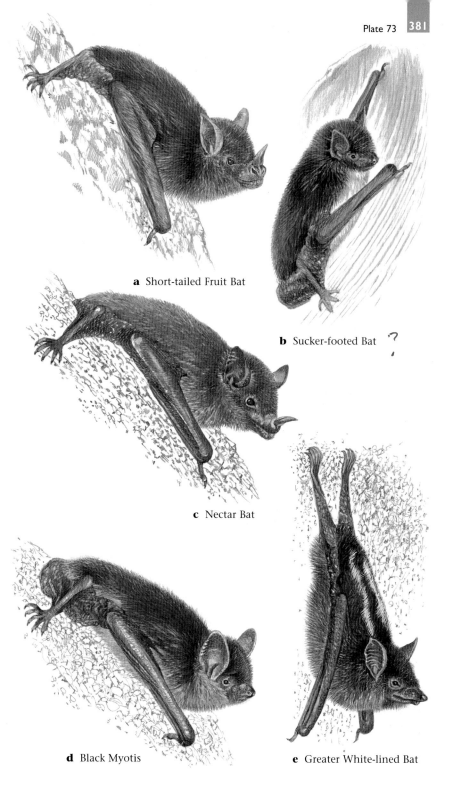

a Short-tailed Fruit Bat

b Sucker-footed Bat

c Nectar Bat

d Black Myotis

e Greater White-lined Bat

Plate 74a

Red-backed Squirrel Monkey
(also called Central American Squirrel Monkey)
Saimiri oerstedii
Mono Tití = marmoset monkey
Mono Ardilla = squirrel monkey
ID: A small, orange-gold monkey with yellowish green shoulders and hips; black head with white face mask; white chin, throat, ears; to 30 cm (12 in), plus very long, black-tipped, nonprehensile tail.

HABITAT: Wet forests of southern Pacific slope; arboreal.

PARKS: CONP, MANP

Note: This species is endangered, CITES Appendix I and USA ESA listed.

Plate 74b

White-faced Capuchin
(also called White-throated Capuchin)
Cebus capucinus
Mono Carablanca = whiteface monkey
ID: A mid-sized black monkey with whitish face, neck, shoulders, and upper arms; to 46 cm (18 in), plus long tail; males larger than females.

HABITAT: Wet and dry forests, Caribbean and Pacific slopes; arboreal, but also comes to the ground.

PARKS: BCNP, CABR, CHNP, CNWR, CONP, LANP, LSBR, MANP, MVCR, PVNP, RNVP, SRNP, TONP, WIBG

Note: This species regulated for conservation purposes, CITES Appendix II listed.

Plate 74c

Mantled Howler Monkey
Alouatta palliata
Mono Aullador = howling monkey
Mono Congo = congo monkey
ID: Large black monkey with a more-or-less noticeable fringe (mantle) of pale or chestnut hair on back, sides, belly; to 55 cm (22 in), plus long, prehensile tail; males larger than females.

HABITAT: Wet and dry forests, Caribbean and Pacific slopes; arboreal, usually in upper reaches of trees.

PARKS: ARVL, BCNP, CABR, CHNP, CNWR, CONP, LANP, LSBR, MANP, MVCR, PONP, PVNP, RNVP, SRNP, TONP, WIBG

Note: This species is endangered, Cites Appendix I and USA ESA listed.

Plate 74d

Central American Spider Monkey
(also called Geoffroy's Spider Monkey)
Ateles geoffroyi
Mono Colorado = reddish monkey
Mono Araña = spider monkey
ID: A large monkey, brown, chestnut or silver; lighter-colored belly; dark or black lower legs, feet, hands, and forearms; pale skin around eyes and nose; to 63 cm (25 in), plus long, prehensile tail.

HABITAT: Wet and dry forests, Caribbean and Pacific slopes; arboreal.

PARKS: ARVL, BCNP, CABR, CHNP, CNWR, CONP, LANP, LSBR, MANP, MVCR, PVNP, RNVP, SRNP, TONP, WIBG

Note: This species is endangered, CITES Appendix I and USA ESA listed.

Plate 74   383

a Red-backed Squirrel Monkey

b White-faced Capuchin

c Mantled Howler Monkey

d Central American Spider Monkey

Plate 75 (*See also*: Anteaters, Armadillos, and Sloths, p. 205)

Plate 75a

Hoffman's Two-toed Sloth
Choloepus hoffmanni
Perezoso de Dos Dedos = two-toed sloth
Perico Ligero = fast parakeet
Cúcula

ID: A brown or tan mammal with long, coarse hair; sometimes fur has a greenish tinge; round head with short snout; face light brown; two long, curved claws on each front leg, three on each rear leg; to 70 cm (28 in).

HABITAT: Wet and drier forests, Caribbean and Pacific slopes; arboreal, often in trees crowded with epiphytes and vines; hangs upside down from tree branches; nocturnal; by day, curled up on tree branch or in fork.

PARKS: ARVL, BCNP, CABR, CHNP, CNWR, CONP, LANP, LSBR, MANP, MVCR, PVNP, RNVP, SRNP, TONP, WIBG

Note: This species regulated in Costa Rica for conservation purposes, CITES Appendix III listed.

Plate 75b

Brown-throated Three-toed Sloth
(also called Three-toed Sloth)
Bradypus variegatus
Perezoso de Tres Dedos = three-toed sloth
Perico Ligero = fast parakeet
Cúcula

ID: A light brown and whitish mammal with long, coarse hair; sometimes fur has a greenish tinge; round head; white face with black mask; three long, curved claws on each leg; 40 to 80 cm (16 to 31 in).

HABITAT: Low and middle elevation forests, Caribbean and Pacific slopes; arboreal; usually hangs from tree branch by its claws; diurnal and nocturnal.

PARKS: BCNP, CABR, CHNP, CNWR, CONP, LSBR, MANP, MVCR, SRNP, TONP, WIBG

Plate 75c

Nine-banded Armadillo
Dasypus novemcinctus
Armadillo
Cusuco

ID: Gray to yellowish body; hairless back consisting of hard, bony plates; about 9 movable bands in midsection; long snout; large ears; scales on head, legs; to 57 cm (22 in), plus long, ringed tail.

HABITAT: Forests, scrub areas, and thickets, Caribbean and Pacific slopes; nocturnal; terrestrial.

PARKS: ARVL, BCNP, CABR, CHNP, CNWR, CONP, IVNP, LANP, LSBR, MANP, MVCR, PONP, PVNP, RNVP, SRNP, TONP, WIBG

Plate 75d

Silky Anteater
(also called Pygmy Anteater)
Cyclopes didactylus
Serafin de Platanar = banana tree angel
Gato de Balso = woolly cat
Tapacara = cover-face
Ceibita = little kapok

ID: Small anteater with gray, brownish, or yellowish dense, silky fur; darker on top, with a dark line running from top of head along the back; to 18 cm (7 in), plus thick, prehensile tail as long as or longer than body.

HABITAT: Low and middle elevation wet forests, Caribbean and Pacific slopes; nocturnal; arboreal; especially found among vines and thin tree branches.

PARKS: BCNP, CHNP, CNWR, CONP, LSBR, MANP, MVCR, TONP, WIBG

Plate 75e

Northern Tamandua
Tamandua mexicana
Oso Hormiguero = anteater bear
Oso Mielero = honey bear
Oso Colmenero = beehive bear
Oso Jaceta

ID: Mid-sized anteater with long, pointed snout; brown or yellowish head and legs with a black "vest" on belly and back that encircles body; 47 to 77 cm (18 to 30 in) long, plus tail as long as body; last section of tail is bare.

HABITAT: Low and middle elevation forests, Caribbean and Pacific slopes; active both nocturnally and during the day; found in trees and on the ground.

PARKS: BCNP, CABR, CHNP, CNWR, CONP, LANP, LSBR, MANP, MVCR, PVNP, RNVP, SRNP, TONP, WIBG

Plate 75 385

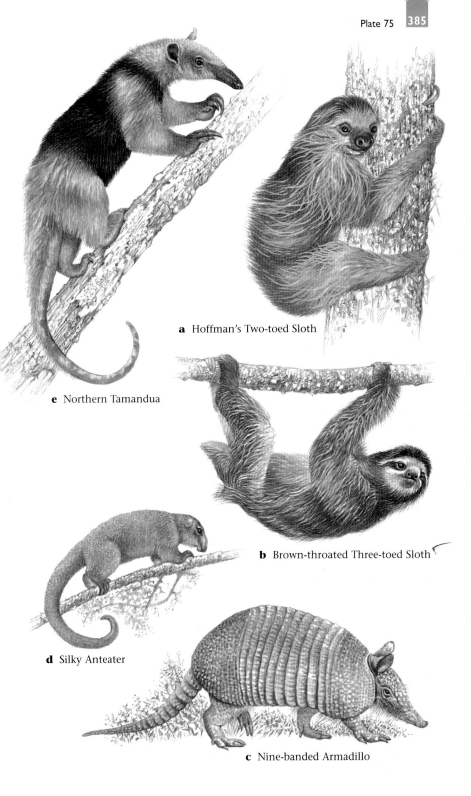

a Hoffman's Two-toed Sloth

e Northern Tamandua

b Brown-throated Three-toed Sloth

d Silky Anteater

c Nine-banded Armadillo

Plate 76a

Red-tailed Squirrel
Sciurus granatensis
Granadera = passion-fruit eater
Ardilla Roja = red squirrel
Ardilla = squirrel
Chisa

ID: Short-haired squirrel with reddish brown back and sides (some are darker-colored), and with a rust-red tail, sometimes black-tipped; 20 to 28 cm (8 to 11 in), plus long, bushy tail.

HABITAT: Wet forests, Caribbean and Pacific slopes; found in trees and on the ground.

PARKS: ARVL, BCNP, CHNP, CNWR, CONP, IVNP, LANP, LSBR, MVCR, PONP, RNVP, TONP, WIBG

Plate 76b

Variegated Squirrel
Sciurus variegatoides
Ardilla = squirrel
Chisa

ID: Large squirrel with longish fur; body color highly variable, some blackish, some yellowish gray; tail is black/white "grizzled;" about 22 to 33 cm (9 to 13 in), plus long, bushy tail.

HABITAT: Low and some mid-elevation forest edge and more open sites, especially in drier areas, Caribbean and Pacific slopes; in trees and on the ground.

PARKS: BCNP, CABR, CHNP, CNWR, CONP, LSBR, MANP, MVCR, PVNP, SRNP, TONP, WIBG

Plate 76c

Central American Dwarf Squirrel
(also called Alfaro's Pygmy Squirrel)
Microsciuris alfari
Ardilla = squirrel
Chisa

ID: Small squirrel, usually with short hair; back and sides brown, olive-brown or blackish; very short ears; tail dark or lighter-colored; 12 to 16 cm (5 to 6 in), plus tail almost as long as body.

HABITAT: Low, middle, and higher elevation wet forests, Caribbean and Pacific slopes; arboreal; but also found on the ground.

PARKS: ARVL, BCNP, CHNP, CNWR, CONP, IVNP, LANP, LSBR, MANP, MVCR, PONP, RNVP, TONP, WIBG

Plate 76d

Mexican Hairy Porcupine
(also called Prehensile-tailed Porcupine)
Coendou mexicanus
Puercoespín = porcupine
Cuerpoespín = thorny body

ID: Small brown or black porcupine with long prehensile tail which is bare at the end; spines ("quills") are largely hidden by long, soft hair; usually 30 to 40 cm (12 to 16 in), plus tail.

HABITAT: Low, middle, and some higher elevation forests and more open areas, Caribbean and Pacific slopes; nocturnal; mostly arboreal but also found on the ground.

PARKS: ARVL, BCNP, CABR, CNWR, CONP, LANP, LSBR, MANP, MVCR, PVNP, RNVP, SRNP, TONP, WIBG

Plate 76e

Paca
Agouti paca
Tepezcuintle

ID: Large, pig-like rodent; brown or blackish with horizontal rows of whitish spots on sides; 60 to 80 cm (24 to 31 in) long, plus tiny tail.

HABITAT: Low and middle elevation wet forests and drier areas near watercourses, Caribbean and Pacific slopes; nocturnal; found on the ground.

PARKS: ARVL, BCNP, CABR, CHNP, CNWR, CONP, LANP, LSBR, MVCR, PONP, PVNP, SRNP, TONP, WIBG

Plate 76f

Central American Agouti
Dasyprocta punctata
Guatusa

ID: Large, pig-like rodent; reddish brown, brown, or blackish back and sides; 40 to 62 cm (16 to 24 in) long, plus tiny tail.

HABITAT: Low and middle elevation forests, Caribbean and Pacific slopes; diurnal; found on the ground.

PARKS: ARVL, BCNP, CABR, CHNP, CNWR, CONP, LANP, LSBR, MANP, MVCR, PVNP, RNVP, SRNP, TONP, WIBG

Plate 76   **387**

a Red-tailed Squirrel

c Central American Dwarf Squirrel

b Variegated Squirrel

d Mexican Hairy Porcupine

e Paca

f Central American Agouti

Plate 77 (*See also*: Carnivores, p. 212)

Plate 77a

Coyote
Canis latrans
Coyote

ID: Medium-sized and dog-like; coat color varies from grayish to yellow-beige, often with "grizzled" or salt-and-pepper appearance; to about 75 cm (30 in) long, plus tail (sometimes black-tipped).

HABITAT: Forested and open areas of northern Pacific lowlands (Guanacaste region); active day or night; often seen during early morning.

PARKS: MVCR, PVNP, SRNP

Plate 77b

Gray Fox
Urocyon cinereoargenteus
Zorro Gris = gray fox

ID: Small, silver-gray, dog-like mammal, with reddish ears and shoulders; to 52 to 64 cm (20 to 24 in) long, plus tail.

HABITAT: Forested and open areas of northern Pacific lowlands (Guanacaste region); active day or night; often seen during early morning.

PARKS: MVCR, PVNP, SRNP

Plate 77c

Ocelot
Leopardus pardalis
Mano Gordo = fat hand
Ocelote

ID: Medium-sized yellow/tawny cat with black spots and lines; tail shorter than rear leg; to 70 to 85 cm (28 to 34 in) long, plus tail.

HABITAT: Low and middle elevation wet and dry forests of Caribbean and Pacific slopes; mostly nocturnal; found on the ground or in trees (where it sleeps).

PARKS: BCNP, CABR, CHNP, CNWR, CONP, LANP, LSBR, MANP, MVCR, PVNP, SRNP, TONP, WIBG

Note: This species listed as endangered, CITES Appendix I and USA ESA.

Plate 77d

Margay
Leopardus wiedii
Tigrillo = little tiger
Caucél

ID: Small to mid-sized yellowish, tawny, or brownish gray cat with black spots and lines; tail longer than rear leg; to 50 to 70 cm (20 to 28 in) long, plus tail.

HABITAT: Low and middle elevation forests, countrywide; nocturnal; found mostly in trees but also on the ground.

PARKS: ARVL, BCNP, CABR, CHNP, CNWR, CONP, LANP, LSBR, MANP, MVCR, PVNP, SRNP, TONP, WIBG

Note: This species listed as endangered, CITES Appendix I and USA ESA.

Plate 77e

Jaguar
Panthera onca
Tigre = tiger

ID: A large or very large cat, yellowish/tawny with black spots; to 1.1 to 1.8 m (3.5 to 6 ft) long, plus tail; you will know it when you see it.

HABITAT: Low and middle elevation forests and semi-open areas, countrywide; active day or night.

PARKS: ARVL, BCNP, CABR, CHNP, CNWR, CONP, LANP, LSBR, MANP, MVCR, PVNP, RNVP, SRNP, TONP, WIBG

Note: This species listed as endangered, CITES Appendix I and USA ESA.

Plate 77f

Jaguarundi
Herpailurus yaguarondi
León Breñero = craggy ground lion
Gatillo de Monte = little mountain cat

ID: Smallish to mid-sized slender cat without spots; gray, brown, or reddish; to 50 to 65+ cm (20 to 25+ in), plus long tail.

HABITAT: Wet and dry forests, countrywide; active day or night; usually seen on the ground, but also climbs.

PARKS: ARVL, BCNP, CABR, CHNP, CNWR, CONP, LANP, LSBR, MANP, MVCR, PONP, PVNP, RNVP, SRNP, TONP, WIBG

Note: This species listed as endangered, CITES Appendix I and USA ESA.

Plate 77 **389**

f Jaguarundi

c Ocelot

d Margay

e Jaguar

b Gray Fox

a Coyote

Plate 78a

Tayra
Eira barbara
Gato de Monte = mountain cat
Tolumuco
ID: Medium-sized, weasel-like mammal, resembling a large mink; black or brown body; tan, brown, or yellowish head and neck; most with large yellowish spot on chest/throat; to 52 to 70 cm (20 to 28 in), plus long, densely-furred tail.

HABITAT: Wet forests, drier areas, and agricultural areas, countrywide; day- and dusk-active; found in trees or on the ground.

PARKS: ARVL, BCNP, CABR, CHNP, CNWR, CONP, LANP, LSBR, MANP, MVCR, PVNP, SRNP, TONP, WIBG

Plate 78b

Striped Hog-nosed Skunk
Conepatus semistriatus
Zorrillo = skunk
Zorrillo hediondo = little stinky fox
ID: Black or brown, long-snouted mammal with wide white stripe on top of head and neck, dividing to 2 white stripes along back; bushy white tail; 30 to 49 cm (12 to 19 in), plus tail.

HABITAT: Found countrywide in most forests but more usually in cleared areas, gardens, agricultural areas; nocturnal; found on the ground.

PARKS: ARVL, BCNP, CABR, CHNP, CNWR, CONP, IVNP, LANP, LSBR, MANP, MVCR, PONP, PVNP, RNVP, SRNP, TONP, WIBG

Plate 78c

Hooded Skunk
Mephitis macroura
Zorrillo = skunk
Zorrillo hediondo = little stinky fox
ID: All black or black and white skunk, usually mostly black with 2 white stripes along each side; long, bushy tail; 28 to 38 cm (11 to 15 in) long, plus tail.

HABITAT: Lowland forests and open areas over northern Pacific slope, Nicoya Peninsula; nocturnal; found on the ground.

PARKS: PVNP, SRNP

Plate 78d

Neotropical Otter
Lutra longicaudis
Lobito del Río = little river wolf
Lobito de Plata = little silver wolf
Perro de Agua = water dog
ID: Short-legged, short-haired brown mammal with whitish throat and belly; first half of tail very thick; webbed feet; 45 to 75 cm (18 to 30 in) long, plus tail.

HABITAT: Found in and around rivers and streams, countrywide; active day and night.

PARKS: BCNP, CABR, CHNP, CNWR, CONP, IVNP, LANP, LSBR, MVCR, PVNP, RNVP, SRNP, TONP, WIBG

Note: This species listed as endangered, CITES Appendix I and USA ESA.

Plate 78e

Grison
(also called Huron)
Galictis vittata
Tejón = badger
Grisón
ID: A weasel-like mammal with short legs; grayish or "grizzled" above and on sides; black muzzle, throat, chest, and limbs; 45 to 55 cm (18 to 21 in) long, plus short tail.

HABITAT: Low elevation forests, especially near waterways, countrywide; night and morning-active; found on the ground.

PARKS: BCNP, CABR, CHNP, CNWR, CONP, LSBR, PVNP, SRNP, TONP

Note: This species regulated in Costa Rica for conservation purposes, CITES Appendix III listed.

Plate 78f

Long-tailed Weasel
Mustela frenata
Comadreja = weasel
ID: Small dark brown weasel with orangish or cream-colored throat, chest, and belly; white markings on blackish head; tip of tail black; 18 to 30 cm (7 to 12 in), plus tail.

HABITAT: Low, middle, and higher elevation forests, drier cleared areas, and agricultural areas, countrywide; active day or night; usually found on the ground but also climbs.

PARKS: ARVL, BCNP, CABR, CHNP, CNWR, CONP, IVNP, LANP, LSBR, MANP, MVCR, PONP, PVNP, RNVP, SRNP, TONP, WIBG

Plate 78 391

a Tayra

c Hooded Skunk

b Striped Hog-nosed Skunk

d Neotropical Otter

e Grison

f Long-tailed Weasel

Plate 79a

Northern Raccoon
Procyon lotor
Mapache = raccoon
Osito Lavador = little washing bear

ID: Gray-black back with "grizzled" appearance; whitish face with black mask; gray forearms and thighs; light gray/white feet; pointed muzzle; 45 to 64 cm (18 to 25 in), plus ringed tail.

HABITAT: Low and middle elevation forests and open areas, primarily near seashores and inland waterways and marshes; nocturnal; found on the ground and in trees.

PARKS: BCNP, CABR, CHNP, CNWR, CONP, LANP, LSBR, MANP, MVCR, PVNP, SRNP, TONP, WIBG

Plate 79b

Crab-eating Raccoon
Procyon cancrivorus
Mapache = raccoon
Osito Lavador = little washing bear

ID: Brownish or grayish raccoon with shortish fur; gray and whitish face with black mask; pointed muzzle; brown legs and feet; 55 to 70 cm (21 to 28 in) long, plus ringed tail.

HABITAT: Lowland forests and more open areas, but primarily near rivers, streams, lakes, marshes, seashores, southern Pacific slope; nocturnal; found on the ground and in trees.

PARKS: CONP, MANP, PVNP, WIBG

Plate 79c

White-nosed Coati
Nasua narica
Pizote

ID: Light-, dark-, or reddish brown raccoon-like mammal with grayish or yellowish shoulders; white muzzle, chin, and throat; 45 to 70 cm (18 to 27 in), plus very long, faintly ringed tail.

HABITAT: Low and middle elevation wet and dry forests and forest edge areas, countrywide; day active; found on the ground and in trees.

PARKS: BCNP, CABR, CHNP, CNWR, CONP, LANP, LSBR, MANP, MVCR, PVNP, SRNP, TONP, WIBG

Plate 79d

Kinkajou
Potos flavus
Mico de Noche = night monkey
Martilla = hammer

ID: Grayish or reddish brown, short-haired mammal, sometimes with a darker stripe along back; roundish head with short muzzle; short legs; 40 to 55 cm (16 to 22 in), plus very long, prehensile tail.

HABITAT: Low and middle elevation forests, plantations, Caribbean and Pacific slopes; nocturnal; found in trees, often in canopy.

PARKS: BCNP, CABR, CHNP, CNWR, CONP, LANP, LSBR, MANP, MVCR, PVNP, SRNP, TONP, WIBG

Plate 79e

Olingo
(also called Bushy-tailed Olingo)
Bassaricyon gabbii

ID: A light brown, densely furred mammal with a shortish, pointed, often grayish, muzzle; 35 to 42 cm (14 to 16 in), plus long, bushy, faintly ringed tail. (Another species, the Cacomistle, *Bassariscus sumichrasti*, resembles the Olingo, but has a white mask around its eyes and dark lower legs and feet; it is found in higher-elevation wet forests.)

HABITAT: Low and middle elevation wet forests, Caribbean and Pacific slopes; nocturnal; found in trees.

PARKS: BCNP, CABR, CHNP, CNWR, CONP, LANP, LSBR, MVCR, TONP, WIBG

Note: This species regulated in Costa Rica for conservation purposes, CITES Appendix III listed.

Plate 79 393

e Olingo

d Kinkajou

b Crab-eating Raccoon

a Northern Raccoon

c White-nosed Coati

Plate 80a
Baird's Tapir
Tapirus bairdii
Macho de Monte = mountain male
Danta

ID: Large mammal, brownish, black, or grayish, with short, often sparse, hair; lighter-colored throat and chest; vaguely horse-like head with large, hanging, upper lip, or "proboscis;" to 1.8 to 2.0 m (5.8 to 6.5 ft); weight to 200+ kg (440+ lb).

HABITAT: Low, middle, and higher elevation wet forests and swampy areas, Caribbean and Pacific slopes; active day or night; found on land or in shallow water.

PARKS: BCNP, CNWR, CONP, LANP, LSBR, MVCR, RNVP, SRNP, TONP

Note: This species listed as endangered, CITES Appendix I and USA ESA.

Plate 80b
Collared Peccary
Tayassu tajacu
Saíno

ID: A pig-like animal, gray or blackish, with long, coarse hair; white or yellowish "collar" around shoulders; to 80 to 92 cm (31 to 36 in).

HABITAT: Low and middle elevation wet and dry forests, agricultural areas, countrywide; day active.

PARKS: BCNP, CABR, CHNP, CNWR, CONP, LANP, LSBR, MVCR, PVNP, SRNP, TONP

Note: This species regulated for conservation purposes, CITES Appendix II listed.

Plate 80c
White-lipped Peccary
Tayassu pecari
Puerco de Monte = mountain pig
Cariblanco = whiteface

ID: Black or brown pig-like animal with long, coarse hair; white lower cheek and throat; to 92 to 110 cm (36 to 43 in).

HABITAT: Low and middle elevation wet and dry forests in protected areas; day active.

PARKS: BCNP, CNWR, CONP, LANP, MVCR, RNVP, SRNP, TONP

Note: This species regulated for conservation purposes, CITES Appendix II listed.

Plate 80d
White-tailed Deer
Odocoileus virginianus
Venado Cola Blanca = white-tailed deer
Venado = deer

ID: Mid-sized light-, dark-, or grayish brown deer with white belly, white under tail, and, often, white chin/throat; males with branched antlers; 1 to 1.8 m (3 to 6 ft) long; about 1 m (3.3 ft) high at shoulders.

HABITAT: Low, middle, and higher elevation forest edge areas and more open areas, Caribbean and Pacific slopes; active day or night.

PARKS: BCNP, CABR, CHNP, CNWR, CONP, LANP, LSBR, MANP, MVCR, PVNP, RNVP, SRNP, TONP

Plate 80e
Red Brocket Deer
Mazama americana
Cabro de Monte = mountain goat
Venado Colorado = reddish deer

ID: Small reddish or reddish brown deer with dark brown head and neck, and brownish belly; white under tail; males with small, straight antlers; 1 to 1.4 m (3.4 to 4.6 ft) long; 70 cm (28 in) high at shoulders.

HABITAT: Low and middle elevation wet forests, forest edge areas, and plantations, Caribbean and Pacific slopes; active day or night.

PARKS: ARVL, BCNP, CHNP, CNWR, CONP, LANP, LSBR, MVCR, RNVP, TONP, WIBG

Plate 80 395

a Baird's Tapir

b Collared Peccary

c White-lipped Peccary

d White-tailed Deer

e Red Brocket Deer

WCS Conservation Work in Latin America

The Conservation Challenge in Latin America

From Mexico to Tierra del Fuego, Latin America is a land of superlatives. Vast tropical rain forests, rivers comprising the largest freshwater systems on Earth, towering mountains and deep oceans are home to animals and plants found nowhere else in the world. Perhaps no other region on Earth presents such a variety of ecosystems and astonishing array of wildlife.

Latin American conservation efforts, however, face difficult social, economic, and environmental challenges. The region's human population has tripled since 1950. South America alone has lost almost a quarter of its forests, while more than 60 percent of Mexico's woodlands have fallen. Increased hunting, fishing, mining, and other natural resource exploitation threaten already stressed ecosystems.

Patagonia's elephant seals travel as far as the South Georgia Islands, staying at sea for up to eight months. (Photograph with permission from William Conway and WCS.)

These problems, compounded by too few trained conservation professionals and a chronic lack of funding for natural resource management, have both pushed many species to the brink of extinction, and reduced the land's ability to support human life.

Working to reverse these trends, the Wildlife Conservation Society has supported conservation work in Latin America since 1909 with its landmark field studies in Trinidad, Venezuela, and the Galapagos Islands. Today WCS conservationists, working mainly through local projects run by nationals, are uniquely positioned to understand local conditions and conservation opportunities. WCS has developed hundreds of innovative conservation projects, from field studies of endangered species such as the Andean mountain tapir, to the protection of

WCS scientists conceived a network of protected areas in Central America called Paseo Pantera – the Meso-America biological corridor. By protecting these areas, the vast ecological diversity of the region will be preserved. Red-eyed treefrogs, tapirs and small hawksbill turtles are among the thousands of species found in the Paseo Pantera. (Photographs with permission from S. Matola, A. Meylan and WCS)

immense areas through the Patagonian Coastal Zone Management Plan and Central America's Paseo Pantera Project. Today, WCS operates more than 100 Latin American projects in 17 countries, from Mexico to Argentina.

All of these projects depend critically on scientific research. Field staff survey wildlife and assess biodiversity to determine how species interact with their habitats and their human neighbours. Projects lasting several years allow researchers to uncover trends and patterns not apparent in short-term research and to build relationships with local communities and governments. Local conservationists are trained to be responsible for the stewardship of their land and Government participation is encouraged.

Crossing Political Boundaries for Regional Conservation

The Biological Corridors of Paseo Pantera

Whether called panther, cougar, mountain lion, puma, or pantera, the New World's premier big cat ranges from Patagonia to northern Canada. The Central American Land Bridge joining North and South America, rose from the sea some three million years ago, allowing the panther and thousands of other species to expand their range and thrive in new territories. To protect this 'biological highway', WCS has pioneered a conservation strategy called 'Paseo Pantera' – Path of the Panther – to connect an unbroken corridor of parks and refuges throughout Central America.

The pumas and jaguars require huge expanses of unbroken habitat. Biological corridors in Central America are a key solution to preserving the range of these big cats along with many other threatened species. (Photograph with permission from A. Rabinowitz and WCS.)

Just a few decades ago, upland rain forests and dense vegetation covered much of Central America, and mangrove swamps and coral reefs lined its two coasts, forming a chain of natural areas between North and South America. Subsequent human development and population growth has pushed wildlife into dwindling, isolated patchworks of habitat. Working with all seven countries in the Paseo Pantera region, WCS seeks to improve management of existing parks and to restore degraded habitat for migratory wildlife. In Belize, WCS aims to establish new reserves along the Belize Barrier Reef. In reserves in the western Maya Mountains, researchers are developing guidelines to preserve biodiversity. WCS assists Guatemala in the management of the 3.1-million-acre Maya Biosphere Reserve. In Honduras, WCS musters resources to improve the management of protected coastal areas, including the Bay Islands and the Rio Platano Biosphere Reserve – one of the largest protected areas in Central America. In El Salvador, damaged areas are restored and in Nicaragua, plans have been developed to protect Bosawas, Miskito Cat, and the Si-A-Paz. WCS and several other organisations have helped Costa Rica expand Tortuguero National Park to four times its original size. And Panama is investing in conservation projects in the coastal bays of Bocas del Toro.

Manu Reserve in Peru contains incredible diversity of wildlife, including flocks of Scarlet Macaws, shown here at a lick. (Photographs with permission from C. Munn and E. Nycander.)

In 1994, all seven Central American countries signed an agreement affirming the Central American Biological Corridor as a conservation priority – Paseo Pantera will help sustain the region's unique mixture of wildlife well into the future.

Working with Nations to Protect Habitat

Bolivia Creates Two Massive Parks

When wildlife surveys in Bolivia revealed an extraordinary wealth of species in two diverse regions, WCS joined the Bolivian Government, local conservation organisations, and indigenous people to protect these areas. Two massive parks were declared in 1995 spanning 20,000 square miles – an area larger than Switzerland.

The first park, Kaa-Iya del Gran Chaco in southeast Bolivia, protects a vast 8.6 million acres of the Chaco – a unique dry forest and thorn-scrub habitat second only to the Amazon rain forest in size. Agricultural clearing has destroyed most of the original Chaco, which once covered much of northern Argentina and Paraguay, leaving sparsely populated Bolivia with the last great expanse. Since 1984, WCS has catalogued 46 species of large mammals in Bolivia's Chaco, including giant armadillos, maned wolves, several big cat and primate species, and the rare Chacoan peccary, thought extinct until 1975.

The second park, Alto Madidi in northwest Bolivia, covers 4.7 million acres of glaciers, mountain and lowland rain forests, and Pampas del Heath savannas. It could be the most biologically rich region in the world with almost 1,200 species of birds, Andean bears, jaguars, giant otters, anacondas, black caimans, and thousands of other animal and plant species.

Today, illegal hunting threatens wildlife. This jaguar skin was found in the Mamiráua Reserve. (Photograph with permission from J. Thorbjarnarson.)

Making these two parks a reality required several years of research and co-operation between the various interested parties. In the huge Chaco park, WCS is supporting the efforts of native peoples to develop management plans, foster eco-tourism possibilities and explore other economic incentives to local inhabitants. The Tacana Indians, who have long supported conservation efforts in the Madidi region, will similarly help manage their new park.

Stewardship Through Community Involvement

Mamirauá Lake Ecological Station

Amazonian Brazil boasts one of the most extraordinary, yet least studied ecosystems in the world – the seasonally flooded forest known as the várzea – an area larger than Florida. Rare uakari monkeys and umbrella birds forage in the canopy, while pink river dolphins, caimans, and Amazonian manatees swim among submerged trees. WCS has recorded over 200 species of fish, nearly 300 species of birds, and an exceptional diversity of trees in this unique environment.

In response to threats such as commercial logging and overfishing, WCS launched one of its most unique Latin American projects: the Mamirauá Lake Ecological Station, a 2.8 million-acre reserve. Brazilian and international scientists gather information and monitor the resource demands of the 2,000 local inhabitants. Research projects include surveys of wildlife, plants, and fish; and measure the effects of timber extraction, fishing, and subsistence hunting.

Local people have provided crucial support to this initiative, protecting their livelihood from outside exploitation. Ultimately, local participation is the only way to insure future wise stewardship of this flooded Amazonian forest.

In 1995, $1 million was provided for the establishment of the 'National Institute for the Várzea,' to be built near the reserve in the town of Tefè, the first major Brazilian research institute in the upper Amazon region.

Long term Commitments

Coastal Conservation in Patagonia

Spectacular concentrations of colonial seabirds and marine mammals flourish along Patagonia's rugged 2,000-mile coastline. The plankton-filled Antarctic current supports southern right whales, elephant seals, Magellanic penguins, and one of the planet's most productive fisheries.

WCS has worked here for over 30 years, promoting the declaration of many coastal reserves, among them Punta Tombo and Punta Leon in Chubat Province.

To combat threats from burgeoning petroleum, shipping, fishing, and tourism developments, WCS has helped produce a Patagonian Coastal Zone Management Plan, a collaborative effort with local organisations to manage fast-growing industries while protecting the region's unique ecology.

WCS monitors Elephant seals and Magellanic penguins as indicator species of the southern Atlantic ecosystem. Chronic oil pollution has reduced penguin

Chronic oil pollution has caused a one-third decline in Magellanic penguin populations at Punta Tombo, Patagonia. WCS is working with Argentinean authorities to move oil tanker routes away from delicate breeding areas. WCS President and General Director William Conway pioneered WCS's work in Patagonia some 30 years ago. (Photograph with permission from William Conway.)

numbers by one-third in the past 15 years and WCS advocates that oil tanker routes be moved farther from the coast. Offshore, WCS examines the impact of whale-watching, which has grown 300 percent in seven years, working with local governments and the whale-watching industry to ensure that boats do not disturb the whales and their young. WCS monitors the impacts of commercial fishery 'by-catch' – non-target fish species discarded overboard. Fisheries off Patagonia produce up to 50 to 70 percent by-catch, virtually all of which dies on the decks of the fishing vessels, reducing the food supplies of marine birds and mammals.

Conservation Through Training

WCS teaches scientific know-how to Latin American students and professionals, to create a core of conservationists, scientists, and decision-makers who will be able to protect the region's wildlife. Local people and park guards are taught how to census and monitor wildlife populations and conservation science is taught to university students and professionals. Since 1989, WCS has held courses in Colombia, Venezuela, Ecuador, and Peru.

The WCS Student Grants Program offers graduate and undergraduate conservationists much-needed funding for research projects to solve conservation problems in Latin America. Since 1987, this program has supported more than 140 projects in Peru, Ecuador, Colombia, Bolivia, and Venezuela.

The Scientific Challenge of Sustainable Use

'Sustainable use' – harvesting natural resources while preserving biodiversity – is often seen as the panacea to unite conflicting environmental and economic interests. However, the exploitation of natural resources, even on a sustainable basis, will inevitably involve some biodiversity loss, a problem under WCS scrutiny. WCS is investigating the effects of selective timber harvesting in Bolivia and Venezuela, for example, where some logging interests claim the practice is sustainable. In Ecuador, the Sustainable Utilisation of Biological Resources (SUBIR) project monitors wildlife populations and works with local communities to develop economic alternatives to destroying habitats.

WCS trains park rangers and conservationists throughout Latin America. These Venezuelan park guards help protect world-renowned regions, including Angel Falls in Canaima National Park. (Photograph with permission from A. Grajal.)

$25 ASSOCIATE
- One year of *Wildlife Conservation*, our award-winning magazine filled with breathtaking photographs and articles that will keep you up to date about our worldwide conservation initiatives.

$35 BASIC MEMBERSHIP
Wildlife Conservation magazine plus the benefits of *full membership* including:
- *Notes from the Field*, a quarterly newsletter with project reports from scientists in the field
- Opportunities to travel with WCS scientists
- A membership card that entitles one adult to unlimited admission for one year to all five of our wildlife parks in New York including the world famous Bronx Zoo, as well as passes for free parking where available.

$75 PLUS MEMBERSHIP
All the benefits of Basic and:
- *Passport to Adventure* ... Travel around the world learning about exotic animals without ever leaving home with this interactive, educational package of stickers, fun fact cards, a map and more. Great fun for the entire family!
- A membership card that entitles two additional adults (total of three) and children to unlimited admission for one year to all five of our wildlife parks.

$150 CONSERVATION SUPPORTER
All the benefits of Plus and:
- Limited edition sterling silver antelope pin

JOIN NOW! Mail your membership contribution to:
WILDLIFE CONSERVATION SOCIETY
Membership Department
2300 Southern Boulevard
Bronx, NY 10460–1068, USA

Join using your credit card by calling
1–718–220–5111

or by visiting our website
www.wcs.org

TRAVEL WITH THE EXPERTS!
Wildlife Conservation Society tours take you to wild places with informed escorts who know the country, know the animals and care about wildlife. They have actively participated in establishing national parks or saving endangered species. You'll travel with experts who will share their excitement, wonder and love of wildlife conservation.

From the national parks of Kenya to the rain forest of Peru, WCS travel experts will make your trip an informative, educational and lively adventure.

For more information call or write:
WCS International Travel Program
830 Fifth Avenue
New York, NY 10021 USA
00 1 212–439–6507

Please clip this form and mail it with your gift to Wildlife Conservation Society/2300 Southern Blvd/Bronx, NY 10460–1068, USA.

IMPORTANT: Wildlife Conservation Society is a 401(c)3 organization. Non membership contributions are fully tax-deductible to the extent allowed by law. Membership dues are tax-deductible in excess of benefit value. Magazine is a $12 value, parking passes are an $8 value, *Passport to Adventure* is a $6 value. For a copy of our latest Annual Report you can write to us or to the Office of Charities Registration, 162 Washington Avenue, Albany NY 12231, USA. Your contribution to the Society will be used to support our general programs as described in the Annual Report.

Species Index

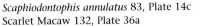

General Index